WELCOME no.10 | TOMO TAKEUCHI
TO THE BALLROOM

Contents

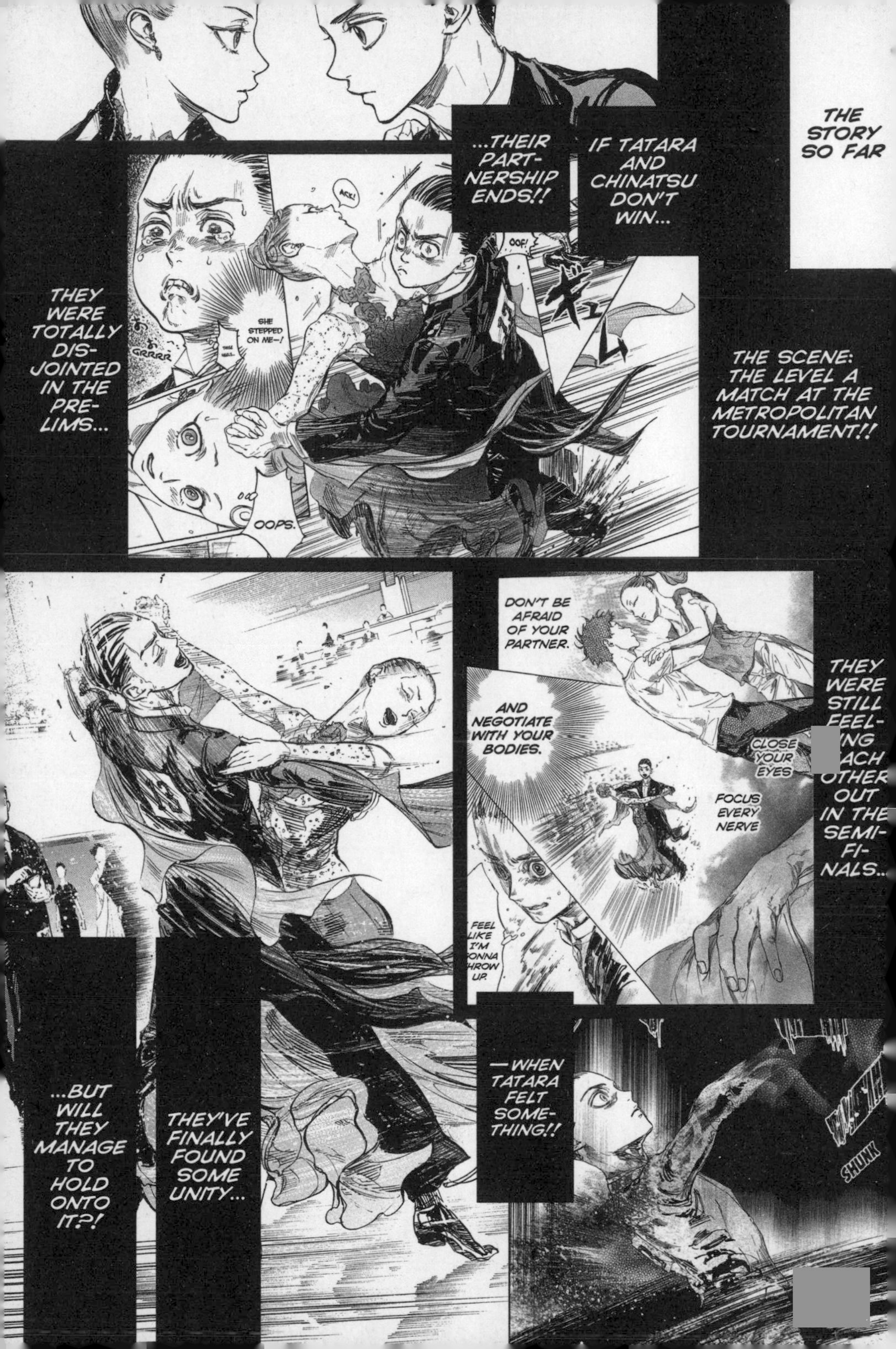
THE STORY SO FAR
THE SCENE: THE LEVEL A MATCH AT THE METROPOLITAN TOURNAMENT!!
IF TATARA AND CHINATSU DON'T WIN...
...THEIR PART-NERSHIP ENDS!!
OOF!
ACK!
SHE STEPPED ON ME—!
THOSE NAILS...
GRRRR
OOPS.
THEY WERE TOTALLY DIS-JOINTED IN THE PRE-LIMS...
THEY WERE STILL FEEL-ING EACH OTHER OUT IN THE SEMI-FI-NALS...
DON'T BE AFRAID OF YOUR PARTNER.
AND NEGOTIATE WITH YOUR BODIES.
CLOSE YOUR EYES
FOCUS EVERY NERVE
I FEEL LIKE I'M GONNA THROW UP.
—WHEN TATARA FELT SOME-THING!!
SHUNK
THEY'VE FINALLY FOUND SOME UNITY...
...BUT WILL THEY MANAGE TO HOLD ONTO IT?!

WELCOME TO THE BALLROOM

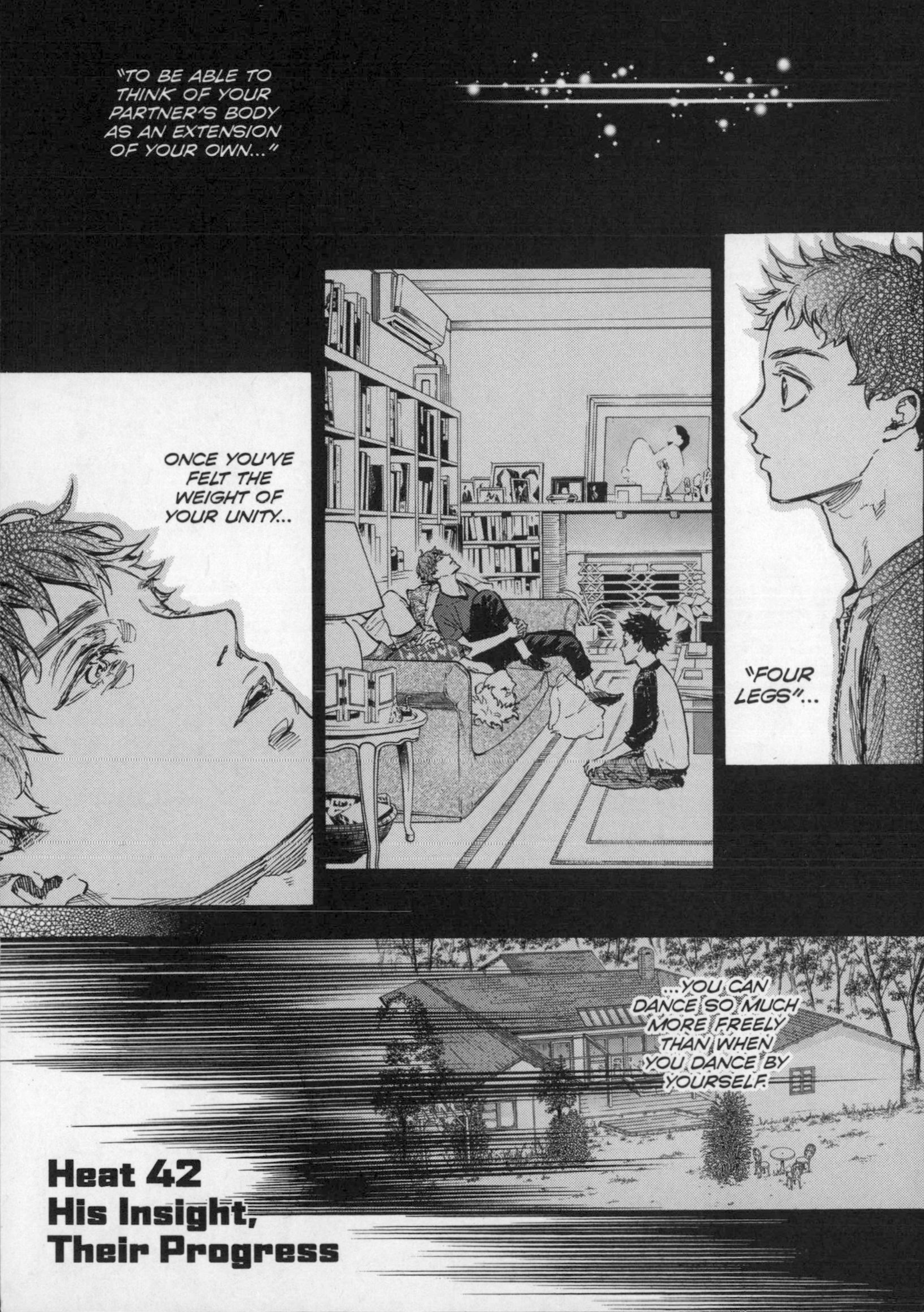
"TO BE ABLE TO THINK OF YOUR PARTNER'S BODY AS AN EXTENSION OF YOUR OWN..."
"FOUR LEGS"...
ONCE YOU'VE FELT THE WEIGHT OF YOUR UNITY...
...YOU CAN DANCE SO MUCH MORE FREELY THAN WHEN YOU DANCE BY YOURSELF.
Heat 42
His Insight, Their Progress

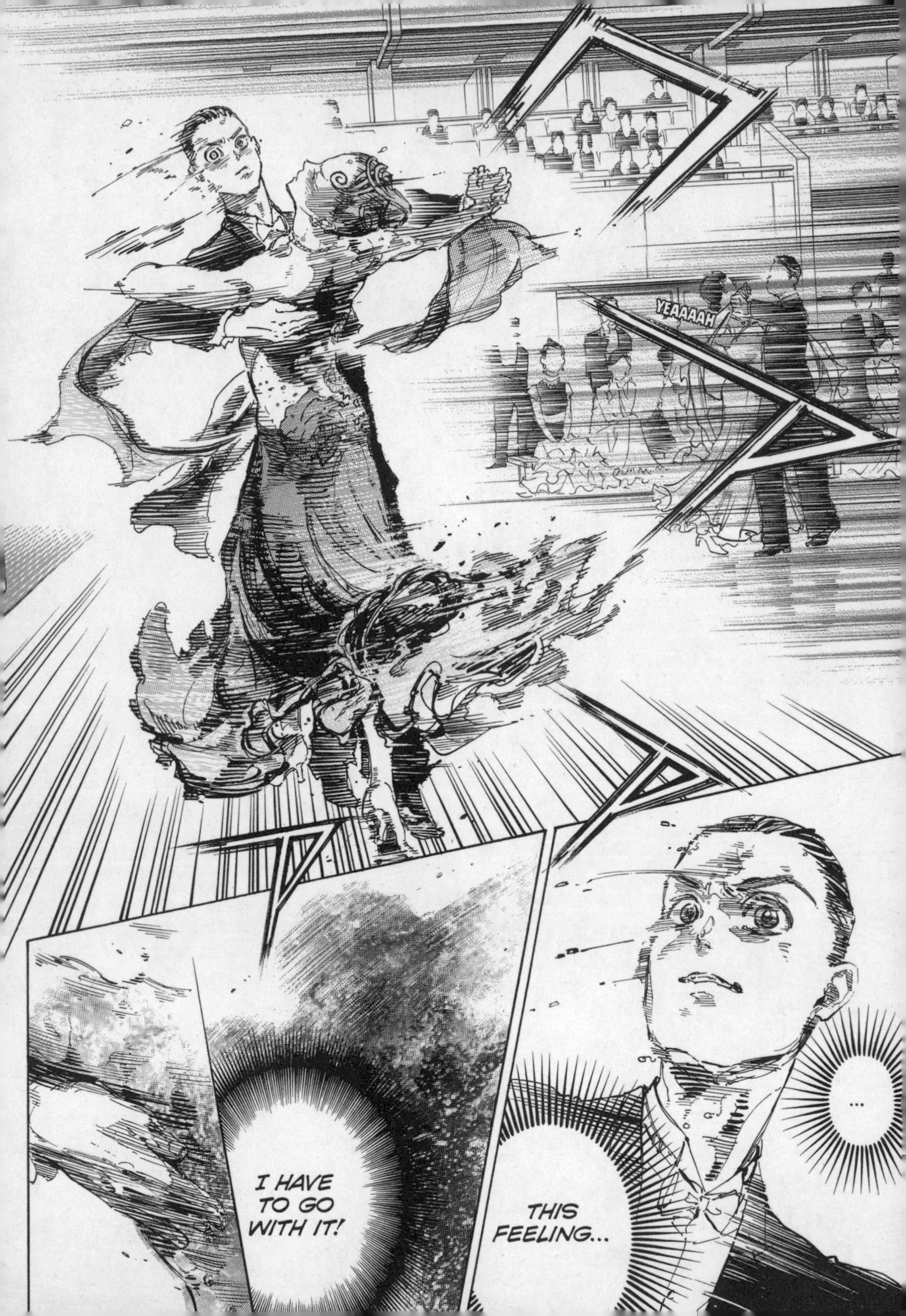
YEAAAAH
...
THIS FEELING...
I HAVE TO GO WITH IT!

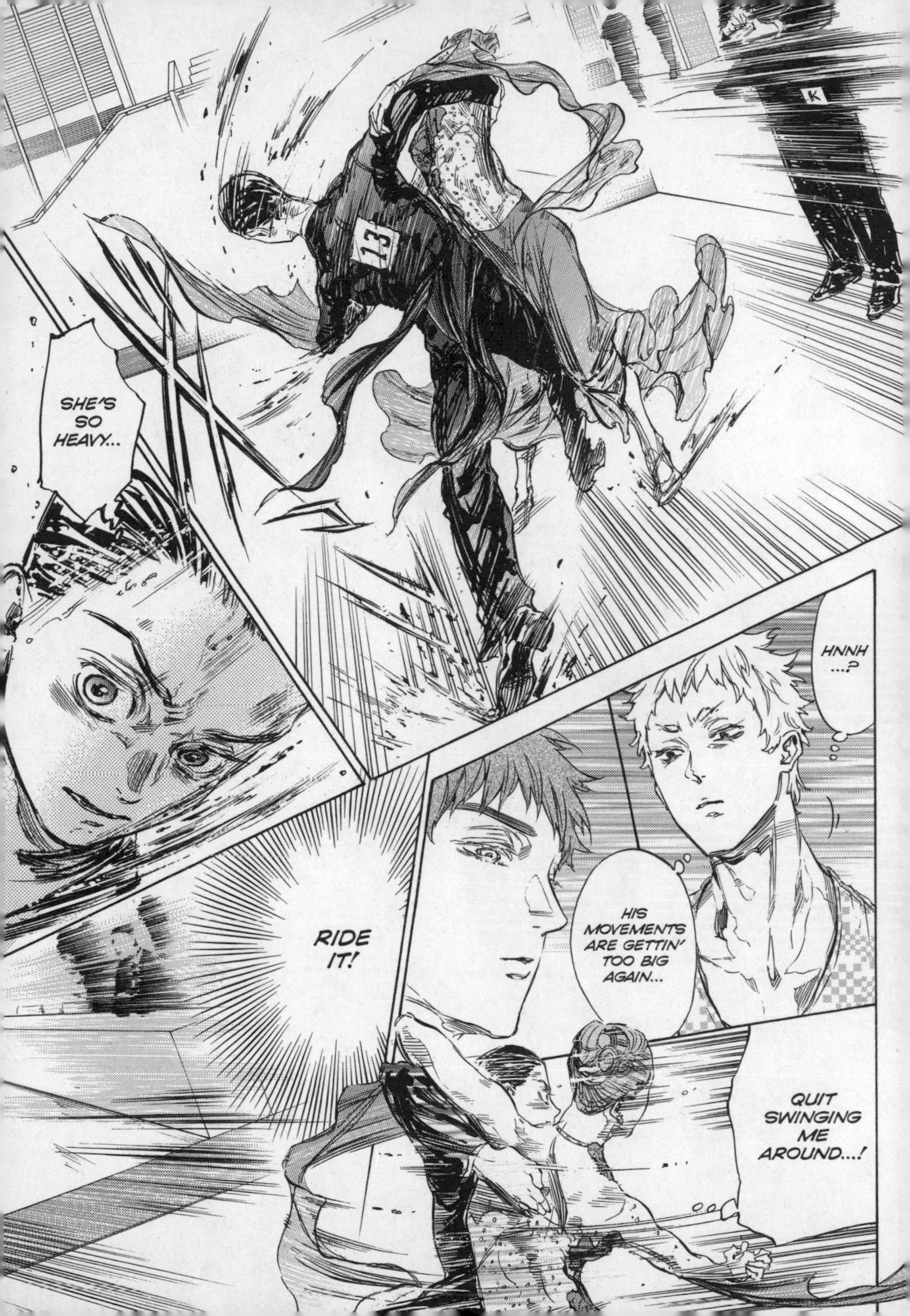
SHE'S SO HEAVY...
HNNH ...?
HIS MOVEMENTS ARE GETTIN' TOO BIG AGAIN...
RIDE IT!
QUIT SWINGING ME AROUND...!

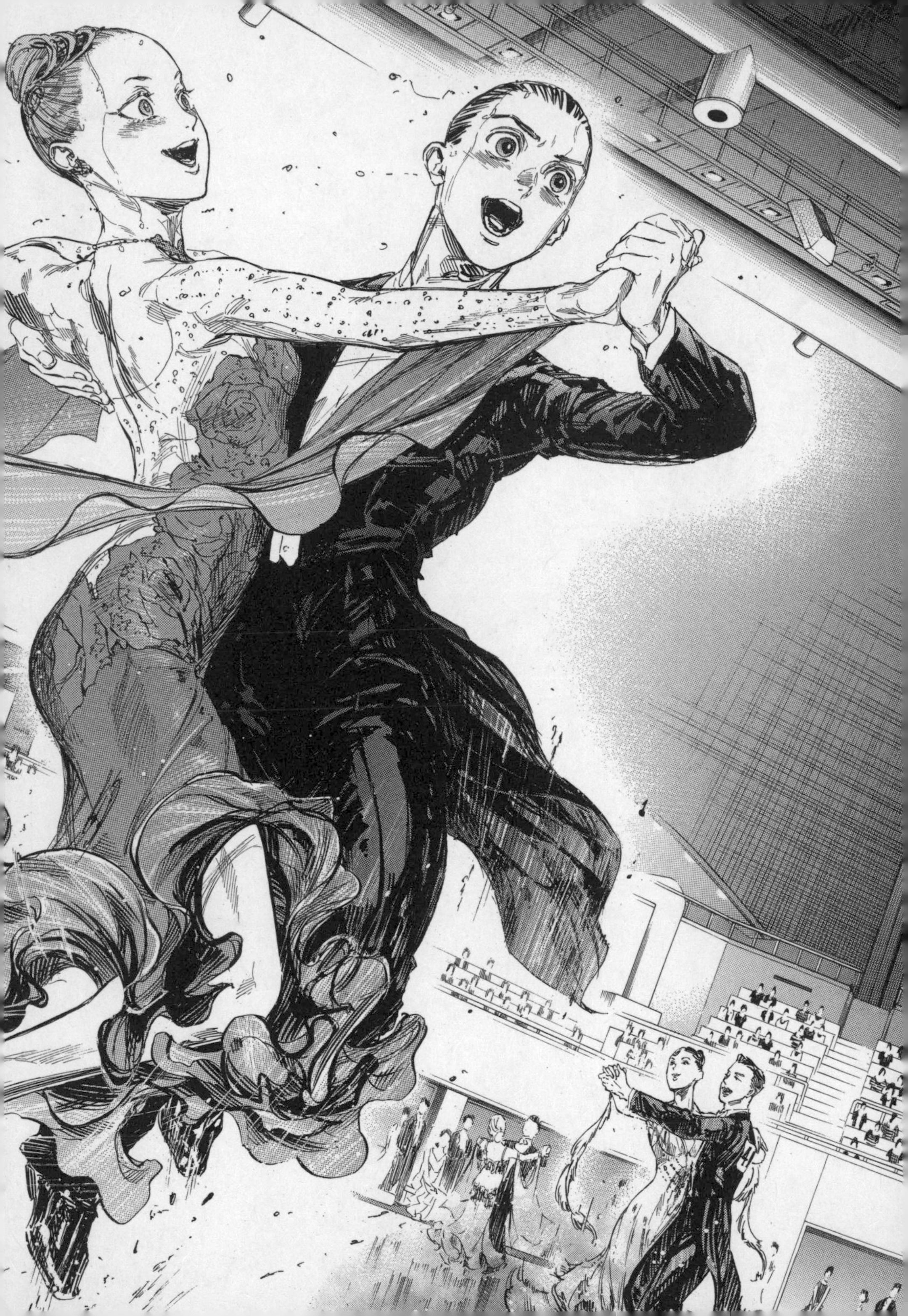

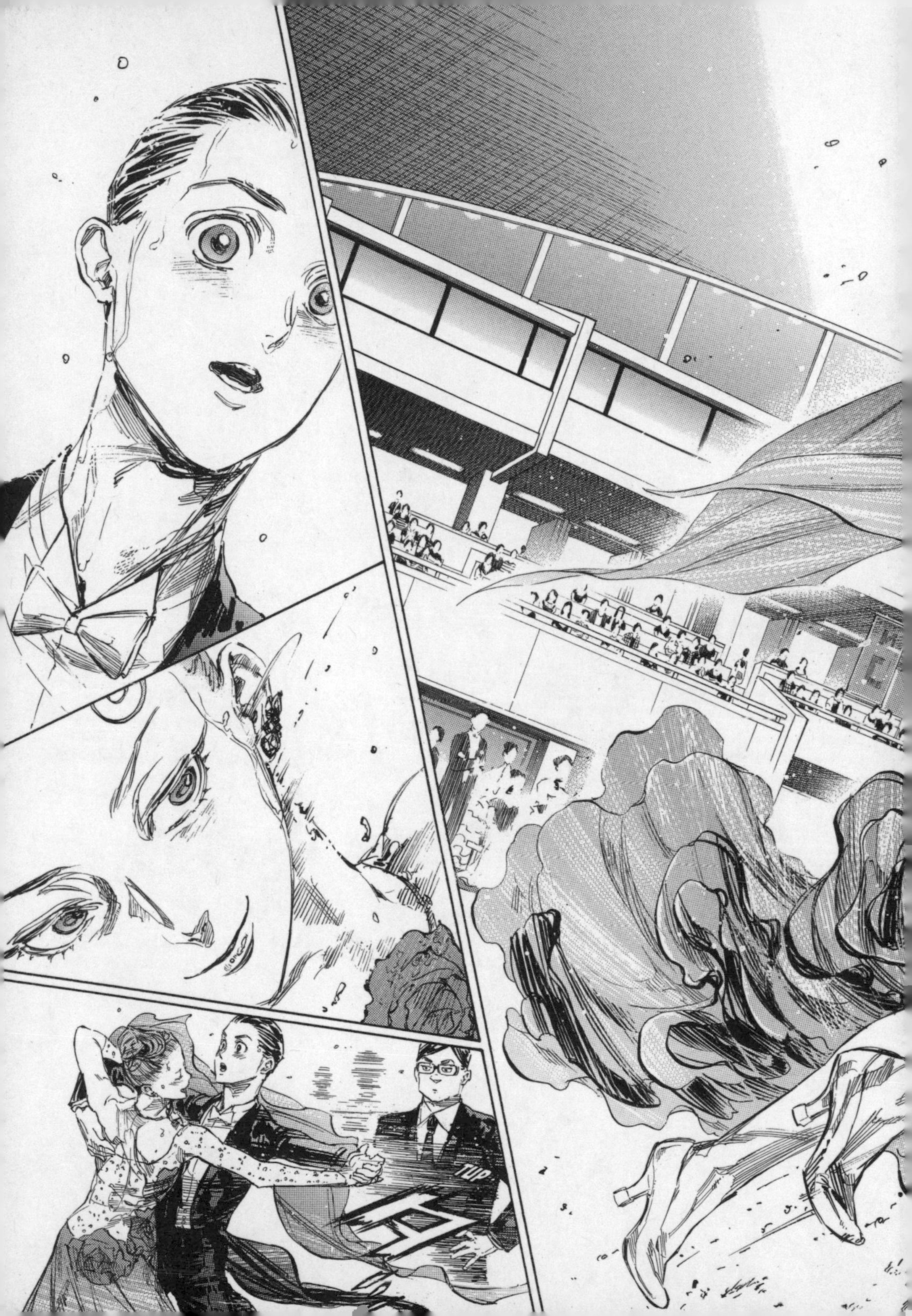
TUP

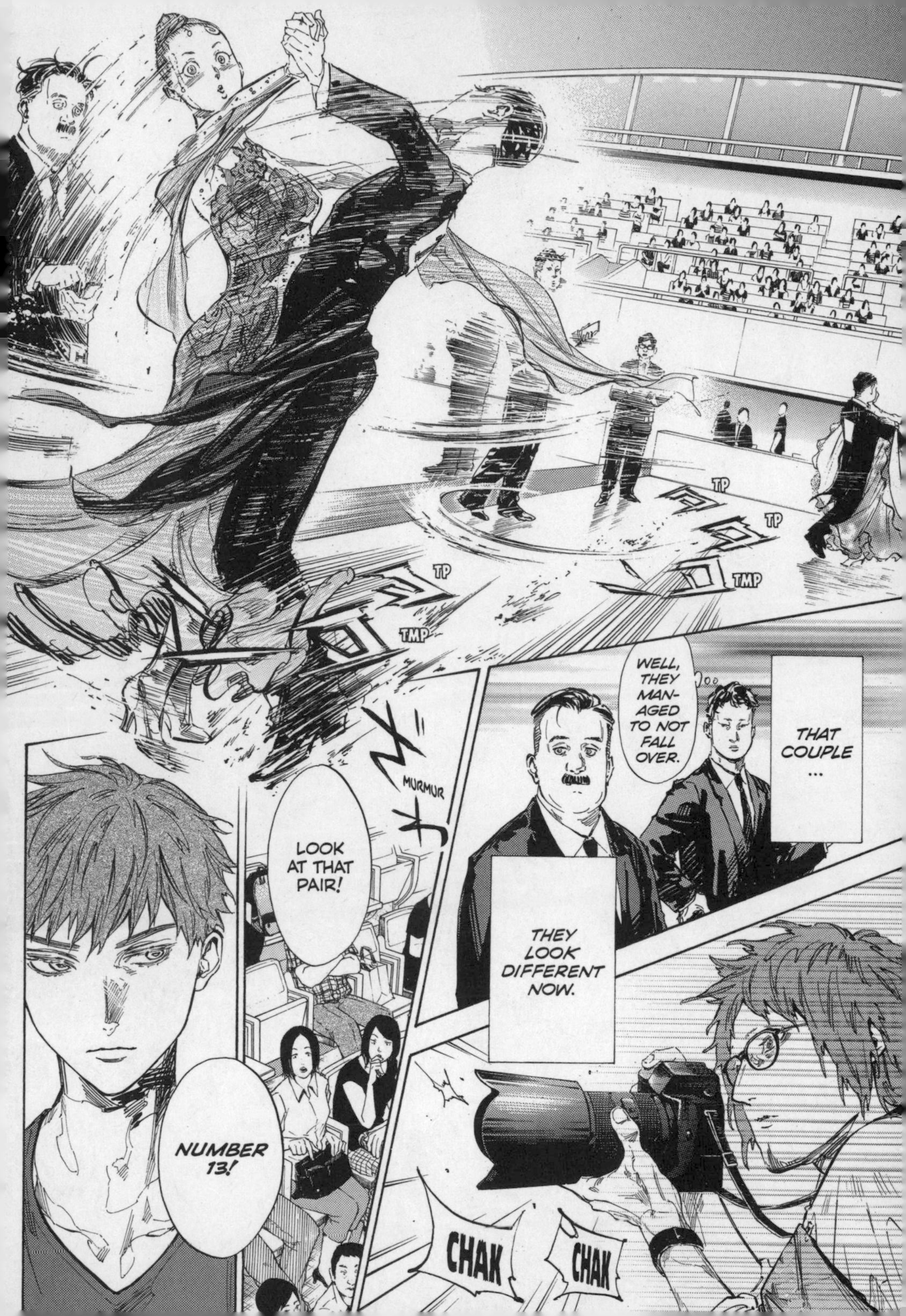
TP
TP
TMP
TP
TMP
THAT COUPLE ...
WELL, THEY MAN-AGED TO NOT FALL OVER.
THEY LOOK DIFFERENT NOW.
CHAK
CHAK
MURMUR
LOOK AT THAT PAIR!
NUMBER 13!

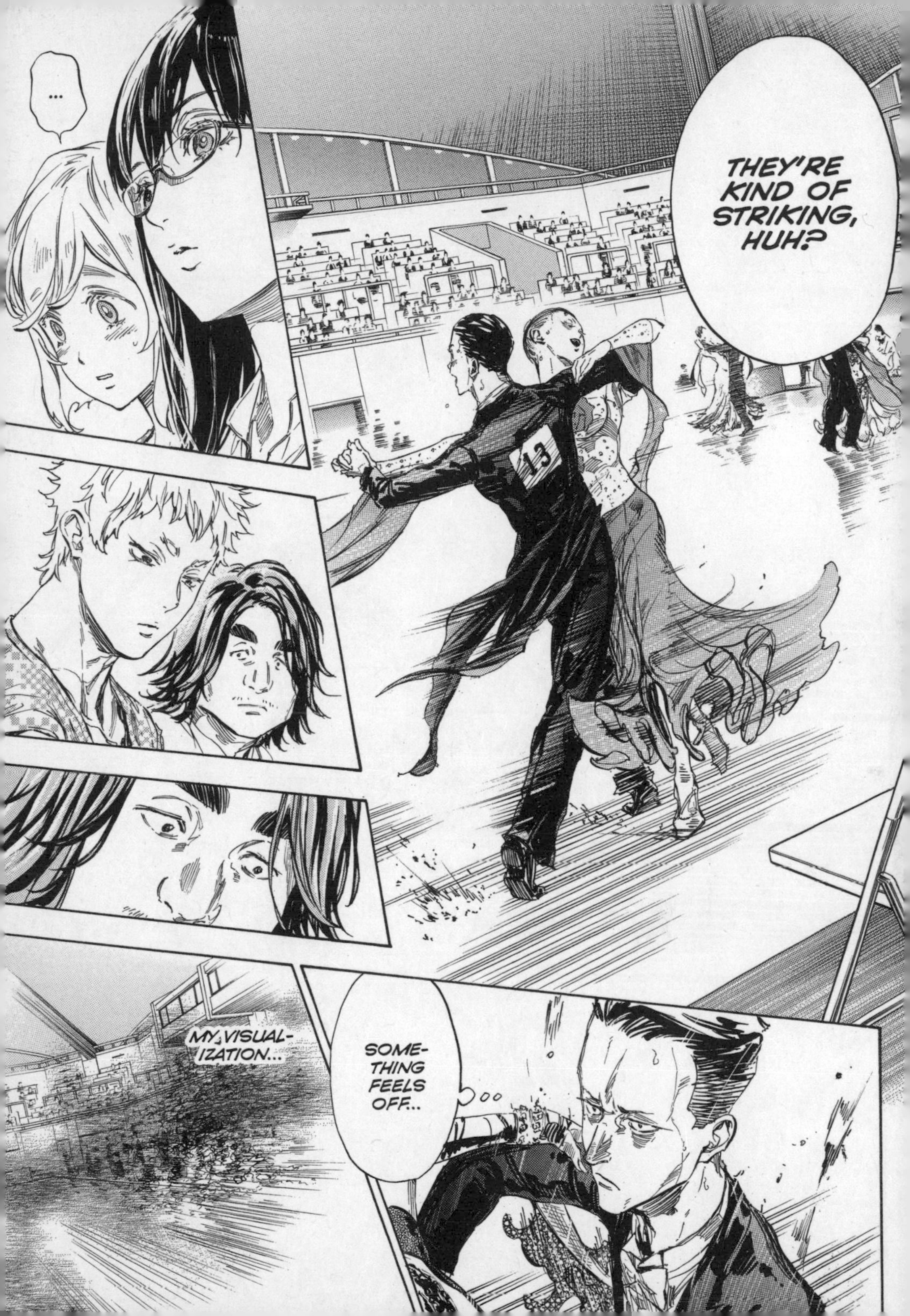
THEY'RE KIND OF STRIKING, HUH?
...
SOME-THING FEELS OFF...
MY VISUAL-IZATION...

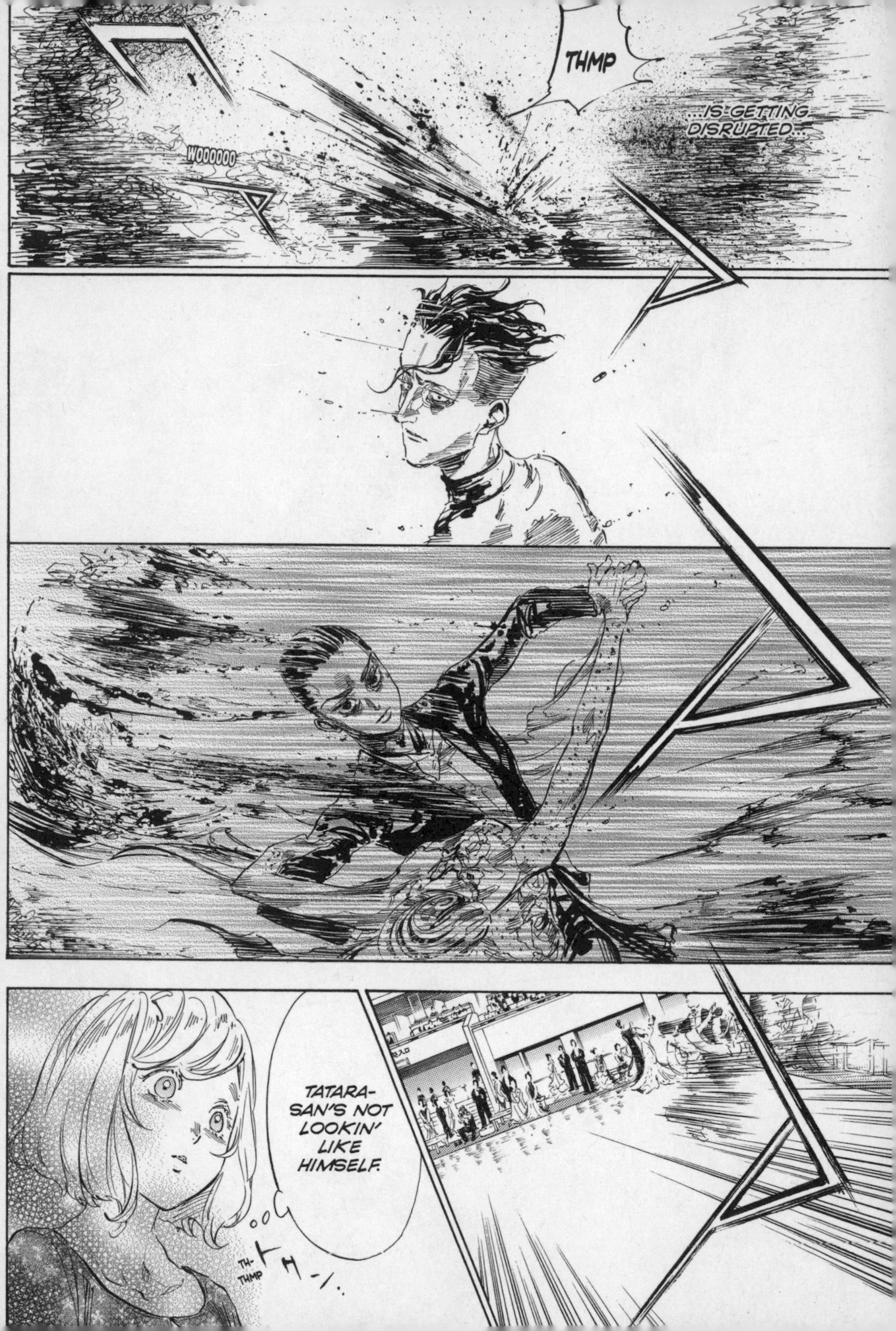
THMP
...IS GETTING DISRUPTED...
WOOOOOO
TATARA-SAN'S NOT LOOKIN' LIKE HIMSELF.
TH-THMP

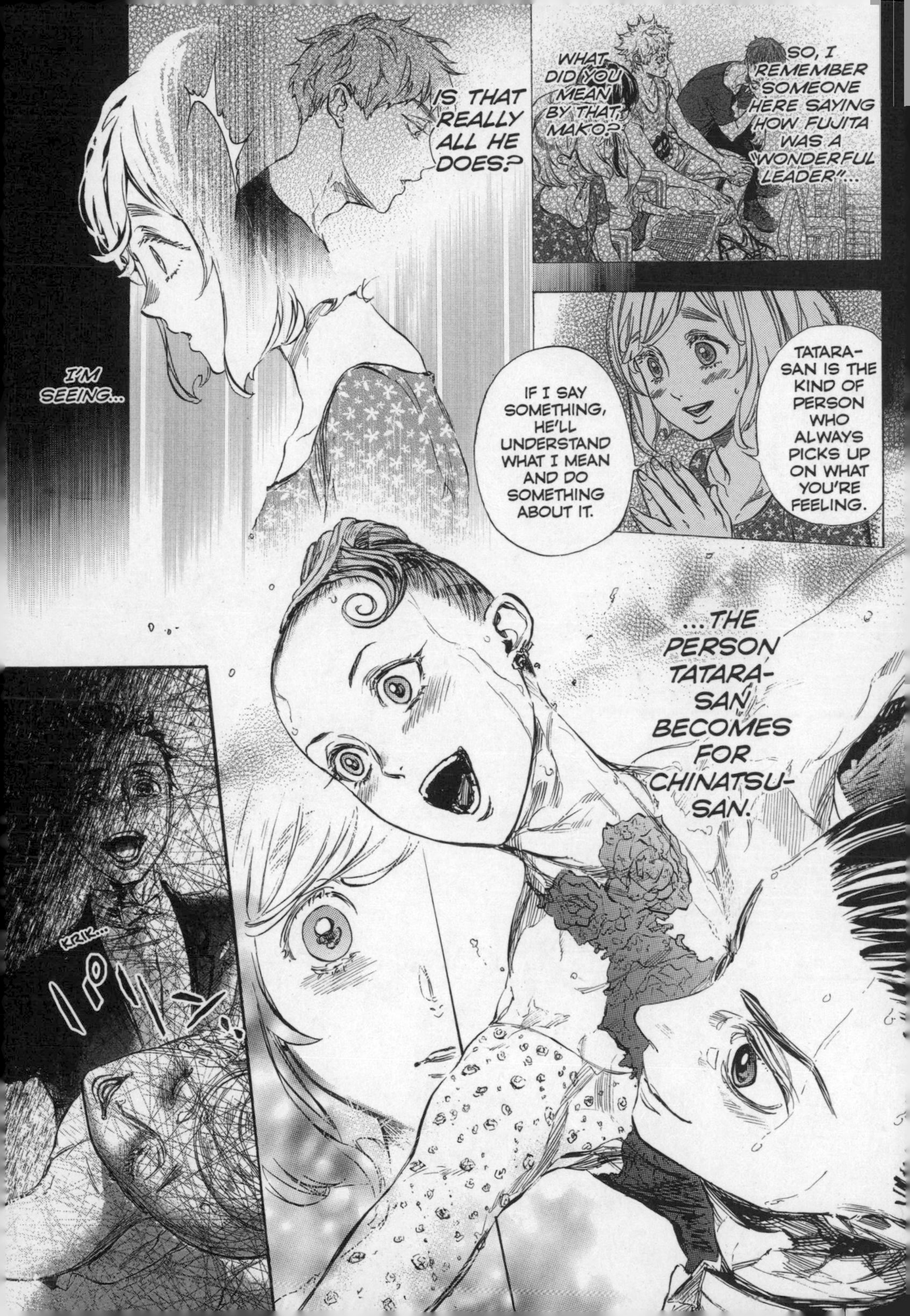
SO, I REMEMBER SOMEONE HERE SAYING HOW FUJITA WAS A "WONDERFUL LEADER"...
WHAT DID YOU MEAN BY THAT, MAKO?
TATARA-SAN IS THE KIND OF PERSON WHO ALWAYS PICKS UP ON WHAT YOU'RE FEELING.
IF I SAY SOMETHING, HE'LL UNDERSTAND WHAT I MEAN AND DO SOMETHING ABOUT IT.
IS THAT REALLY ALL HE DOES?
I'M SEEING...
...THE PERSON TATARA-SAN BECOMES FOR CHINATSU-SAN.
KRIK...

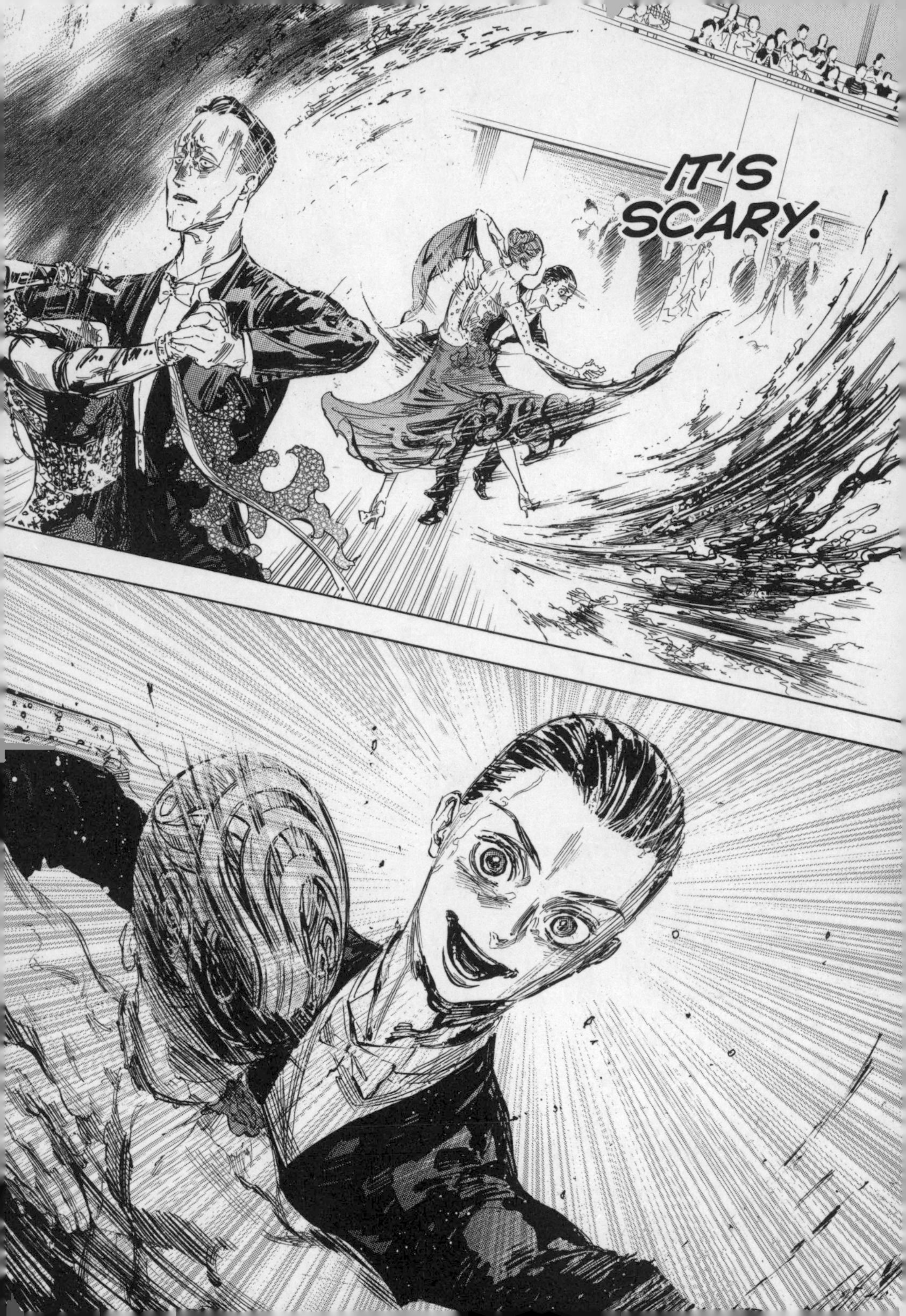
IT'S SCARY.

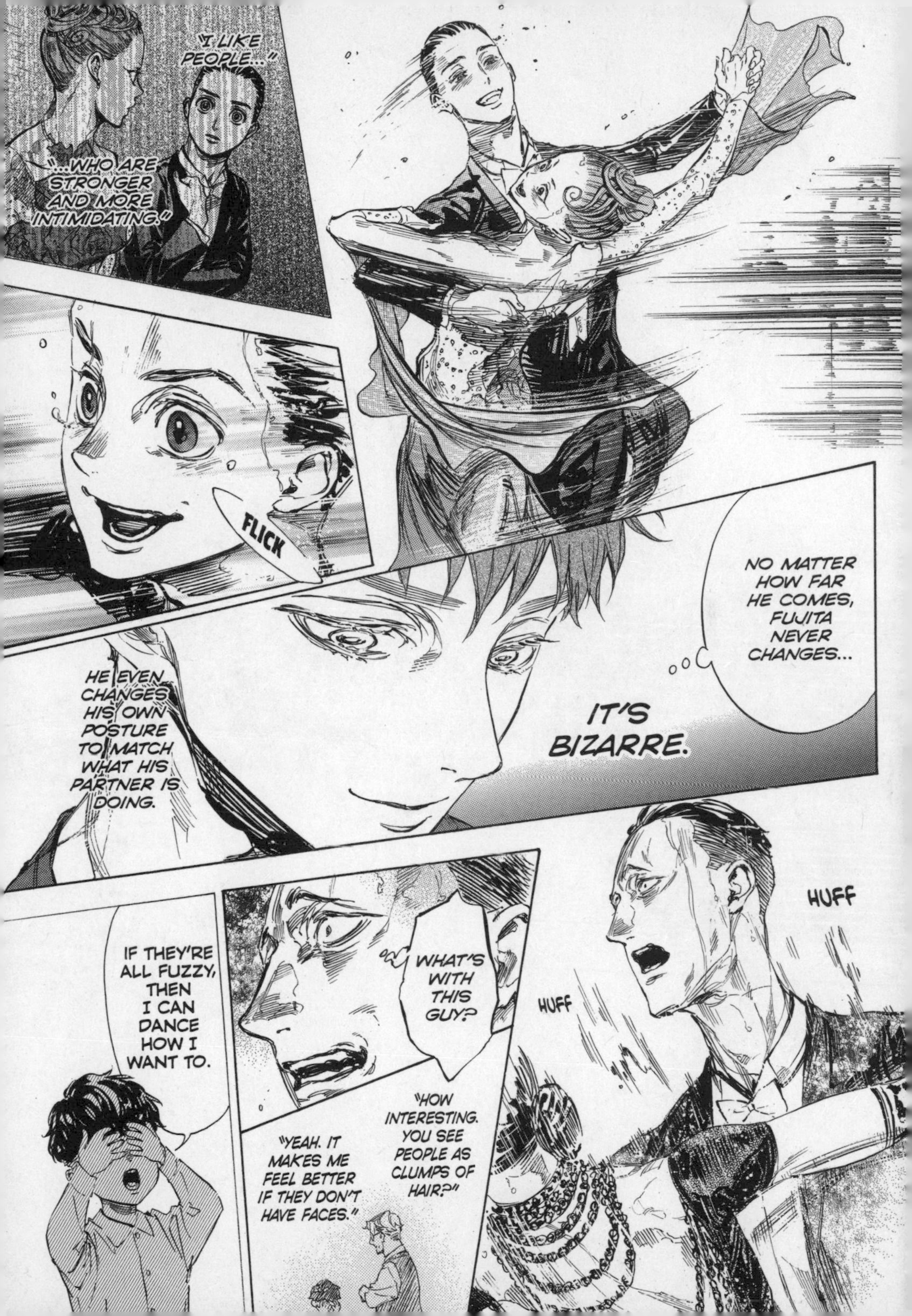
"I LIKE PEOPLE..."
"...WHO ARE STRONGER AND MORE INTIMIDATING."
FLICK
NO MATTER HOW FAR HE COMES, FUJITA NEVER CHANGES...
IT'S BIZARRE.
HE EVEN CHANGES HIS OWN POSTURE TO MATCH WHAT HIS PARTNER IS DOING.
HUFF
HUFF
WHAT'S WITH THIS GUY?
"HOW INTERESTING. YOU SEE PEOPLE AS CLUMPS OF HAIR?"
"YEAH. IT MAKES ME FEEL BETTER IF THEY DON'T HAVE FACES."
IF THEY'RE ALL FUZZY, THEN I CAN DANCE HOW I WANT TO.

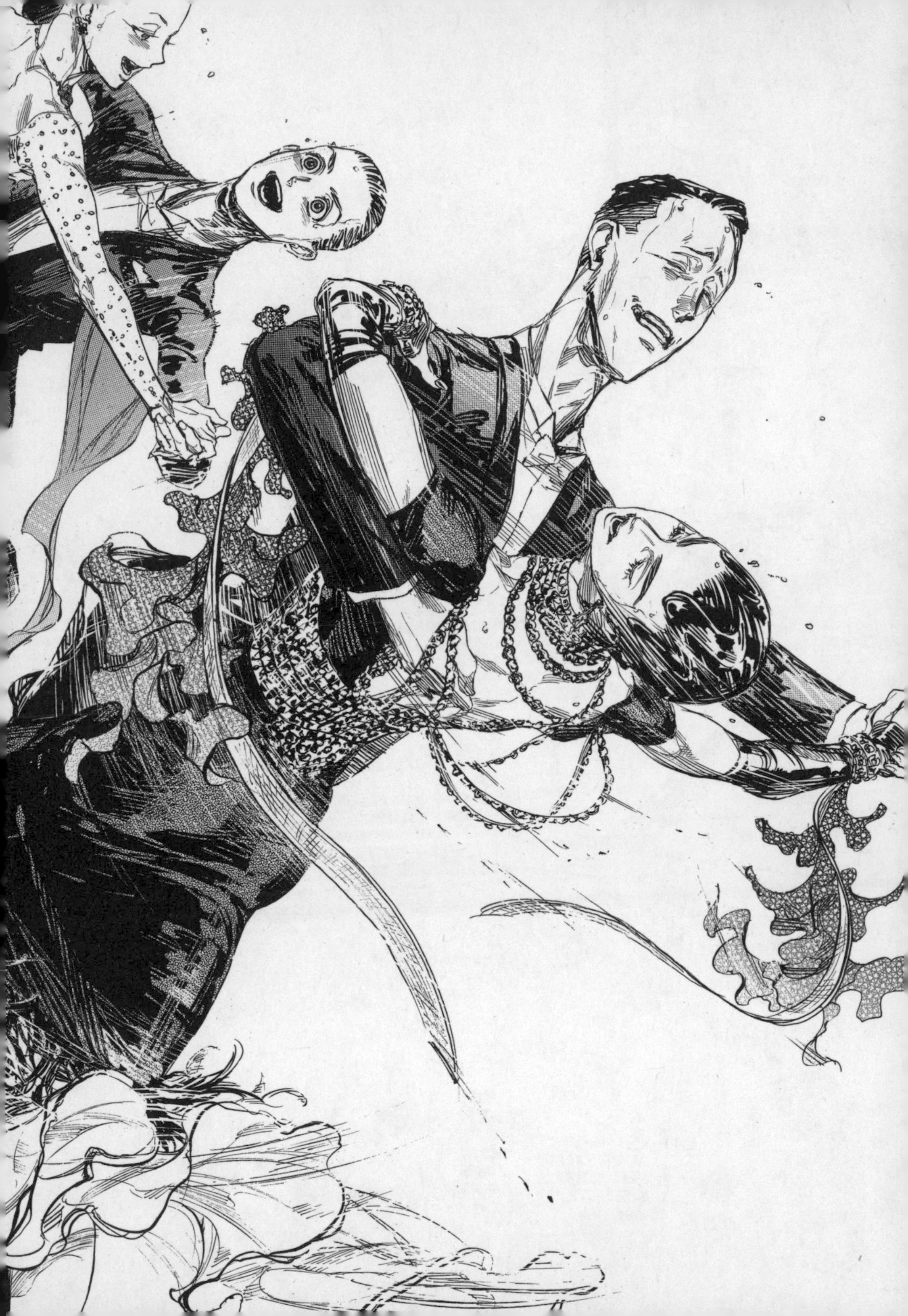

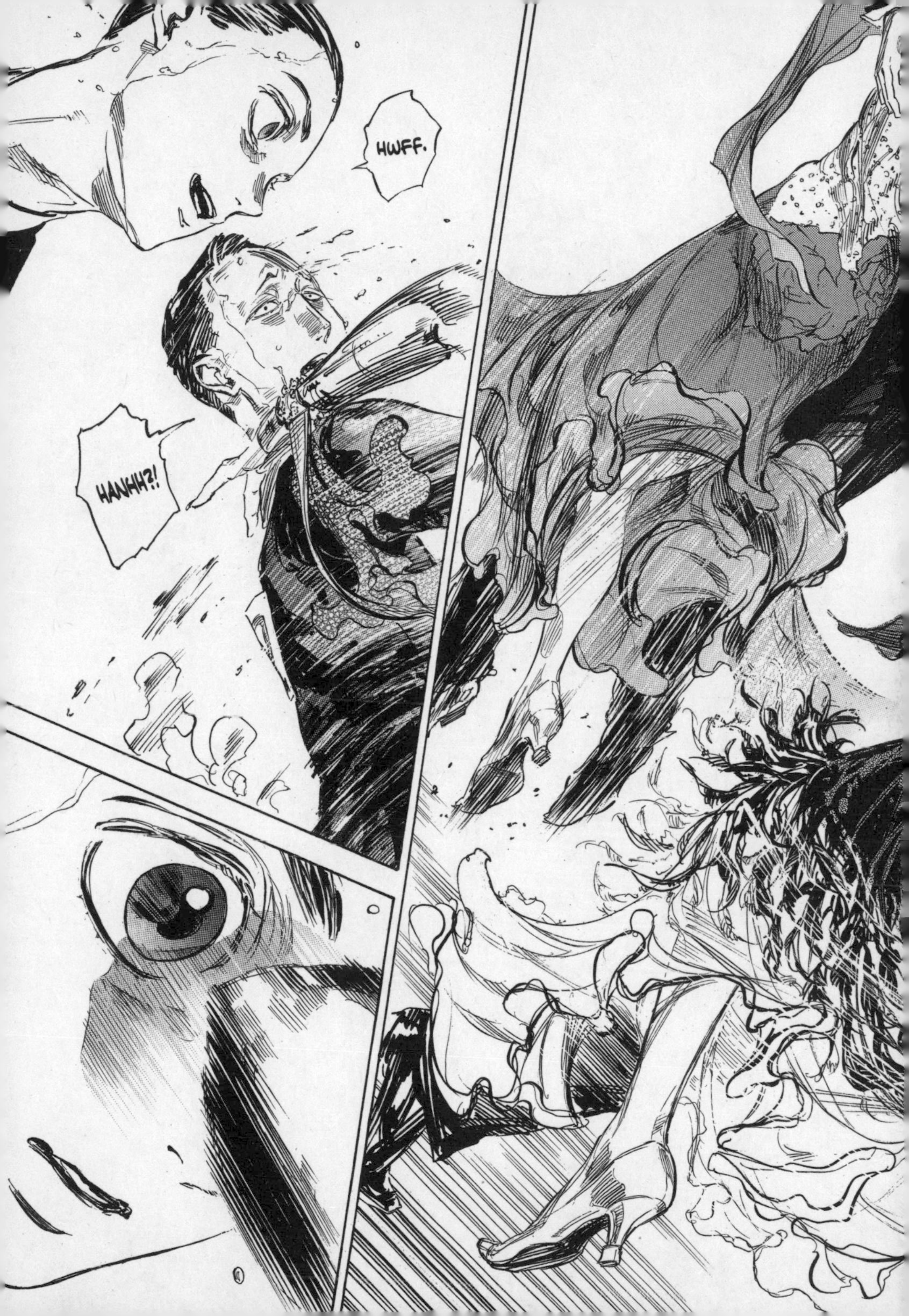
HWFF.
HANHH?!

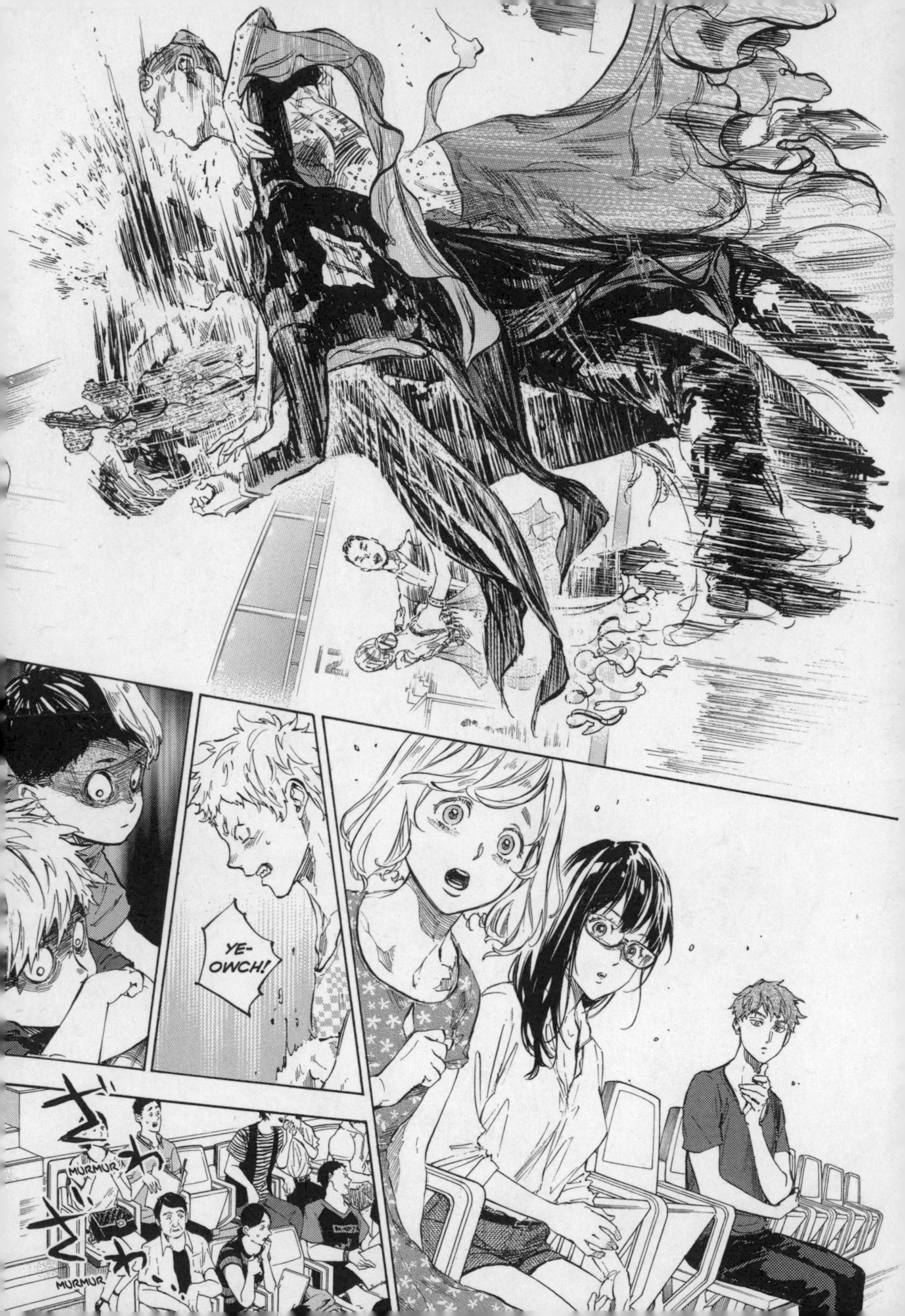
YE-OWCH!
MURMUR
MURMUR

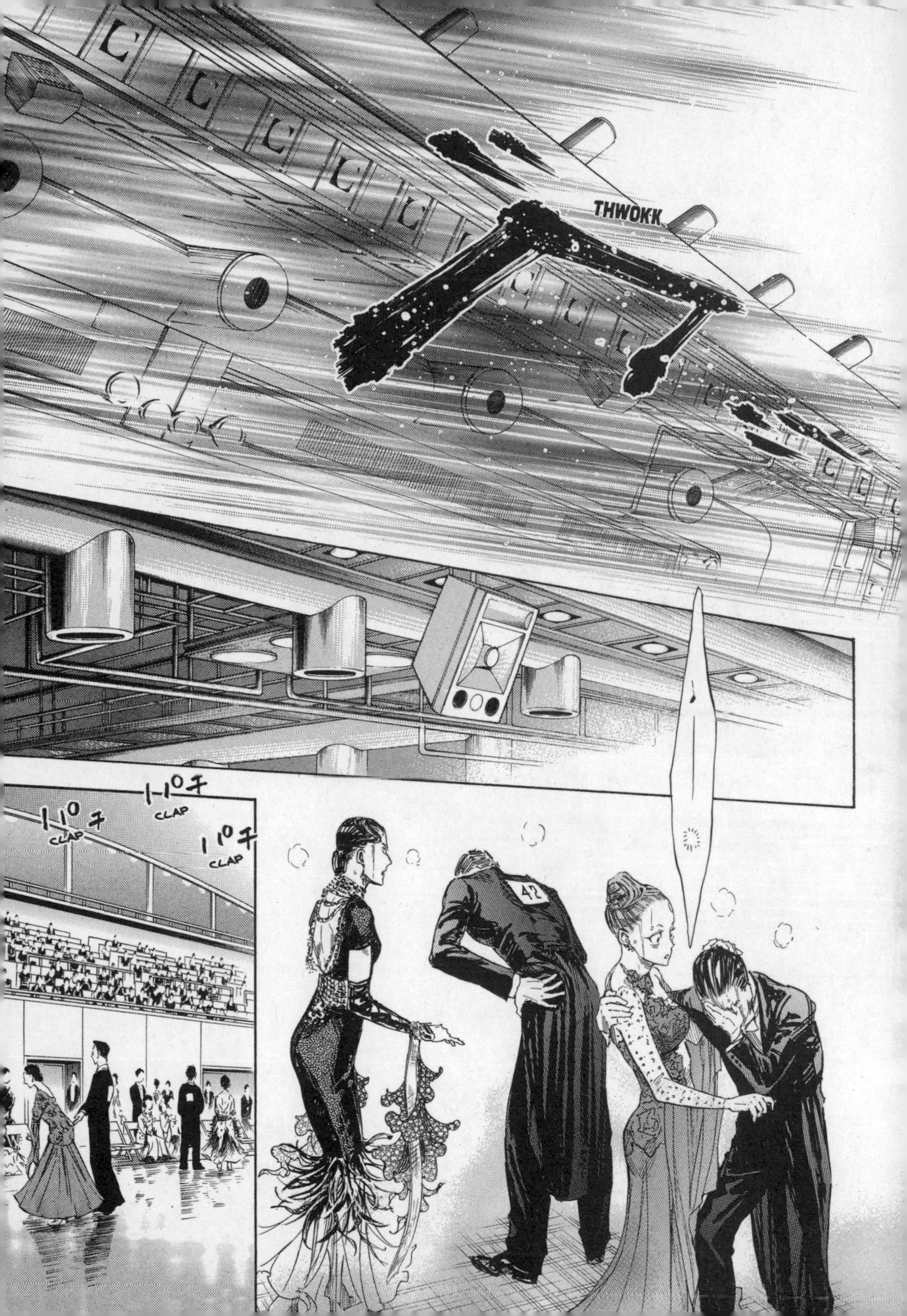
THWOKK
パチ
CLAP
パチ
CLAP
パチ
CLAP

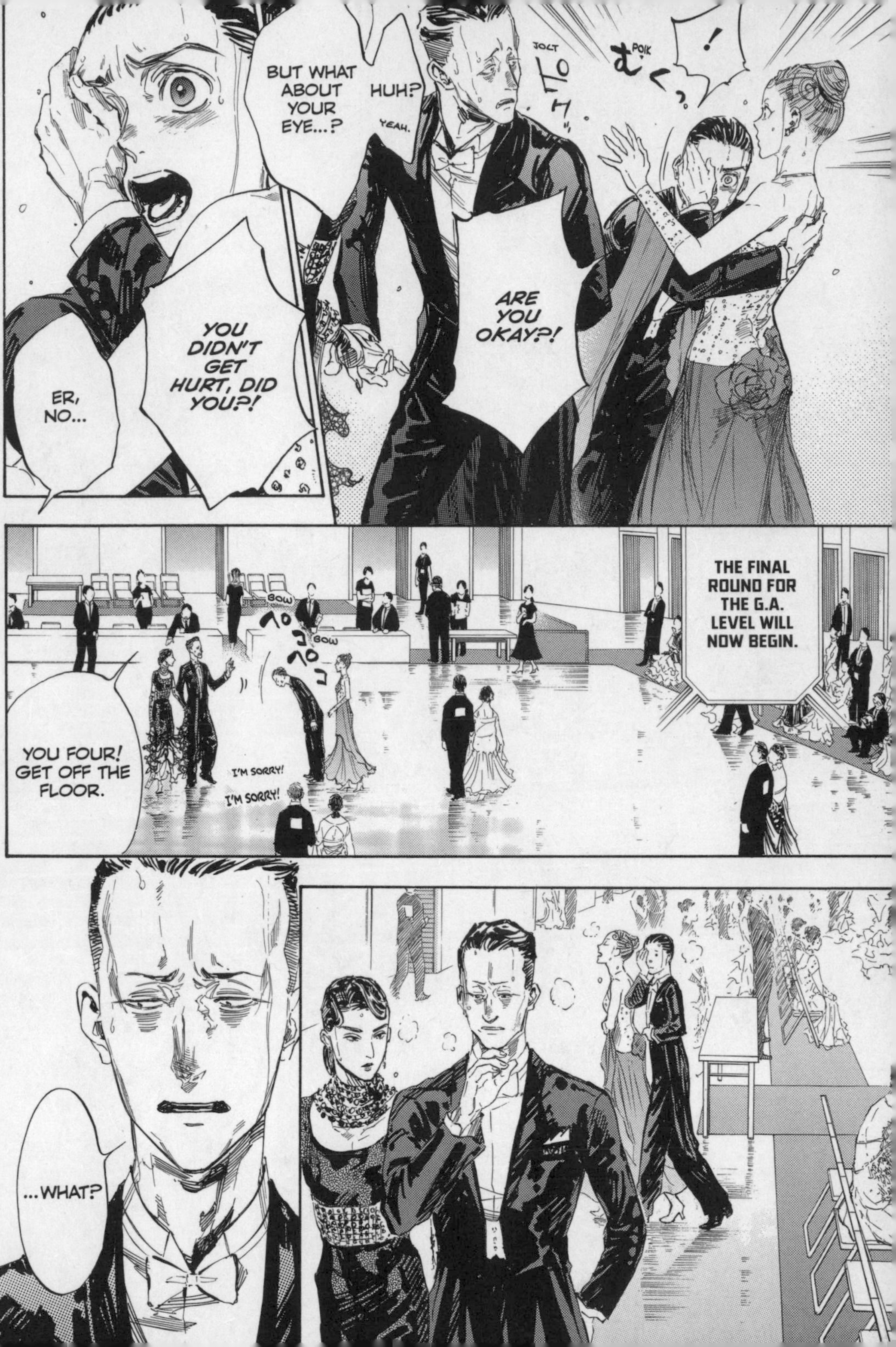
!
POIK
JOLT
HUH?
YEAH.
BUT WHAT ABOUT YOUR EYE...?
ARE YOU OKAY?!
YOU DIDN'T GET HURT, DID YOU?!
ER, NO...
THE FINAL ROUND FOR THE G.A. LEVEL WILL NOW BEGIN.
BOW
BOW
I'M SORRY!
I'M SORRY!
YOU FOUR! GET OFF THE FLOOR.
...WHAT?

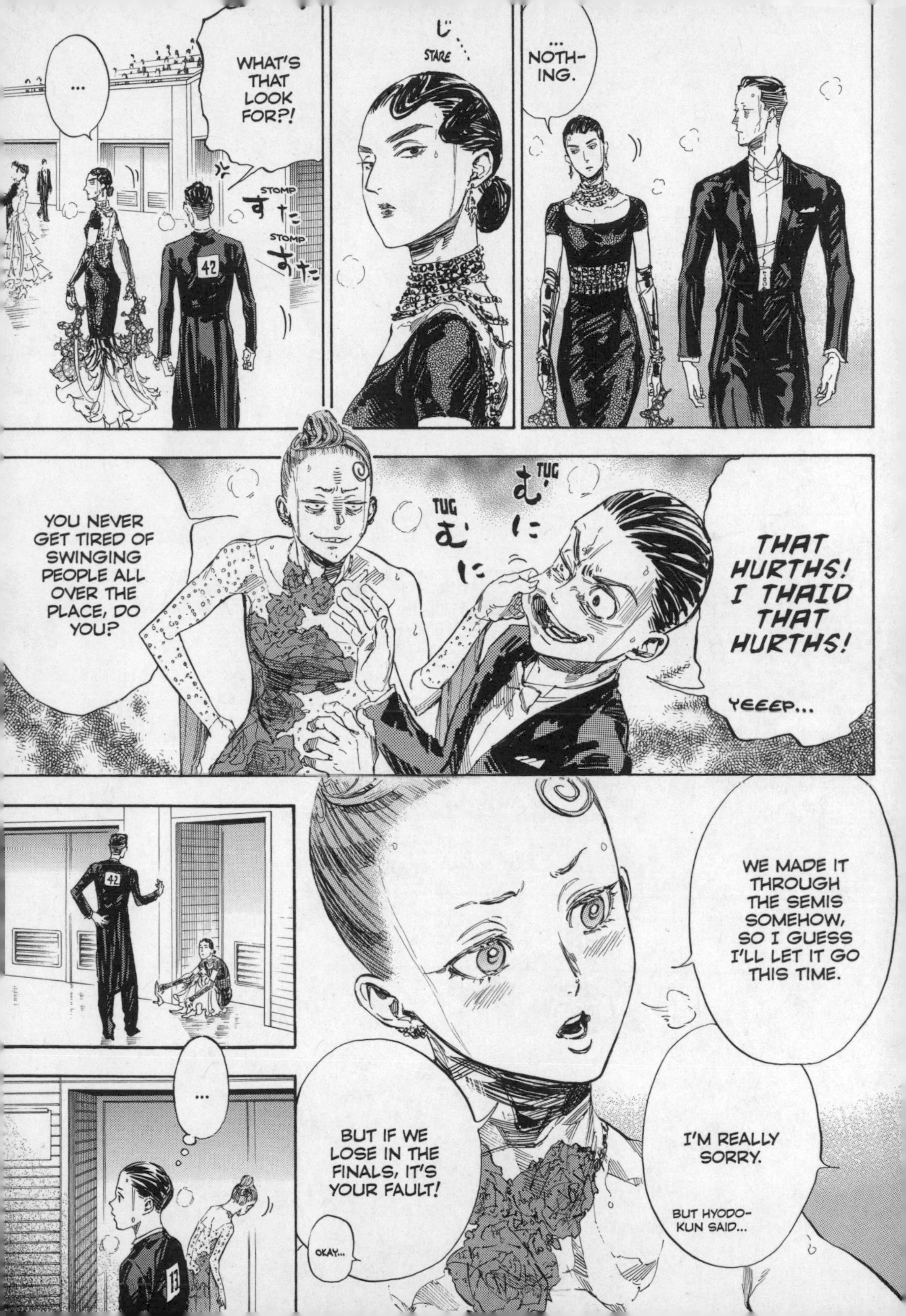
...
WHAT'S THAT LOOK FOR?!
STOMP すた
STOMP すた
じ...
STARE
... NOTH-ING.
YOU NEVER GET TIRED OF SWINGING PEOPLE ALL OVER THE PLACE, DO YOU?
TUG むに
TUG むに
THAT HURTHS! I THAID THAT HURTHS!
YEEEP...
...
WE MADE IT THROUGH THE SEMIS SOMEHOW, SO I GUESS I'LL LET IT GO THIS TIME.
BUT IF WE LOSE IN THE FINALS, IT'S YOUR FAULT!
OKAY...
I'M REALLY SORRY.
BUT HYODO-KUN SAID...

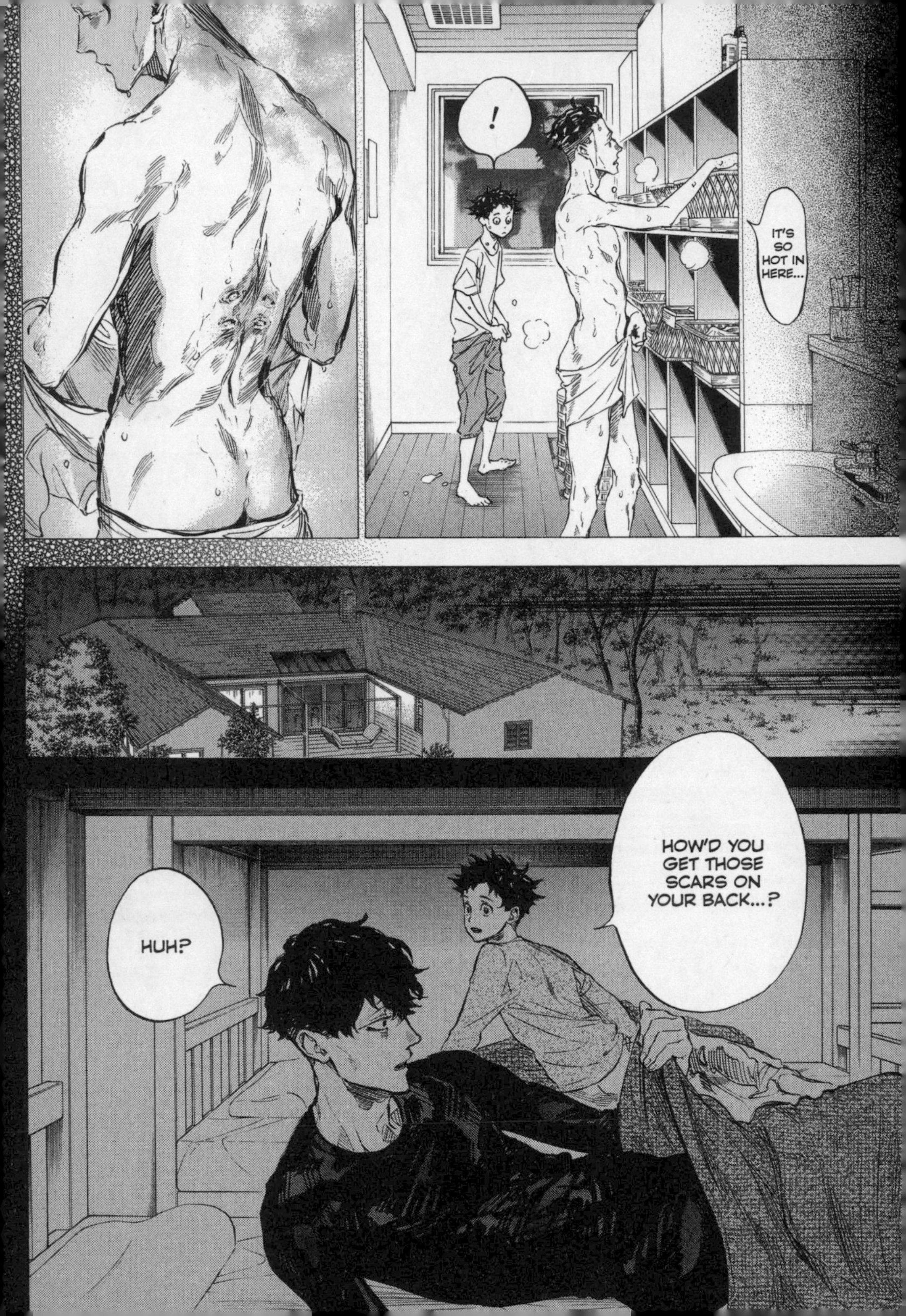
IT'S SO HOT IN HERE...
!
HOW'D YOU GET THOSE SCARS ON YOUR BACK...?
HUH?

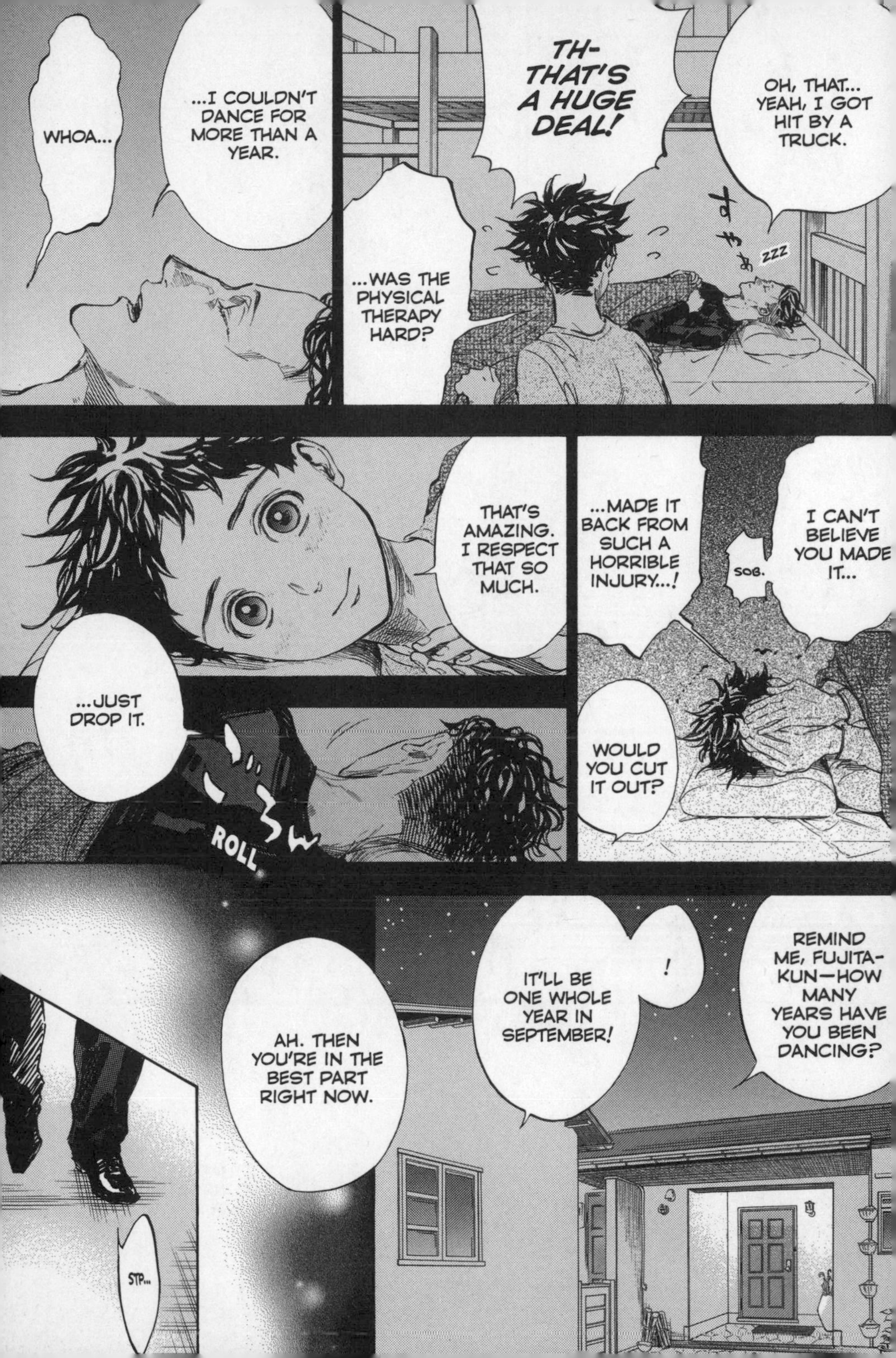
OH, THAT... YEAH, I GOT HIT BY A TRUCK.
ZZZ
TH-THAT'S A HUGE DEAL!
...WAS THE PHYSICAL THERAPY HARD?
...I COULDN'T DANCE FOR MORE THAN A YEAR.
WHOA...
I CAN'T BELIEVE YOU MADE IT...
SOB.
...MADE IT BACK FROM SUCH A HORRIBLE INJURY...!
WOULD YOU CUT IT OUT?
THAT'S AMAZING. I RESPECT THAT SO MUCH.
...JUST DROP IT.
ROLL
REMIND ME, FUJITA-KUN—HOW MANY YEARS HAVE YOU BEEN DANCING?
!
IT'LL BE ONE WHOLE YEAR IN SEPTEMBER!
AH. THEN YOU'RE IN THE BEST PART RIGHT NOW.
STP...

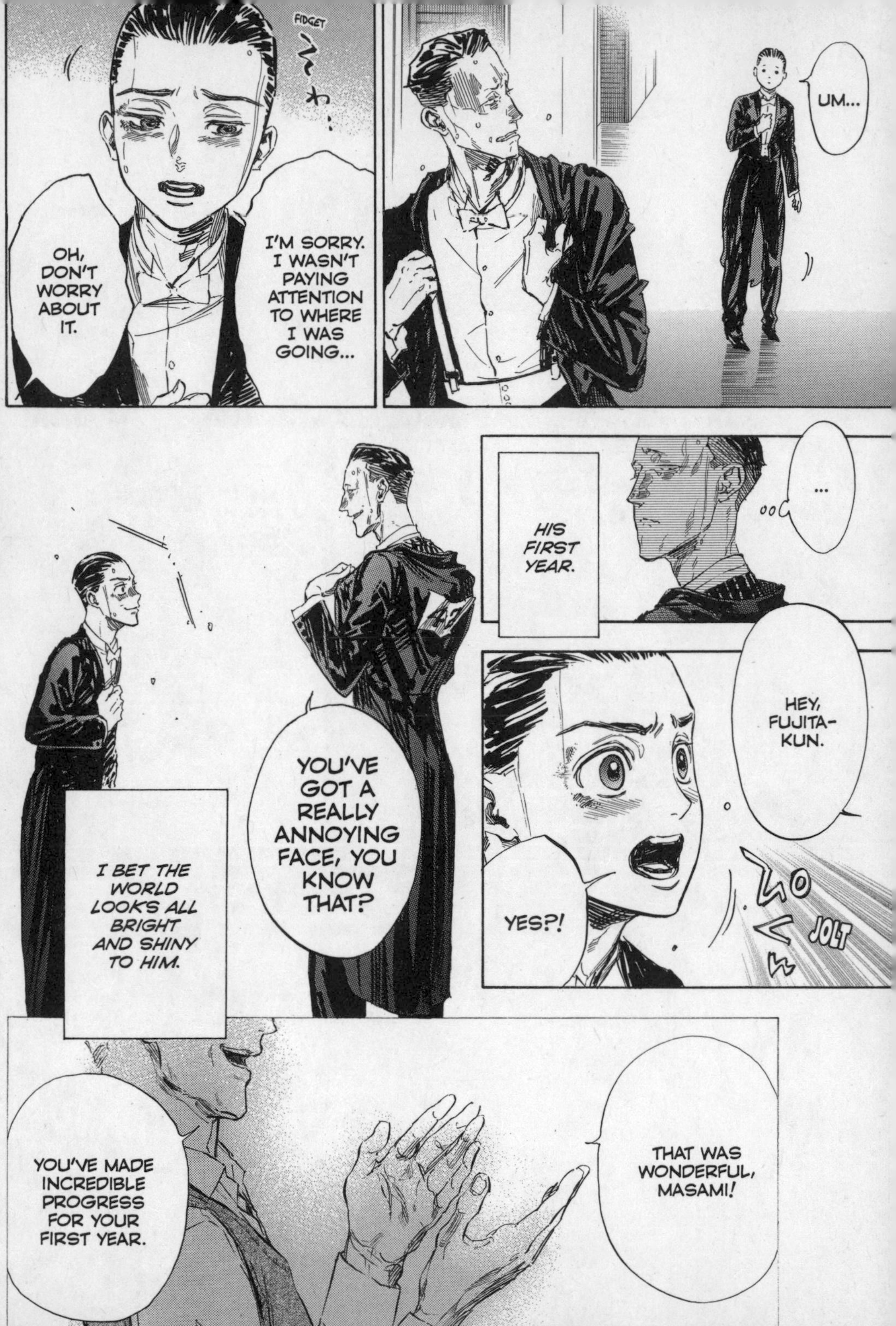
UM...
FIDGET
I'M SORRY. I WASN'T PAYING ATTENTION TO WHERE I WAS GOING...
OH, DON'T WORRY ABOUT IT.
...
HIS FIRST YEAR.
HEY, FUJITA-KUN.
JOLT
YES?!
YOU'VE GOT A REALLY ANNOYING FACE, YOU KNOW THAT?
I BET THE WORLD LOOKS ALL BRIGHT AND SHINY TO HIM.
THAT WAS WONDERFUL, MASAMI!
YOU'VE MADE INCREDIBLE PROGRESS FOR YOUR FIRST YEAR.

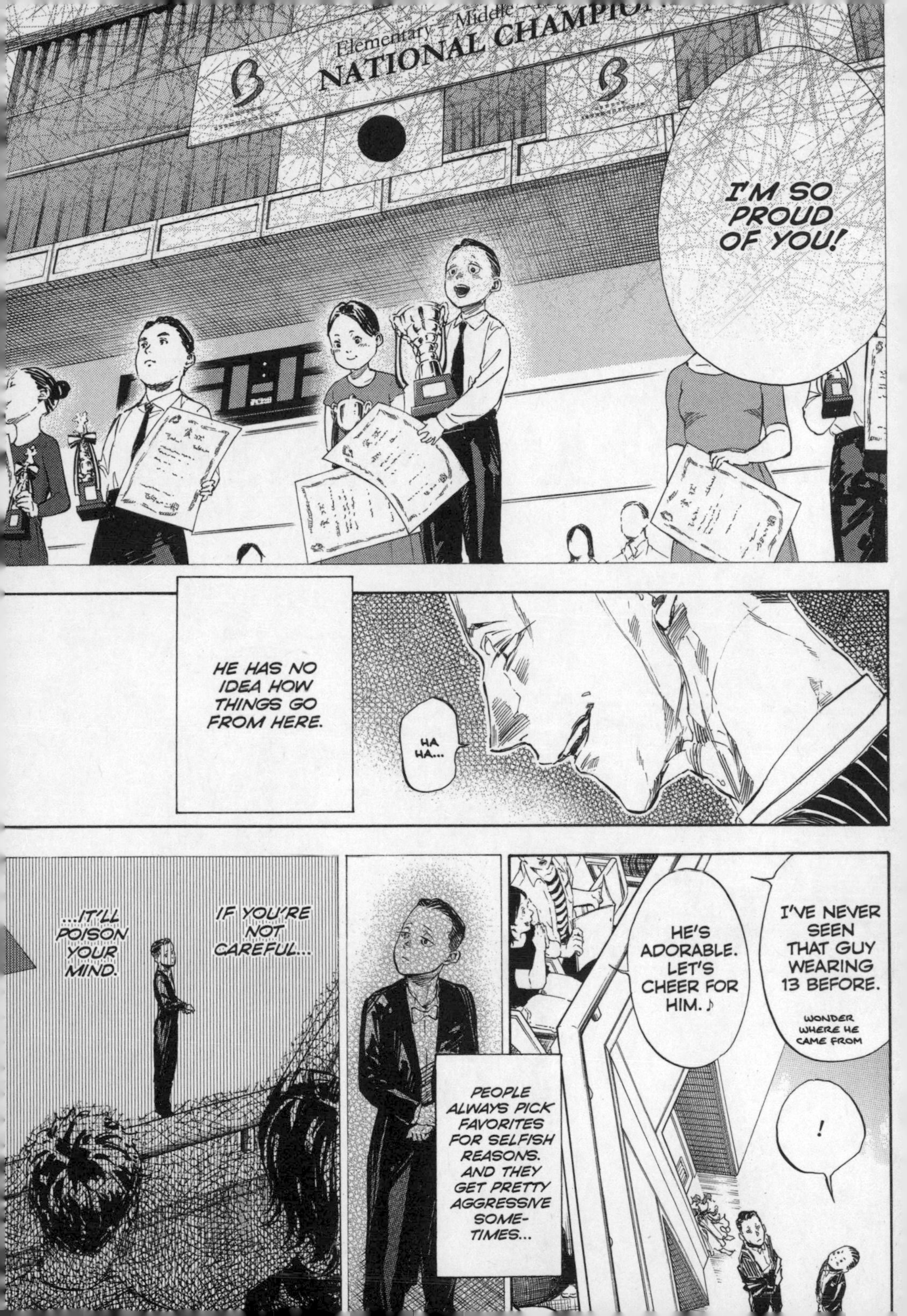
Elementary – Middle
I'M SO PROUD OF YOU!
HA HA...
HE HAS NO IDEA HOW THINGS GO FROM HERE.
I'VE NEVER SEEN THAT GUY WEARING 13 BEFORE.
WONDER WHERE HE CAME FROM
HE'S ADORABLE. LET'S CHEER FOR HIM. ♪
!
PEOPLE ALWAYS PICK FAVORITES FOR SELFISH REASONS. AND THEY GET PRETTY AGGRESSIVE SOME-TIMES...
IF YOU'RE NOT CAREFUL...
...IT'LL POISON YOUR MIND.

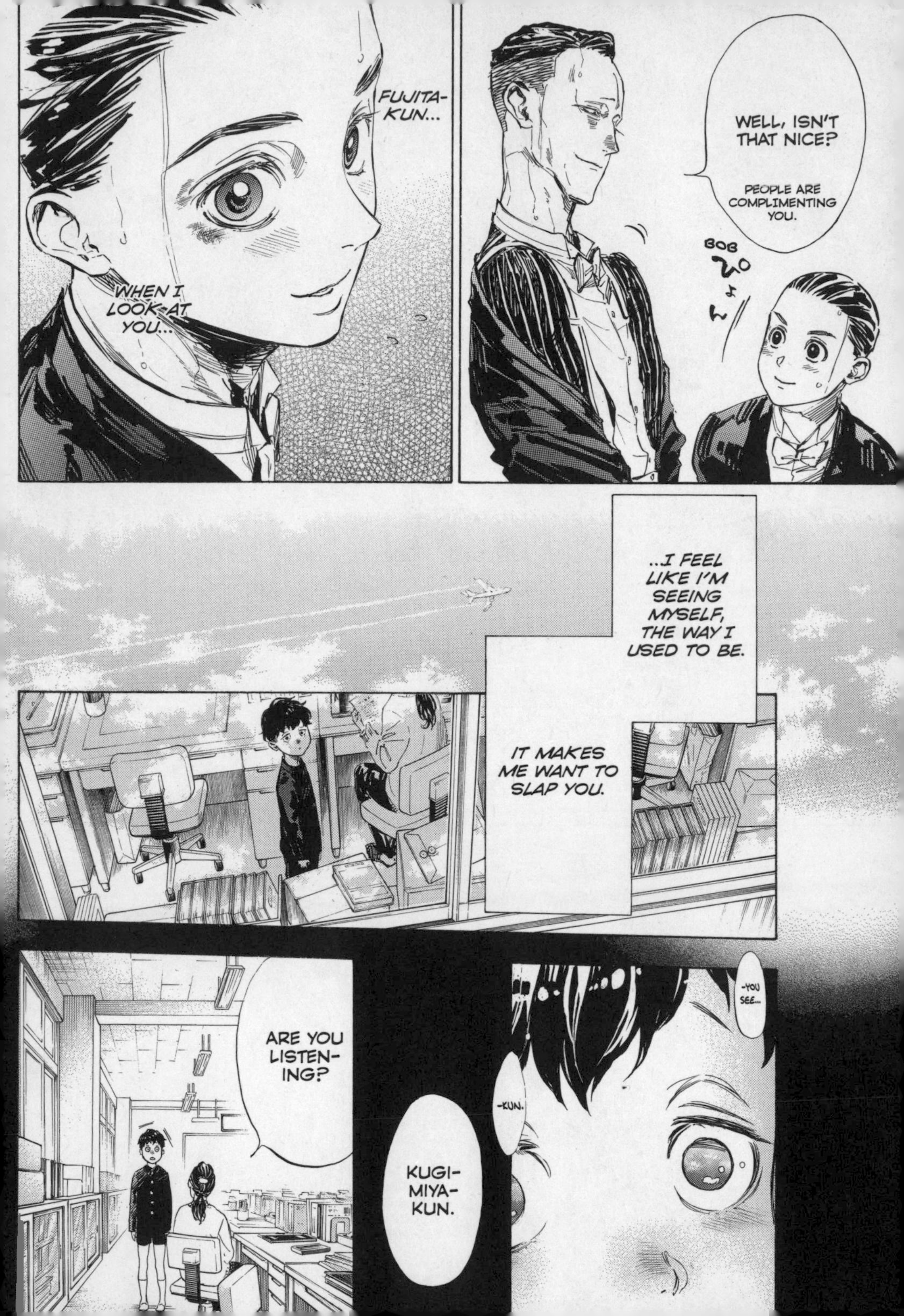
WELL, ISN'T THAT NICE?
PEOPLE ARE COMPLIMENTING YOU.
BOB
ぴょん
FUJITA-KUN...
WHEN I LOOK AT YOU...
...I FEEL LIKE I'M SEEING MYSELF, THE WAY I USED TO BE.
IT MAKES ME WANT TO SLAP YOU.
-YOU SEE...
-KUN.
KUGI-MIYA-KUN.
ARE YOU LISTEN-ING?

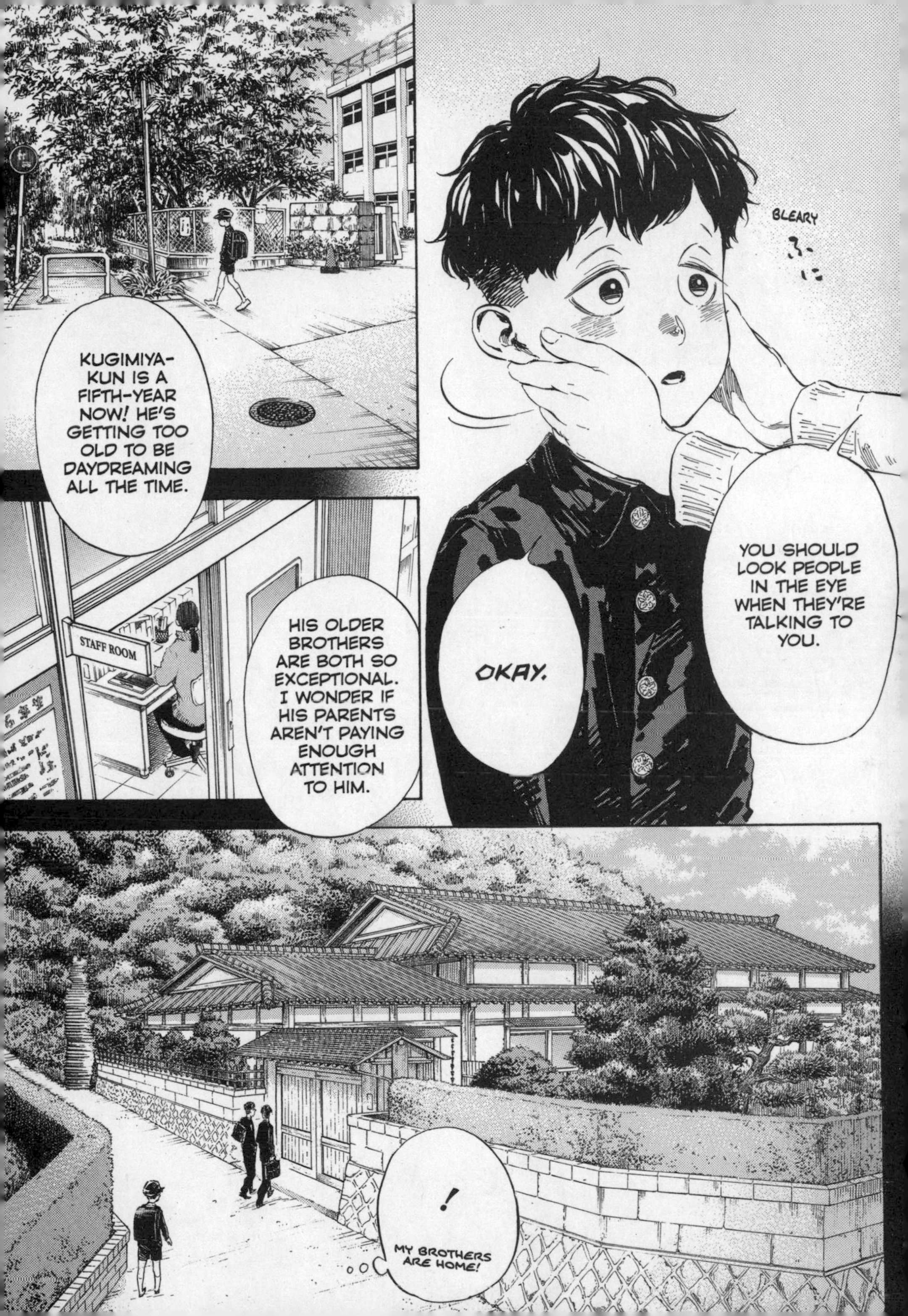
BLEARY
YOU SHOULD LOOK PEOPLE IN THE EYE WHEN THEY'RE TALKING TO YOU.
OKAY.
KUGIMIYA-KUN IS A FIFTH-YEAR NOW! HE'S GETTING TOO OLD TO BE DAYDREAMING ALL THE TIME.
STAFF ROOM
HIS OLDER BROTHERS ARE BOTH SO EXCEPTIONAL. I WONDER IF HIS PARENTS AREN'T PAYING ENOUGH ATTENTION TO HIM.
!
MY BROTHERS ARE HOME!

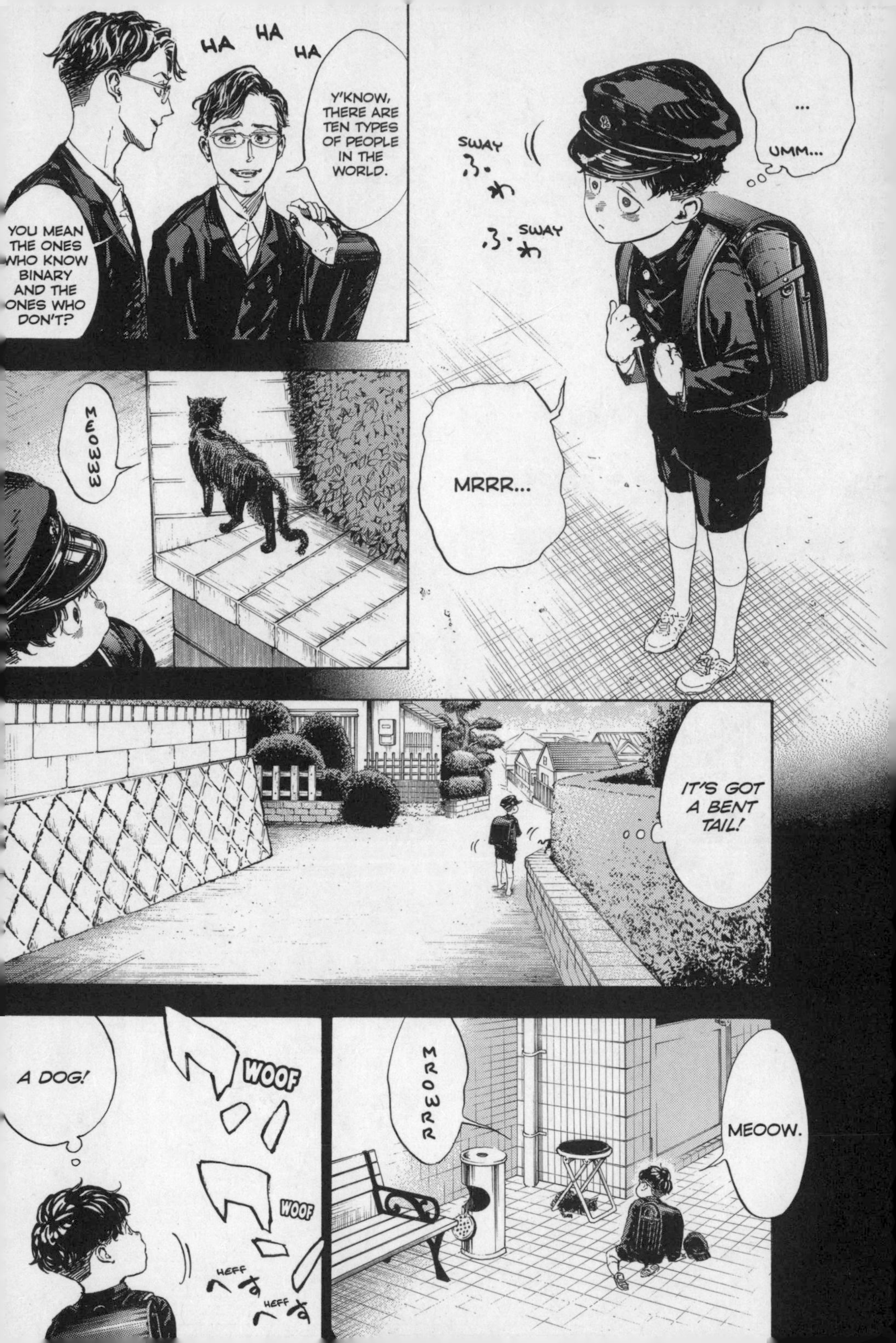
...
UMM...
SWAY ふわ
SWAY ふわ
MRRR...
HA HA HA
Y'KNOW, THERE ARE TEN TYPES OF PEOPLE IN THE WORLD.
YOU MEAN THE ONES WHO KNOW BINARY AND THE ONES WHO DON'T?
MEOWWW
IT'S GOT A BENT TAIL!
MEOOW.
MROWRR
WOOF
A DOG!
WOOF
HEFF へす
HEFF へす

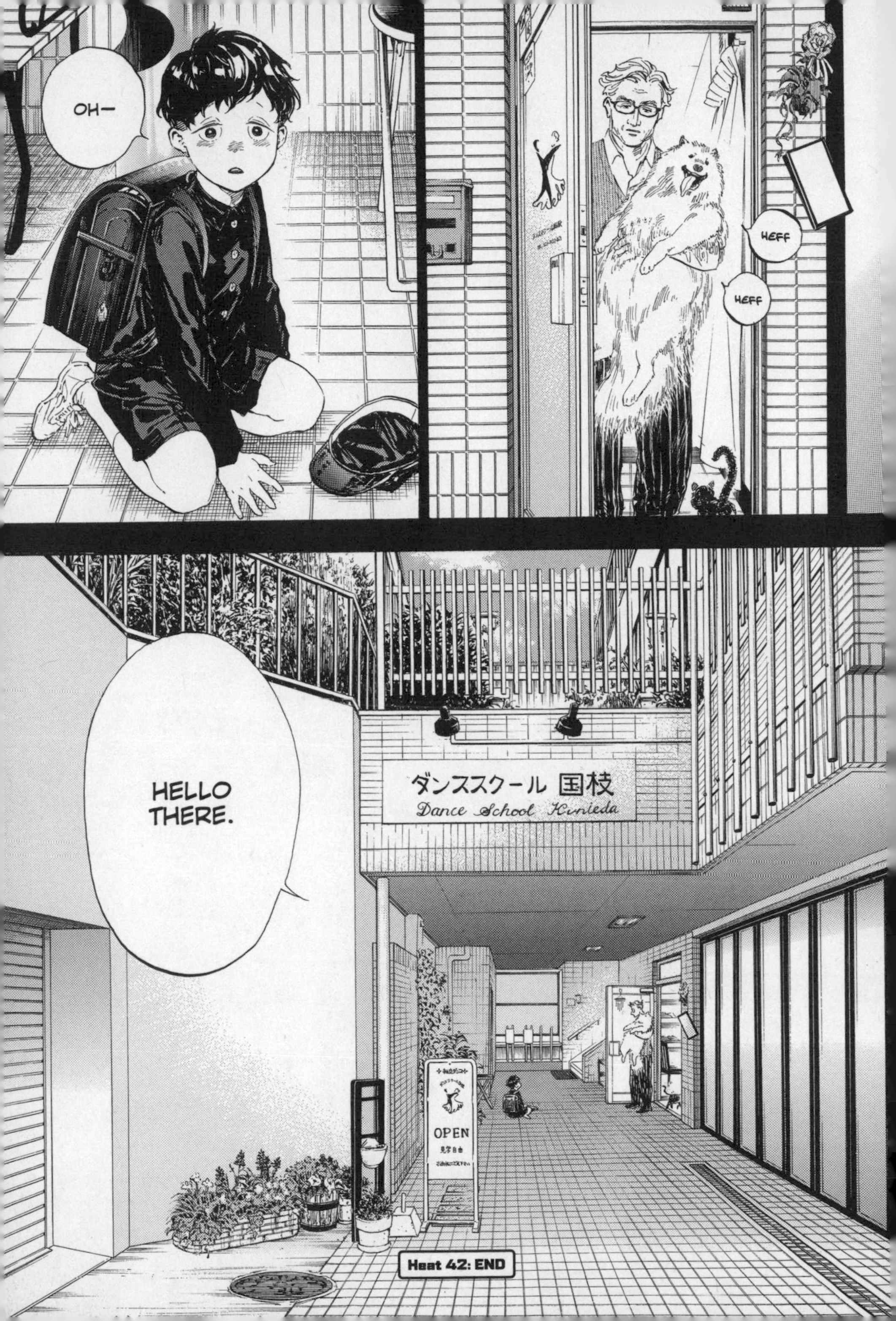
HEFF
HEFF
OH—
HELLO THERE.
ダンススクール 国枝
Dance School Kunieda
OPEN
Heat 42: END

WELCOME TO THE BALLROOM

Heat 43
Captivity

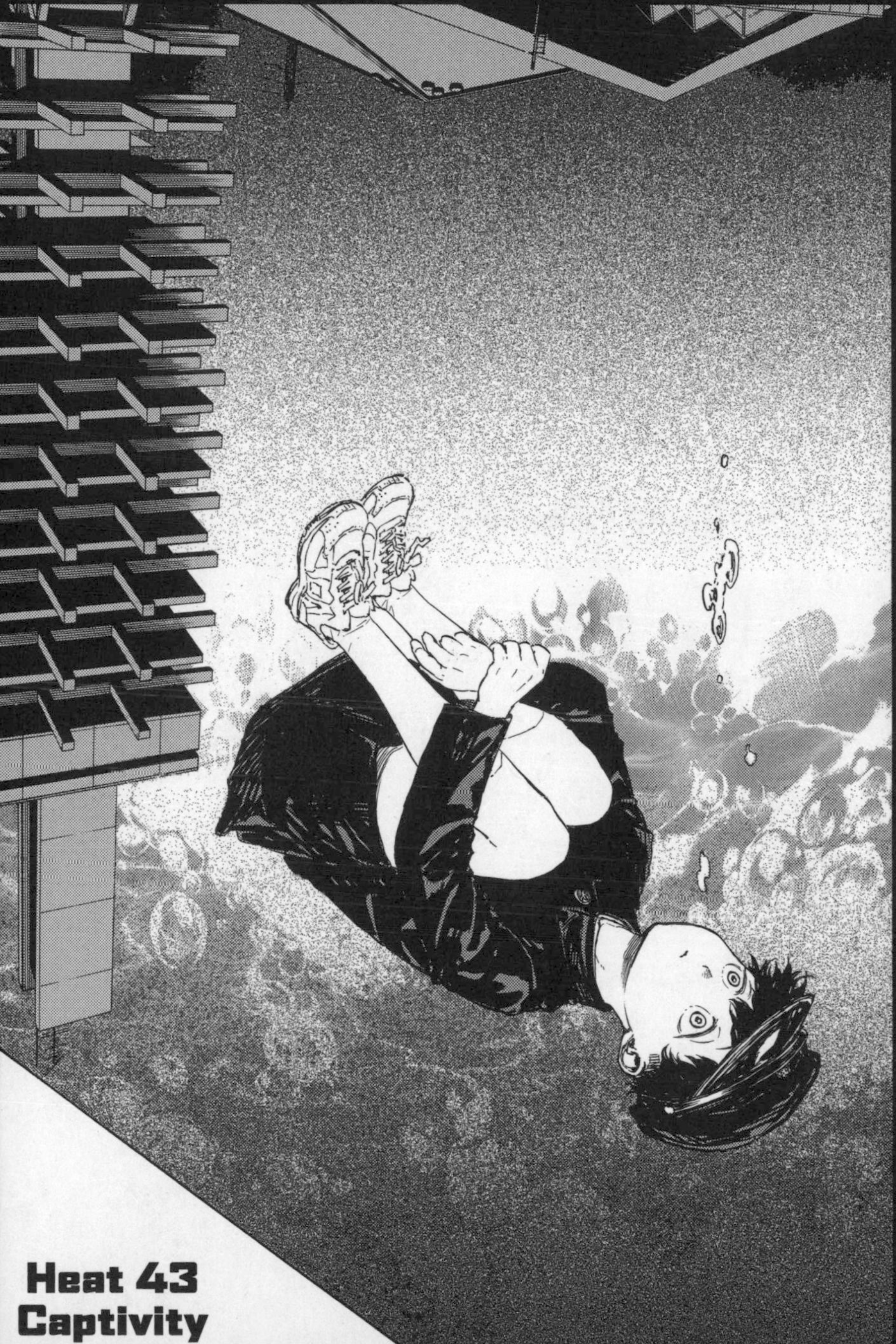

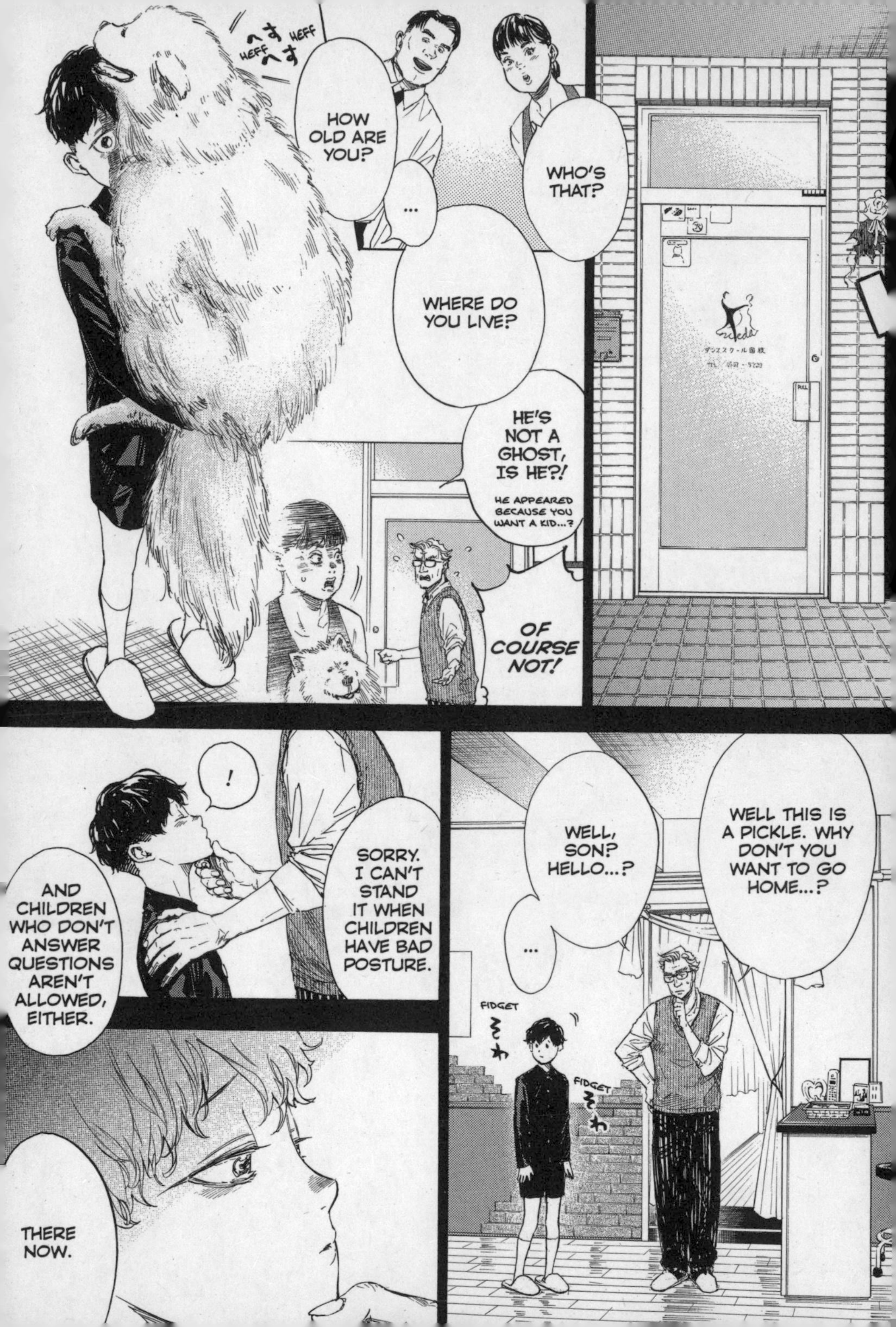
WHO'S THAT?
HOW OLD ARE YOU?
...
WHERE DO YOU LIVE?
HEFF へす HEFF へす
HE'S NOT A GHOST, IS HE?!
HE APPEARED BECAUSE YOU WANT A KID...?
OF COURSE NOT!
WELL THIS IS A PICKLE. WHY DON'T YOU WANT TO GO HOME...?
WELL, SON? HELLO...?
...
FIDGET そわ
FIDGET そわ
!
SORRY. I CAN'T STAND IT WHEN CHILDREN HAVE BAD POSTURE.
AND CHILDREN WHO DON'T ANSWER QUESTIONS AREN'T ALLOWED, EITHER.
THERE NOW.

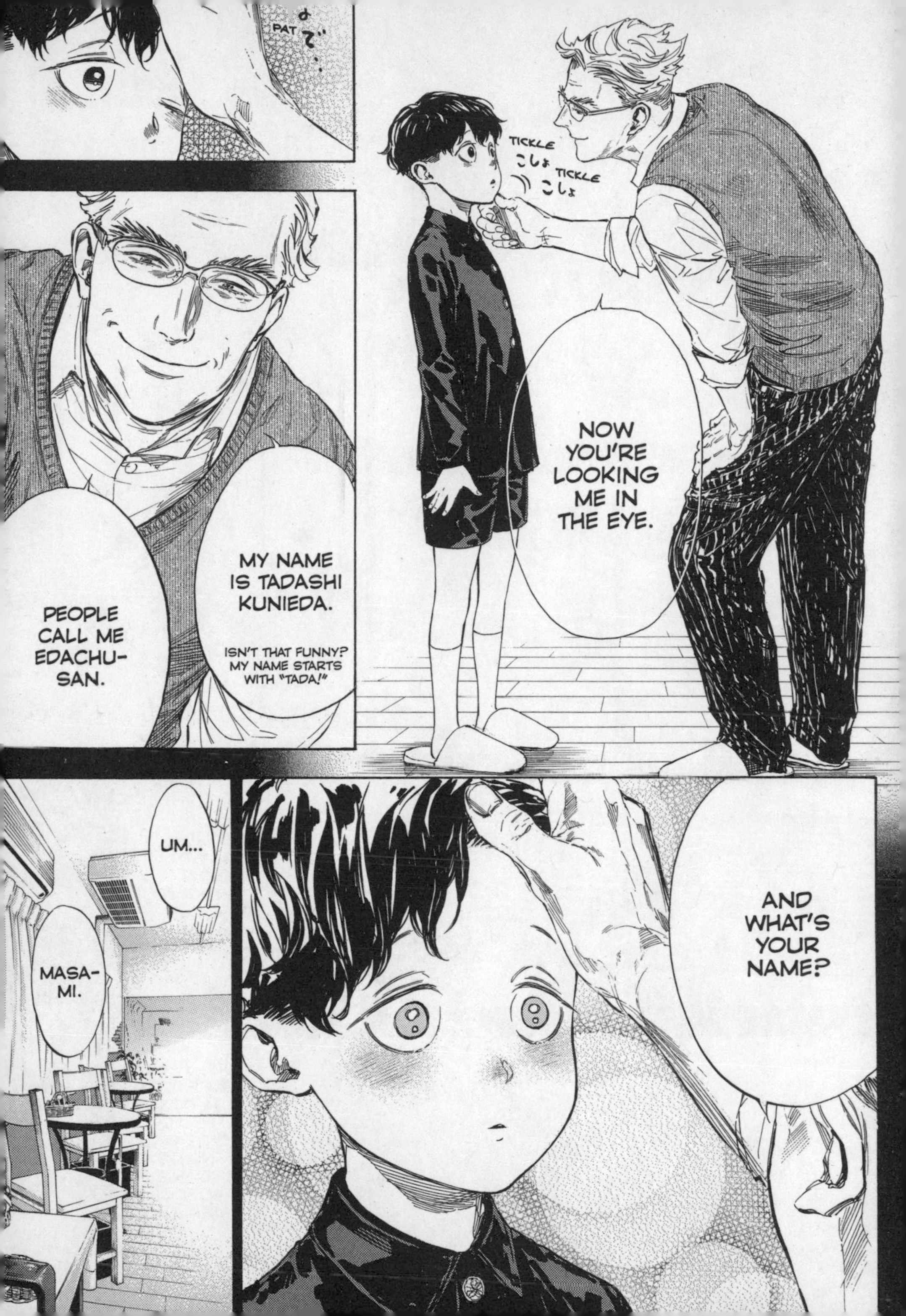
TICKLE
こしょ
TICKLE
こしょ
NOW YOU'RE LOOKING ME IN THE EYE.
PAT
MY NAME IS TADASHI KUNIEDA.
ISN'T THAT FUNNY? MY NAME STARTS WITH "TADA!"
PEOPLE CALL ME EDACHU-SAN.
AND WHAT'S YOUR NAME?
UM...
MASA-MI.

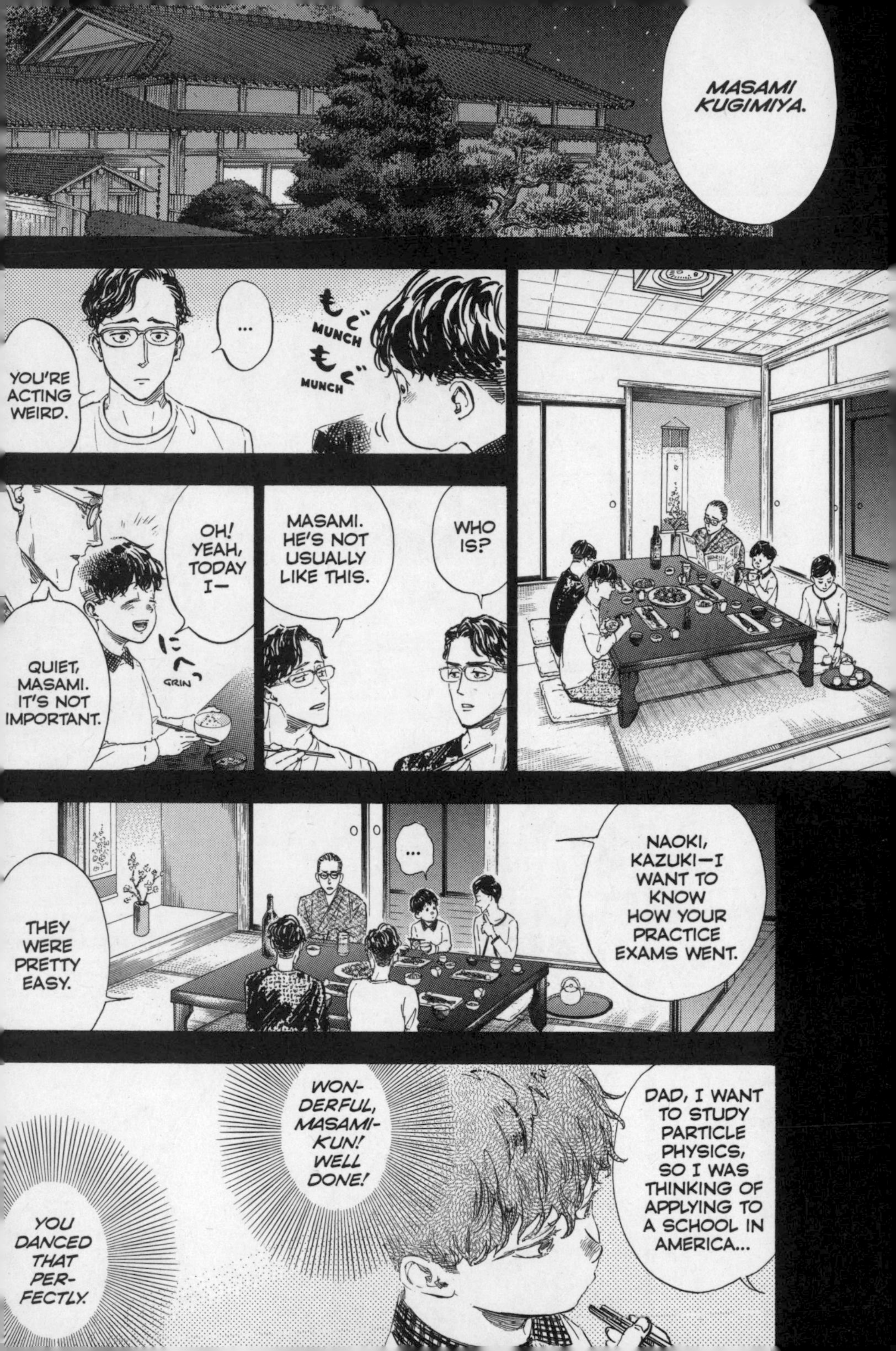
MASAMI KUGIMIYA.
もぐ MUNCH
もぐ MUNCH
...
YOU'RE ACTING WEIRD.
WHO IS?
MASAMI. HE'S NOT USUALLY LIKE THIS.
OH! YEAH, TODAY I—
GRIN
QUIET, MASAMI. IT'S NOT IMPORTANT.
NAOKI, KAZUKI—I WANT TO KNOW HOW YOUR PRACTICE EXAMS WENT.
...
THEY WERE PRETTY EASY.
DAD, I WANT TO STUDY PARTICLE PHYSICS, SO I WAS THINKING OF APPLYING TO A SCHOOL IN AMERICA...
WON-DERFUL, MASAMI-KUN! WELL DONE!
YOU DANCED THAT PER-FECTLY.

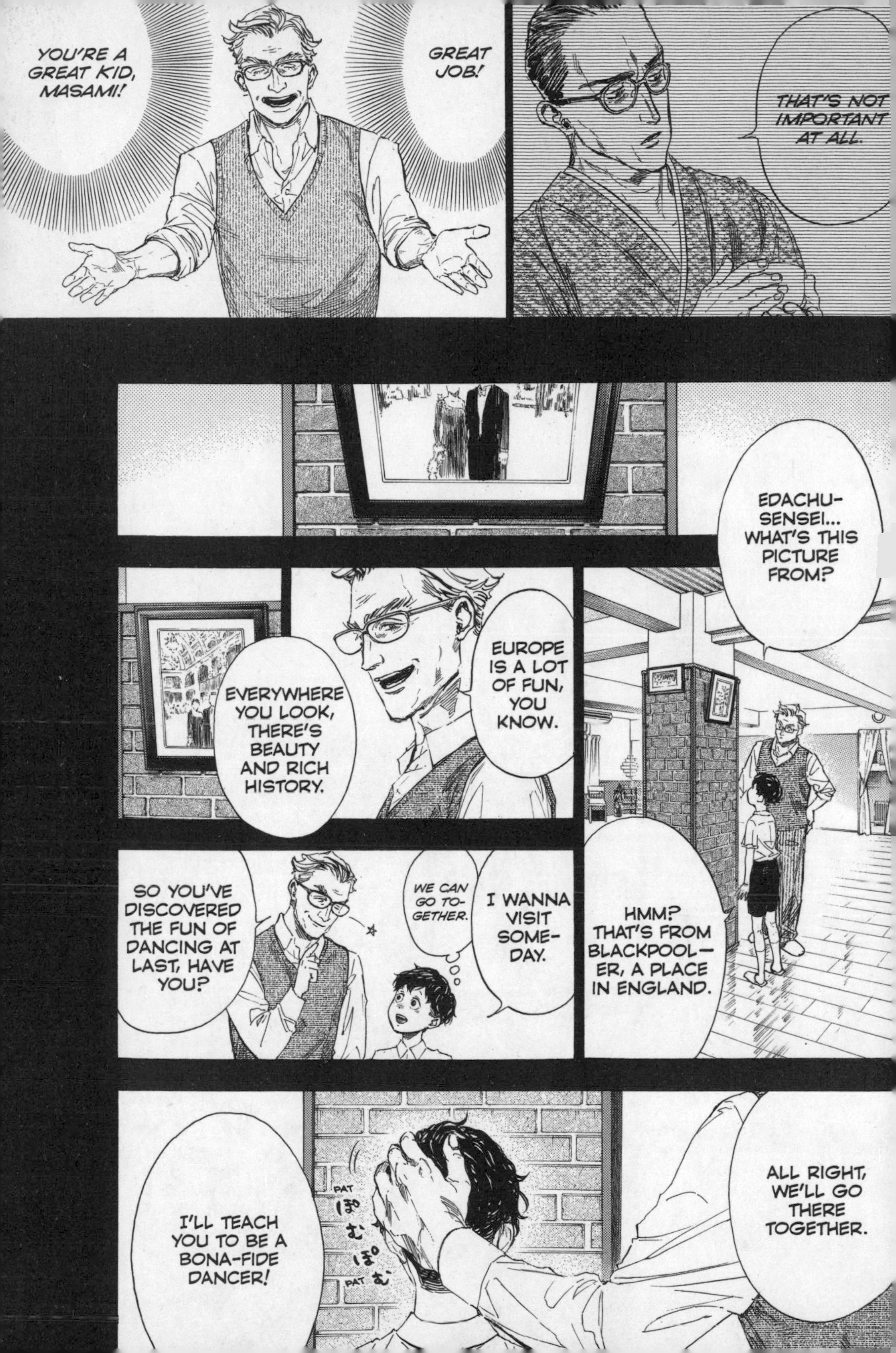
THAT'S NOT IMPORTANT AT ALL.
GREAT JOB!
YOU'RE A GREAT KID, MASAMI!
EDACHU-SENSEI... WHAT'S THIS PICTURE FROM?
HMM? THAT'S FROM BLACKPOOL-ER, A PLACE IN ENGLAND.
EUROPE IS A LOT OF FUN, YOU KNOW.
EVERYWHERE YOU LOOK, THERE'S BEAUTY AND RICH HISTORY.
I WANNA VISIT SOME-DAY.
WE CAN GO TO-GETHER.
SO YOU'VE DISCOVERED THE FUN OF DANCING AT LAST, HAVE YOU?
ALL RIGHT, WE'LL GO THERE TOGETHER.
PAT ぽむ
ぽむ PAT
I'LL TEACH YOU TO BE A BONA-FIDE DANCER!

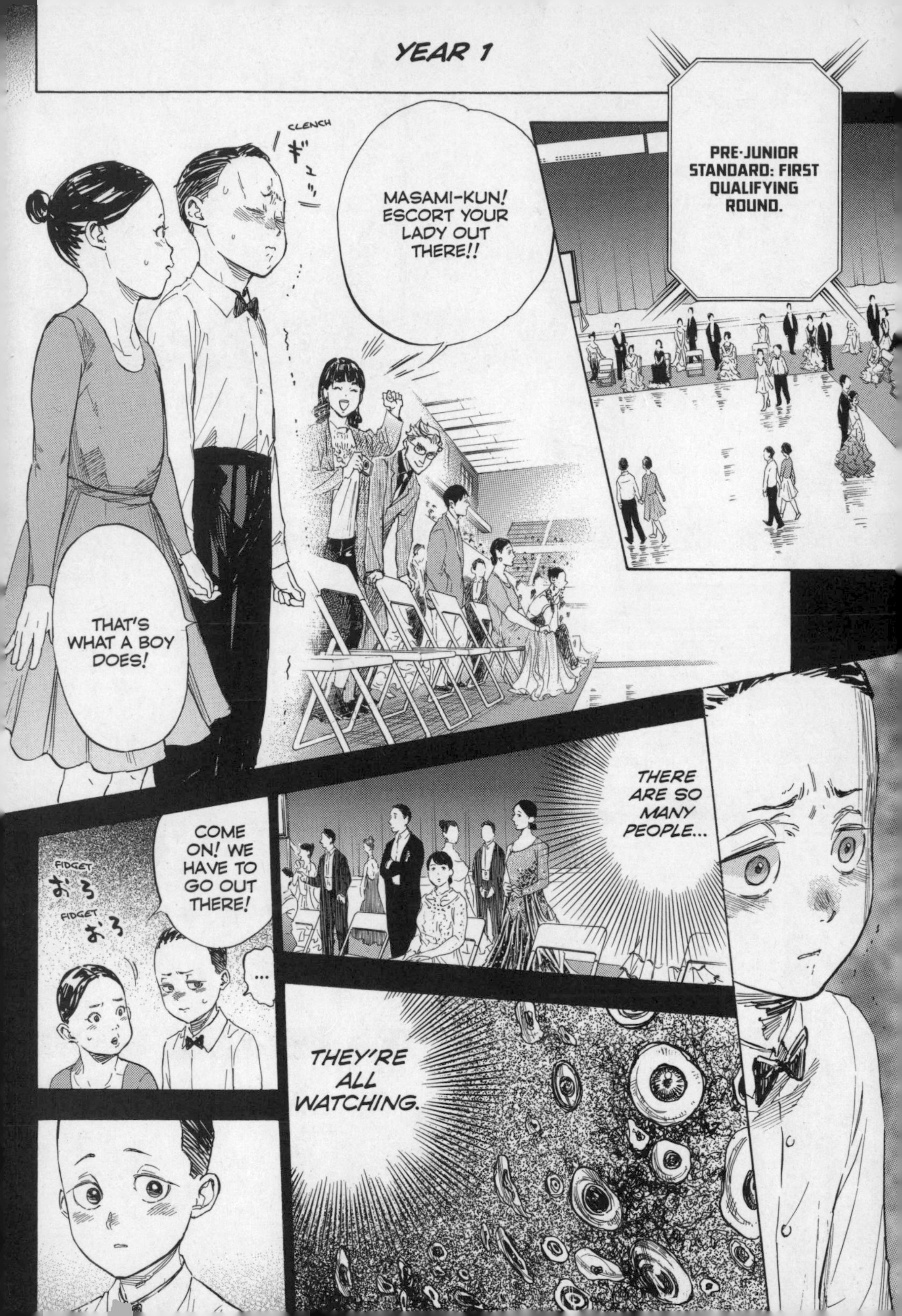
YEAR 1
PRE-JUNIOR STANDARD: FIRST QUALIFYING ROUND.
MASAMI-KUN! ESCORT YOUR LADY OUT THERE!!
CLENCH
THAT'S WHAT A BOY DOES!
THERE ARE SO MANY PEOPLE...
THEY'RE ALL WATCHING.
COME ON! WE HAVE TO GO OUT THERE!
FIDGET
FIDGET
...

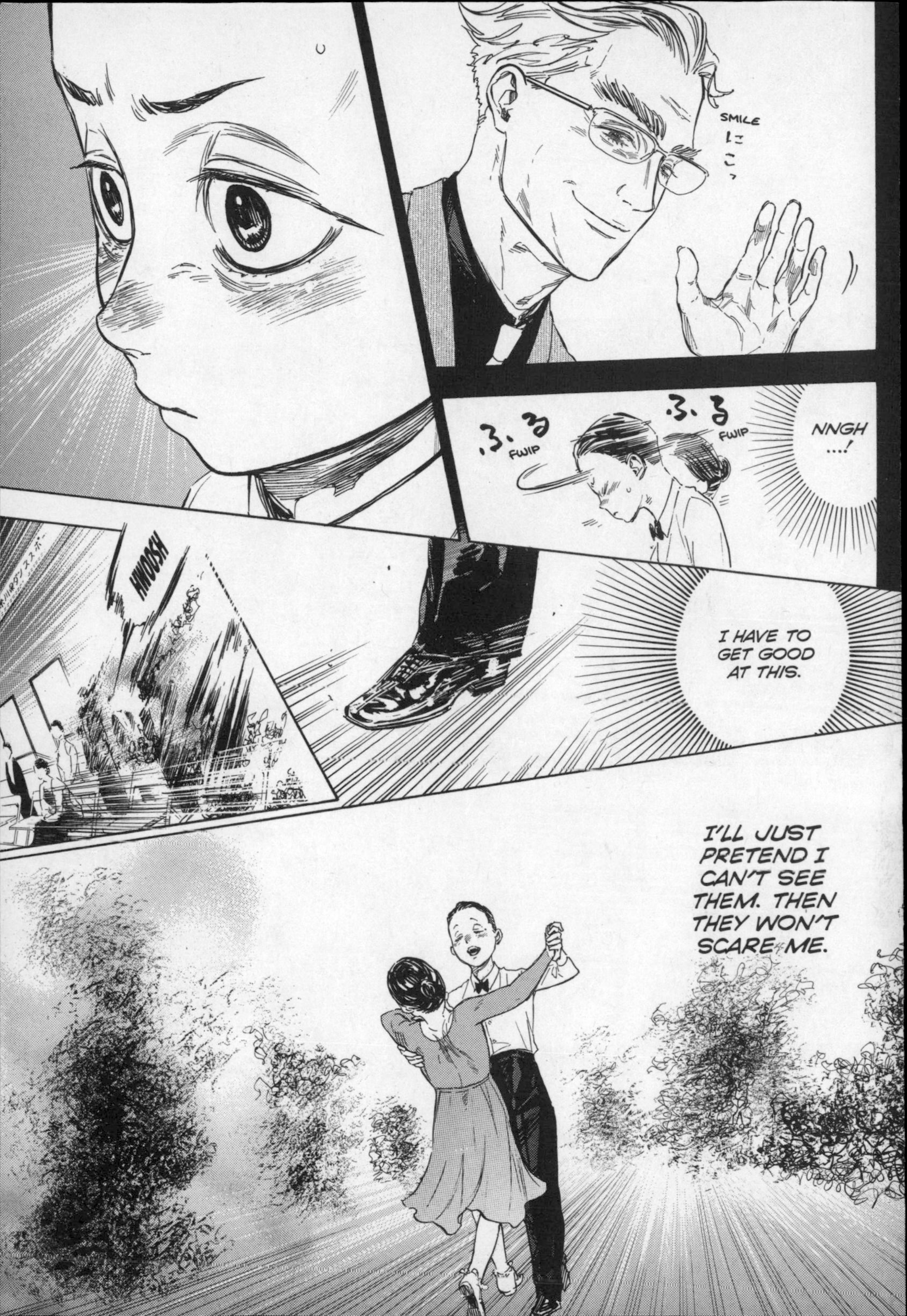
SMILE
にこっ
NNGH ...!
ふる
FWIP
ふる
FWIP
I HAVE TO GET GOOD AT THIS.
HWOOSH
I'LL JUST PRETEND I CAN'T SEE THEM. THEN THEY WON'T SCARE ME.

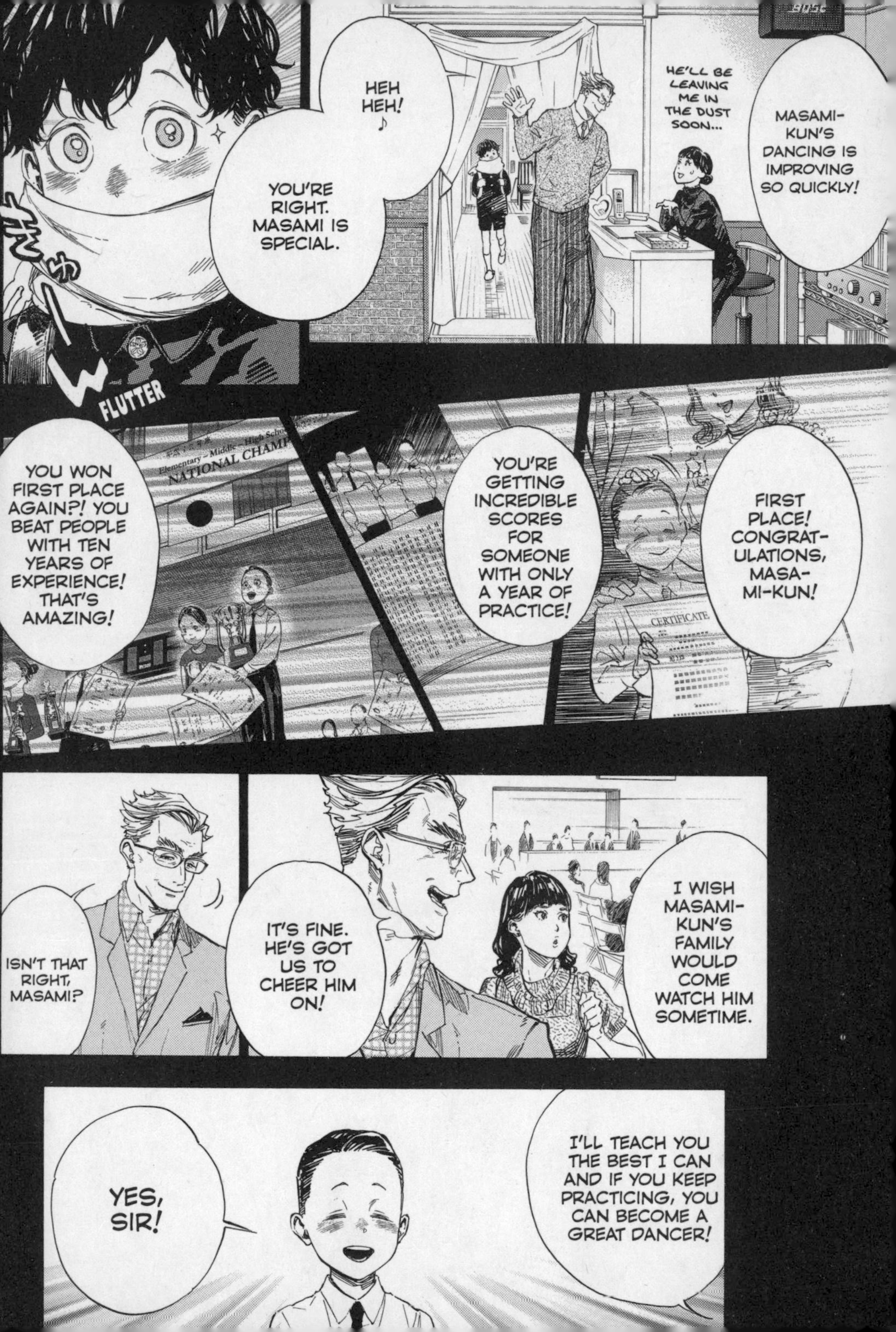
MASAMI-KUN'S DANCING IS IMPROVING SO QUICKLY!
HE'LL BE LEAVING ME IN THE DUST SOON...
HEH HEH! ♪
YOU'RE RIGHT. MASAMI IS SPECIAL.
FLUTTER
FIRST PLACE! CONGRAT-ULATIONS, MASA-MI-KUN!
CERTIFICATE
YOU'RE GETTING INCREDIBLE SCORES FOR SOMEONE WITH ONLY A YEAR OF PRACTICE!
YOU WON FIRST PLACE AGAIN?! YOU BEAT PEOPLE WITH TEN YEARS OF EXPERIENCE! THAT'S AMAZING!
I WISH MASAMI-KUN'S FAMILY WOULD COME WATCH HIM SOMETIME.
IT'S FINE. HE'S GOT US TO CHEER HIM ON!
ISN'T THAT RIGHT, MASAMI?
I'LL TEACH YOU THE BEST I CAN AND IF YOU KEEP PRACTICING, YOU CAN BECOME A GREAT DANCER!
YES, SIR!

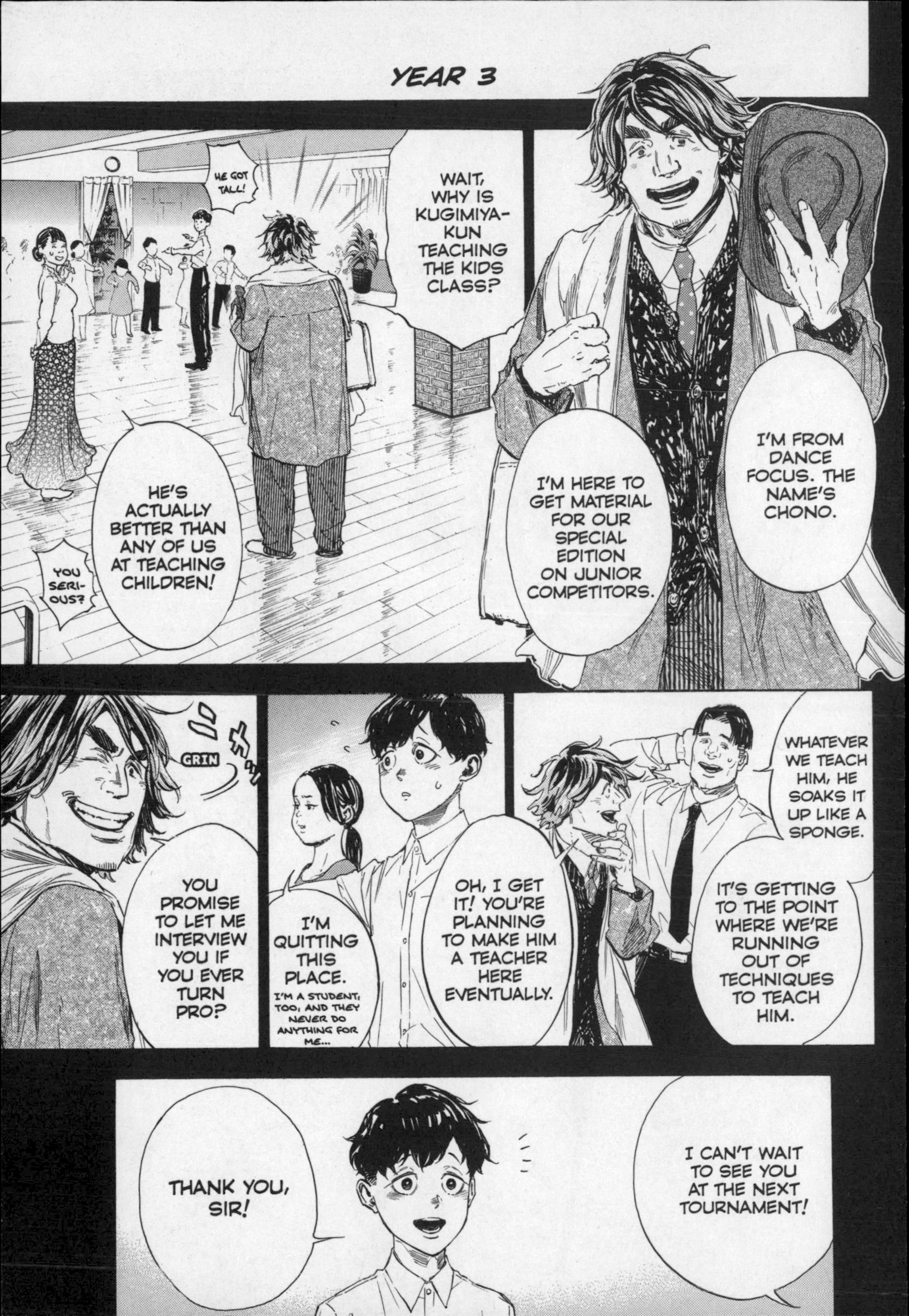
YEAR 3
I'M FROM DANCE FOCUS. THE NAME'S CHONO.
I'M HERE TO GET MATERIAL FOR OUR SPECIAL EDITION ON JUNIOR COMPETITORS.
WAIT, WHY IS KUGIMIYA-KUN TEACHING THE KIDS CLASS?
HE GOT TALL!
HE'S ACTUALLY BETTER THAN ANY OF US AT TEACHING CHILDREN!
YOU SERI-OUS?
WHATEVER WE TEACH HIM, HE SOAKS IT UP LIKE A SPONGE.
IT'S GETTING TO THE POINT WHERE WE'RE RUNNING OUT OF TECHNIQUES TO TEACH HIM.
OH, I GET IT! YOU'RE PLANNING TO MAKE HIM A TEACHER HERE EVENTUALLY.
I'M QUITTING THIS PLACE.
I'M A STUDENT, TOO, AND THEY NEVER DO ANYTHING FOR ME...
GRIN
YOU PROMISE TO LET ME INTERVIEW YOU IF YOU EVER TURN PRO?
I CAN'T WAIT TO SEE YOU AT THE NEXT TOURNAMENT!
THANK YOU, SIR!

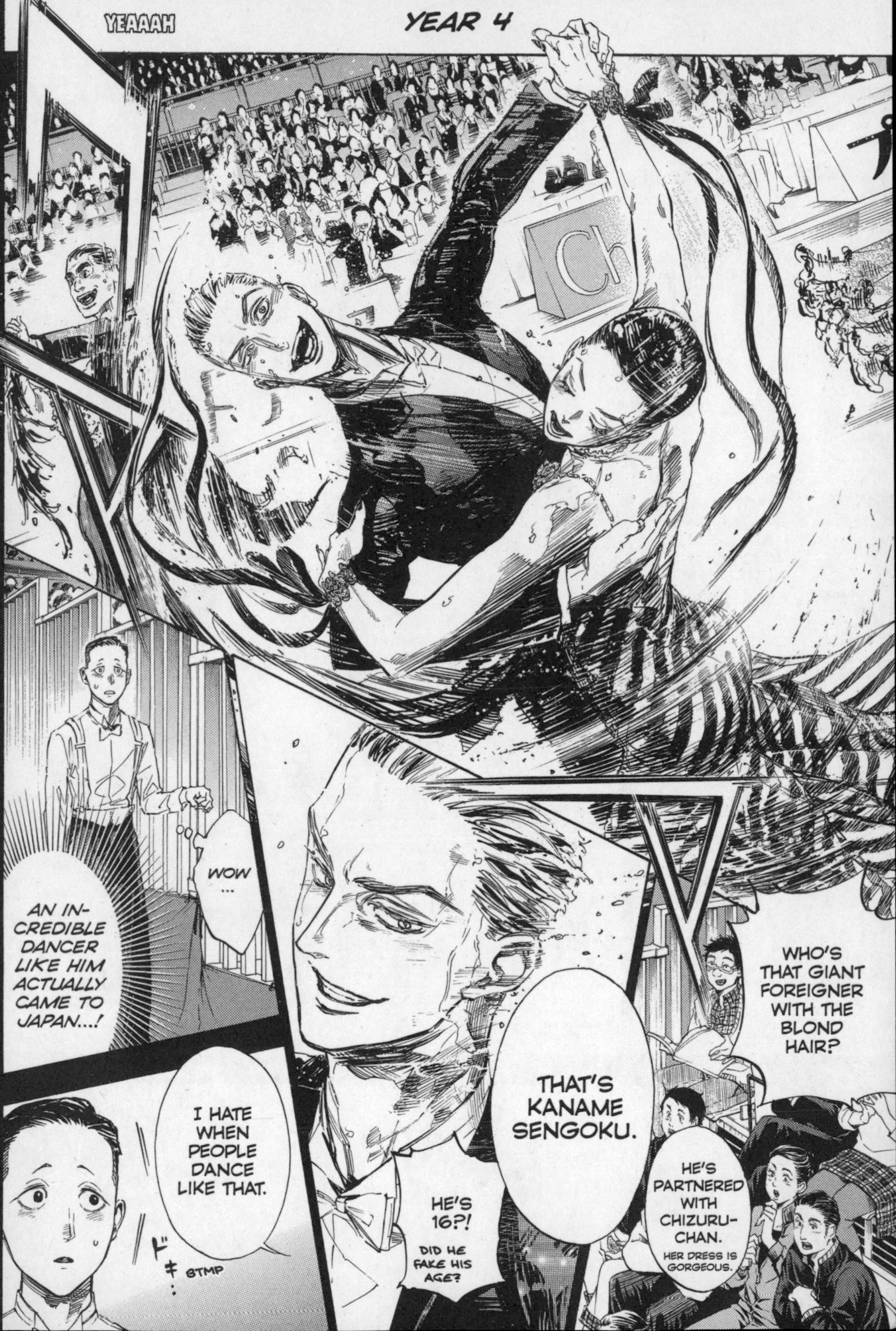
YEAR 4
YEAAAH
WHO'S THAT GIANT FOREIGNER WITH THE BLOND HAIR?
THAT'S KANAME SENGOKU.
HE'S PARTNERED WITH CHIZURU-CHAN.
HER DRESS IS GORGEOUS.
HE'S 16?!
DID HE FAKE HIS AGE?
WOW ...
AN INCREDIBLE DANCER LIKE HIM ACTUALLY CAME TO JAPAN...!
I HATE WHEN PEOPLE DANCE LIKE THAT.
BTMP

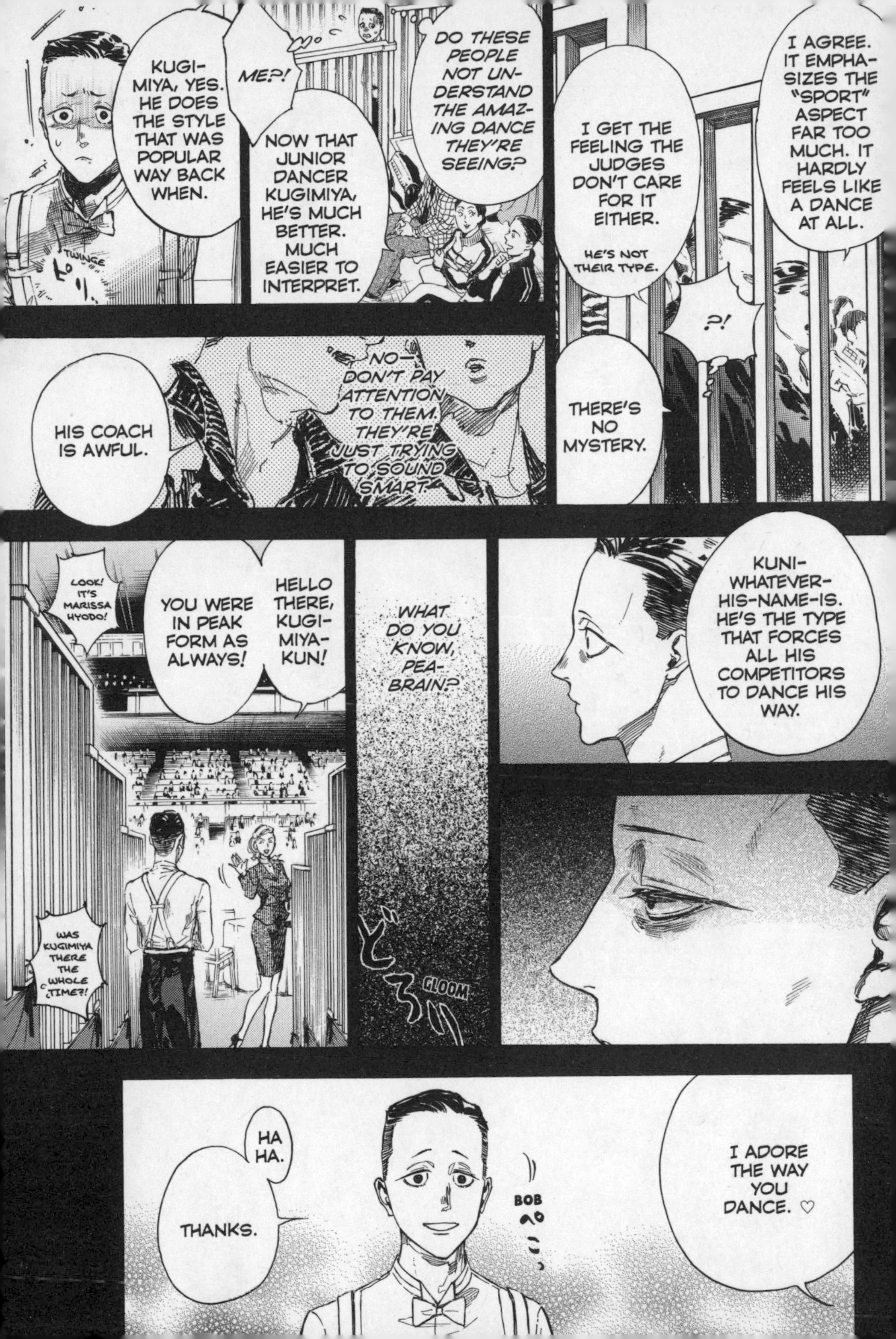
I AGREE. IT EMPHASIZES THE "SPORT" ASPECT FAR TOO MUCH. IT HARDLY FEELS LIKE A DANCE AT ALL.
I GET THE FEELING THE JUDGES DON'T CARE FOR IT EITHER.
HE'S NOT THEIR TYPE.
?!
THERE'S NO MYSTERY.
DO THESE PEOPLE NOT UNDERSTAND THE AMAZING DANCE THEY'RE SEEING?
NOW THAT JUNIOR DANCER KUGIMIYA, HE'S MUCH BETTER. MUCH EASIER TO INTERPRET.
ME?!
KUGIMIYA, YES. HE DOES THE STYLE THAT WAS POPULAR WAY BACK WHEN.
TWINGE
NO—DON'T PAY ATTENTION TO THEM. THEY'RE JUST TRYING TO SOUND SMART.
HIS COACH IS AWFUL.
KUNI-WHATEVER-HIS-NAME-IS. HE'S THE TYPE THAT FORCES ALL HIS COMPETITORS TO DANCE HIS WAY.
WHAT DO YOU KNOW, PEA-BRAIN?
GLOOM
HELLO THERE, KUGIMIYA-KUN!
YOU WERE IN PEAK FORM AS ALWAYS!
LOOK! IT'S MARISSA HYODO!
WAS KUGIMIYA THERE THE WHOLE TIME?!
I ADORE THE WAY YOU DANCE. ♡
BOB
HA HA.
THANKS.

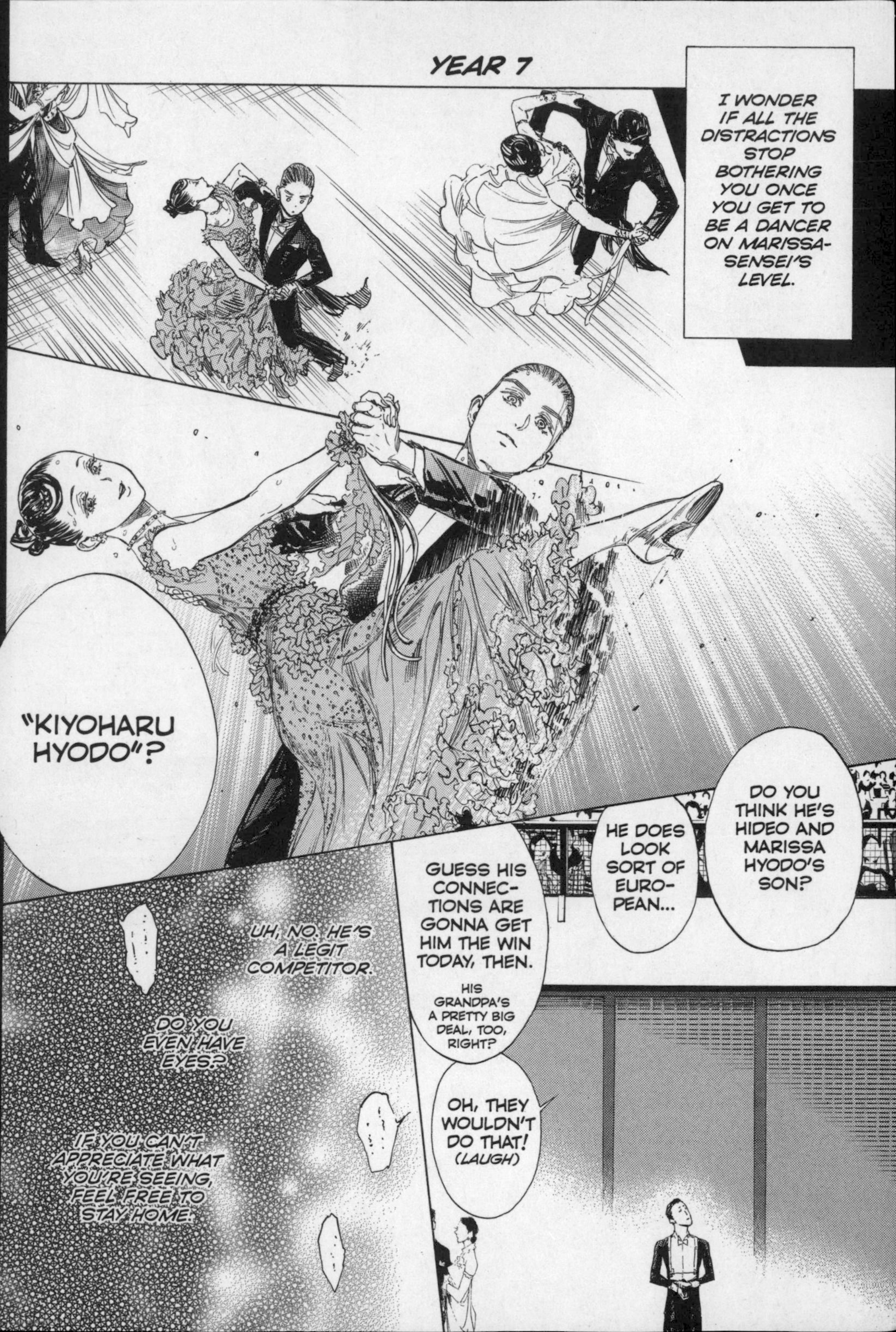
YEAR 7
I WONDER IF ALL THE DISTRACTIONS STOP BOTHERING YOU ONCE YOU GET TO BE A DANCER ON MARISSA-SENSEI'S LEVEL.
"KIYOHARU HYODO"?
DO YOU THINK HE'S HIDEO AND MARISSA HYODO'S SON?
HE DOES LOOK SORT OF EURO-PEAN...
GUESS HIS CONNEC-TIONS ARE GONNA GET HIM THE WIN TODAY, THEN.
HIS GRANDPA'S A PRETTY BIG DEAL, TOO, RIGHT?
OH, THEY WOULDN'T DO THAT! (LAUGH)
UH, NO, HE'S A LEGIT COMPETITOR.
DO YOU EVEN HAVE EYES?
IF YOU CAN'T APPRECIATE WHAT YOU'RE SEEING, FEEL FREE TO STAY HOME.

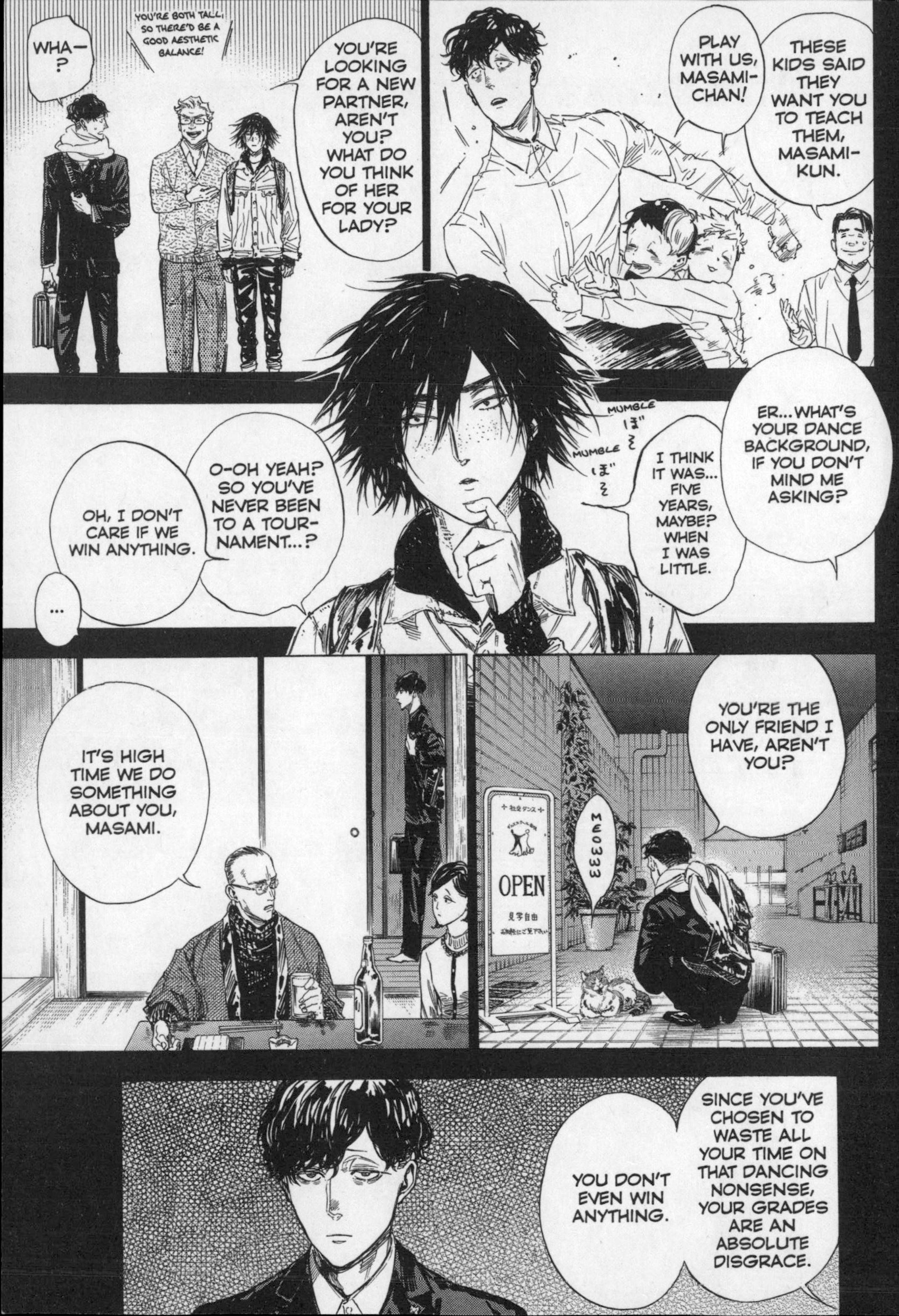
THESE KIDS SAID THEY WANT YOU TO TEACH THEM, MASAMI-KUN.
PLAY WITH US, MASAMI-CHAN!
YOU'RE LOOKING FOR A NEW PARTNER, AREN'T YOU? WHAT DO YOU THINK OF HER FOR YOUR LADY?
YOU'RE BOTH TALL, SO THERE'D BE A GOOD AESTHETIC BALANCE!
WHA— ?
ER...WHAT'S YOUR DANCE BACKGROUND, IF YOU DON'T MIND ME ASKING?
MUMBLE ぼそ
MUMBLE ぼそ
I THINK IT WAS... FIVE YEARS, MAYBE? WHEN I WAS LITTLE.
O-OH YEAH? SO YOU'VE NEVER BEEN TO A TOURNAMENT...?
OH, I DON'T CARE IF WE WIN ANYTHING.
...
YOU'RE THE ONLY FRIEND I HAVE, AREN'T YOU?
MEOWWW
OPEN
IT'S HIGH TIME WE DO SOMETHING ABOUT YOU, MASAMI.
SINCE YOU'VE CHOSEN TO WASTE ALL YOUR TIME ON THAT DANCING NONSENSE, YOUR GRADES ARE AN ABSOLUTE DISGRACE.
YOU DON'T EVEN WIN ANYTHING.

YEAR 10

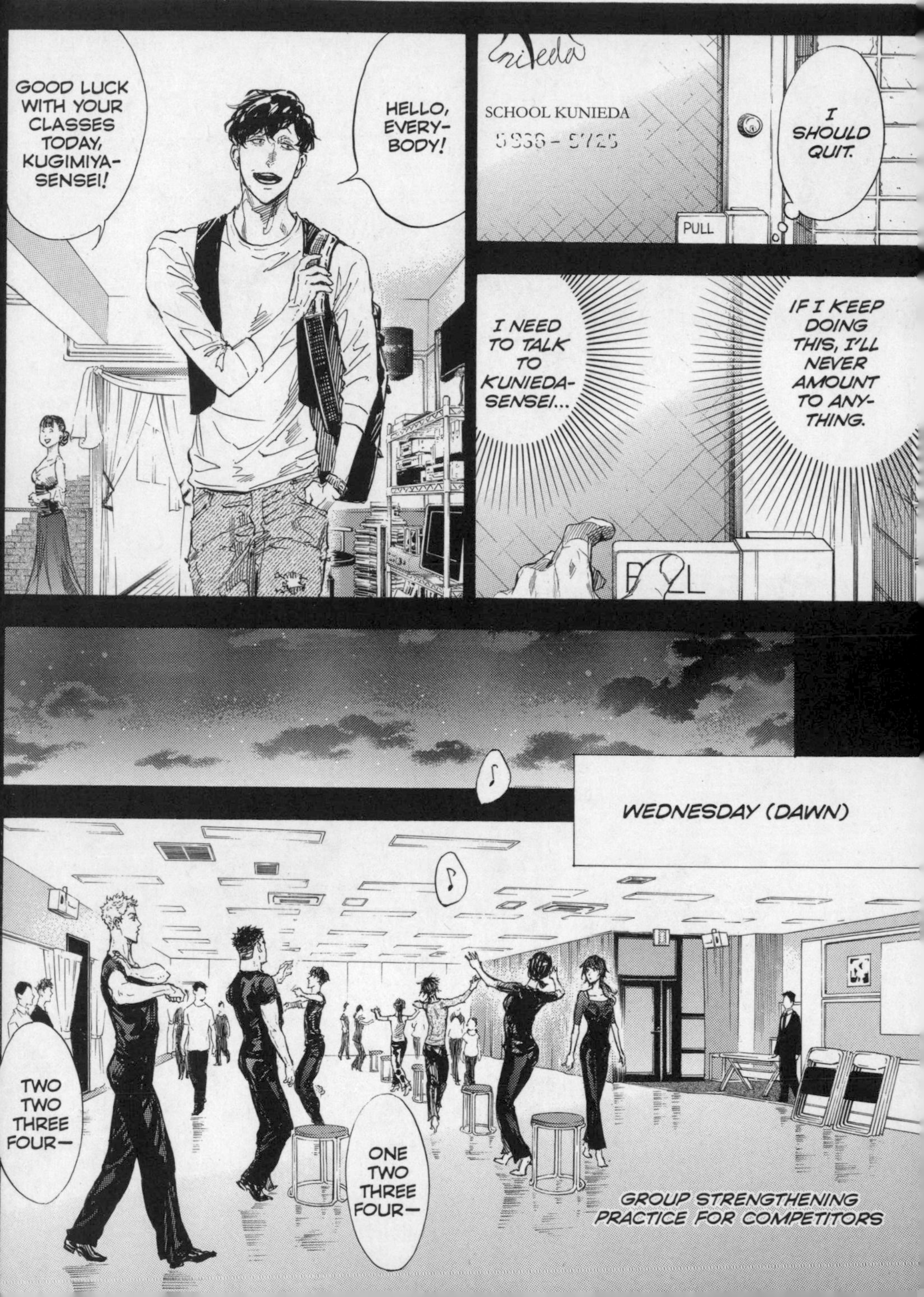
SCHOOL KUNIEDA
5836 - 5725
PULL
I SHOULD QUIT.
IF I KEEP DOING THIS, I'LL NEVER AMOUNT TO ANYTHING.
I NEED TO TALK TO KUNIEDA-SENSEI...
HELLO, EVERYBODY!
GOOD LUCK WITH YOUR CLASSES TODAY, KUGIMIYA-SENSEI!
WEDNESDAY (DAWN)
ONE TWO THREE FOUR—
TWO TWO THREE FOUR—
GROUP STRENGTHENING PRACTICE FOR COMPETITORS

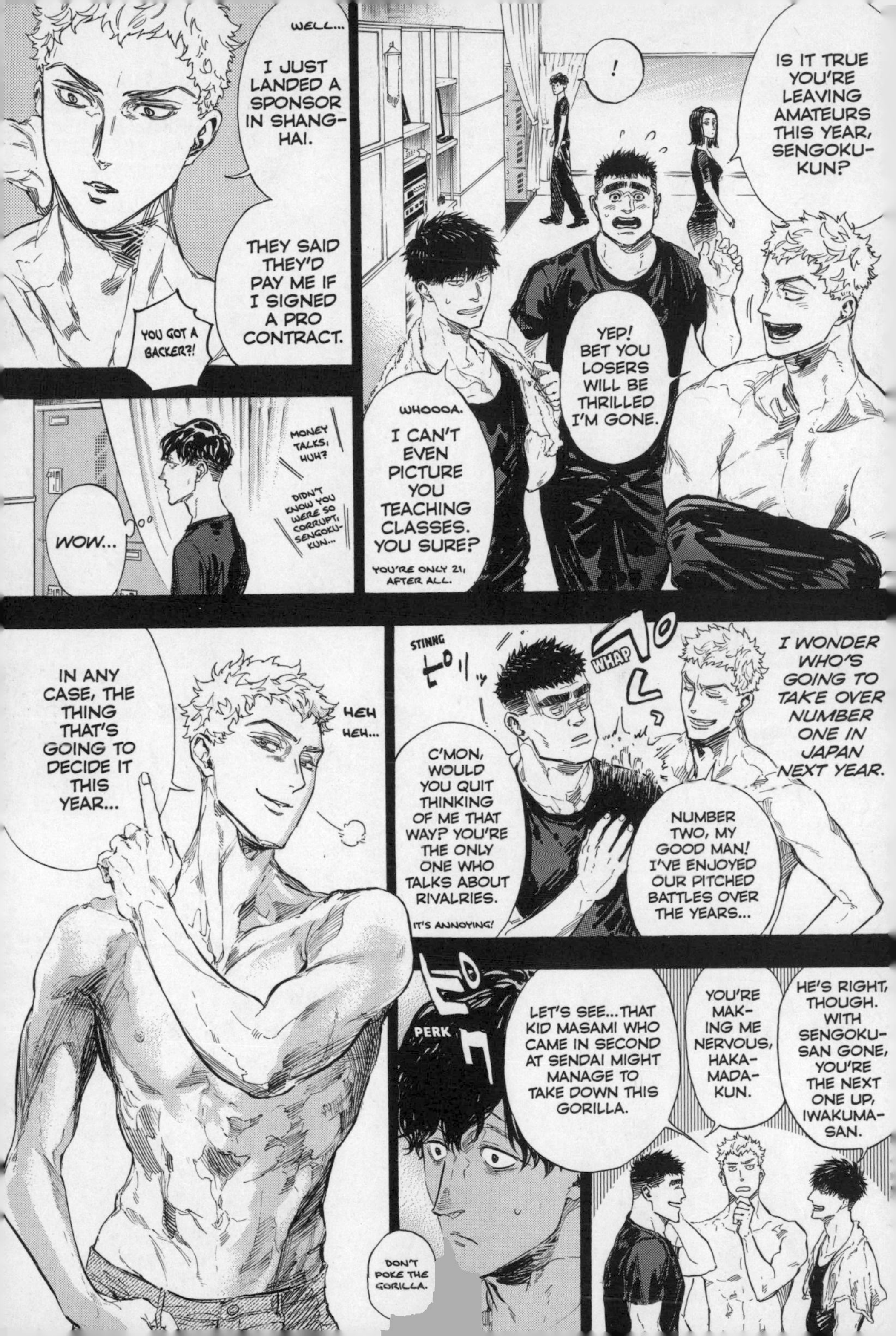
IS IT TRUE YOU'RE LEAVING AMATEURS THIS YEAR, SENGOKU-KUN?
!
YEP! BET YOU LOSERS WILL BE THRILLED I'M GONE.
WHOOOA. I CAN'T EVEN PICTURE YOU TEACHING CLASSES. YOU SURE?
YOU'RE ONLY 21, AFTER ALL.
WELL... I JUST LANDED A SPONSOR IN SHANG-HAI.
THEY SAID THEY'D PAY ME IF I SIGNED A PRO CONTRACT.
YOU GOT A BACKER?!
MONEY TALKS, HUH?
DIDN'T KNOW YOU WERE SO CORRUPT, SENGOKU-KUN...
WOW...
I WONDER WHO'S GOING TO TAKE OVER NUMBER ONE IN JAPAN NEXT YEAR.
WHAP
STINNG
NUMBER TWO, MY GOOD MAN! I'VE ENJOYED OUR PITCHED BATTLES OVER THE YEARS...
C'MON, WOULD YOU QUIT THINKING OF ME THAT WAY? YOU'RE THE ONLY ONE WHO TALKS ABOUT RIVALRIES.
IT'S ANNOYING!
HE'S RIGHT, THOUGH. WITH SENGOKU-SAN GONE, YOU'RE THE NEXT ONE UP, IWAKUMA-SAN.
YOU'RE MAK-ING ME NERVOUS, HAKA-MADA-KUN.
LET'S SEE...THAT KID MASAMI WHO CAME IN SECOND AT SENDAI MIGHT MANAGE TO TAKE DOWN THIS GORILLA.
PERK
DON'T POKE THE GORILLA.
IN ANY CASE, THE THING THAT'S GOING TO DECIDE IT THIS YEAR...
HEH HEH...

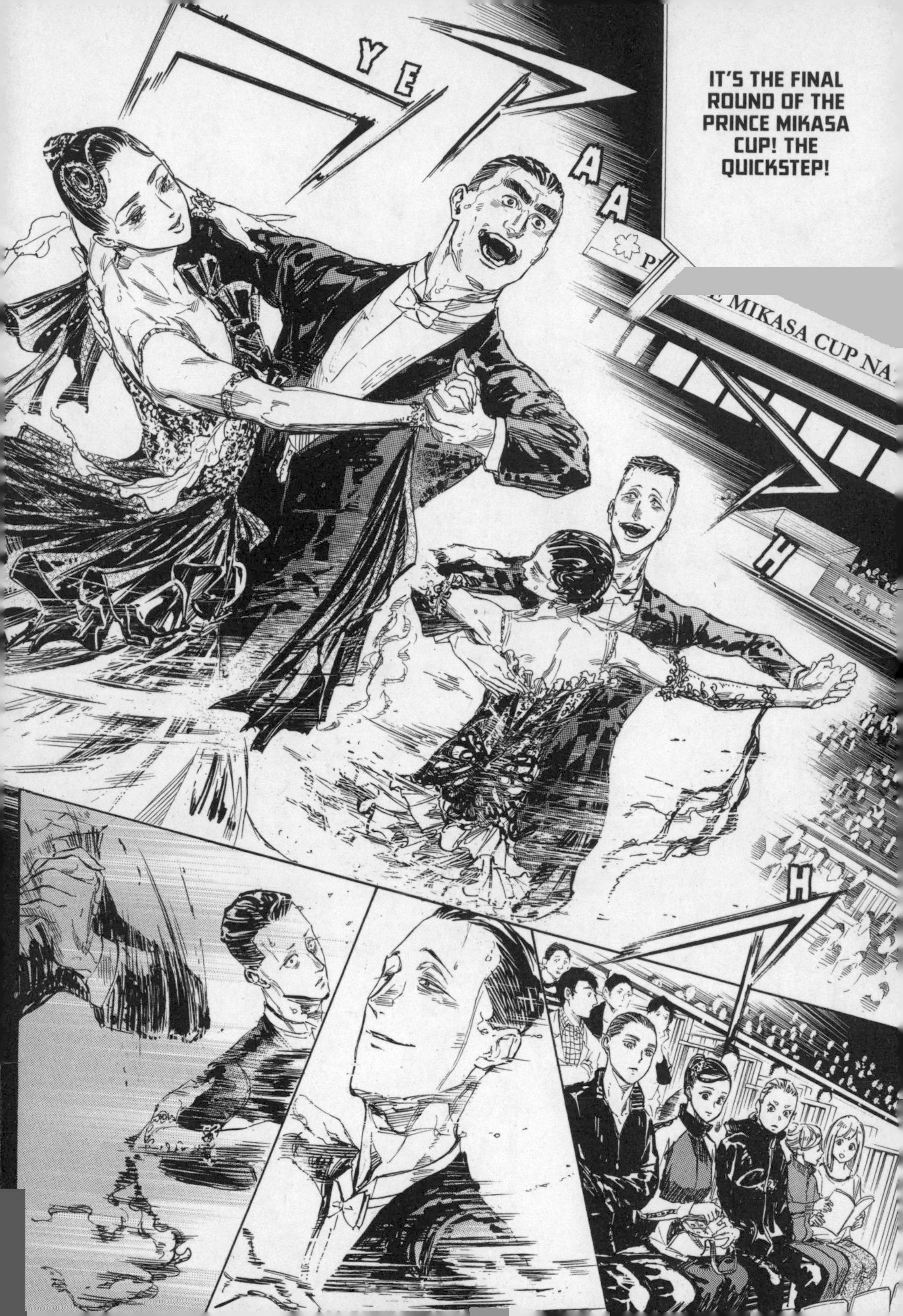
IT'S THE FINAL ROUND OF THE PRINCE MIKASA CUP! THE QUICKSTEP!
YEAAHH

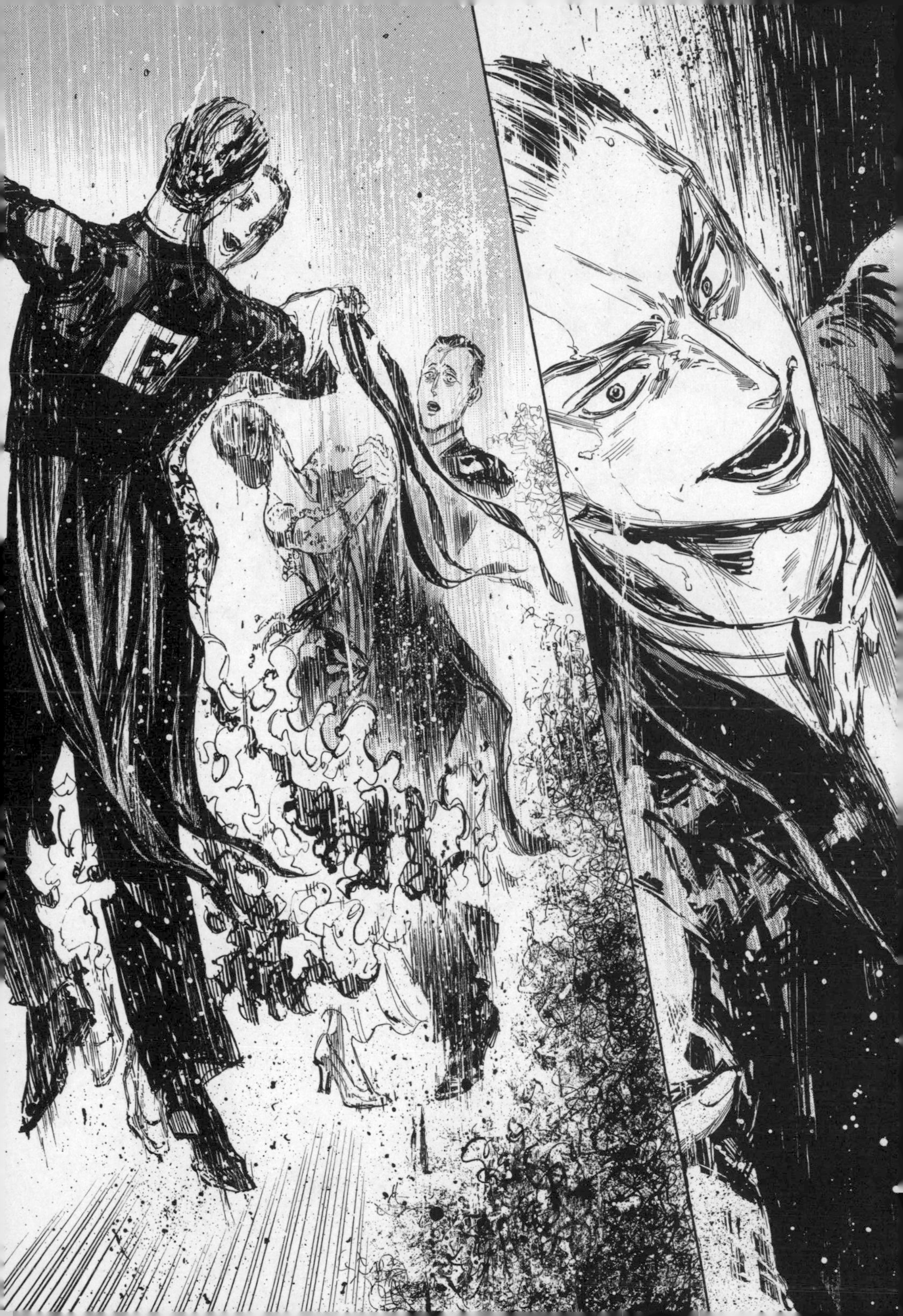

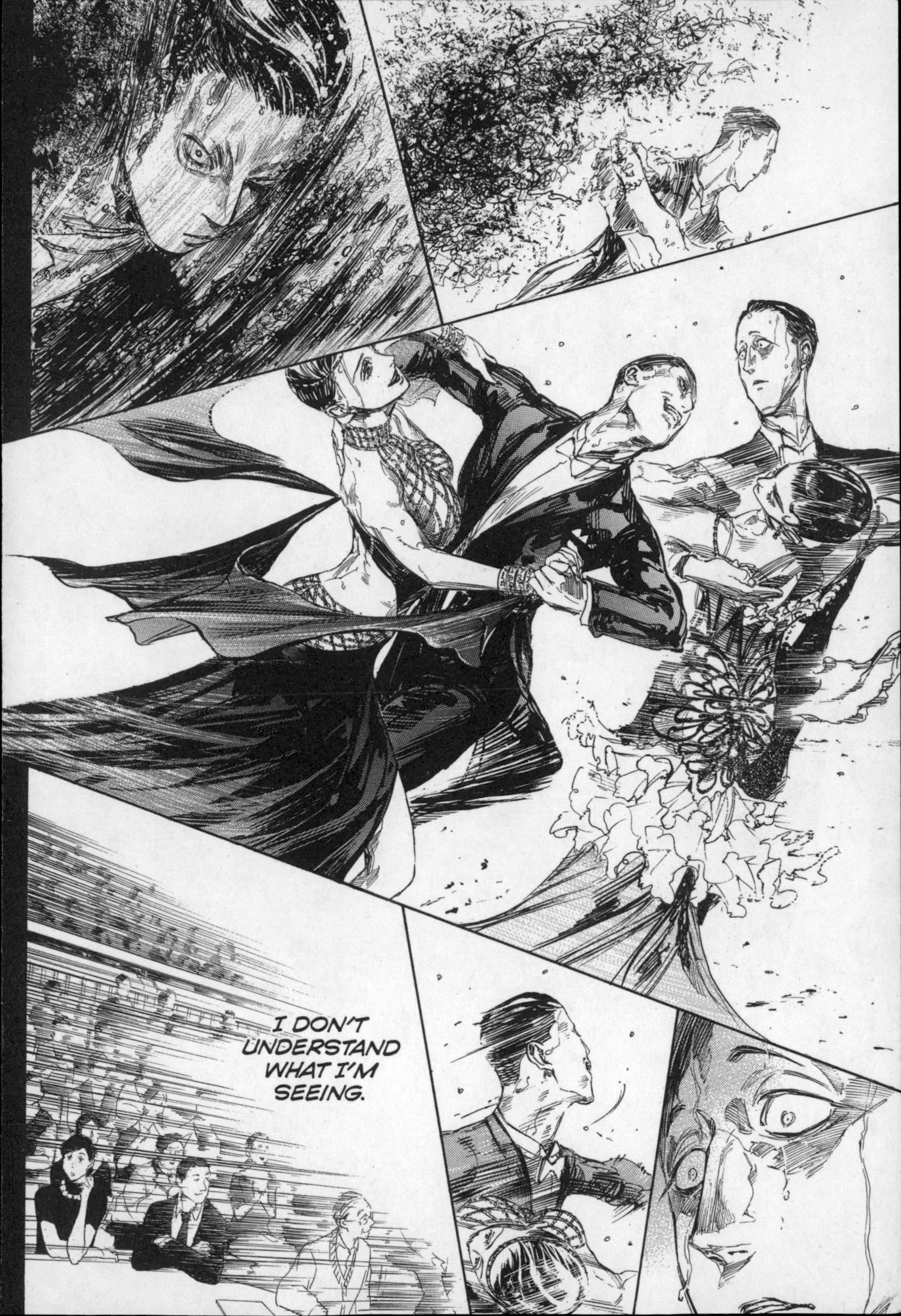
I DON'T UNDERSTAND WHAT I'M SEEING.

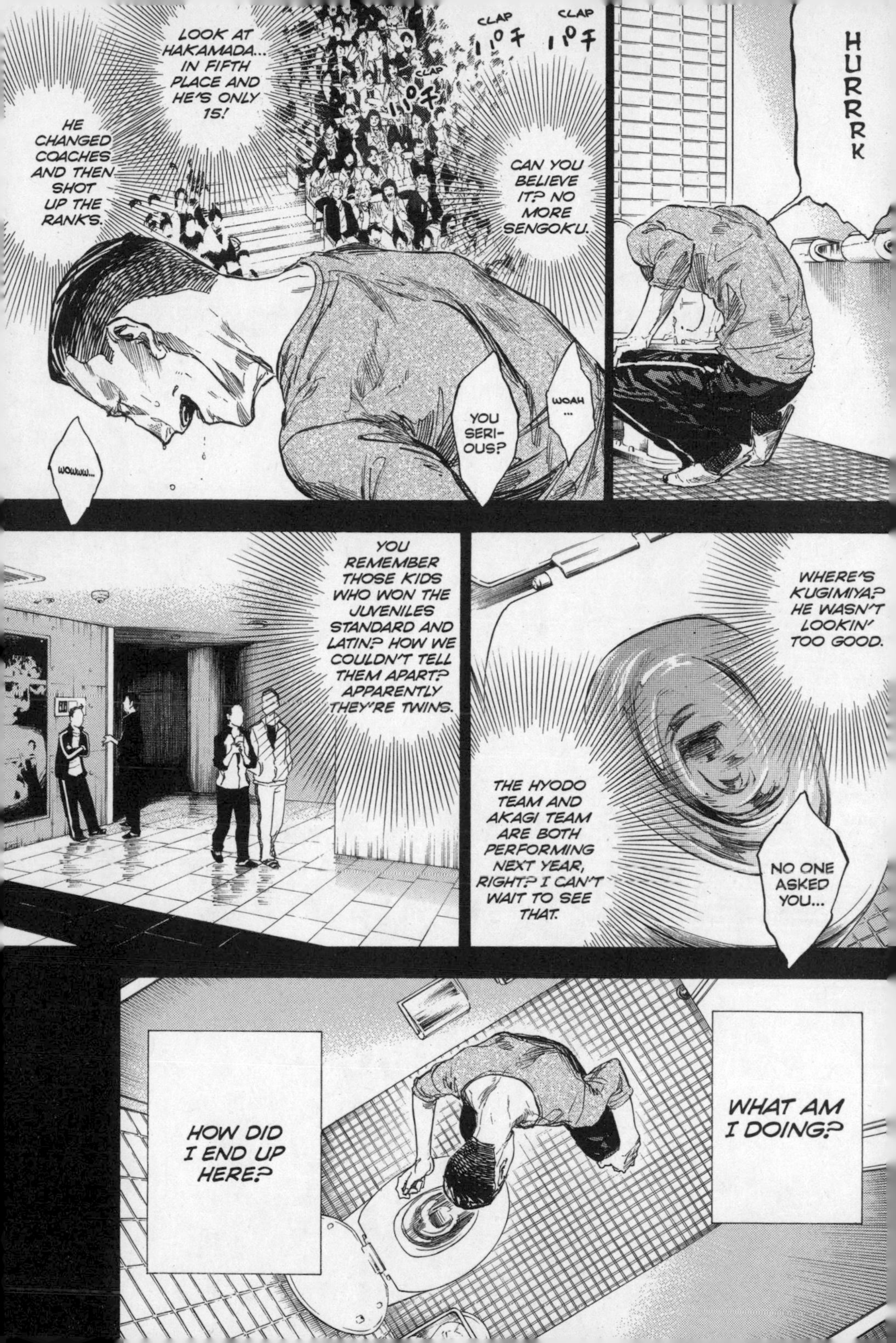

HURRRK
CLAP
パチ
CLAP
パチ
CAN YOU BELIEVE IT? NO MORE SENGOKU.
LOOK AT HAKAMADA... IN FIFTH PLACE AND HE'S ONLY 15!
CLAP
パチ
HE CHANGED COACHES AND THEN SHOT UP THE RANKS.
WOAH...
YOU SERI-OUS?
WOWWW...
WHERE'S KUGIMIYA? HE WASN'T LOOKIN' TOO GOOD.
THE HYODO TEAM AND AKAGI TEAM ARE BOTH PERFORMING NEXT YEAR, RIGHT? I CAN'T WAIT TO SEE THAT.
NO ONE ASKED YOU...
YOU REMEMBER THOSE KIDS WHO WON THE JUVENILES STANDARD AND LATIN? HOW WE COULDN'T TELL THEM APART? APPARENTLY THEY'RE TWINS.
WHAT AM I DOING?
HOW DID I END UP HERE?

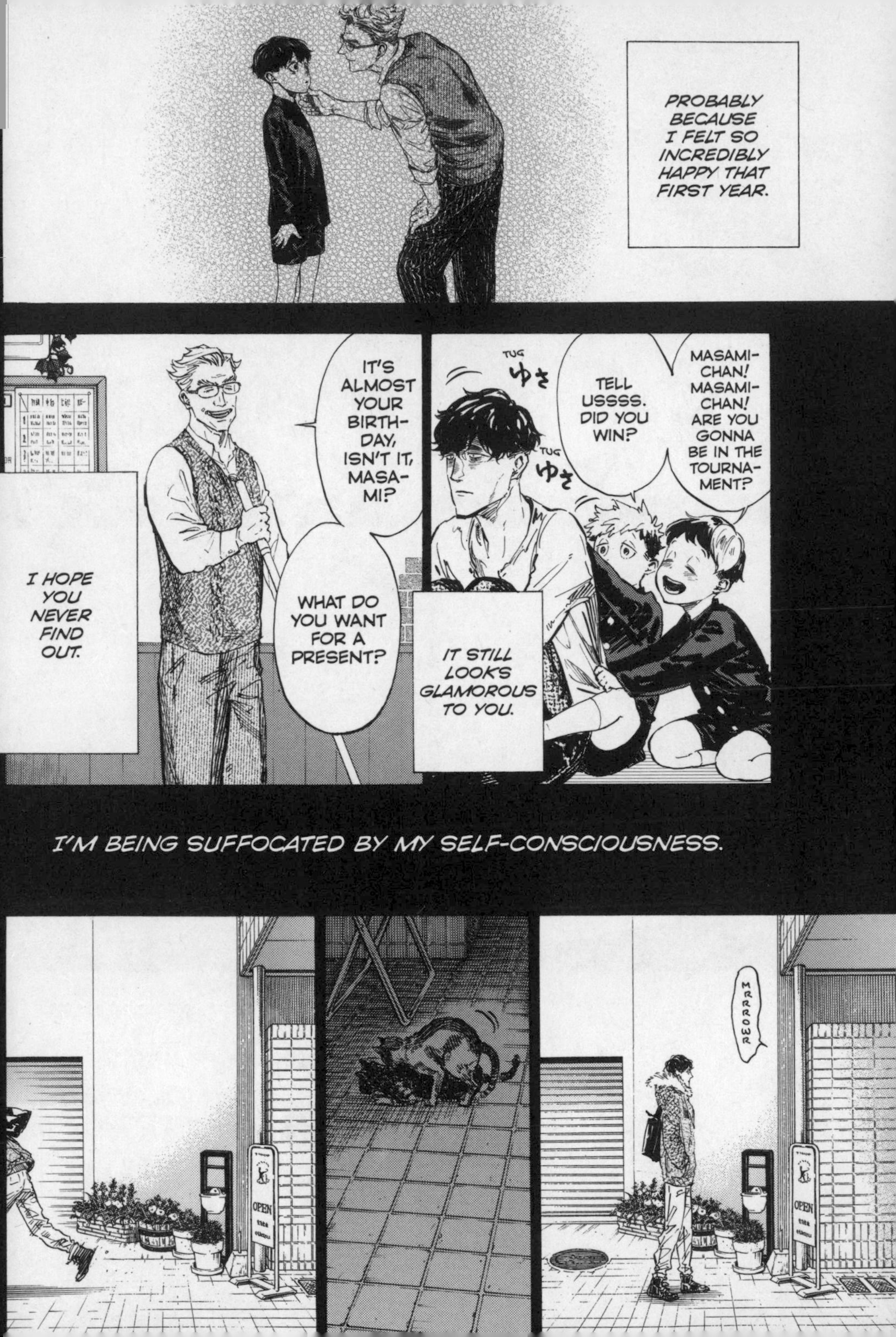

PROBABLY BECAUSE I FELT SO INCREDIBLY HAPPY THAT FIRST YEAR.
MASAMI-CHAN! MASAMI-CHAN! ARE YOU GONNA BE IN THE TOURNAMENT?
TELL USSSS. DID YOU WIN?
TUG ゆさ
TUG ゆさ
IT STILL LOOKS GLAMOROUS TO YOU.
IT'S ALMOST YOUR BIRTHDAY, ISN'T IT, MASAMI?
WHAT DO YOU WANT FOR A PRESENT?
I HOPE YOU NEVER FIND OUT.
I'M BEING SUFFOCATED BY MY SELF-CONSCIOUSNESS.
MRRROWR
OPEN
OPEN

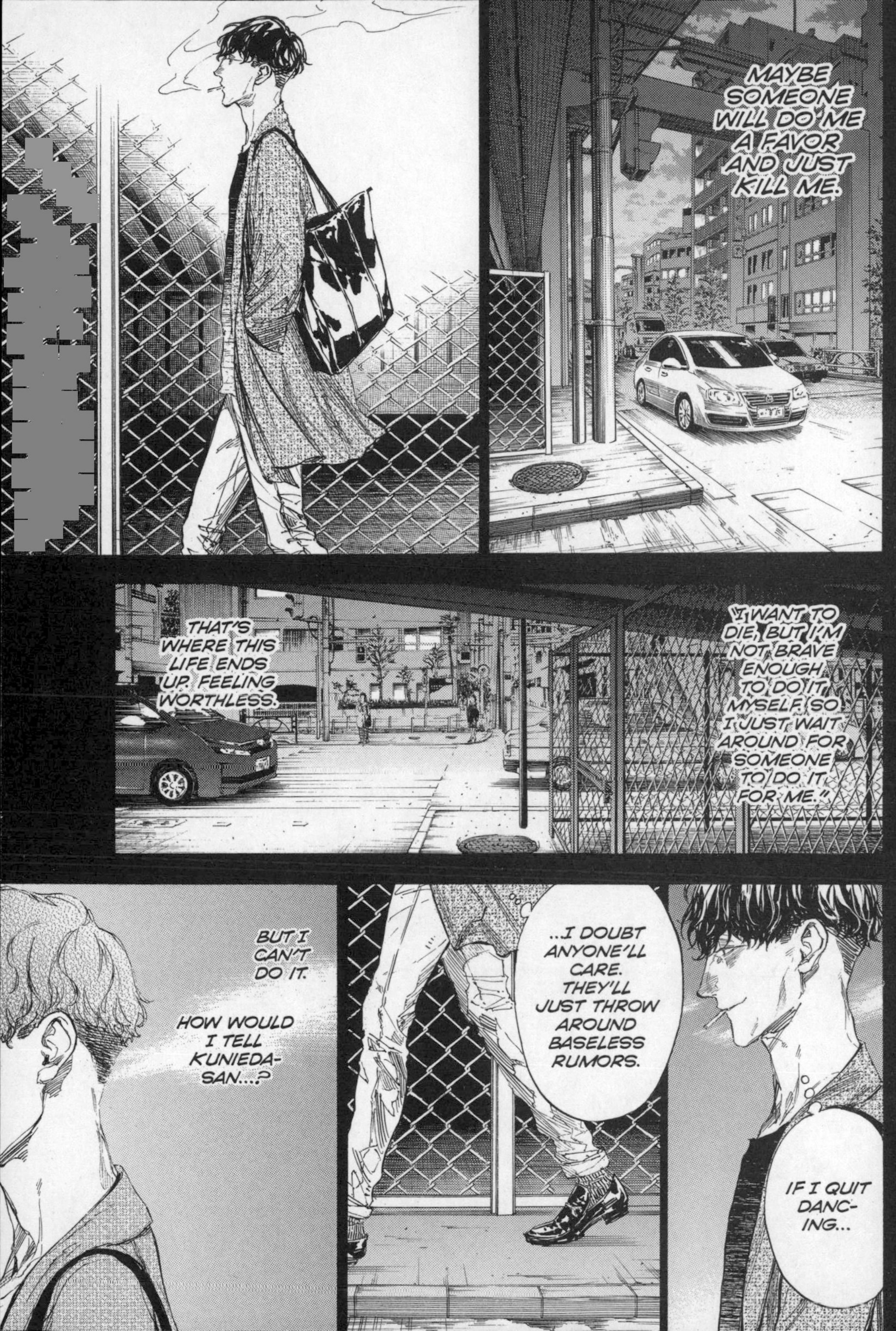
MAYBE SOMEONE WILL DO ME A FAVOR AND JUST KILL ME.
"I WANT TO DIE, BUT I'M NOT BRAVE ENOUGH TO DO IT MYSELF. SO I JUST WAIT AROUND FOR SOMEONE TO DO IT FOR ME."
THAT'S WHERE THIS LIFE ENDS UP. FEELING WORTHLESS.
IF I QUIT DANCING...
...I DOUBT ANYONE'LL CARE. THEY'LL JUST THROW AROUND BASELESS RUMORS.
BUT I CAN'T DO IT.
HOW WOULD I TELL KUNIEDA-SAN...?

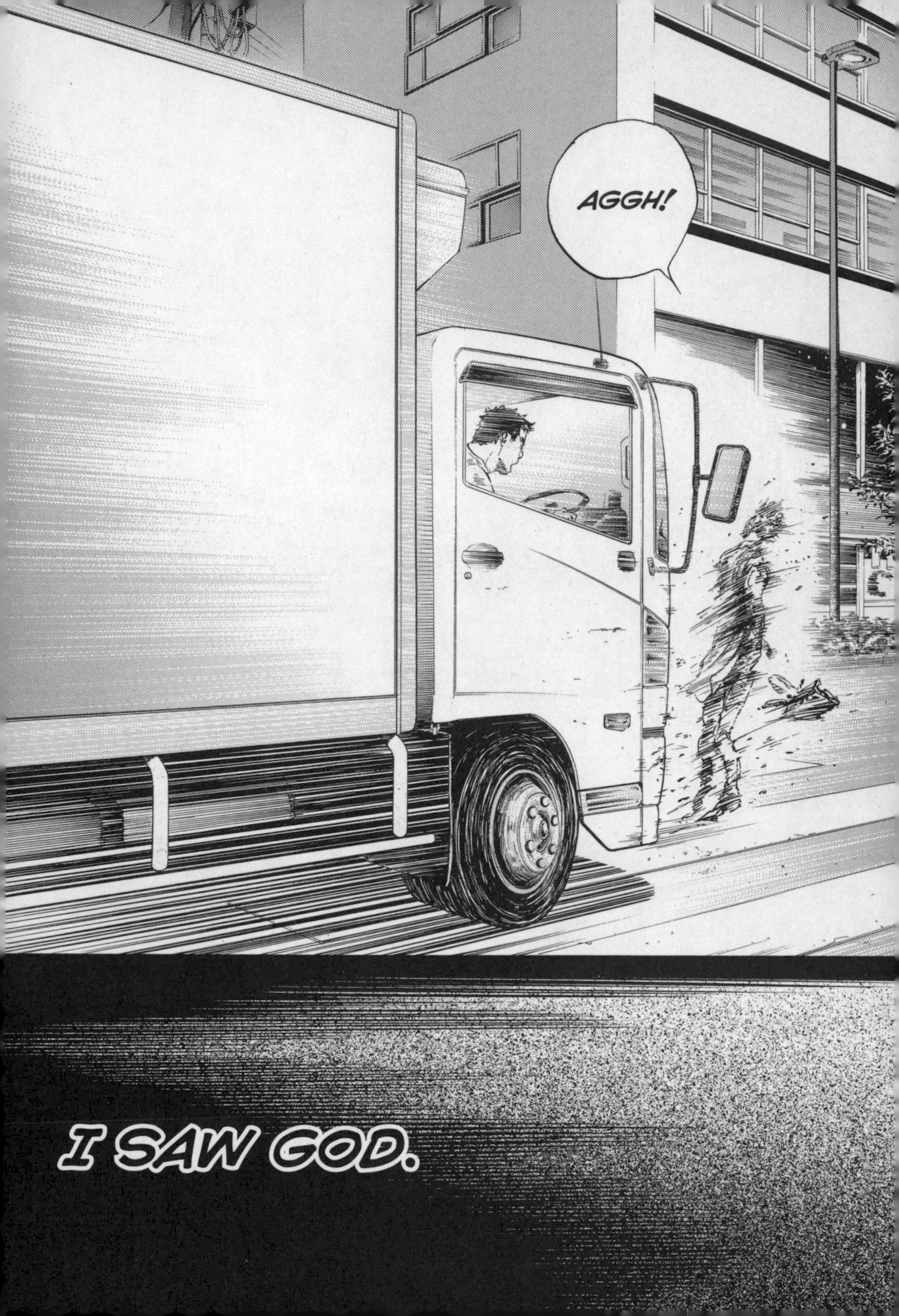
AGGH!
I SAW GOD.

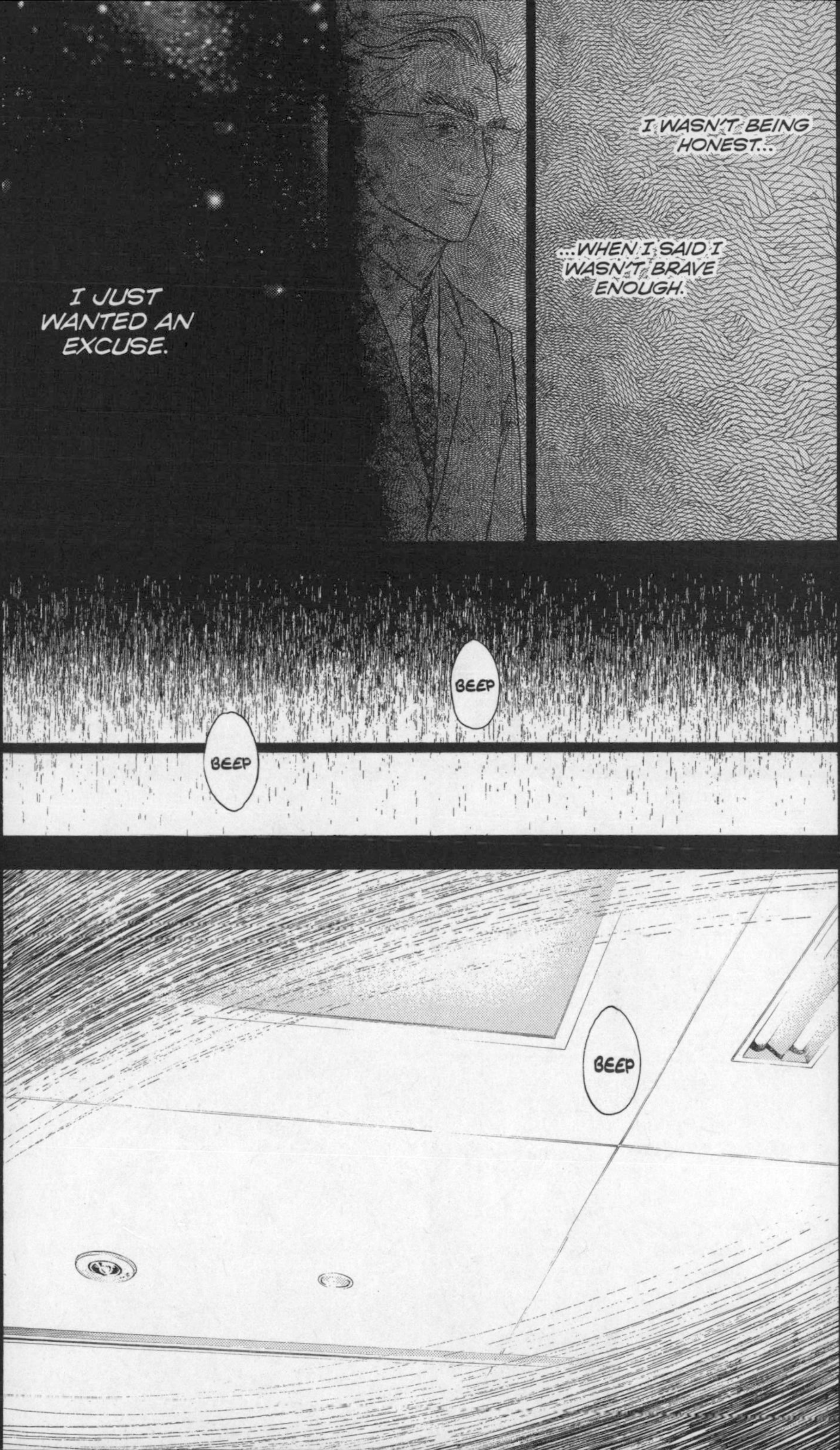
I WASN'T BEING HONEST...
...WHEN I SAID I WASN'T BRAVE ENOUGH.
I JUST WANTED AN EXCUSE.
BEEP
BEEP
BEEP

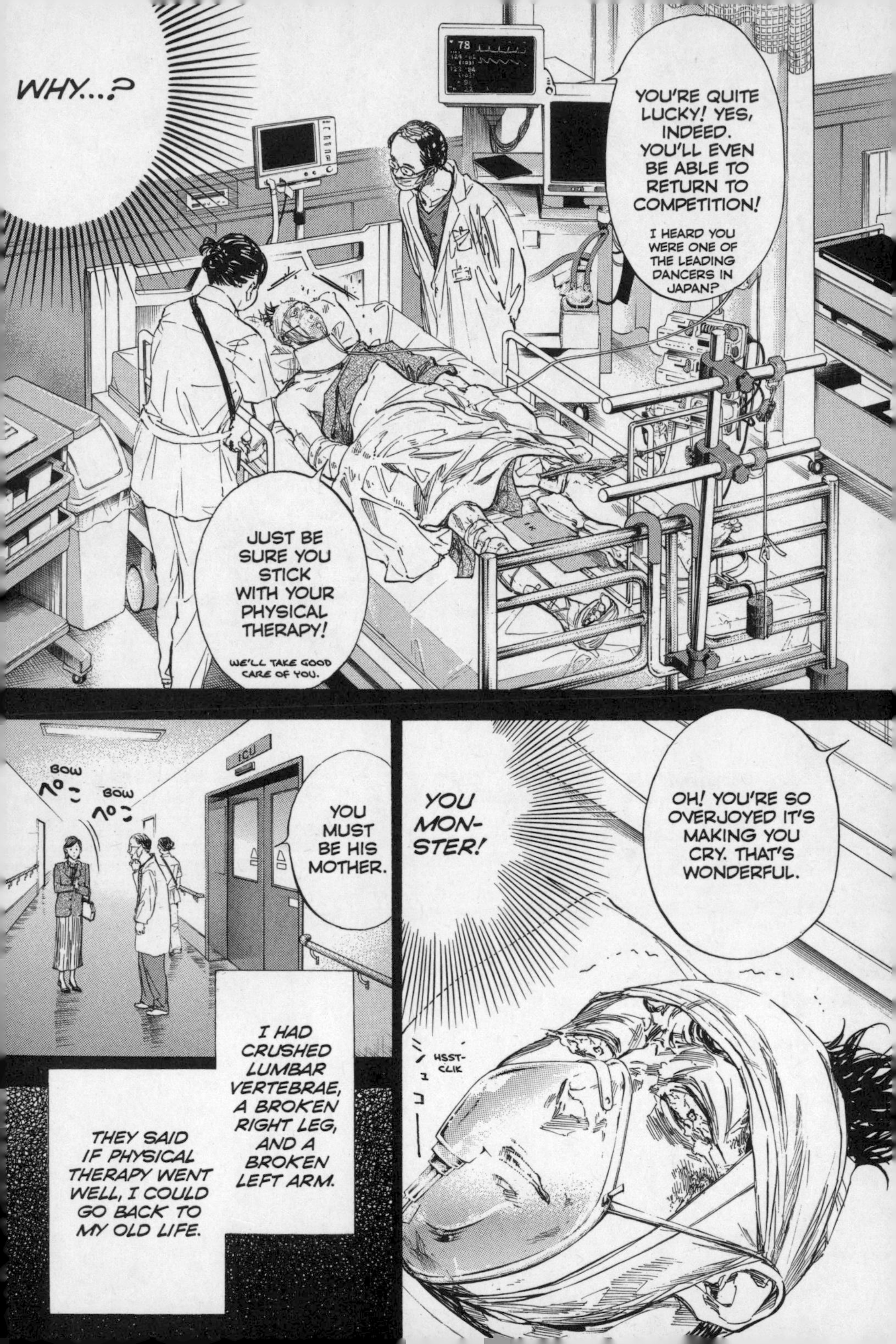
YOU'RE QUITE LUCKY! YES, INDEED. YOU'LL EVEN BE ABLE TO RETURN TO COMPETITION!
I HEARD YOU WERE ONE OF THE LEADING DANCERS IN JAPAN?
WHY...?
JUST BE SURE YOU STICK WITH YOUR PHYSICAL THERAPY!
WE'LL TAKE GOOD CARE OF YOU.
OH! YOU'RE SO OVERJOYED IT'S MAKING YOU CRY. THAT'S WONDERFUL.
YOU MONSTER!
HSST-CLIK
YOU MUST BE HIS MOTHER.
BOW
BOW
ICU
I HAD CRUSHED LUMBAR VERTEBRAE, A BROKEN RIGHT LEG, AND A BROKEN LEFT ARM.
THEY SAID IF PHYSICAL THERAPY WENT WELL, I COULD GO BACK TO MY OLD LIFE.

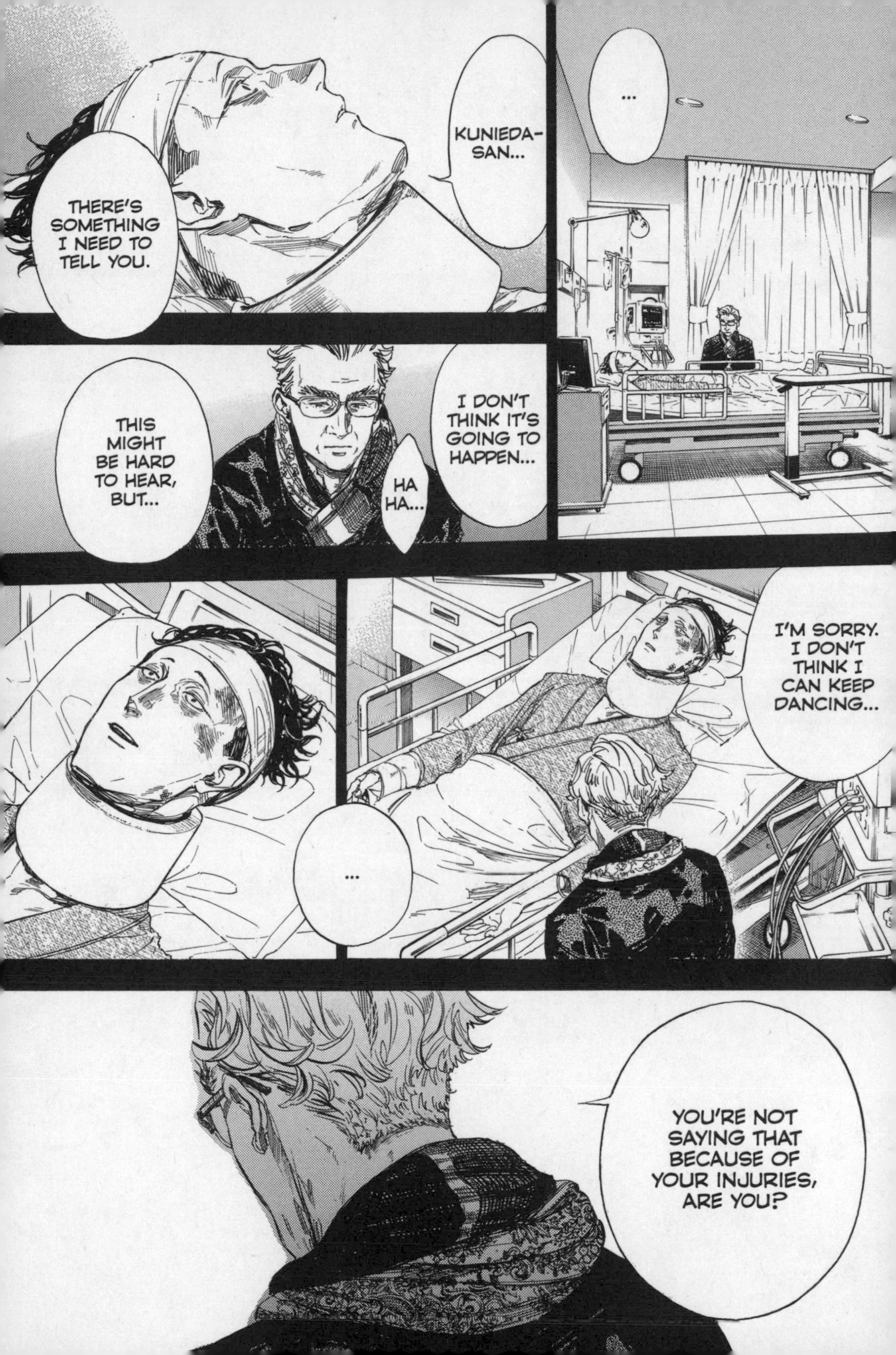
...
KUNIEDA-SAN...
THERE'S SOMETHING I NEED TO TELL YOU.
I DON'T THINK IT'S GOING TO HAPPEN...
HA HA...
THIS MIGHT BE HARD TO HEAR, BUT...
I'M SORRY. I DON'T THINK I CAN KEEP DANCING...
...
YOU'RE NOT SAYING THAT BECAUSE OF YOUR INJURIES, ARE YOU?

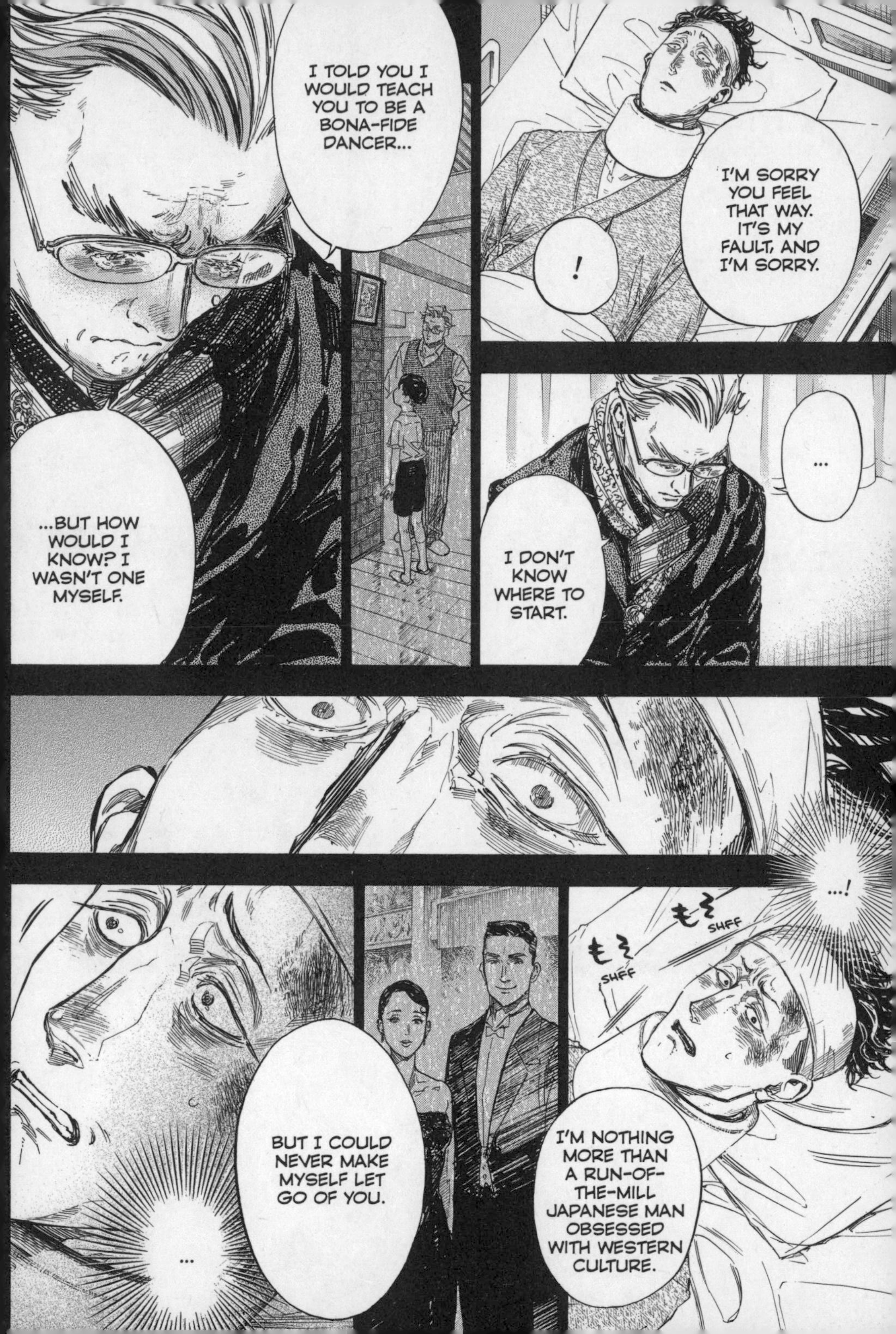
I'M SORRY YOU FEEL THAT WAY. IT'S MY FAULT, AND I'M SORRY.
!
...
I DON'T KNOW WHERE TO START.
I TOLD YOU I WOULD TEACH YOU TO BE A BONA-FIDE DANCER...
...BUT HOW WOULD I KNOW? I WASN'T ONE MYSELF.
...!
もぞ
SHFF
もぞ
SHFF
I'M NOTHING MORE THAN A RUN-OF-THE-MILL JAPANESE MAN OBSESSED WITH WESTERN CULTURE.
BUT I COULD NEVER MAKE MYSELF LET GO OF YOU.
...

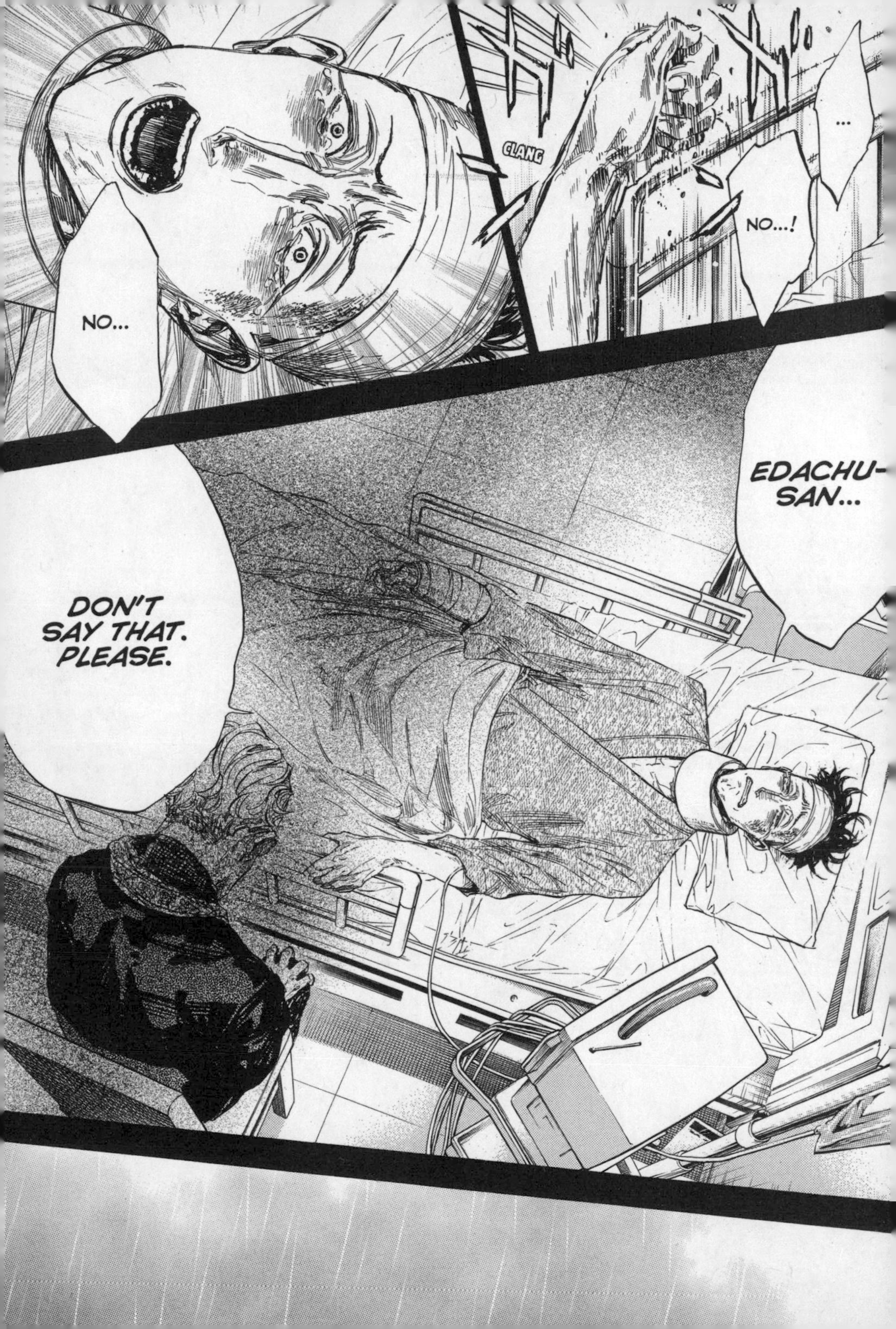
CLANG
...
NO...!
NO...
EDACHU-SAN...
DON'T SAY THAT. PLEASE.

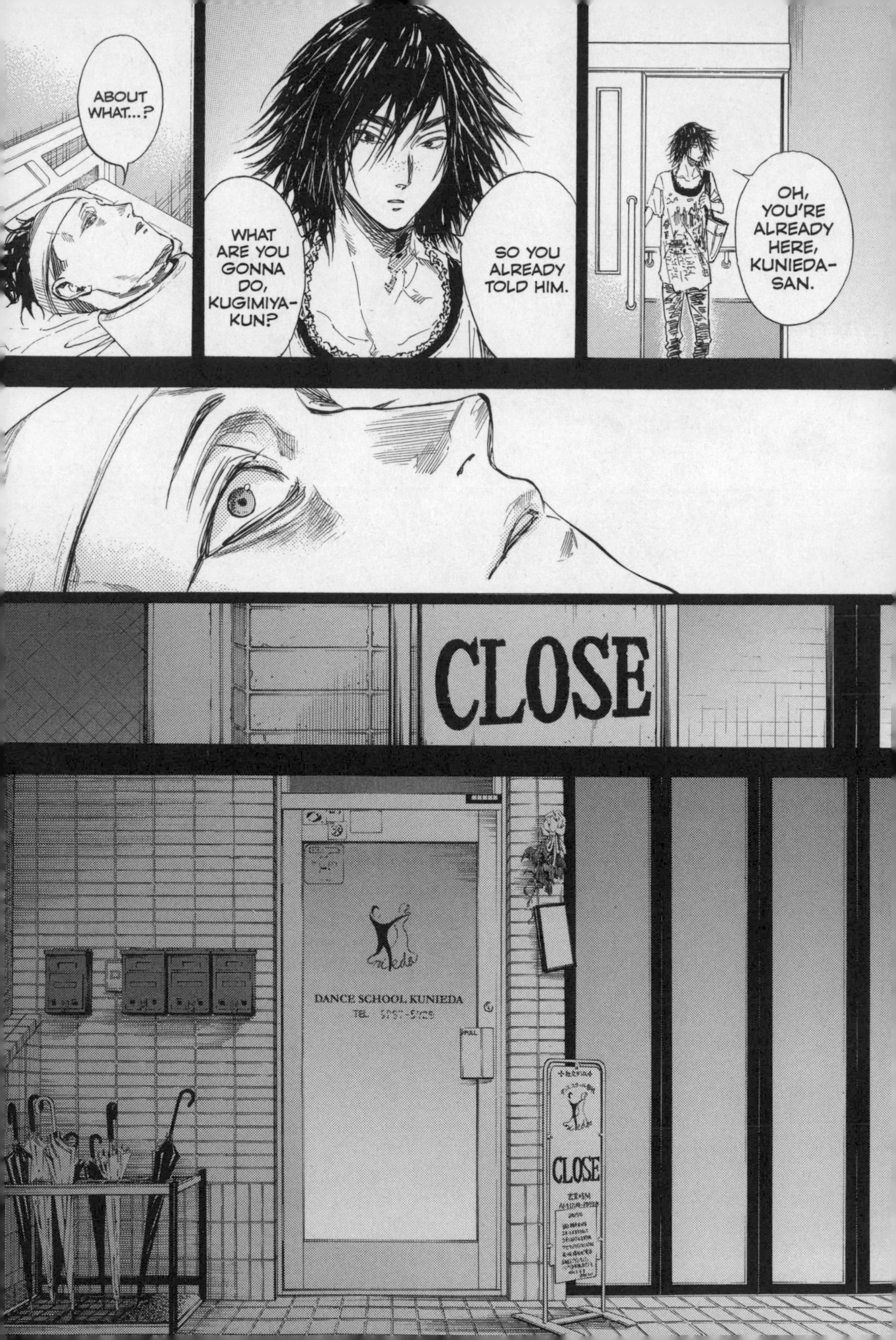
OH, YOU'RE ALREADY HERE, KUNIEDA-SAN.
SO YOU ALREADY TOLD HIM.
WHAT ARE YOU GONNA DO, KUGIMIYA-KUN?
ABOUT WHAT...?
CLOSE
DANCE SCHOOL KUNIEDA
CLOSE

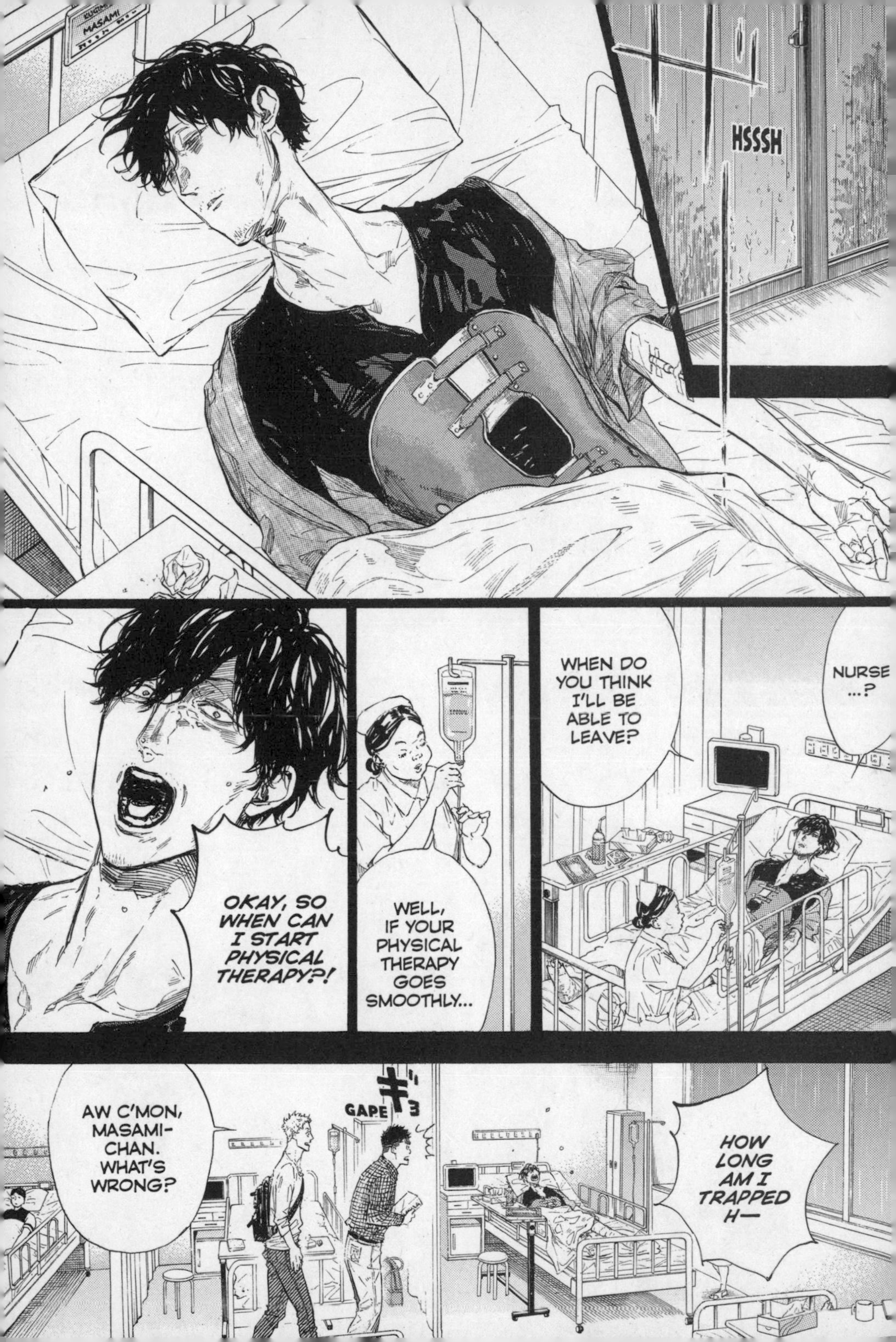
MASAMI
HSSSH
NURSE ...?
WHEN DO YOU THINK I'LL BE ABLE TO LEAVE?
WELL, IF YOUR PHYSICAL THERAPY GOES SMOOTHLY...
OKAY, SO WHEN CAN I START PHYSICAL THERAPY?!
HOW LONG AM I TRAPPED H—
GAPE
AW C'MON, MASAMI-CHAN. WHAT'S WRONG?

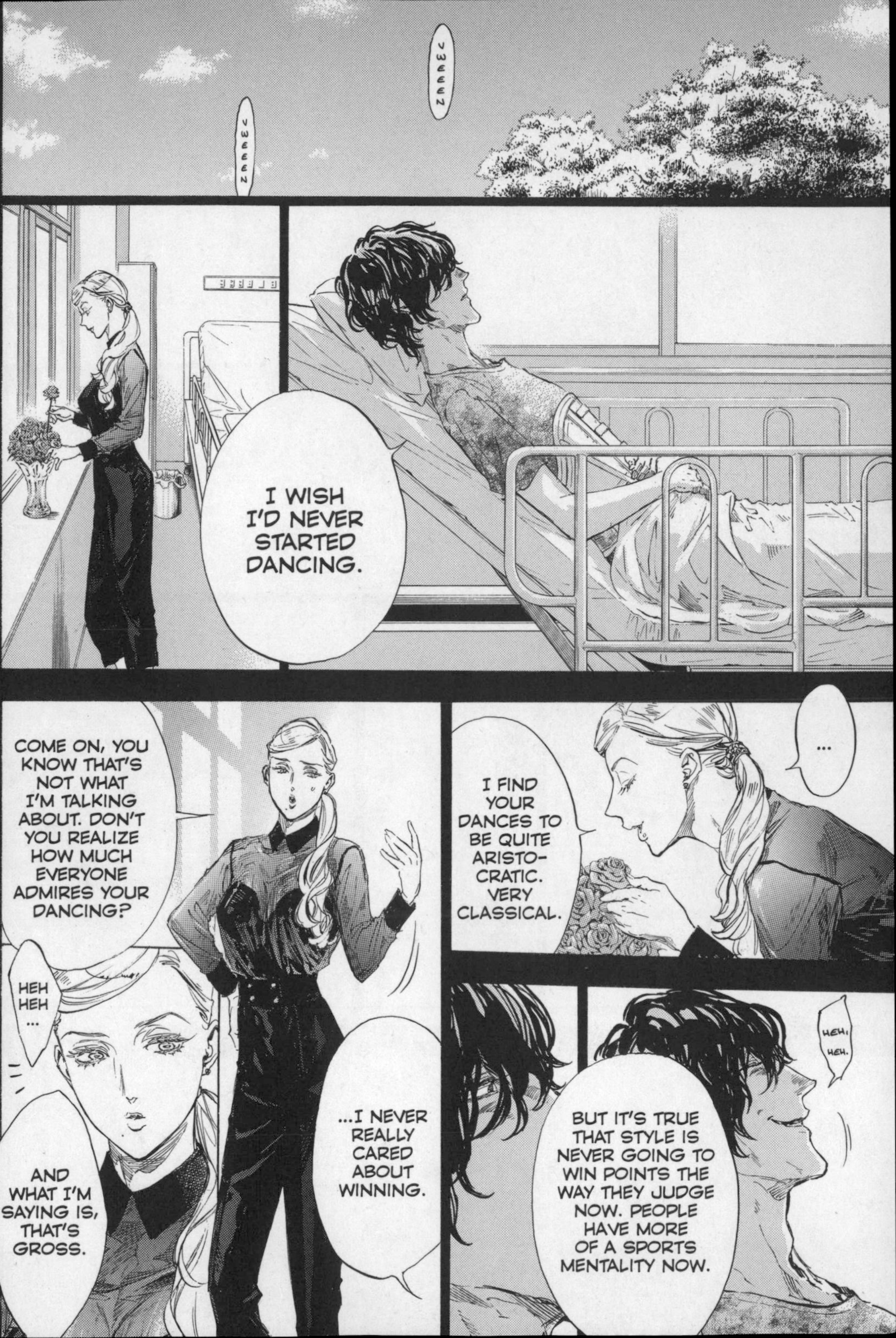
VWEEEN
VWEEEN
I WISH I'D NEVER STARTED DANCING.
...
I FIND YOUR DANCES TO BE QUITE ARISTOCRATIC. VERY CLASSICAL.
HEH, HEH.
BUT IT'S TRUE THAT STYLE IS NEVER GOING TO WIN POINTS THE WAY THEY JUDGE NOW. PEOPLE HAVE MORE OF A SPORTS MENTALITY NOW.
COME ON, YOU KNOW THAT'S NOT WHAT I'M TALKING ABOUT. DON'T YOU REALIZE HOW MUCH EVERYONE ADMIRES YOUR DANCING?
...I NEVER REALLY CARED ABOUT WINNING.
HEH HEH ...
AND WHAT I'M SAYING IS, THAT'S GROSS.

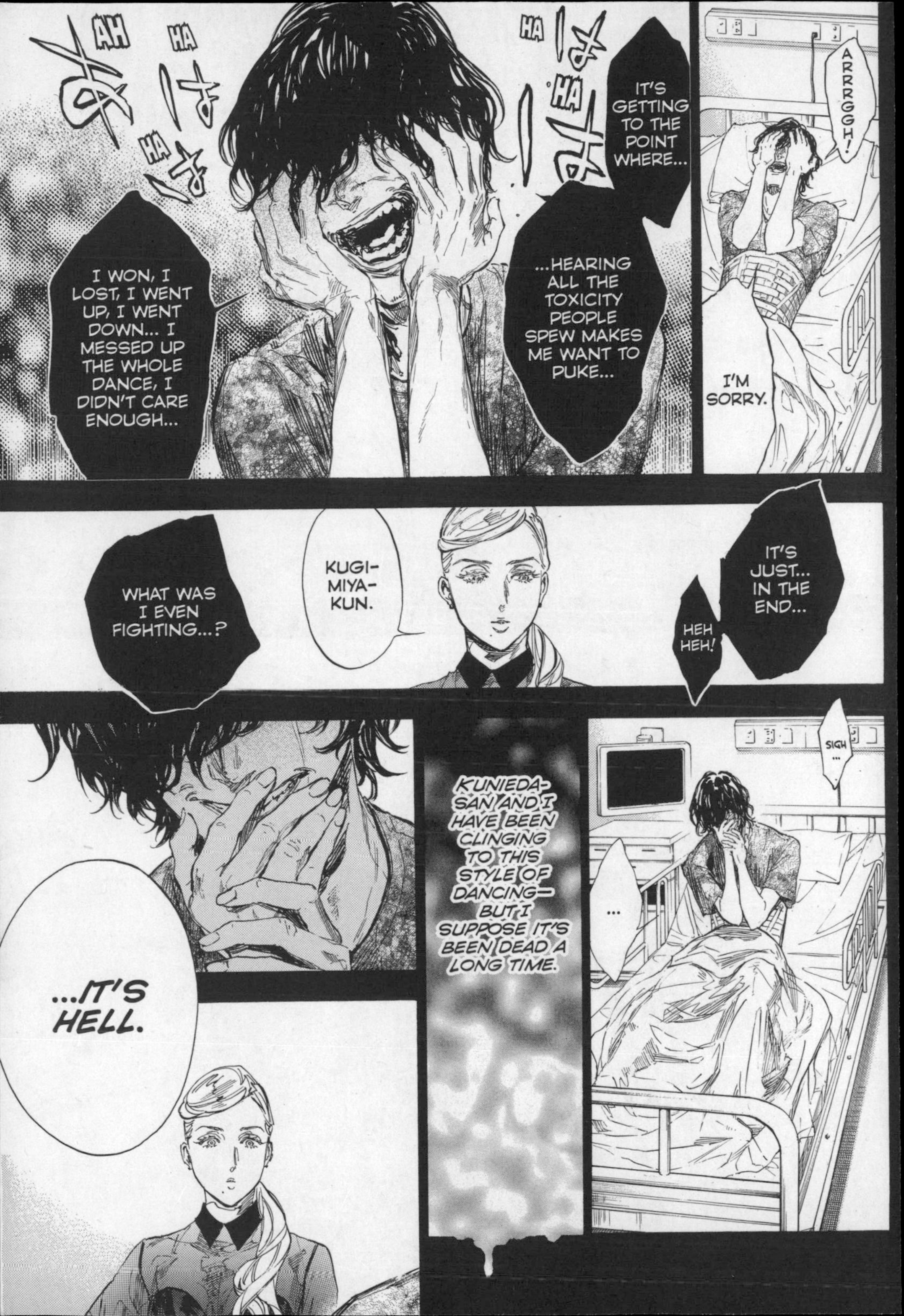
ARRRGGH!
I'M SORRY.
HA HA
HA HA AH
IT'S GETTING TO THE POINT WHERE...
...HEARING ALL THE TOXICITY PEOPLE SPEW MAKES ME WANT TO PUKE...
I WON, I LOST, I WENT UP, I WENT DOWN... I MESSED UP THE WHOLE DANCE, I DIDN'T CARE ENOUGH...
IT'S JUST... IN THE END...
HEH HEH!
KUGI-MIYA-KUN.
WHAT WAS I EVEN FIGHTING...?
SIGH...
...
KUNIEDA-SAN AND I HAVE BEEN CLINGING TO THIS STYLE OF DANCING—BUT I SUPPOSE IT'S BEEN DEAD A LONG TIME.
...IT'S HELL.

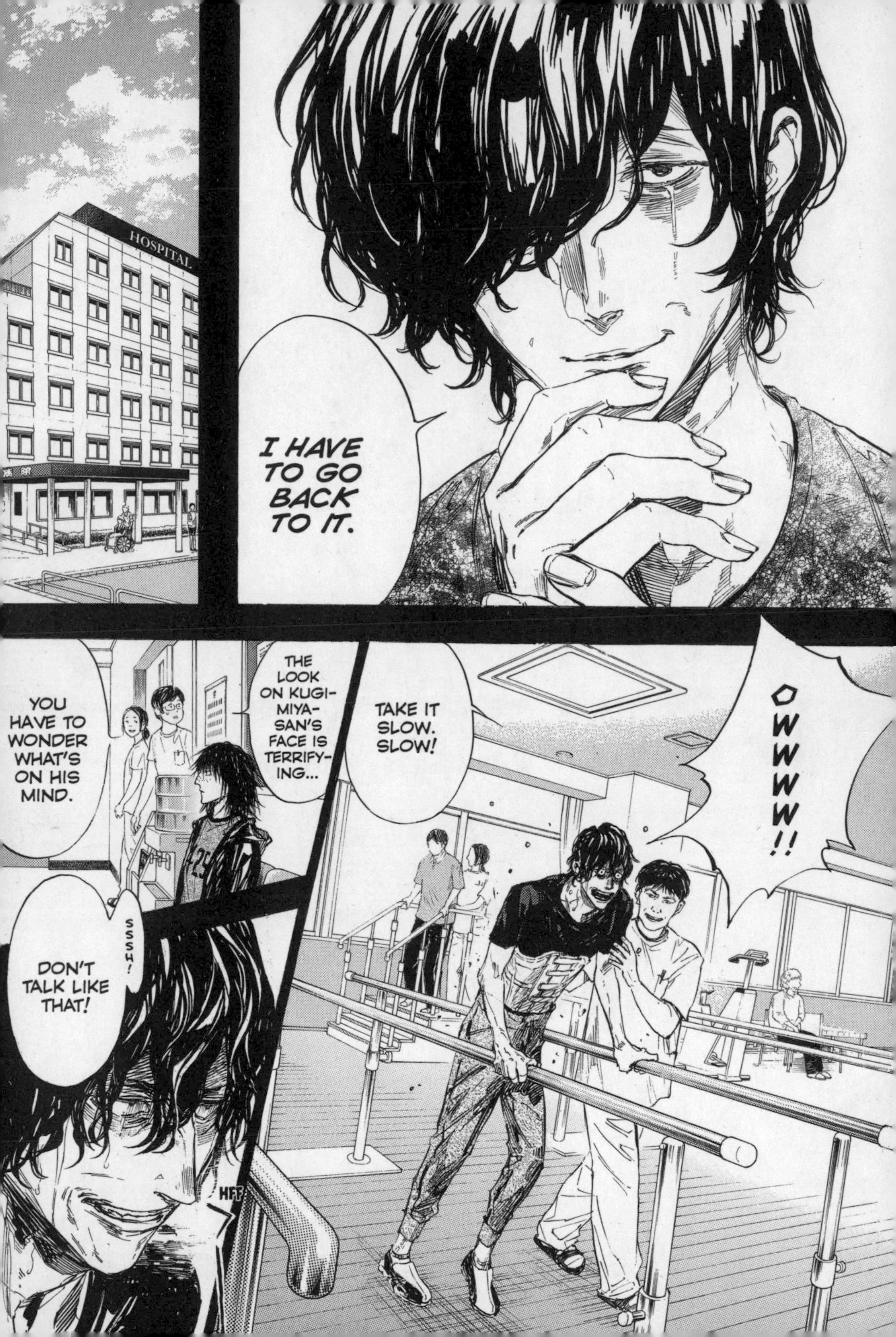
I HAVE TO GO BACK TO IT.
HOSPITAL
OWWWWW!!
TAKE IT SLOW. SLOW!
THE LOOK ON KUGI-MIYA-SAN'S FACE IS TERRIFY-ING...
YOU HAVE TO WONDER WHAT'S ON HIS MIND.
SSSH!
DON'T TALK LIKE THAT!
HFF

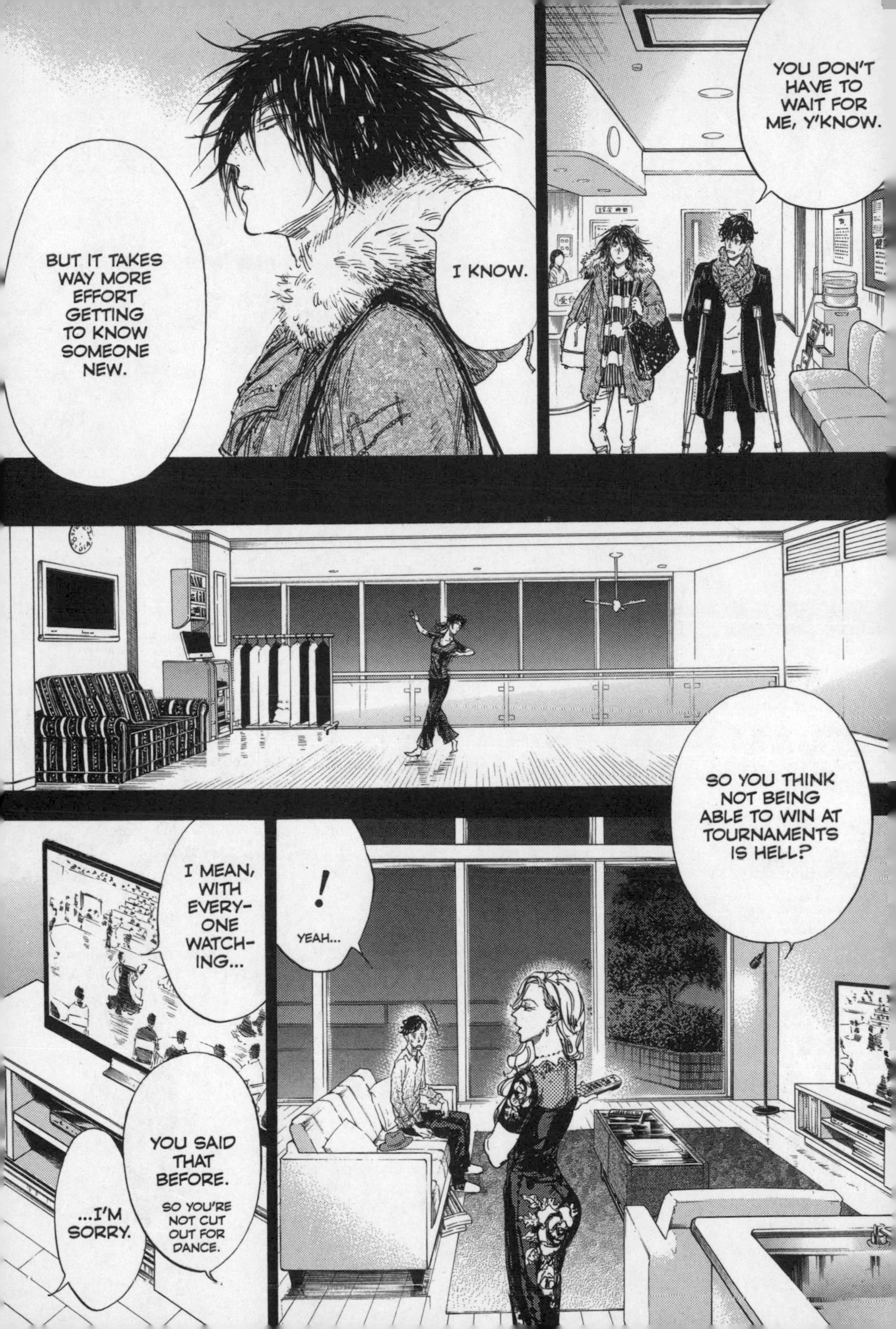
YOU DON'T HAVE TO WAIT FOR ME, Y'KNOW.
I KNOW.
BUT IT TAKES WAY MORE EFFORT GETTING TO KNOW SOMEONE NEW.
SO YOU THINK NOT BEING ABLE TO WIN AT TOURNAMENTS IS HELL?
!
YEAH...
I MEAN, WITH EVERY-ONE WATCHING-ING...
YOU SAID THAT BEFORE.
SO YOU'RE NOT CUT OUT FOR DANCE.
...I'M SORRY.

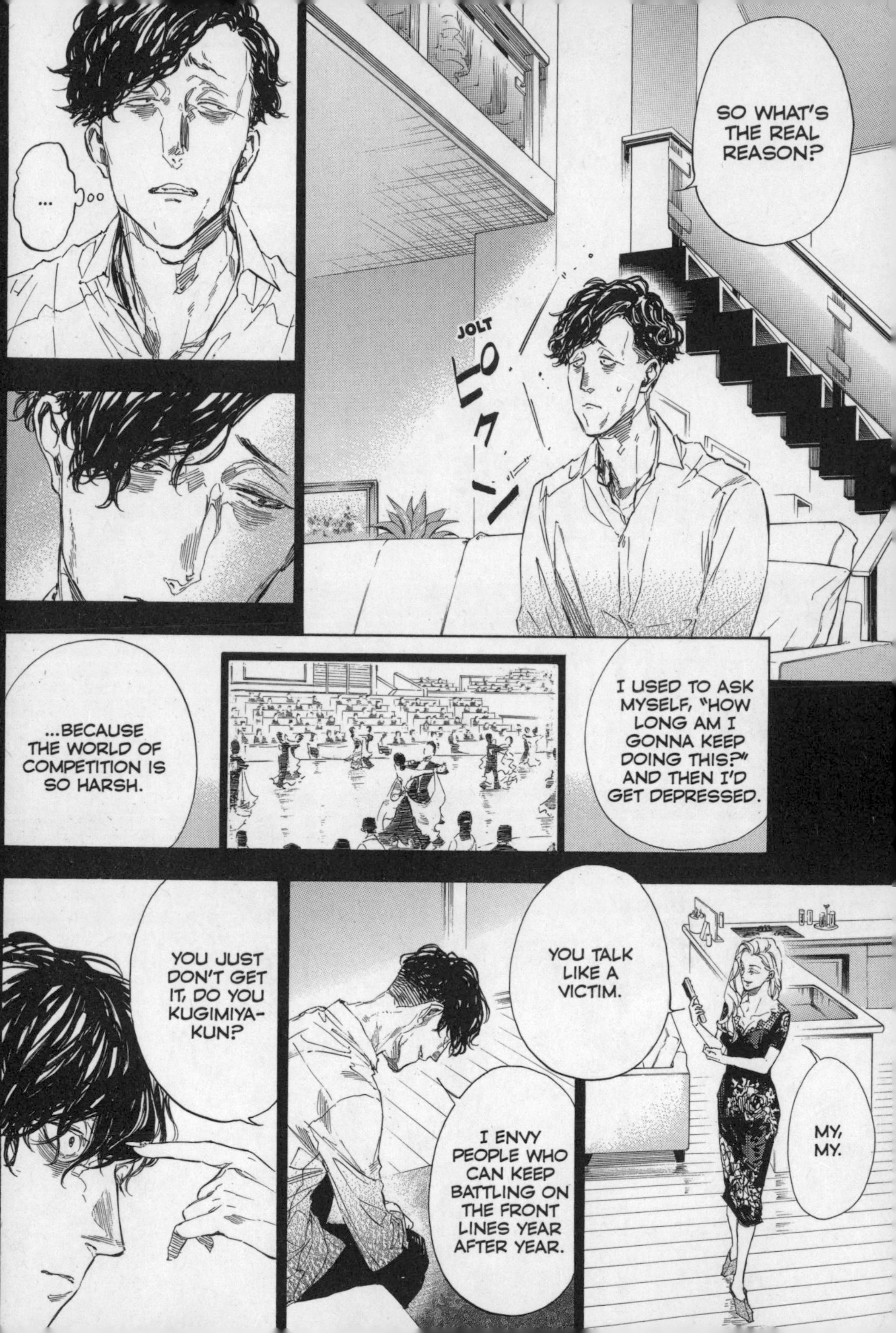
SO WHAT'S THE REAL REASON?
JOLT
...
I USED TO ASK MYSELF, "HOW LONG AM I GONNA KEEP DOING THIS?" AND THEN I'D GET DEPRESSED.
...BECAUSE THE WORLD OF COMPETITION IS SO HARSH.
MY, MY.
YOU TALK LIKE A VICTIM.
I ENVY PEOPLE WHO CAN KEEP BATTLING ON THE FRONT LINES YEAR AFTER YEAR.
YOU JUST DON'T GET IT, DO YOU KUGIMIYA-KUN?

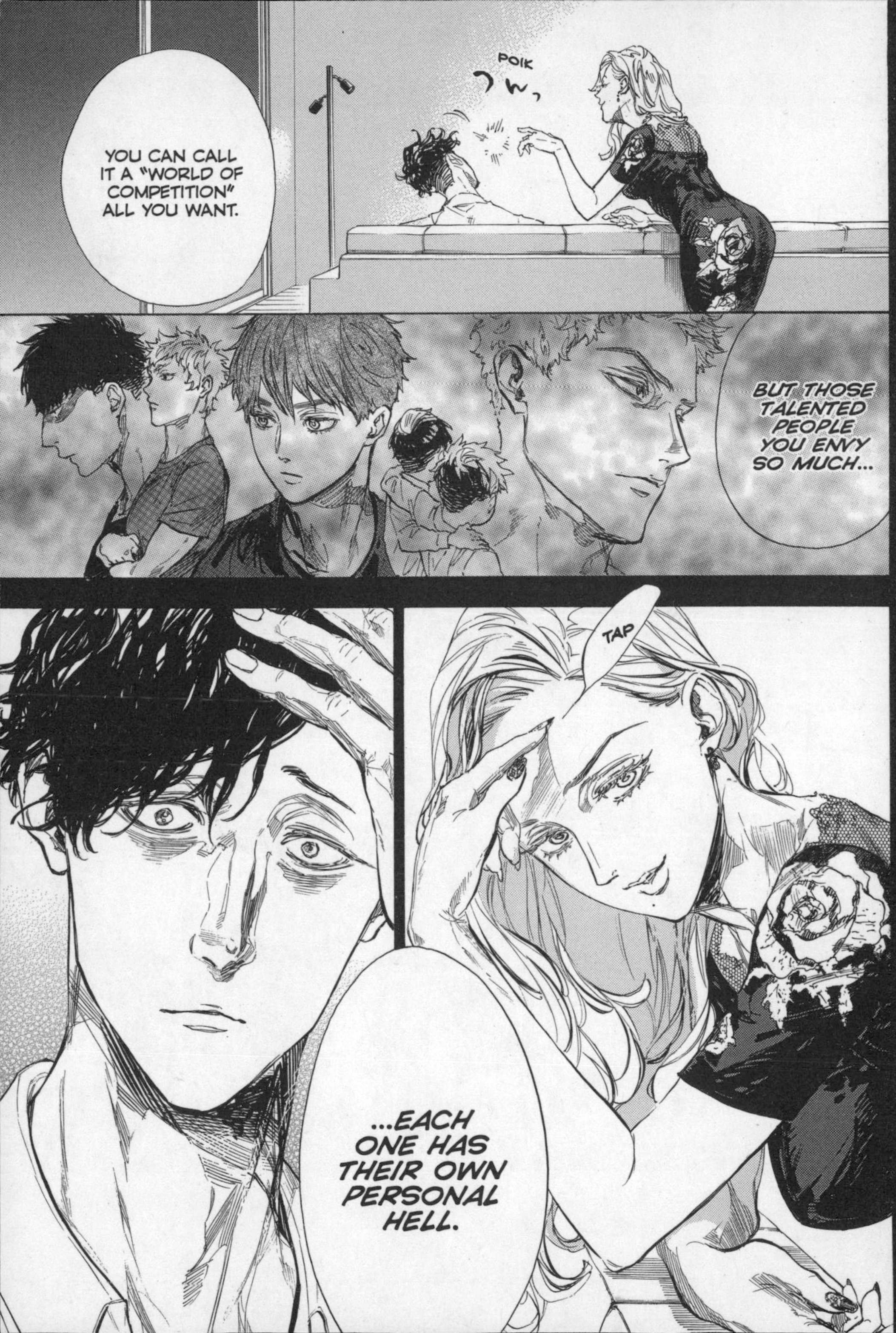
POIK
YOU CAN CALL IT A "WORLD OF COMPETITION" ALL YOU WANT.
BUT THOSE TALENTED PEOPLE YOU ENVY SO MUCH...
TAP
...EACH ONE HAS THEIR OWN PERSONAL HELL.

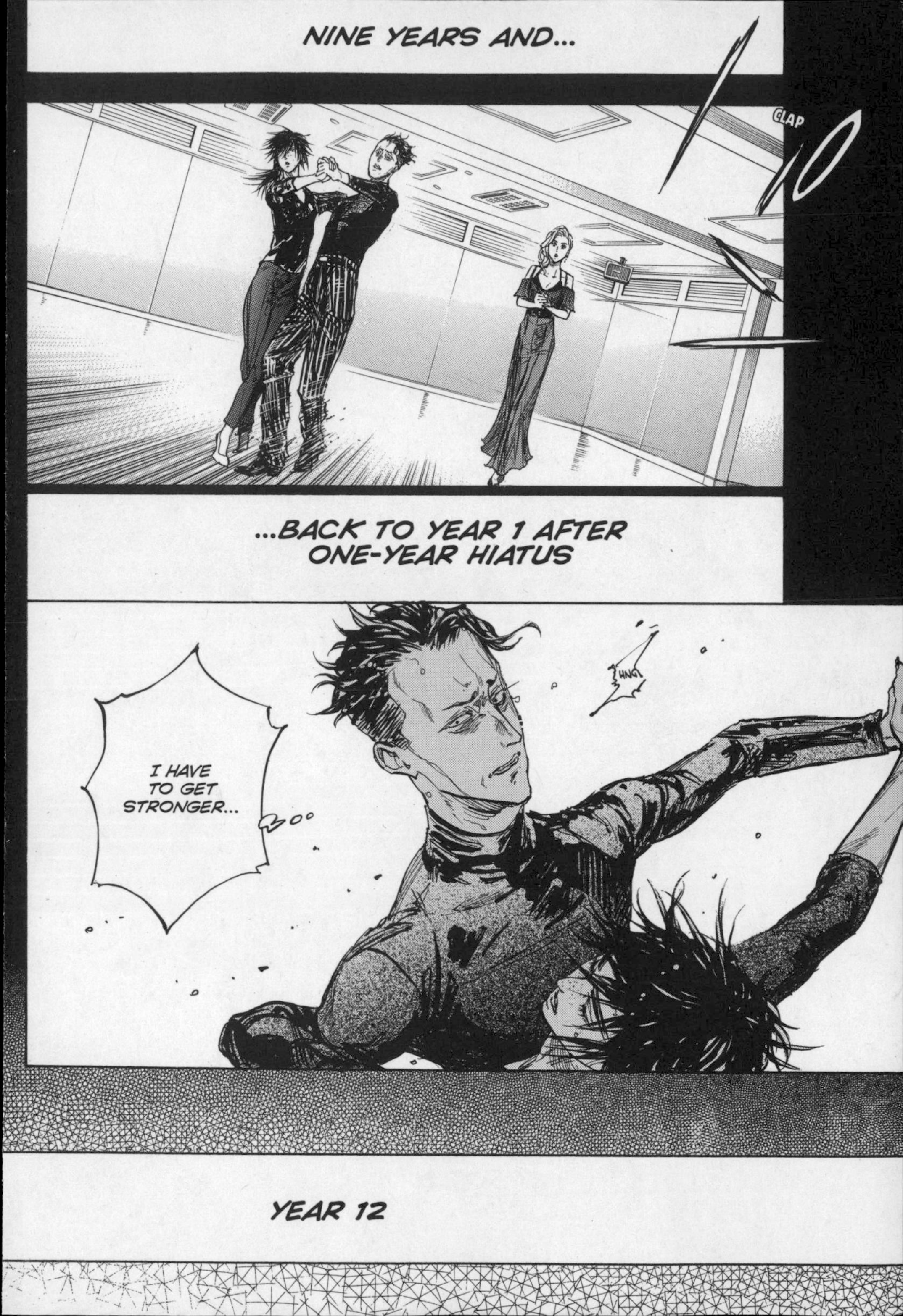
NINE YEARS AND...
CLAP
...BACK TO YEAR 1 AFTER ONE-YEAR HIATUS
HNG!
I HAVE TO GET STRONGER...
YEAR 12

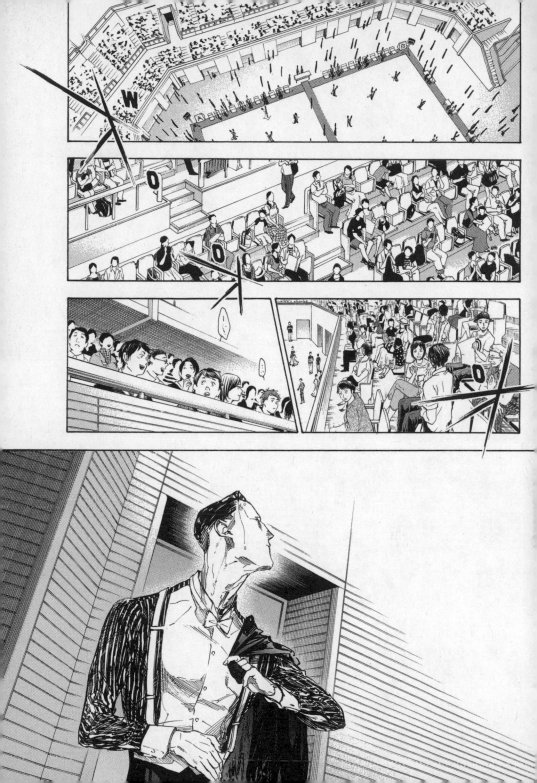

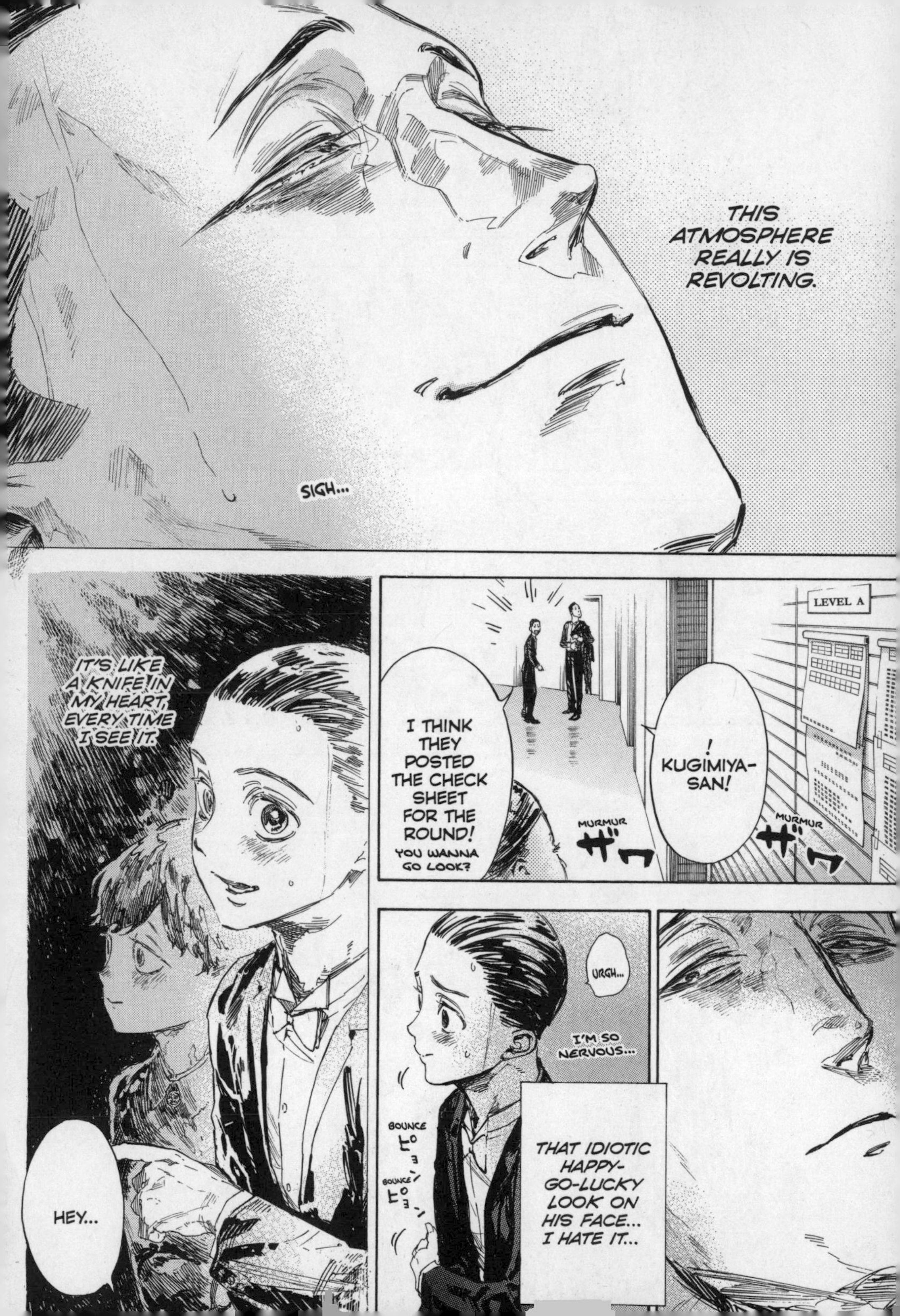

THIS ATMOSPHERE REALLY IS REVOLTING.
SIGH...
LEVEL A
! KUGIMIYA-SAN!
MURMUR ザワ
I THINK THEY POSTED THE CHECK SHEET FOR THE ROUND! YOU WANNA GO LOOK?
MURMUR ザワ
THAT IDIOTIC HAPPY-GO-LUCKY LOOK ON HIS FACE... I HATE IT...
URGH...
I'M SO NERVOUS...
BOUNCE
BOUNCE
IT'S LIKE A KNIFE IN MY HEART, EVERY TIME I SEE IT.
HEY...

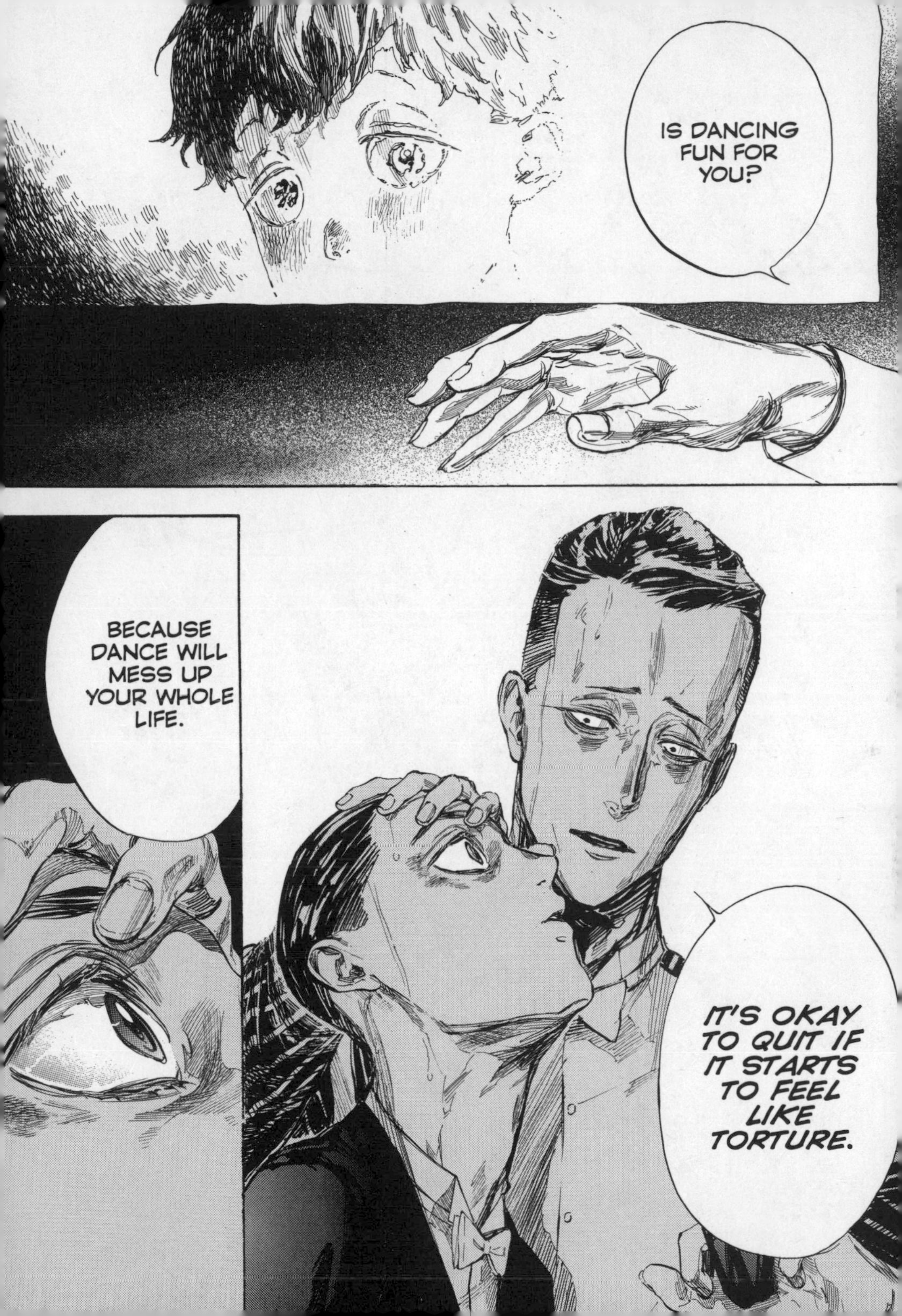
IS DANCING FUN FOR YOU?
IT'S OKAY TO QUIT IF IT STARTS TO FEEL LIKE TORTURE.
BECAUSE DANCE WILL MESS UP YOUR WHOLE LIFE.

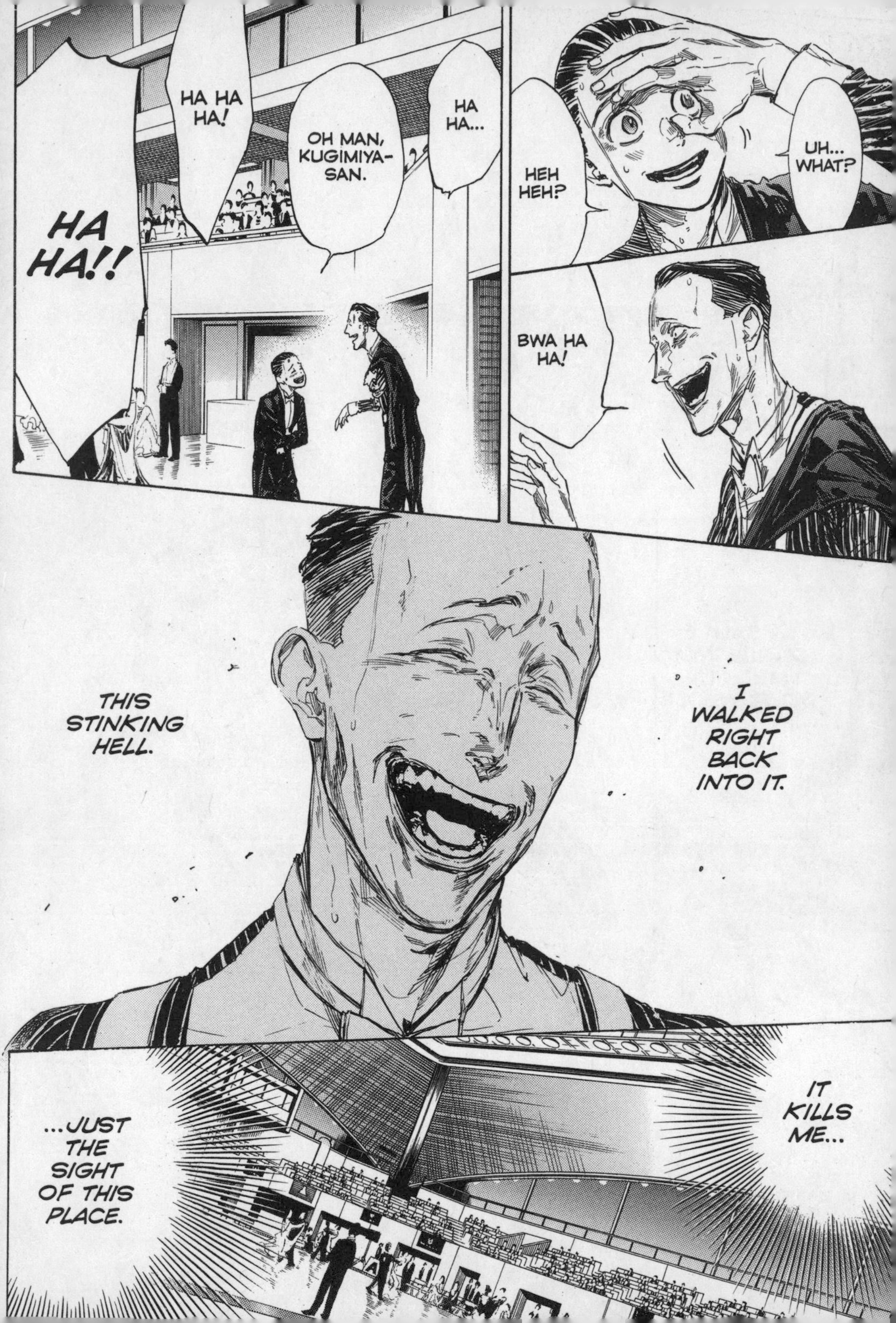
UH... WHAT?
HEH HEH?
BWA HA HA!
HA HA...
OH MAN, KUGIMIYA-SAN.
HA HA HA!
HA HA!!
I WALKED RIGHT BACK INTO IT.
THIS STINKING HELL.
IT KILLS ME...
...JUST THE SIGHT OF THIS PLACE.

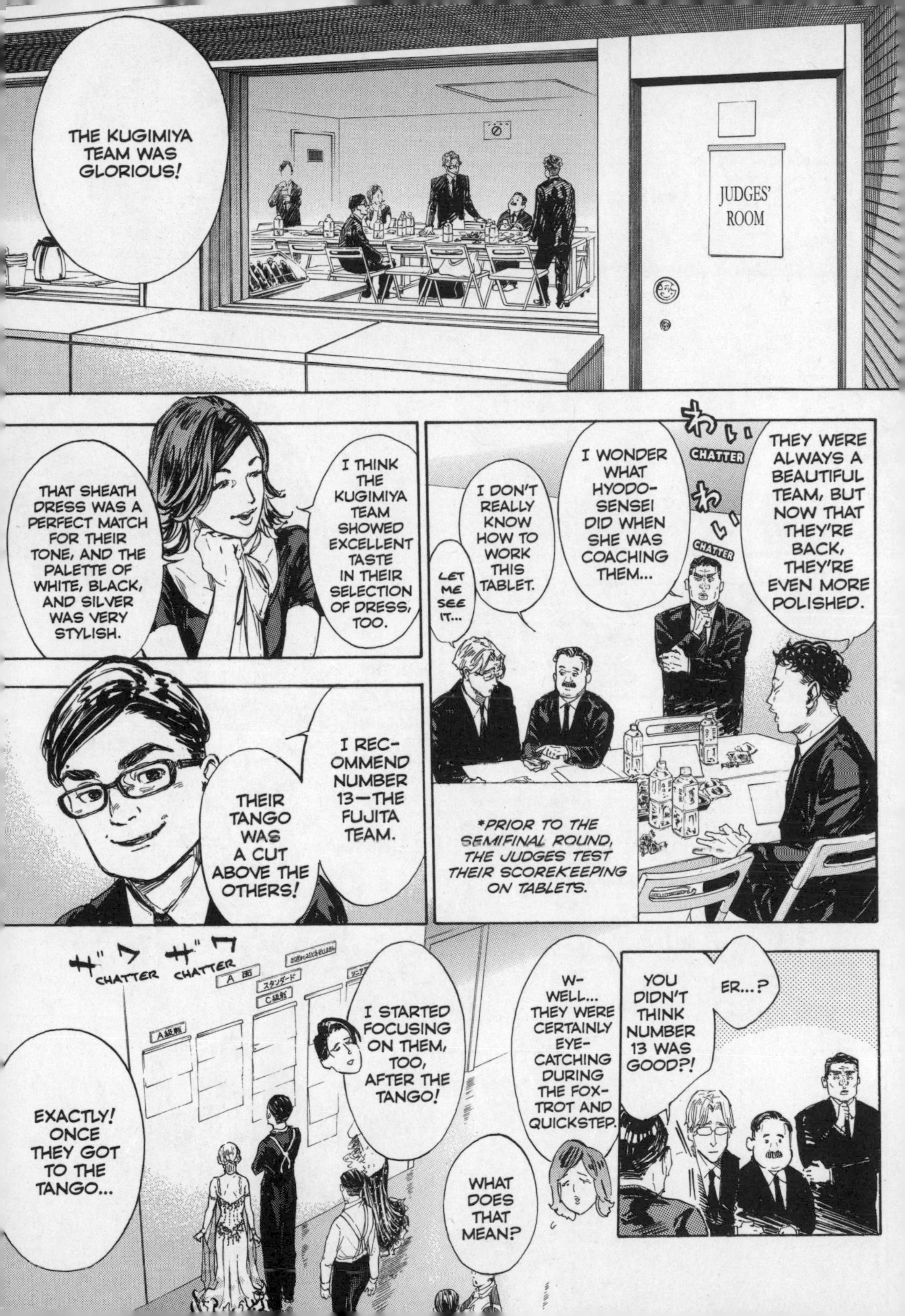
THE KUGIMIYA TEAM WAS GLORIOUS!
JUDGES' ROOM
THEY WERE ALWAYS A BEAUTIFUL TEAM, BUT NOW THAT THEY'RE BACK, THEY'RE EVEN MORE POLISHED.
CHATTER
CHATTER
I WONDER WHAT HYODO-SENSEI DID WHEN SHE WAS COACHING THEM...
I DON'T REALLY KNOW HOW TO WORK THIS TABLET.
LET ME SEE IT...
*PRIOR TO THE SEMIFINAL ROUND, THE JUDGES TEST THEIR SCOREKEEPING ON TABLETS.
I THINK THE KUGIMIYA TEAM SHOWED EXCELLENT TASTE IN THEIR SELECTION OF DRESS, TOO.
THAT SHEATH DRESS WAS A PERFECT MATCH FOR THEIR TONE, AND THE PALETTE OF WHITE, BLACK, AND SILVER WAS VERY STYLISH.
I RECOMMEND NUMBER 13—THE FUJITA TEAM.
THEIR TANGO WAS A CUT ABOVE THE OTHERS!
ER...?
YOU DIDN'T THINK NUMBER 13 WAS GOOD?!
W-WELL... THEY WERE CERTAINLY EYE-CATCHING DURING THE FOX-TROT AND QUICKSTEP.
I STARTED FOCUSING ON THEM, TOO, AFTER THE TANGO!
WHAT DOES THAT MEAN?
CHATTER CHATTER
EXACTLY! ONCE THEY GOT TO THE TANGO...

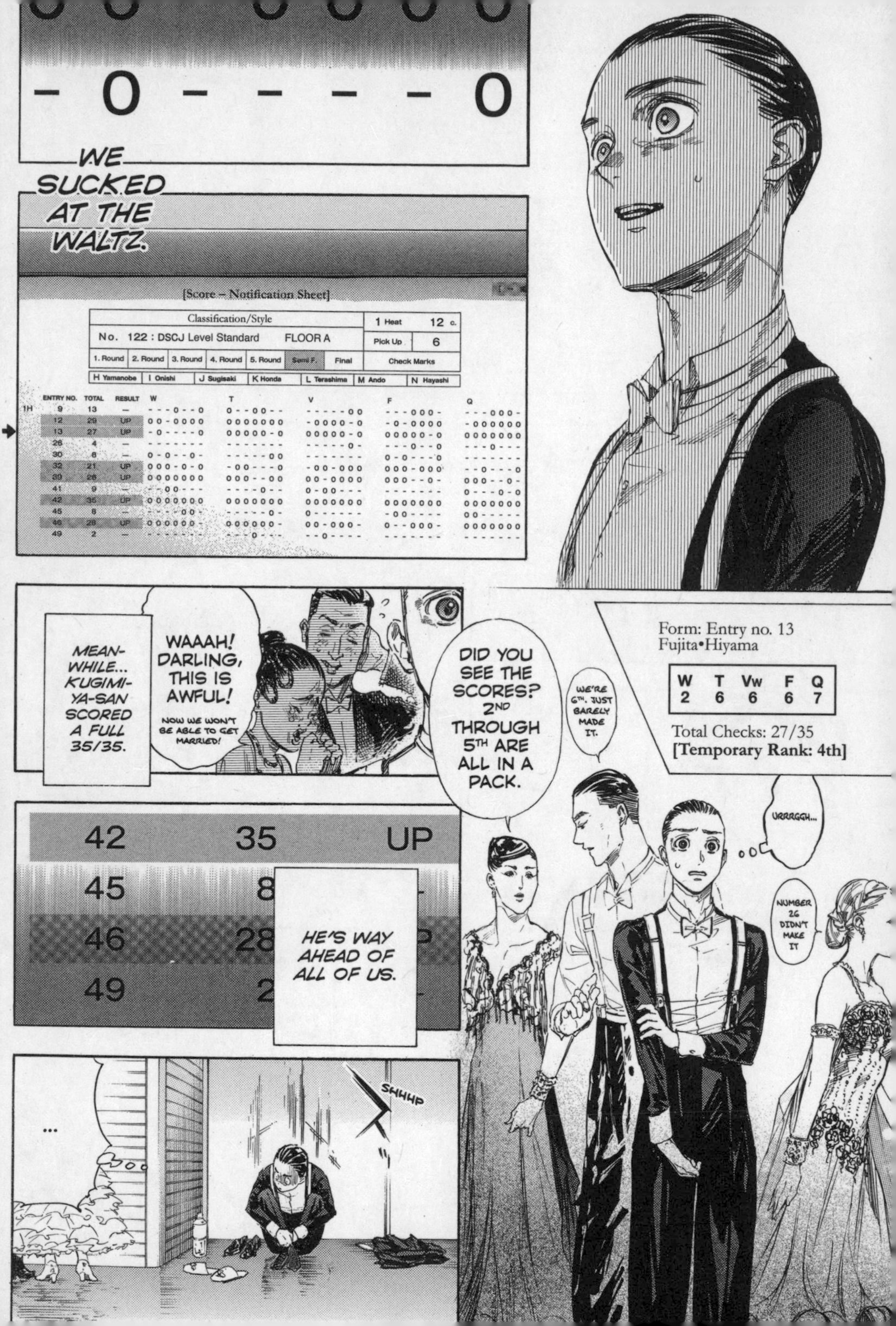
- 0 - - - - 0
WE SUCKED AT THE WALTZ.
[Score – Notification Sheet]

Classification/Style							1 Heat	12 c.
No. 122 : DSCJ Level Standard FLOOR A							Pick Up	6
1. Round	2. Round	3. Round	4. Round	5. Round	Semi F.	Final	Check Marks	
H Yamanobe	I Onishi	J Sugisaki	K Honda	L Terashima	M Ando	N Hayashi		

	ENTRY NO.	TOTAL	RESULT	W	T	V	F	Q
1H	9	13	—	---0--0	0--00--	-----00	---000-	---000-
	12	29	UP	00-0000	0000000	-0000-0	-0-0000	-000000
	13	27	UP	-0----0	00000-0	00000-0	00000-0	0000000
	26	4	—	-------	-------	-----0-	---0--0	---0---
	30	8	—	0-0--0-	-----00	-------	0-0---0	-------
	32	21	UP	000-0-0	-00---0	-00-000	000-000	--0---0
	39	26	UP	0000000	000--00	00-0000	000--0-	000--0-
	41	9	—	--00---	----0--	0-00---	-------	0---0-0
	42	35	UP	0000000	0000000	0000000	0000000	0000000
	45	8	—	----00-	-----0-	0------	-00----	00-----
	46	28	UP	000000-	000000-	00-000-	0--000-	0000000
	49	2	—	-------	---0---	--0----	-------	-------

Form: Entry no. 13
Fujita•Hiyama

W	T	Vw	F	Q
2	6	6	6	7

Total Checks: 27/35
[Temporary Rank: 4th]
URRRGGH...
NUMBER 26 DIDN'T MAKE IT
WE'RE 6TH. JUST BARELY MADE IT.
DID YOU SEE THE SCORES? 2ND THROUGH 5TH ARE ALL IN A PACK.
WAAAH! DARLING, THIS IS AWFUL!
NOW WE WON'T BE ABLE TO GET MARRIED!
MEAN-WHILE... KUGIMIYA-SAN SCORED A FULL 35/35.
42 35 UP
45 8
46 28
49 2
HE'S WAY AHEAD OF ALL OF US.
SHHHP
...

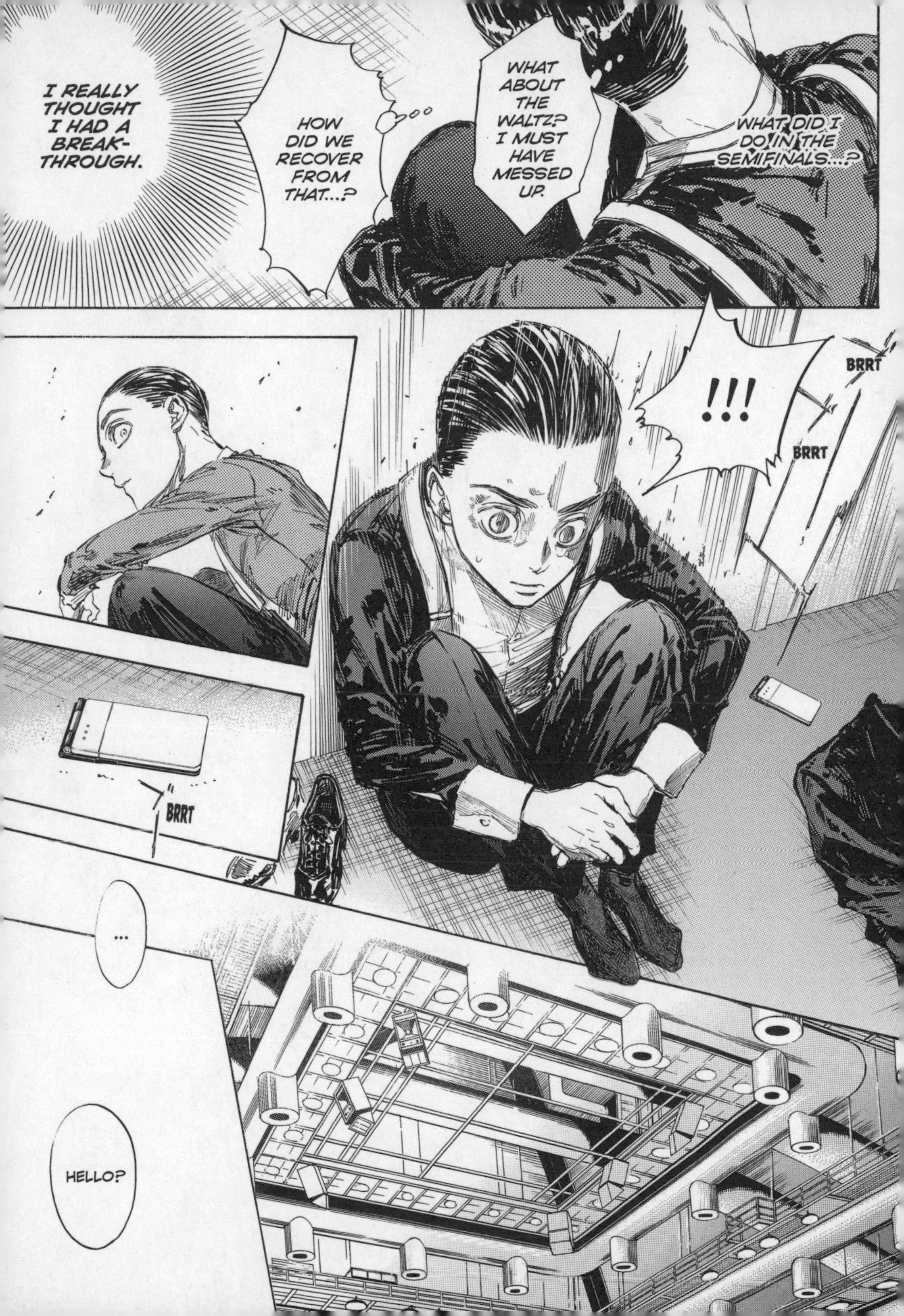
WHAT DID I DO IN THE SEMIFINALS...?
WHAT ABOUT THE WALTZ? I MUST HAVE MESSED UP.
HOW DID WE RECOVER FROM THAT...?
I REALLY THOUGHT I HAD A BREAK-THROUGH.
BRRT
!!!
BRRT
BRRT
...
HELLO?

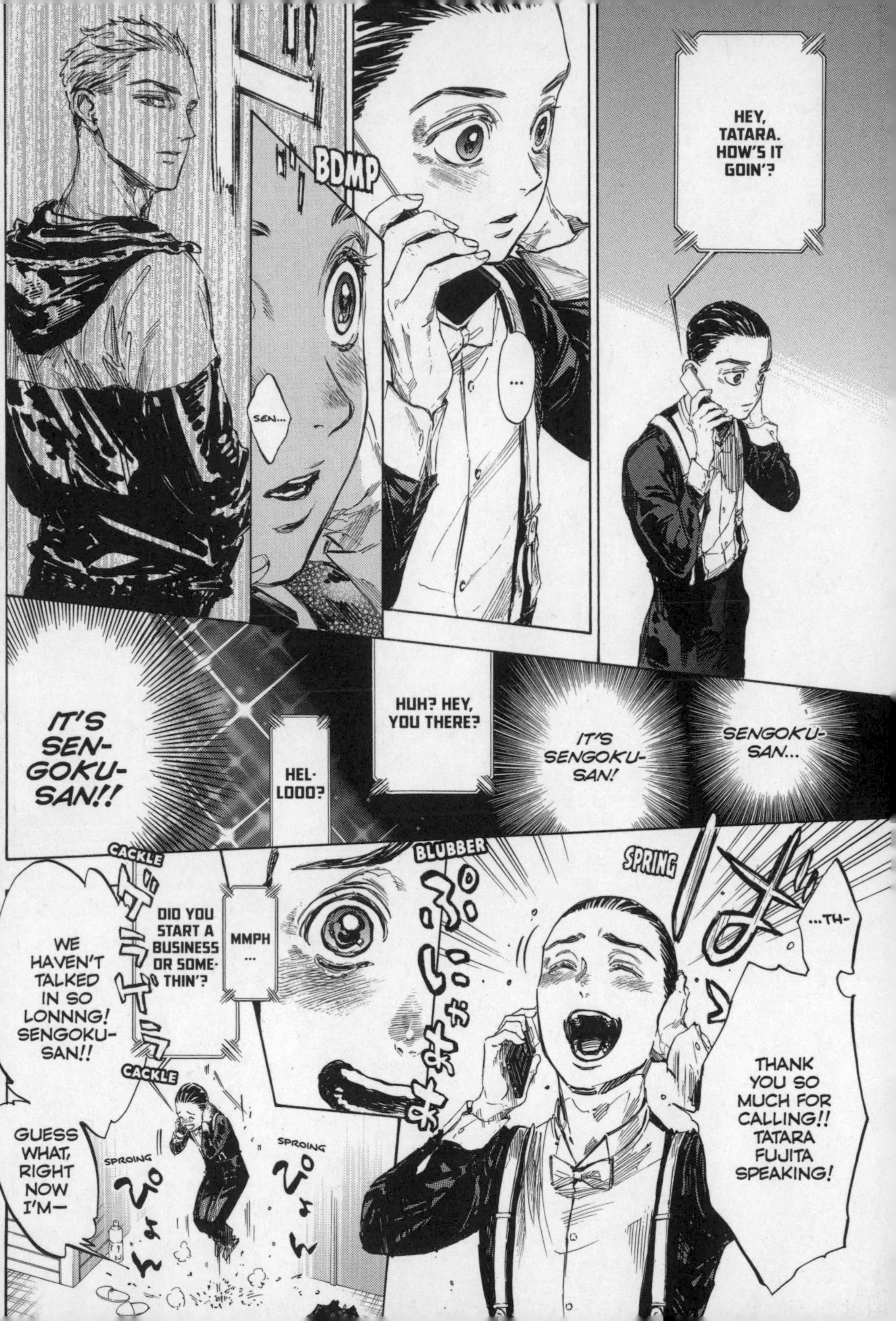
HEY, TATARA. HOW'S IT GOIN'?
...
BDMP
SEN...
SENGOKU-SAN...
IT'S SENGOKU-SAN!
HUH? HEY, YOU THERE?
HEL-LOOO?
IT'S SEN-GOKU-SAN!!
SPRING
...TH-
THANK YOU SO MUCH FOR CALLING!! TATARA FUJITA SPEAKING!
BLUBBER
MMPH ...
DID YOU START A BUSINESS OR SOME-THIN'?
CACKLE
WE HAVEN'T TALKED IN SO LONNNG! SENGOKU-SAN!!
CACKLE
SPROING
GUESS WHAT, RIGHT NOW I'M—
SPROING

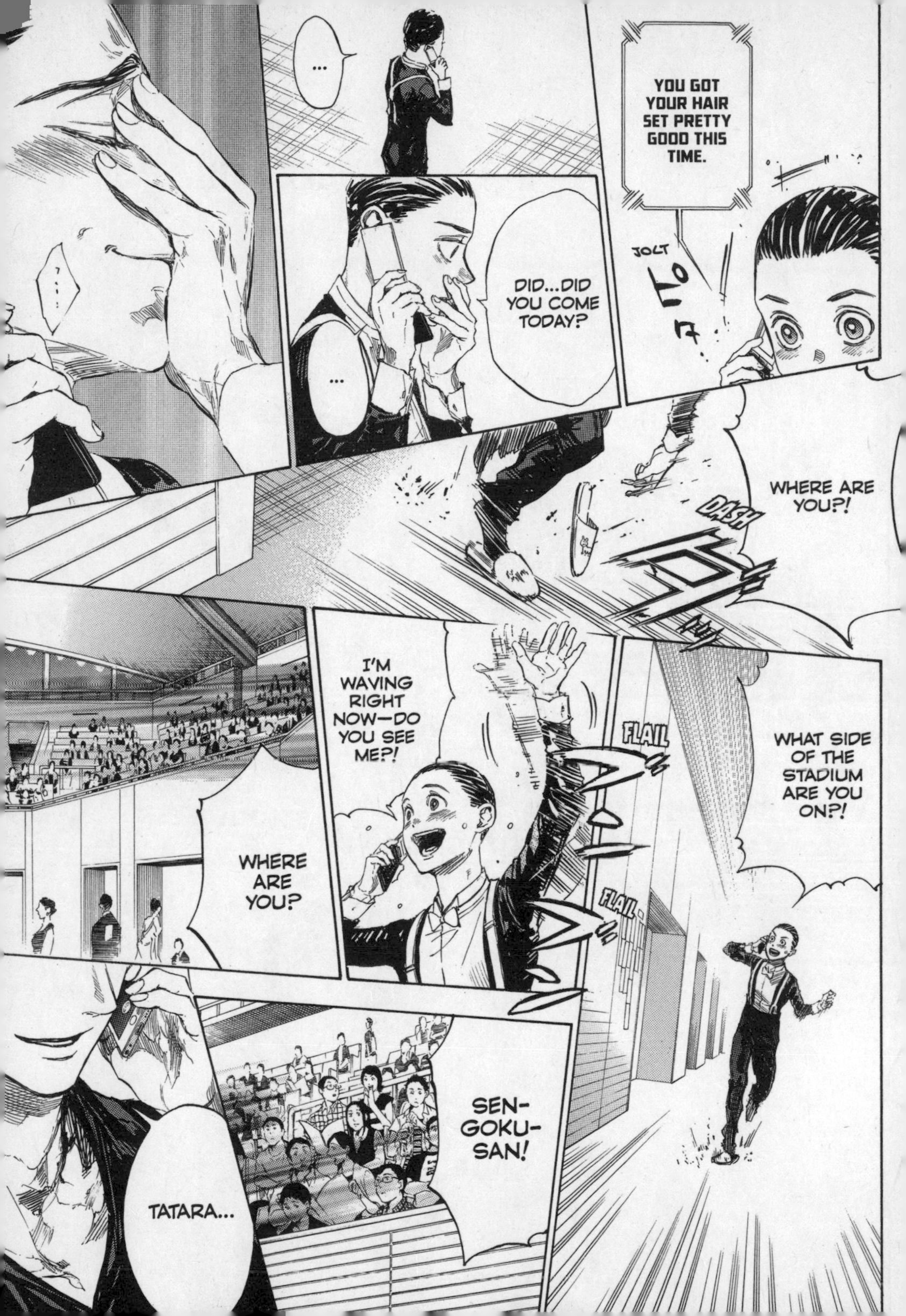
YOU GOT YOUR HAIR SET PRETTY GOOD THIS TIME.
JOLT
...
DID...DID YOU COME TODAY?
...
WHERE ARE YOU?!
DASH
WHAT SIDE OF THE STADIUM ARE YOU ON?!
FLAIL
FLAIL
I'M WAVING RIGHT NOW—DO YOU SEE ME?!
WHERE ARE YOU?
SEN-GOKU-SAN!
TATARA...

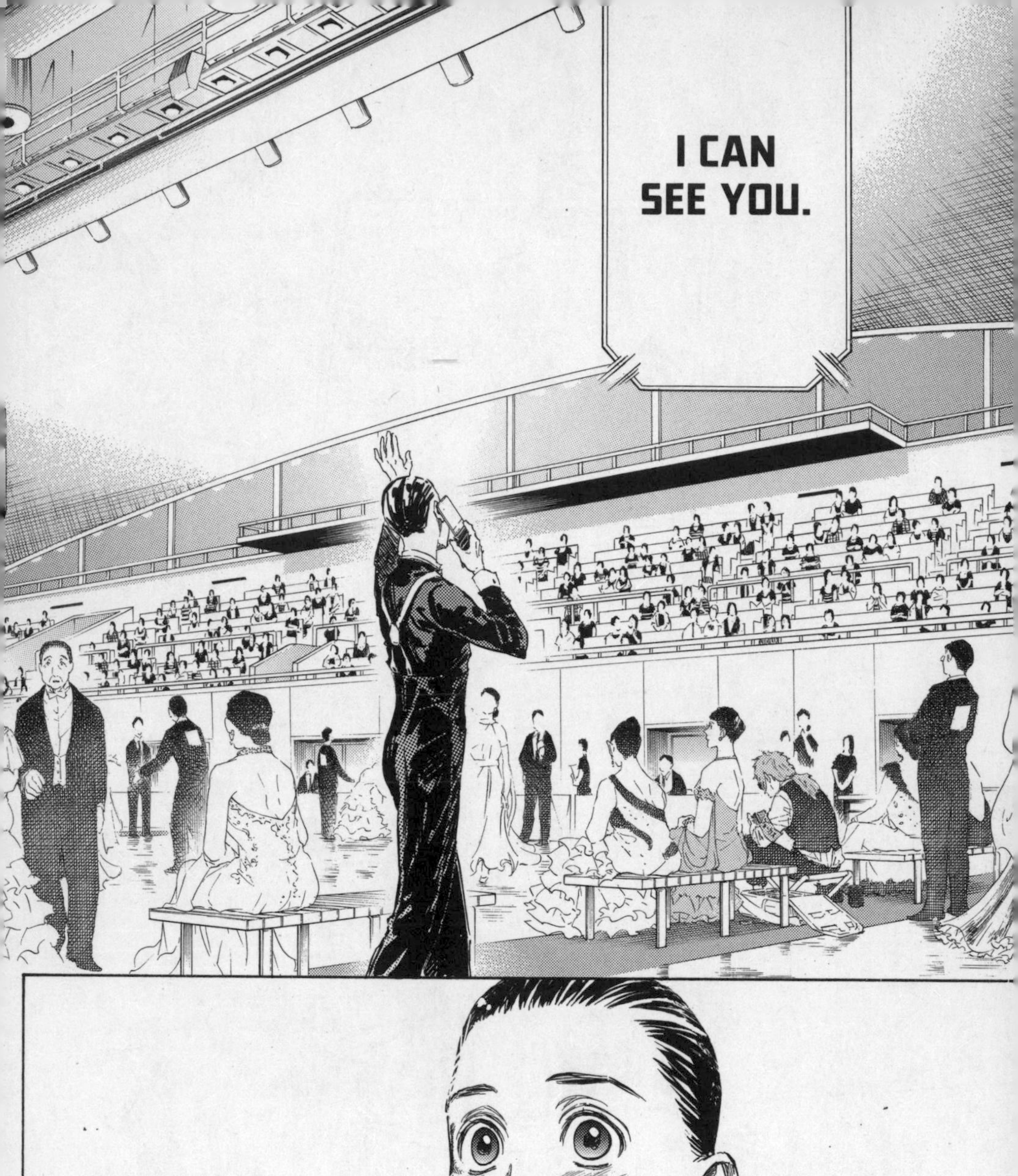
I CAN
SEE YOU.
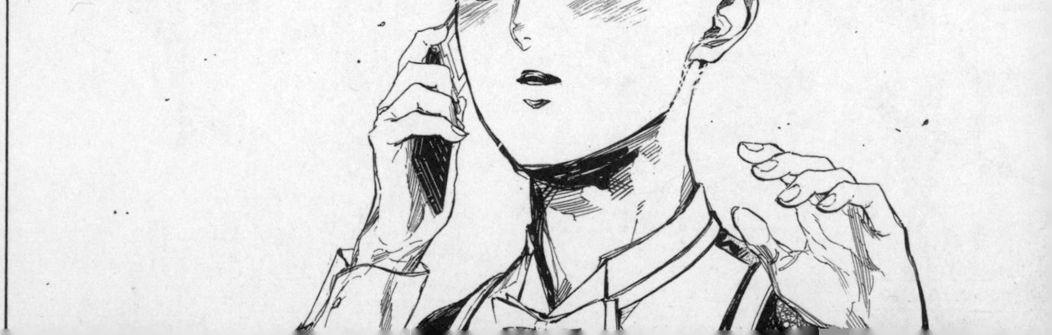

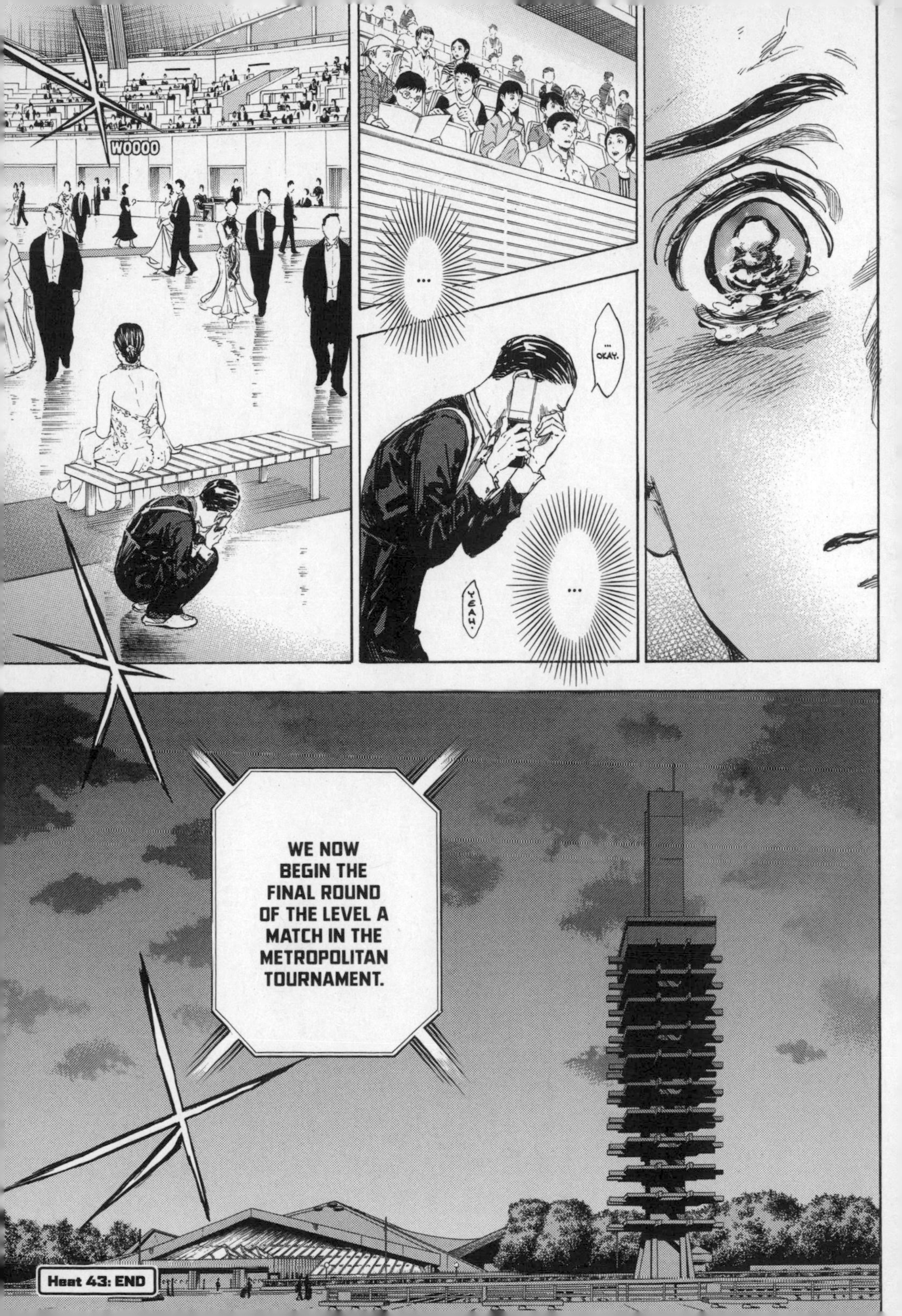
...
... OKAY.
...
YEAH.
WOOOO
WE NOW BEGIN THE FINAL ROUND OF THE LEVEL A MATCH IN THE METROPOLITAN TOURNAMENT.
Heat 43: END

WELCOME TO THE BALLROOM

Heat 44
The Metropolitan Tournament Finals

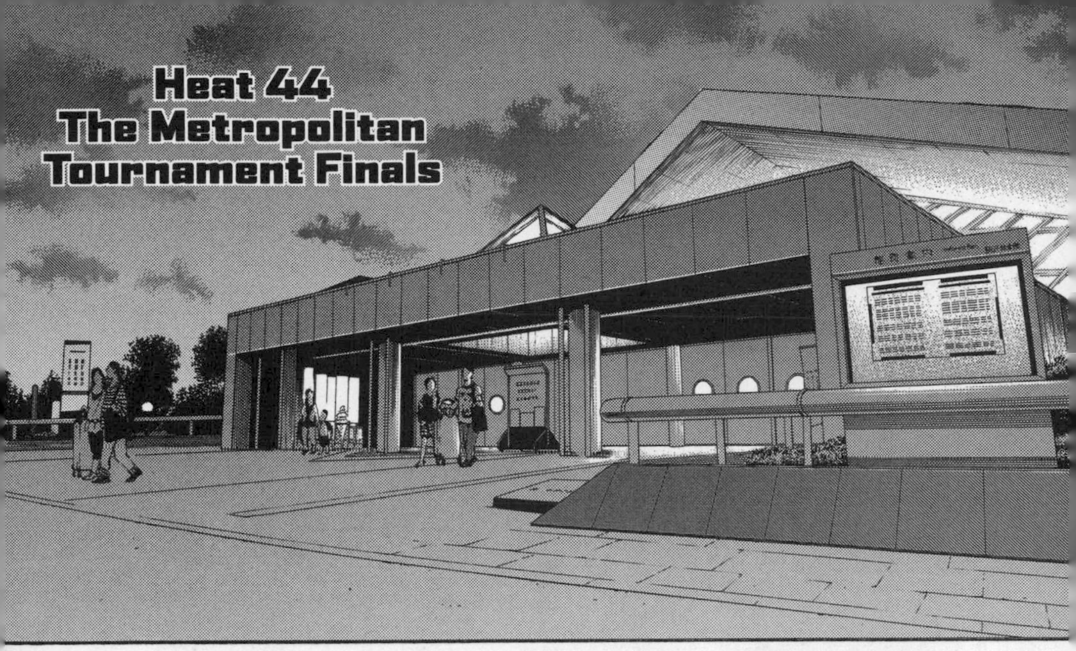

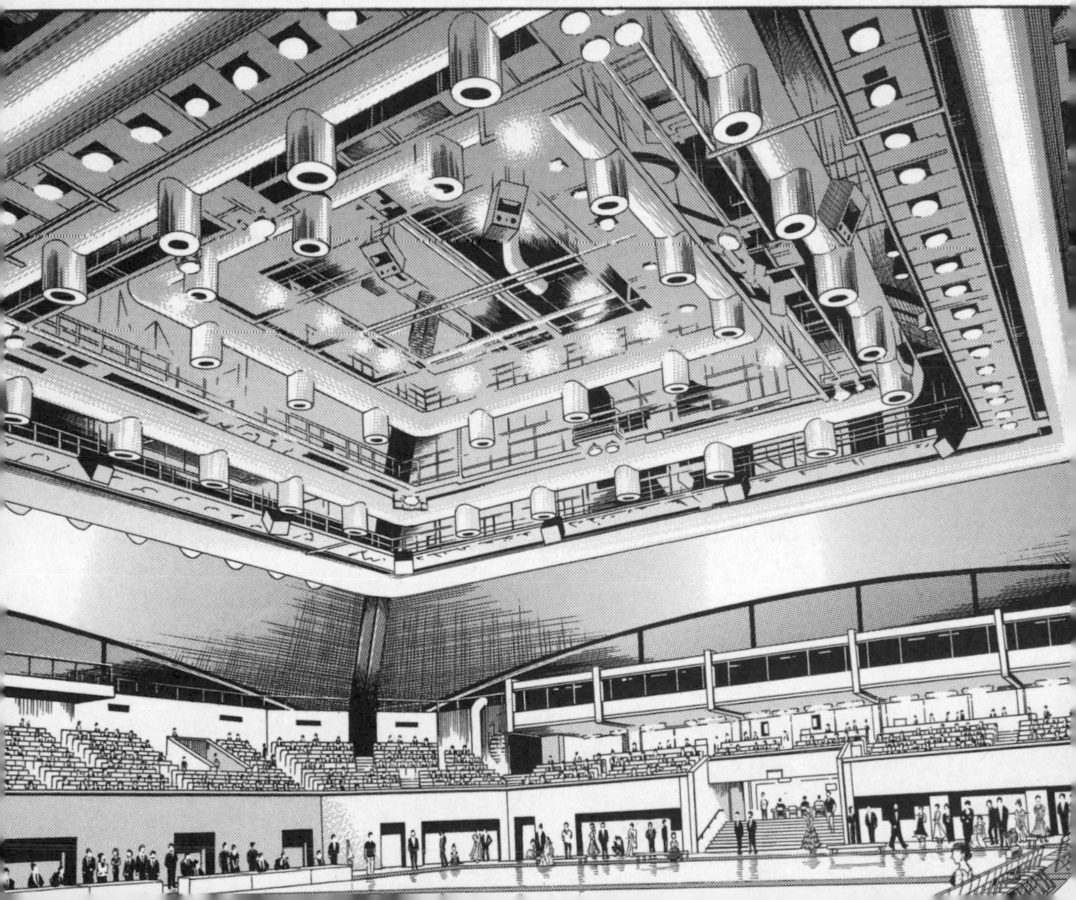

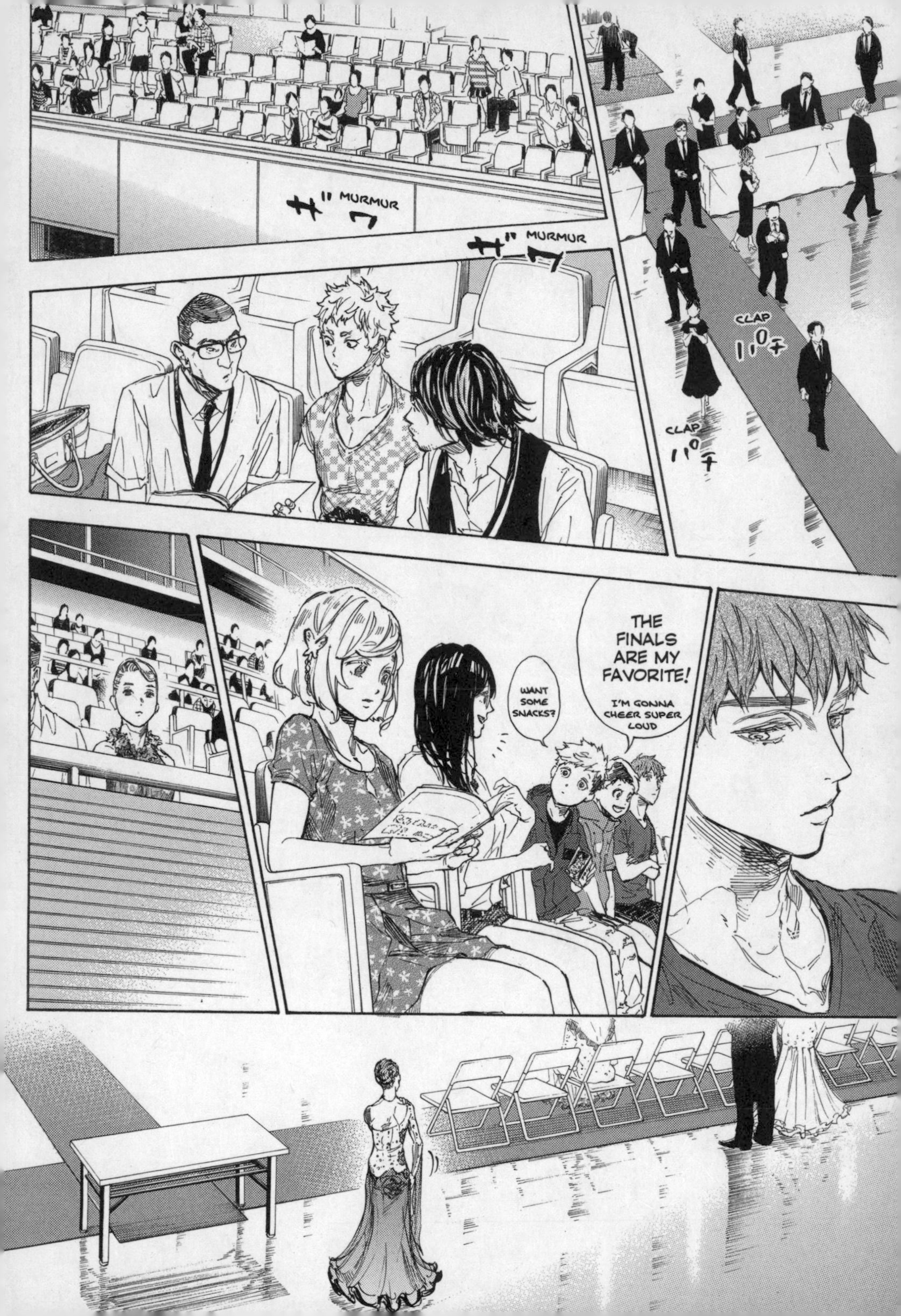
CLAP
CLAP
MURMUR
MURMUR
THE FINALS ARE MY FAVORITE!
I'M GONNA CHEER SUPER LOUD
WANT SOME SNACKS?

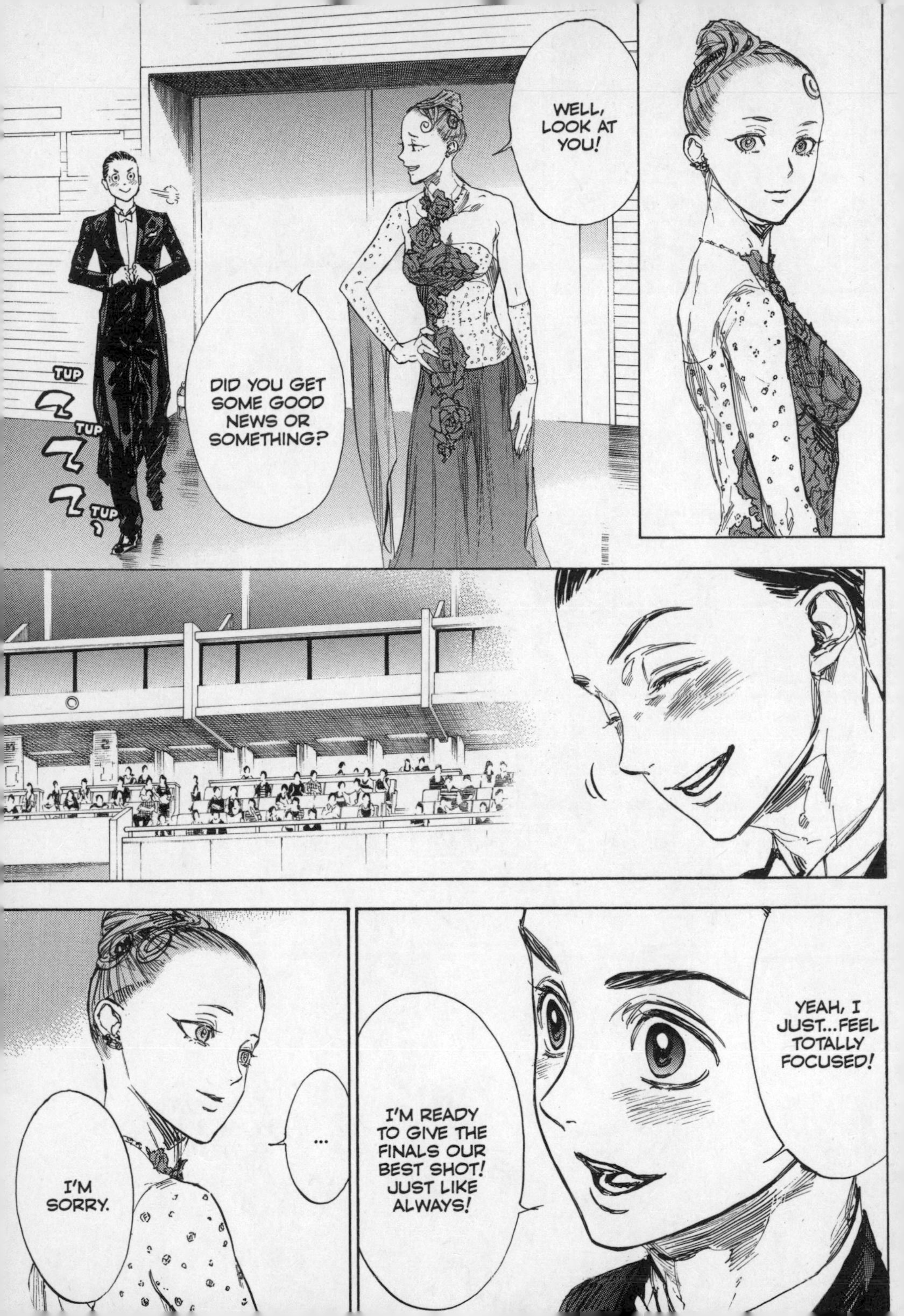
WELL, LOOK AT YOU!
DID YOU GET SOME GOOD NEWS OR SOMETHING?
TUP
TUP
TUP
YEAH, I JUST...FEEL TOTALLY FOCUSED!
I'M READY TO GIVE THE FINALS OUR BEST SHOT! JUST LIKE ALWAYS!
...
I'M SORRY.

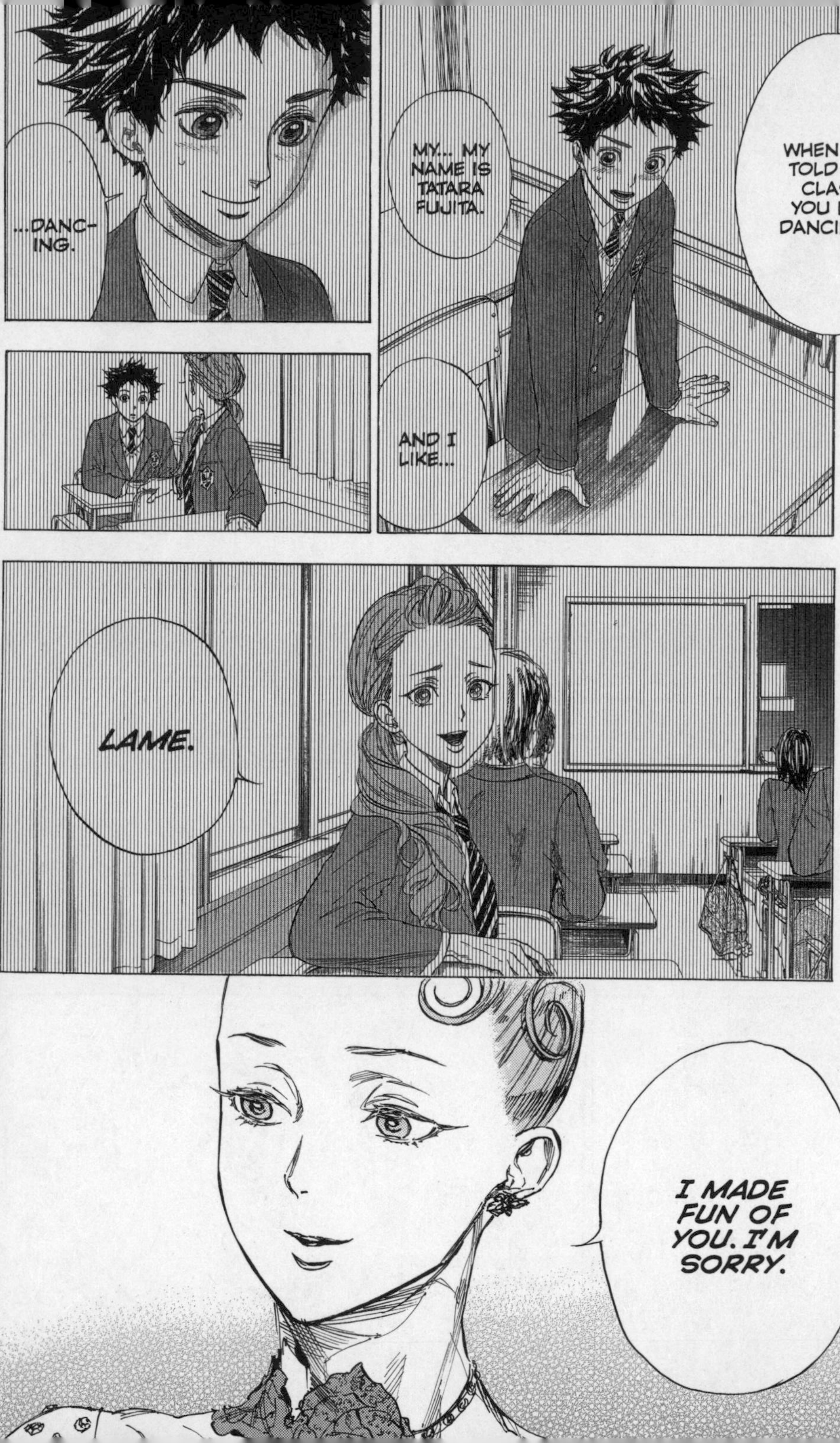
WHEN YOU TOLD THE CLASS YOU LIKE DANCING...
MY... MY NAME IS TATARA FUJITA.
AND I LIKE...
...DANCING.
LAME.
I MADE FUN OF YOU. I'M SORRY.

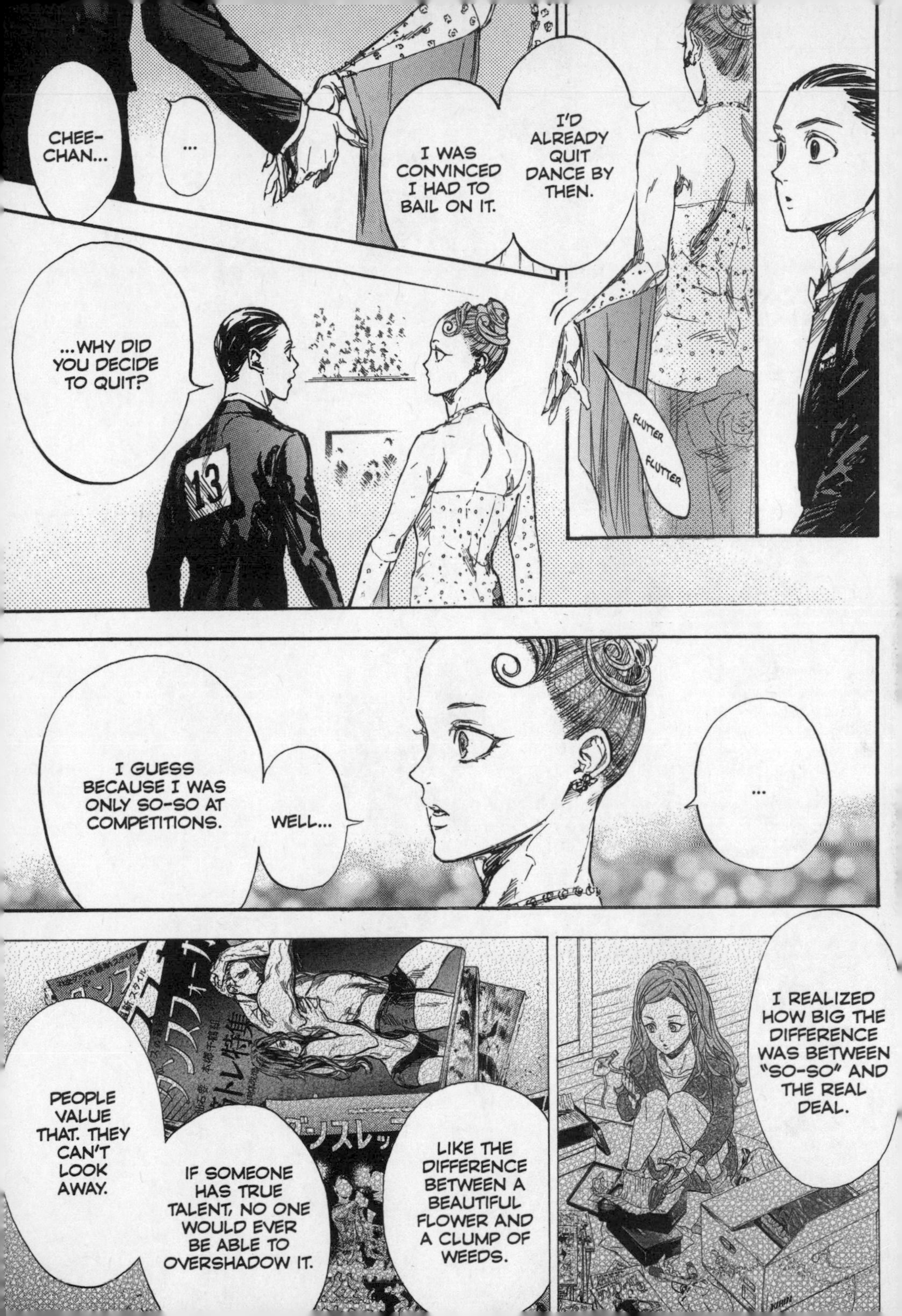
I'D ALREADY QUIT DANCE BY THEN.
I WAS CONVINCED I HAD TO BAIL ON IT.
FLUTTER
FLUTTER
...
CHEE-CHAN...
...WHY DID YOU DECIDE TO QUIT?
...
WELL...
I GUESS BECAUSE I WAS ONLY SO-SO AT COMPETITIONS.
I REALIZED HOW BIG THE DIFFERENCE WAS BETWEEN "SO-SO" AND THE REAL DEAL.
LIKE THE DIFFERENCE BETWEEN A BEAUTIFUL FLOWER AND A CLUMP OF WEEDS.
IF SOMEONE HAS TRUE TALENT, NO ONE WOULD EVER BE ABLE TO OVERSHADOW IT.
PEOPLE VALUE THAT. THEY CAN'T LOOK AWAY.

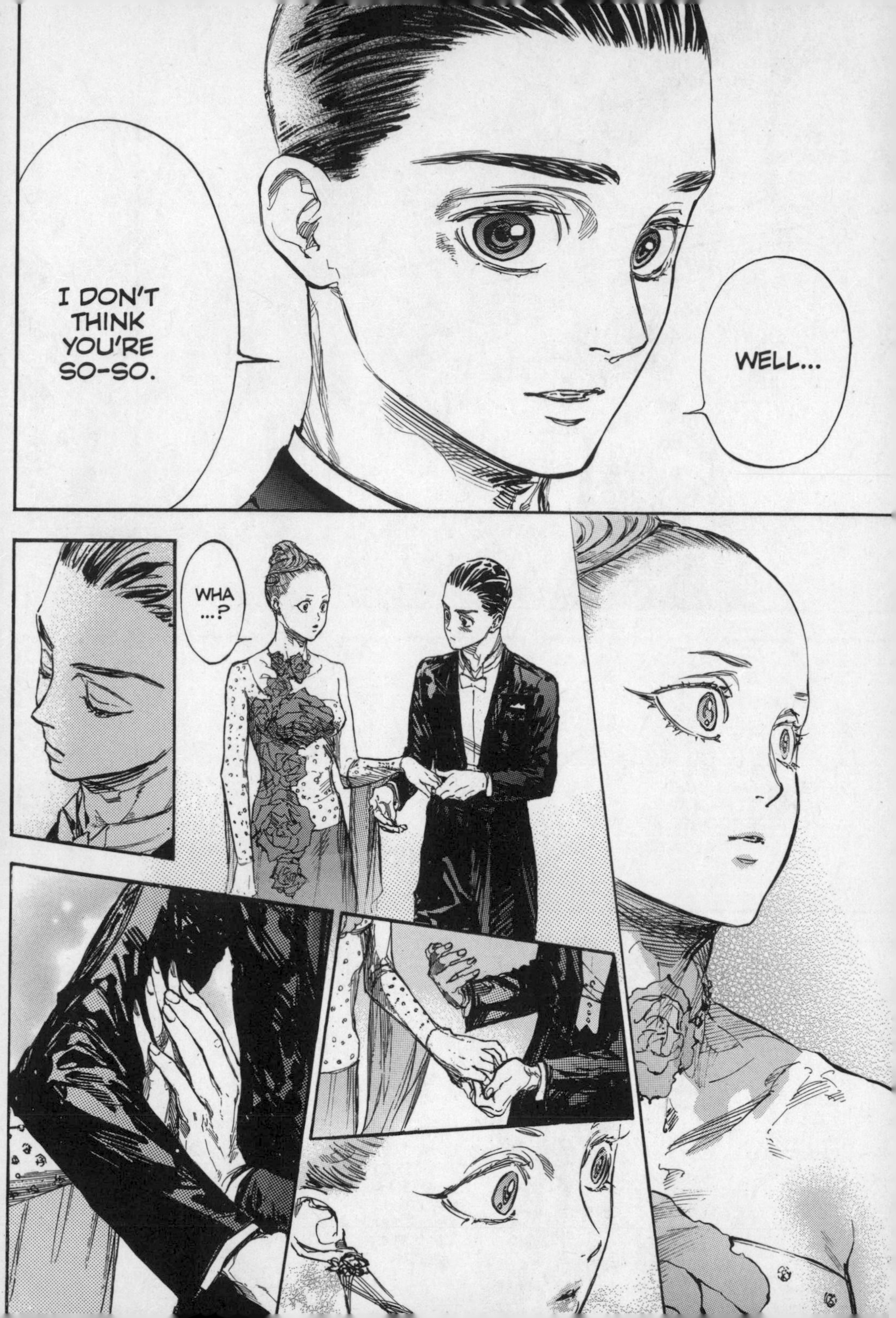
WELL...
I DON'T THINK YOU'RE SO-SO.
WHA ...?

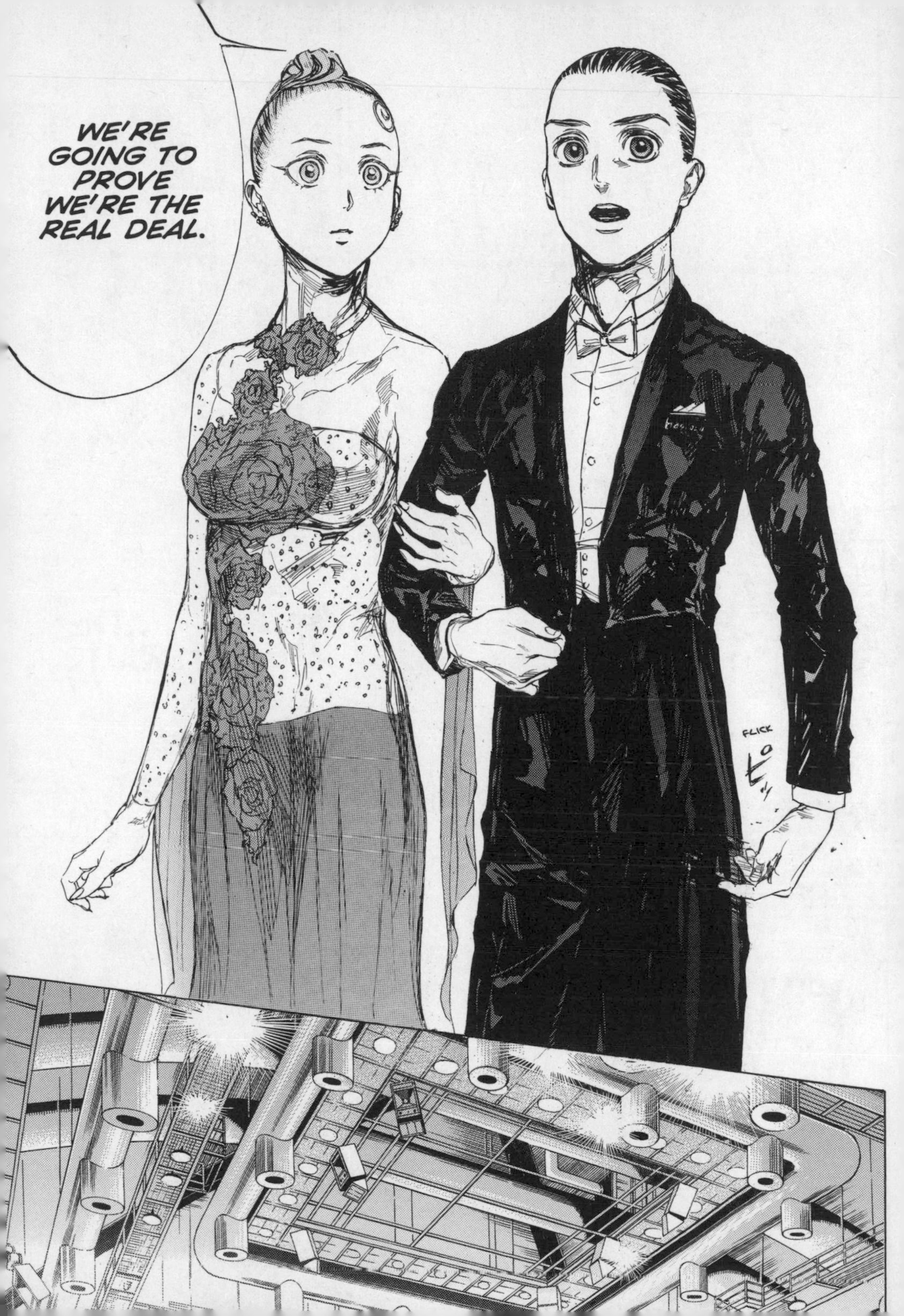
WE'RE GOING TO PROVE WE'RE THE REAL DEAL.
FLICK

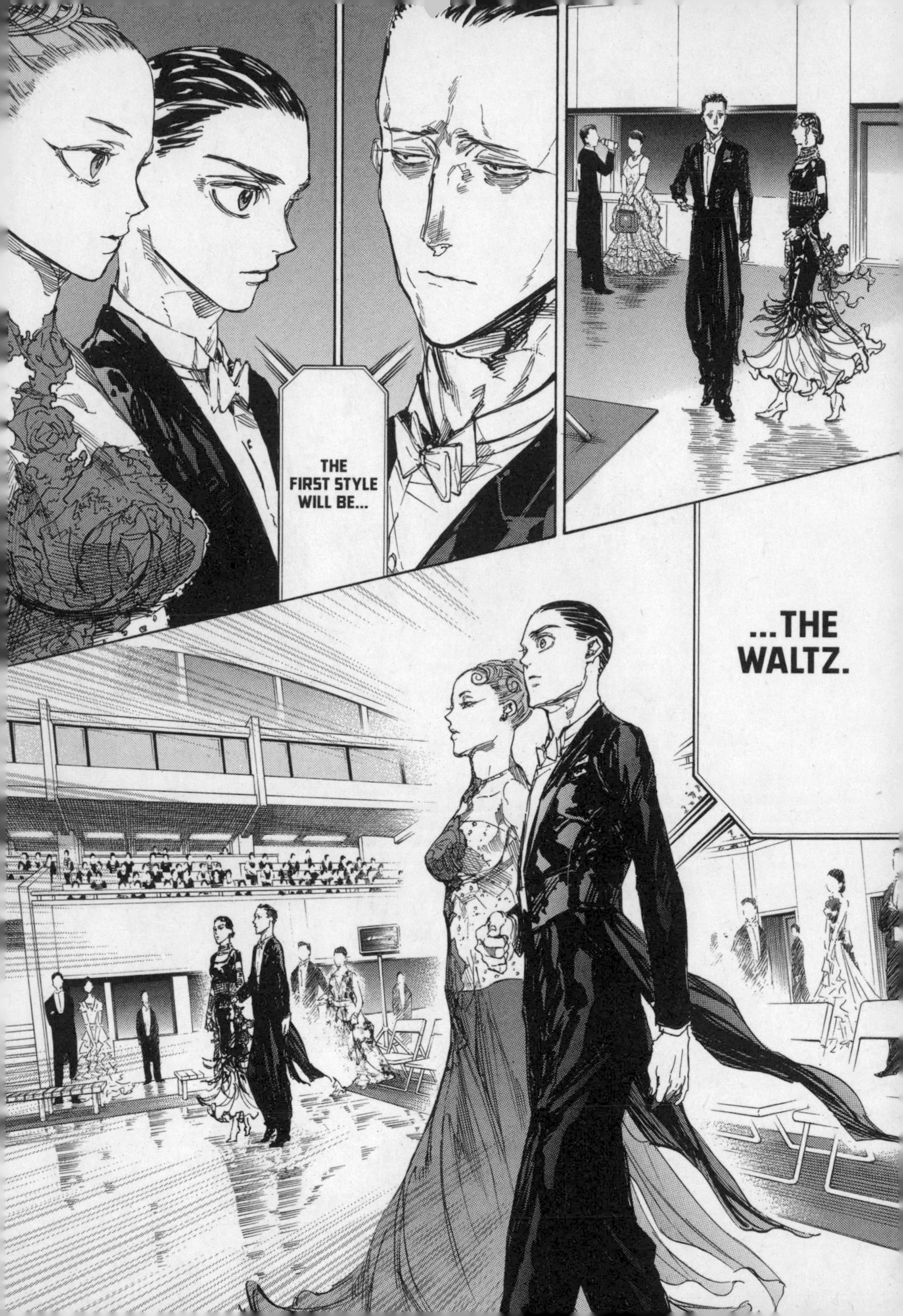
THE FIRST STYLE WILL BE...
...THE WALTZ.

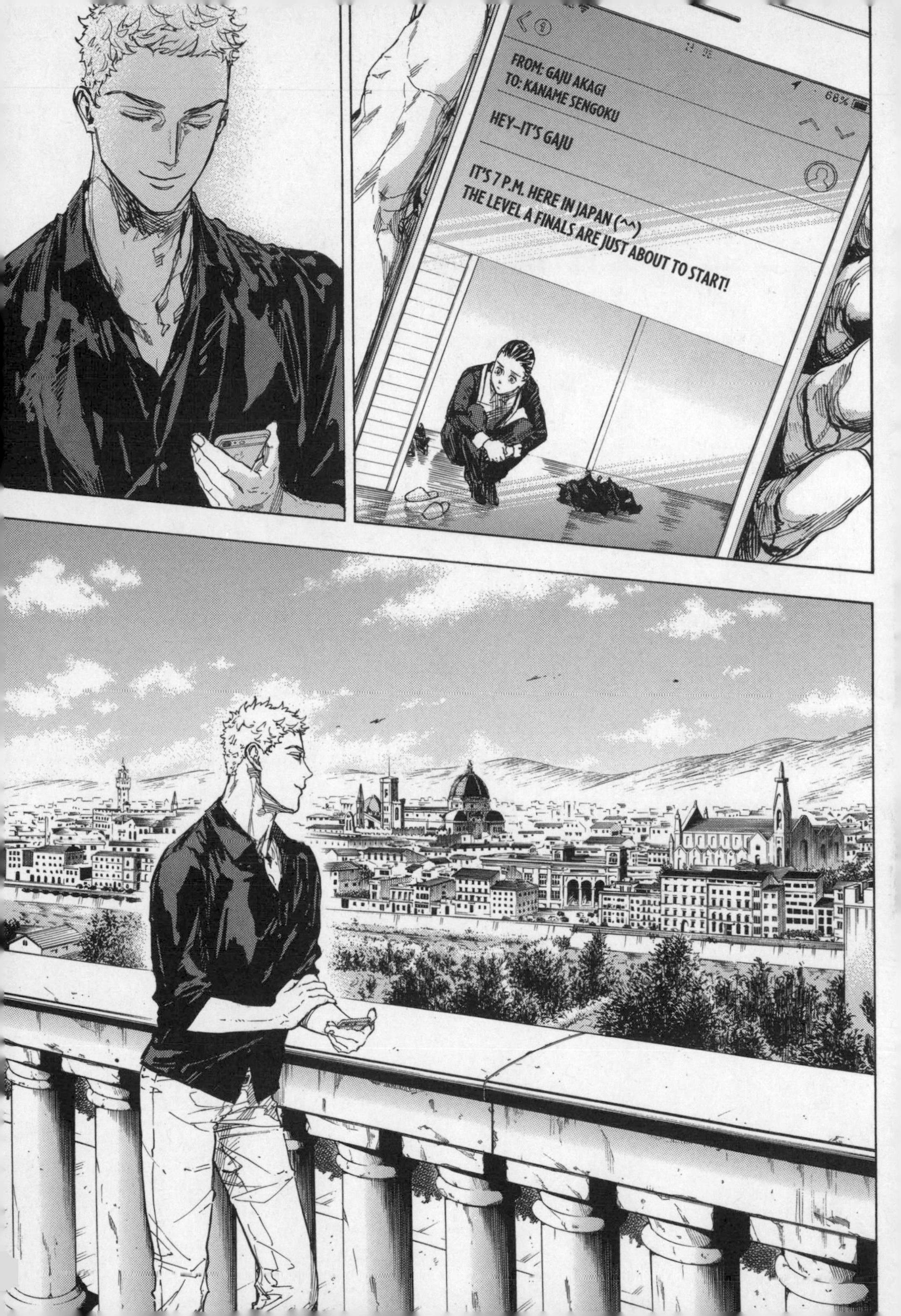
FROM: GAJU AKAGI
TO: KANAME SENGOKU
68%
HEY—IT'S GAJU
IT'S 7 P.M. HERE IN JAPAN (^^)
THE LEVEL A FINALS ARE JUST ABOUT TO START!

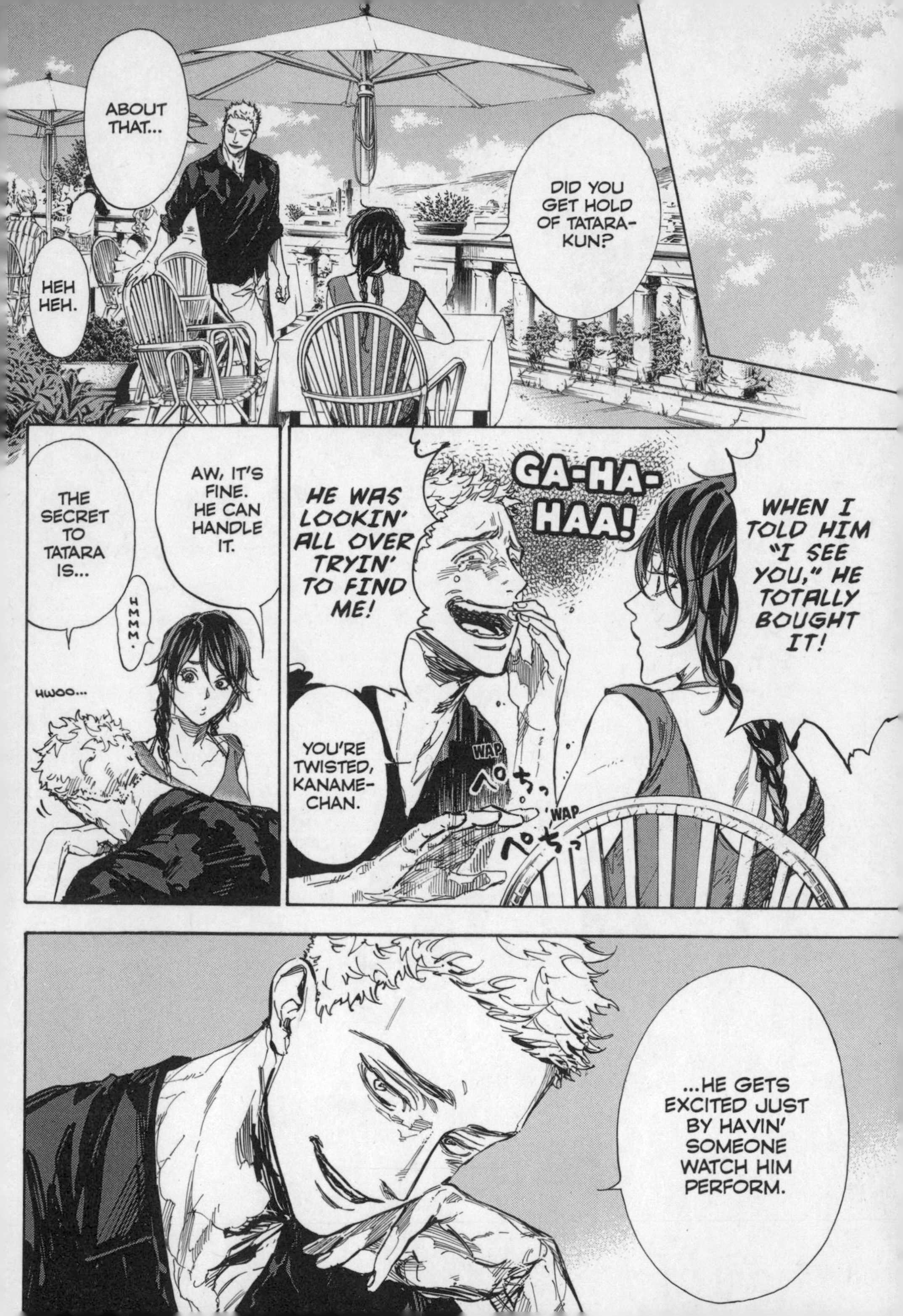
DID YOU GET HOLD OF TATARA-KUN?
ABOUT THAT...
HEH HEH.
WHEN I TOLD HIM "I SEE YOU," HE TOTALLY BOUGHT IT!
GA-HA-HAA!
HE WAS LOOKIN' ALL OVER TRYIN' TO FIND ME!
YOU'RE TWISTED, KANAME-CHAN.
WAP
ぺちっ
WAP
ぺちっ
AW, IT'S FINE. HE CAN HANDLE IT.
HMMM.
THE SECRET TO TATARA IS...
HWOO...
...HE GETS EXCITED JUST BY HAVIN' SOMEONE WATCH HIM PERFORM.

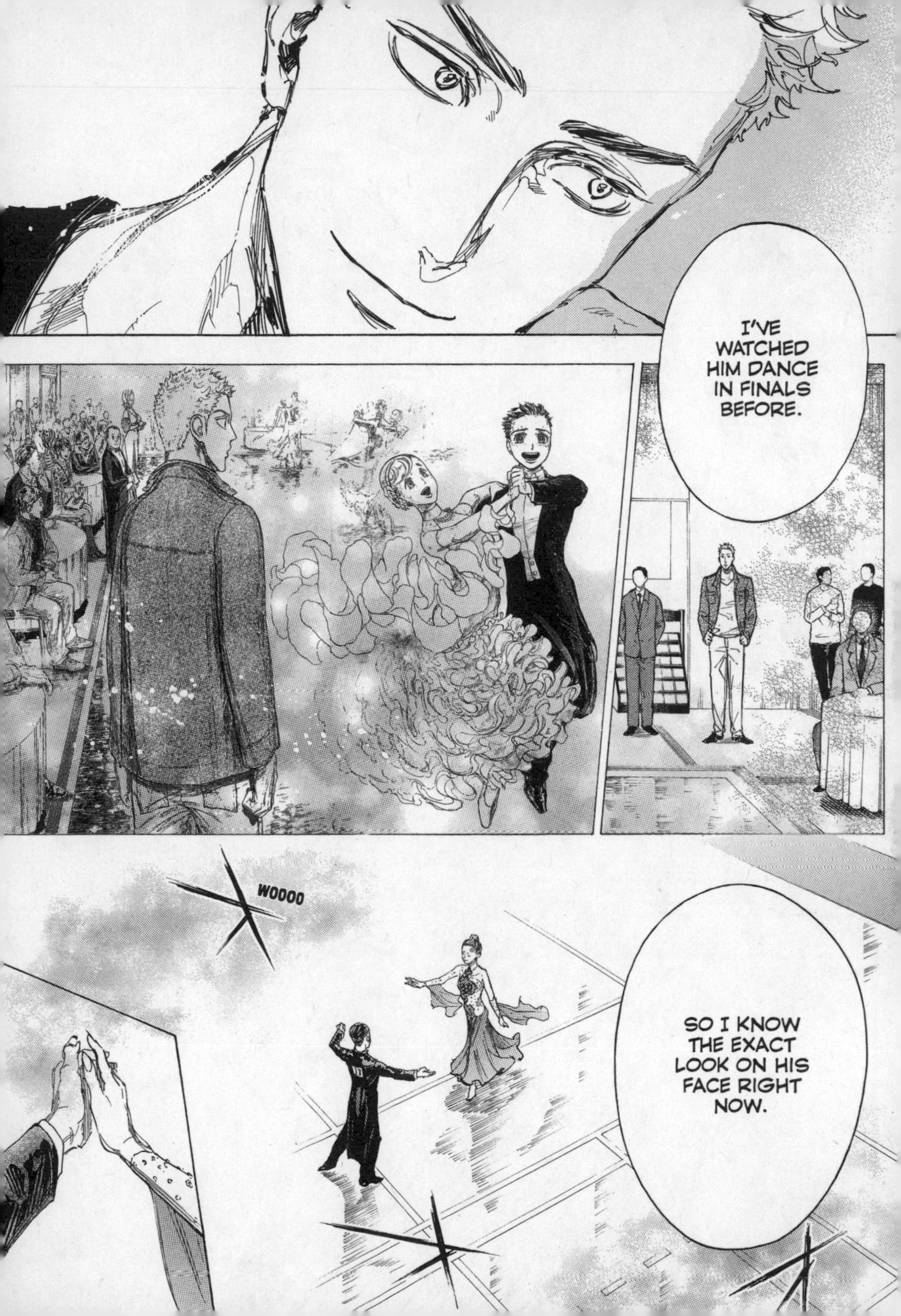
I'VE WATCHED HIM DANCE IN FINALS BEFORE.
WOOOO
SO I KNOW THE EXACT LOOK ON HIS FACE RIGHT NOW.

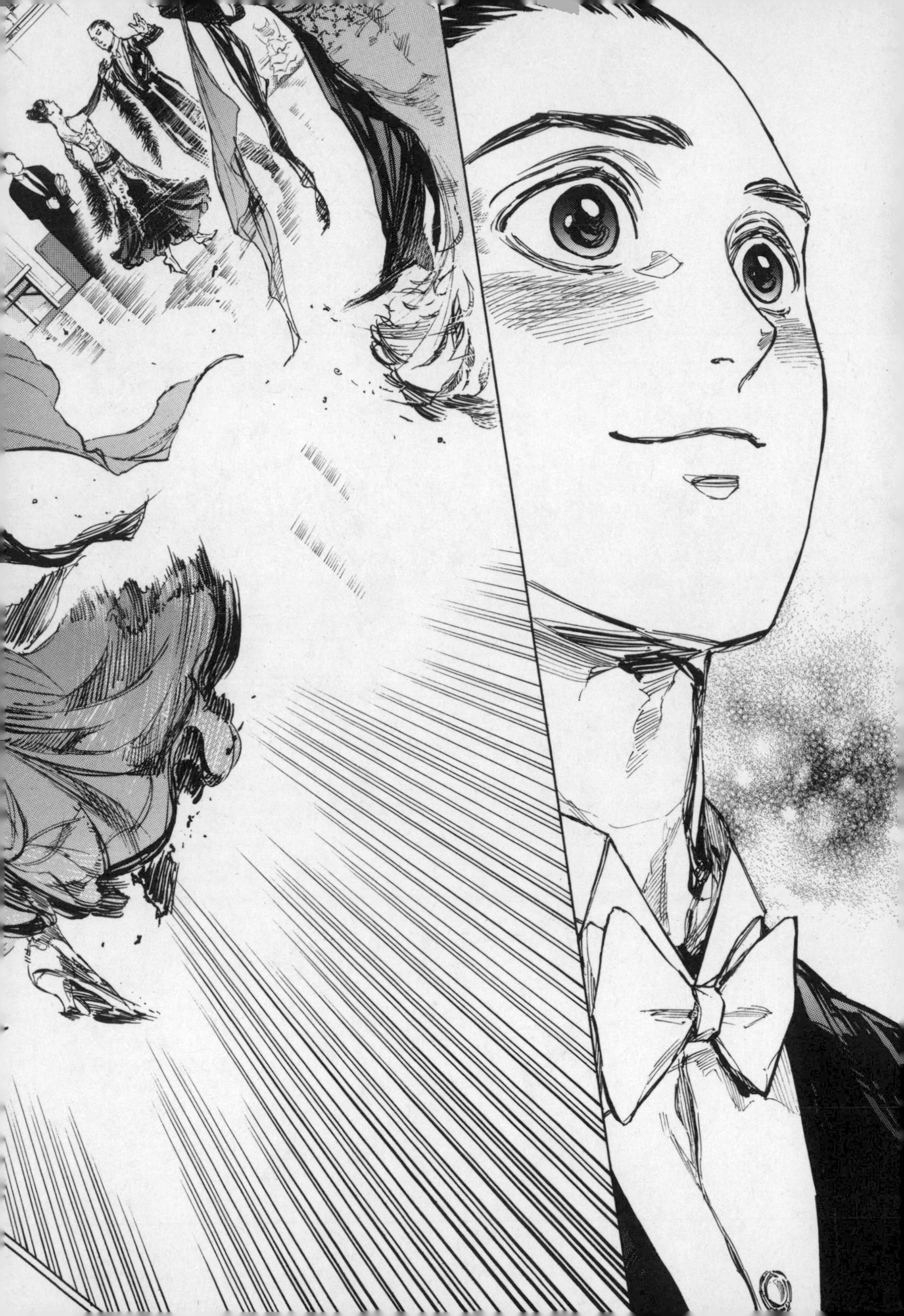

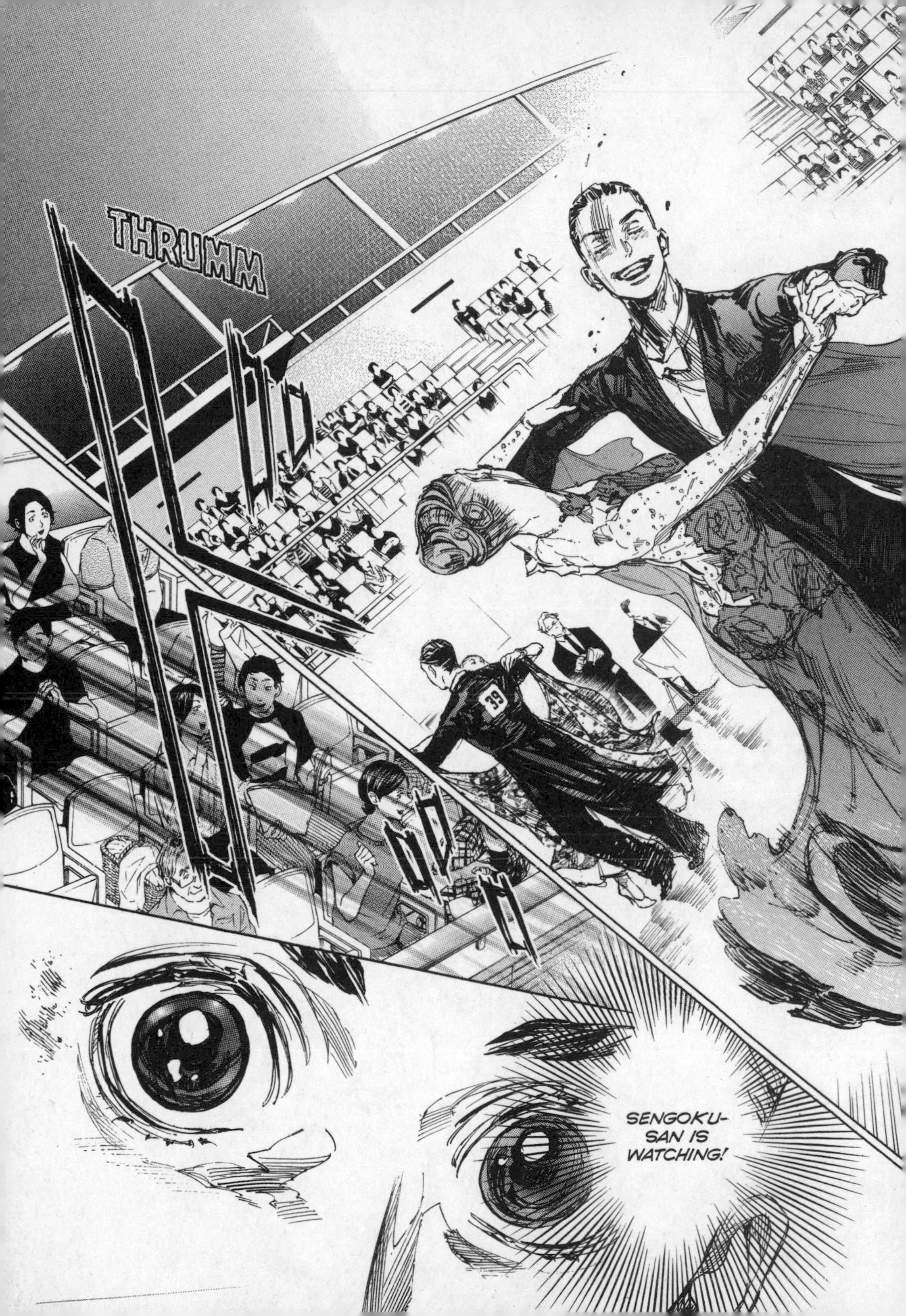
THRUMM
SENGOKU-SAN IS WATCHING!

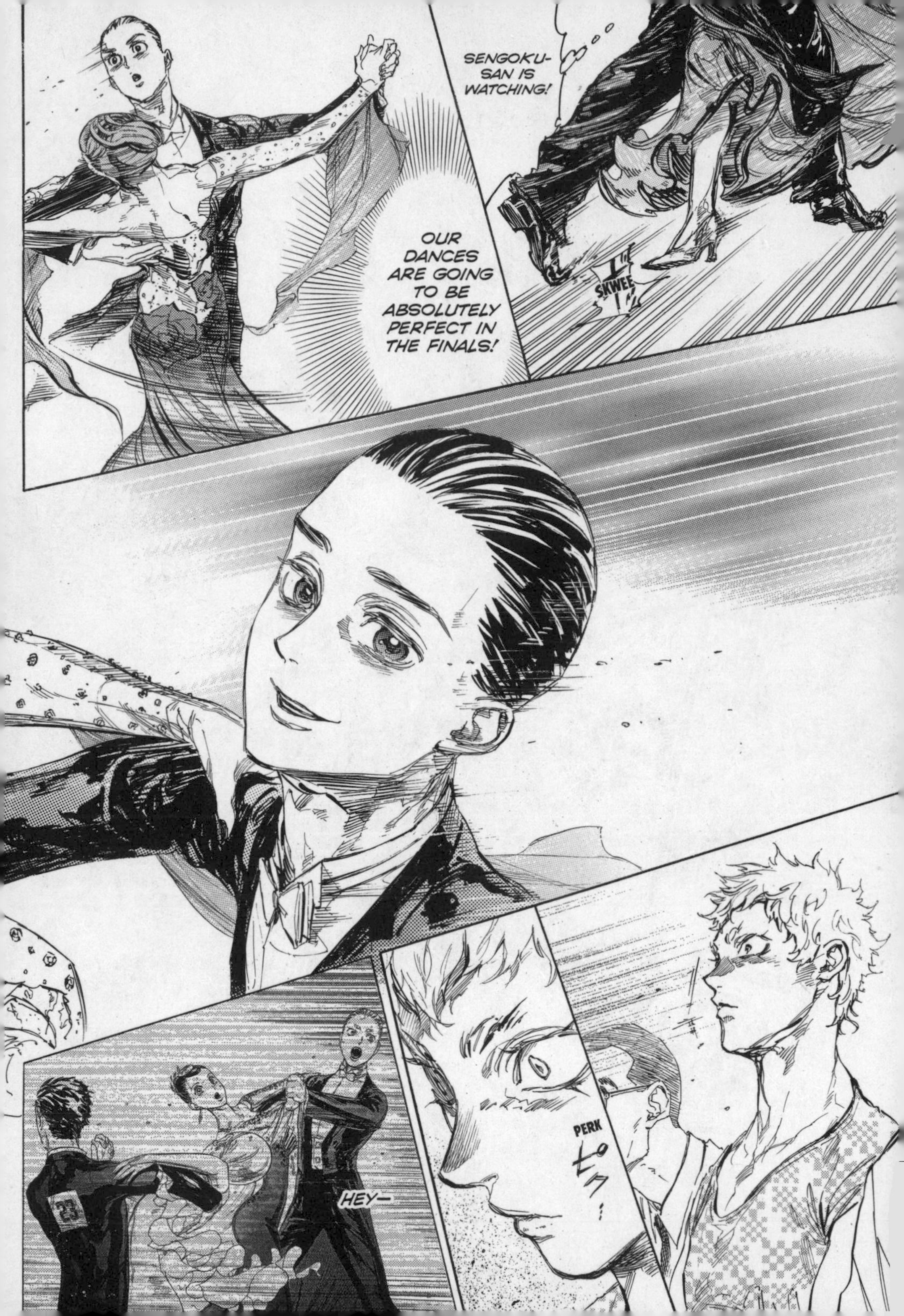
SENGOKU-SAN IS WATCHING!
SKWEE
OUR DANCES ARE GOING TO BE ABSOLUTELY PERFECT IN THE FINALS!
PERK
HEY—

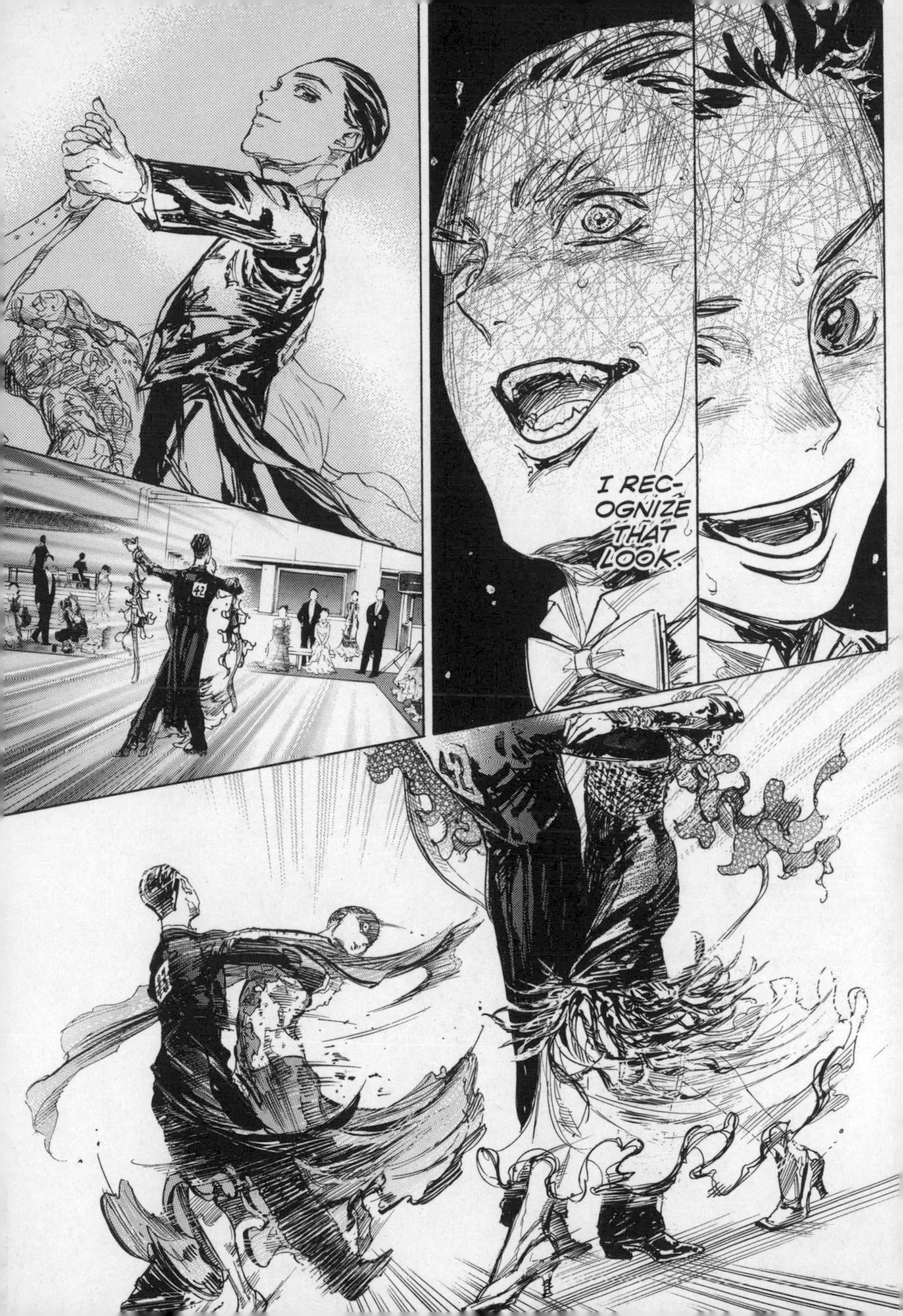
I RECOGNIZE THAT LOOK.

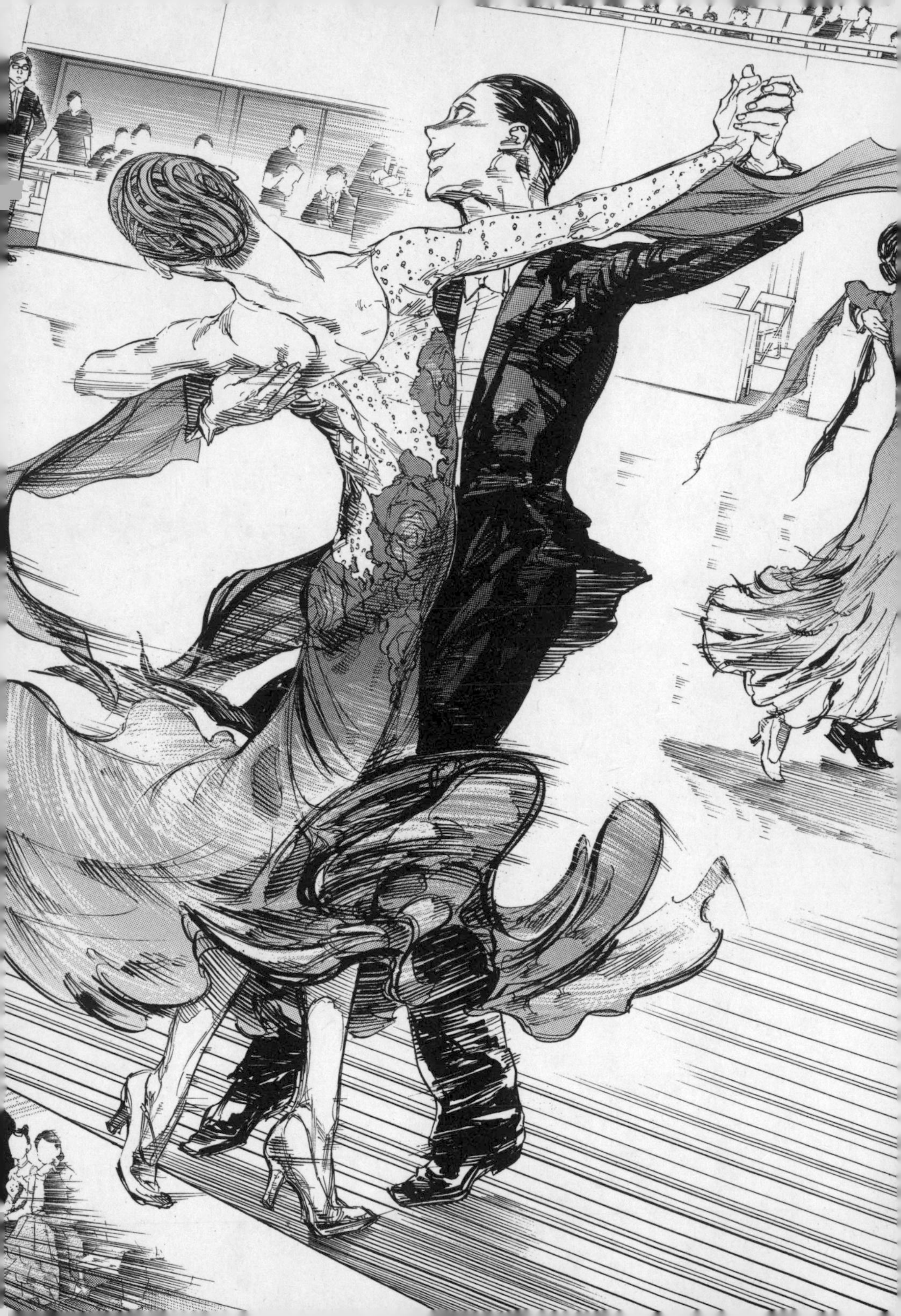

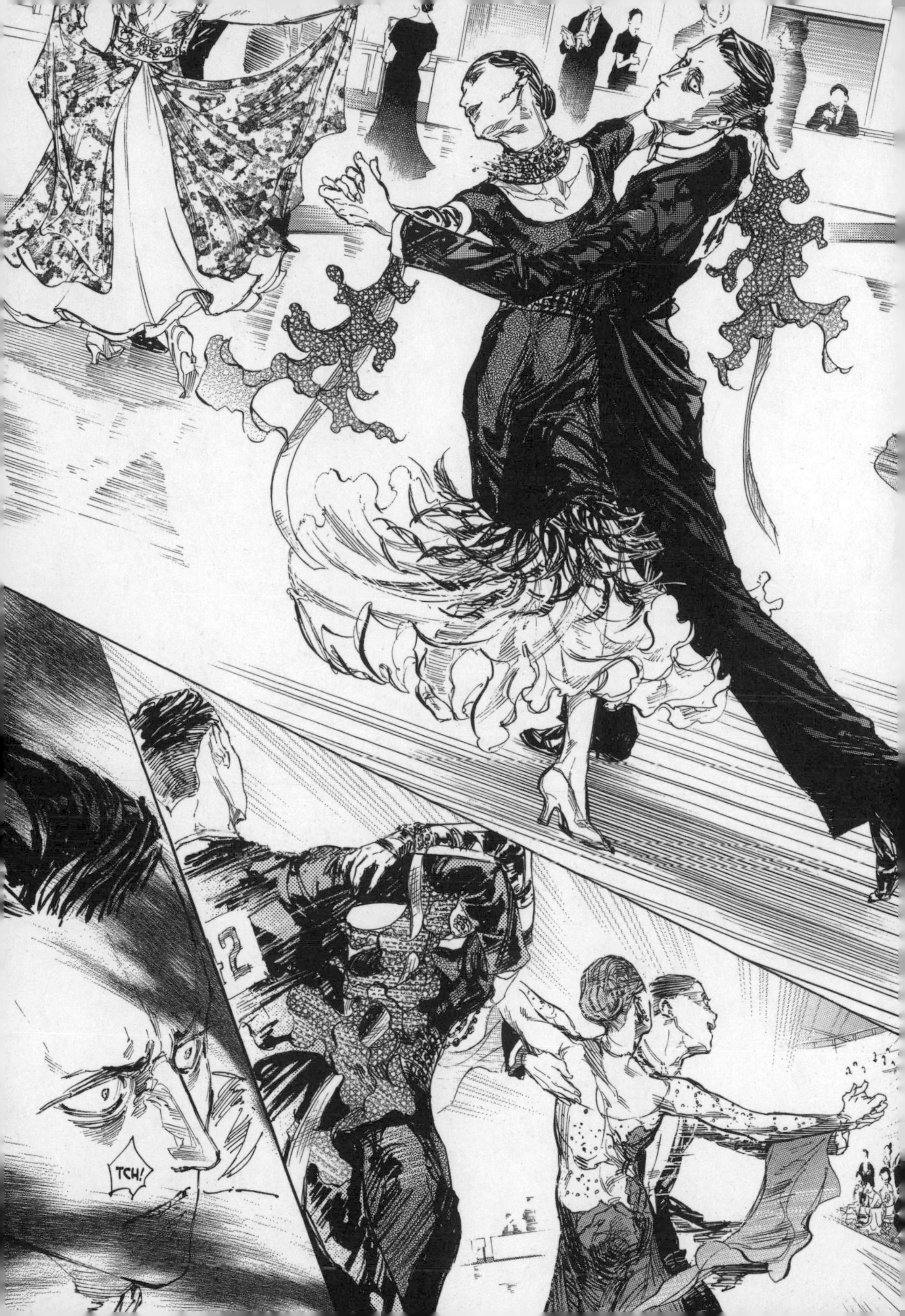
TCH!

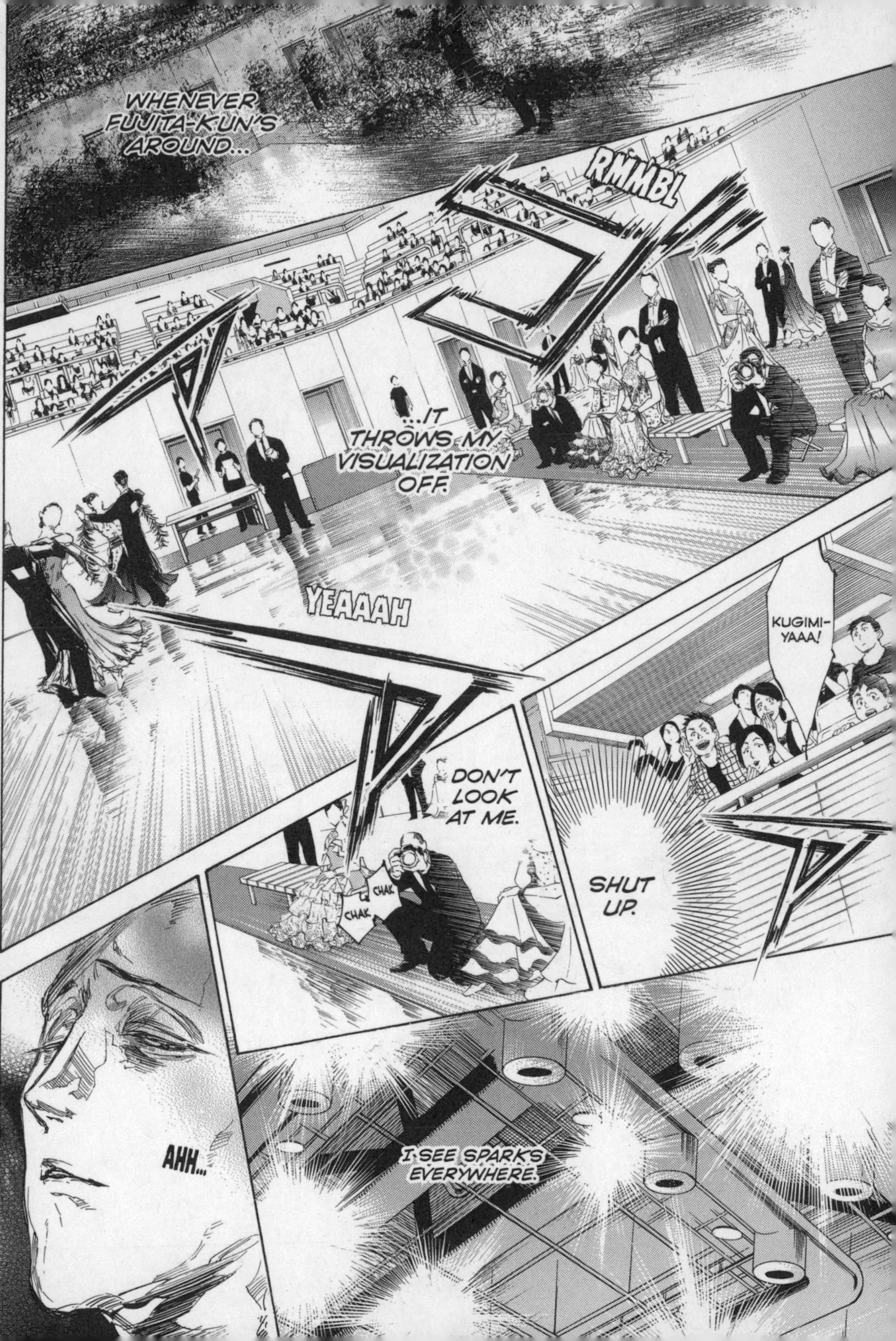
WHENEVER FUJITA-KUN'S AROUND...
RMMBL
...IT THROWS MY VISUALIZATION OFF.
YEAAAH
KUGIMI-YAAA!
SHUT UP.
DON'T LOOK AT ME.
CHAK
CHAK
I SEE SPARKS EVERYWHERE.
AHH...

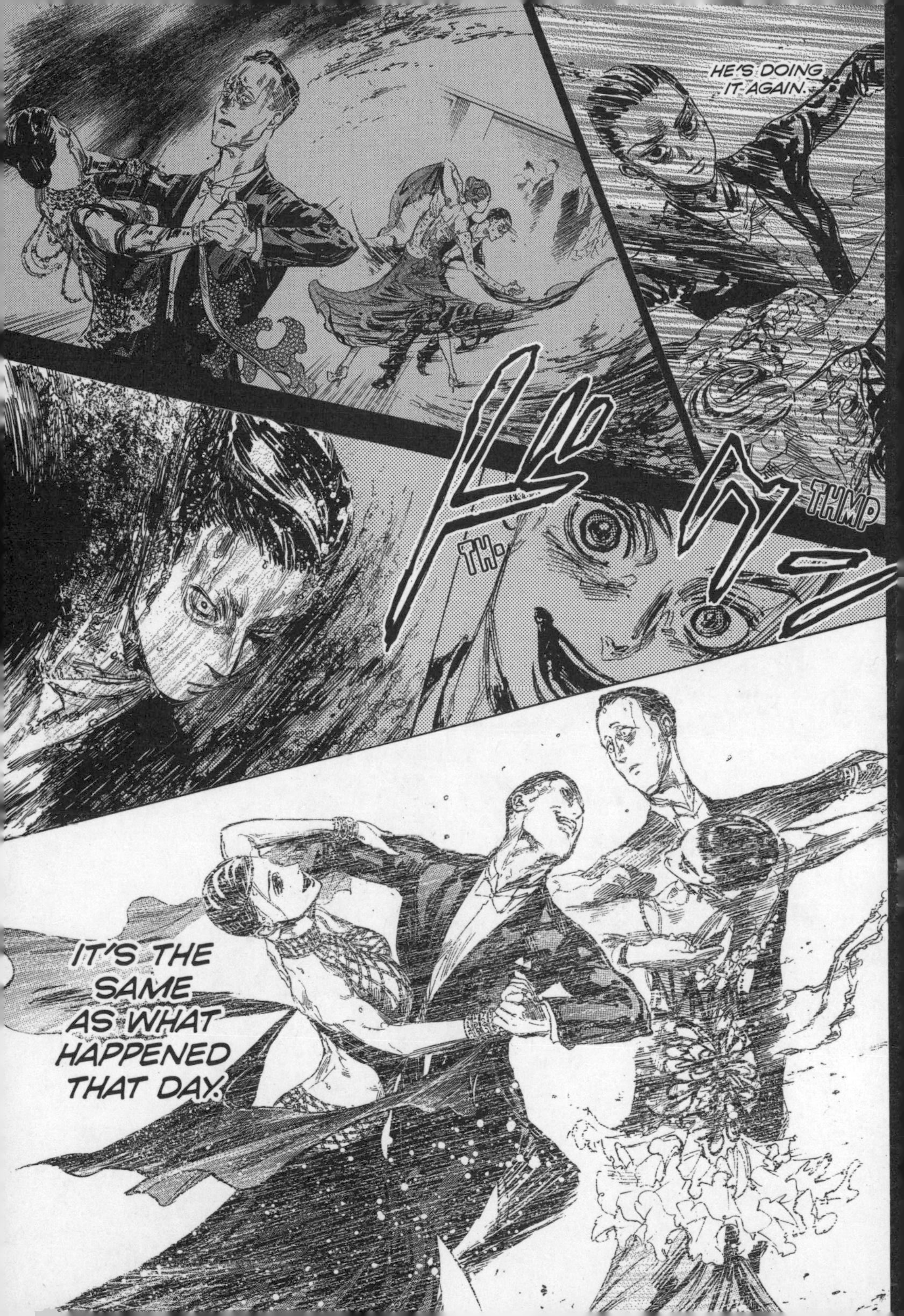
HE'S DOING IT AGAIN.
THMP
TH.
IT'S THE SAME AS WHAT HAPPENED THAT DAY.

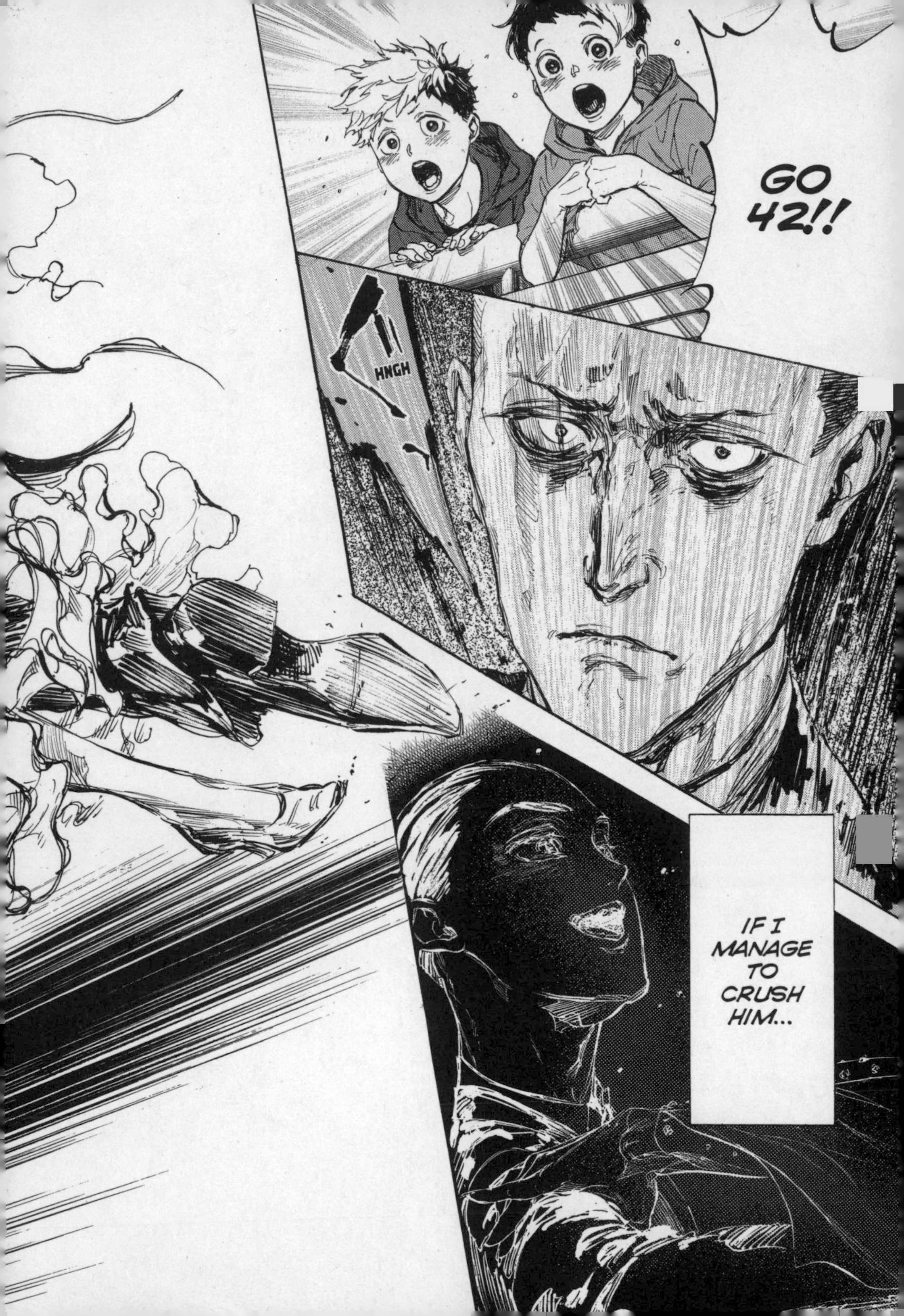
GO 42!!
HNGH
IF I MANAGE TO CRUSH HIM...

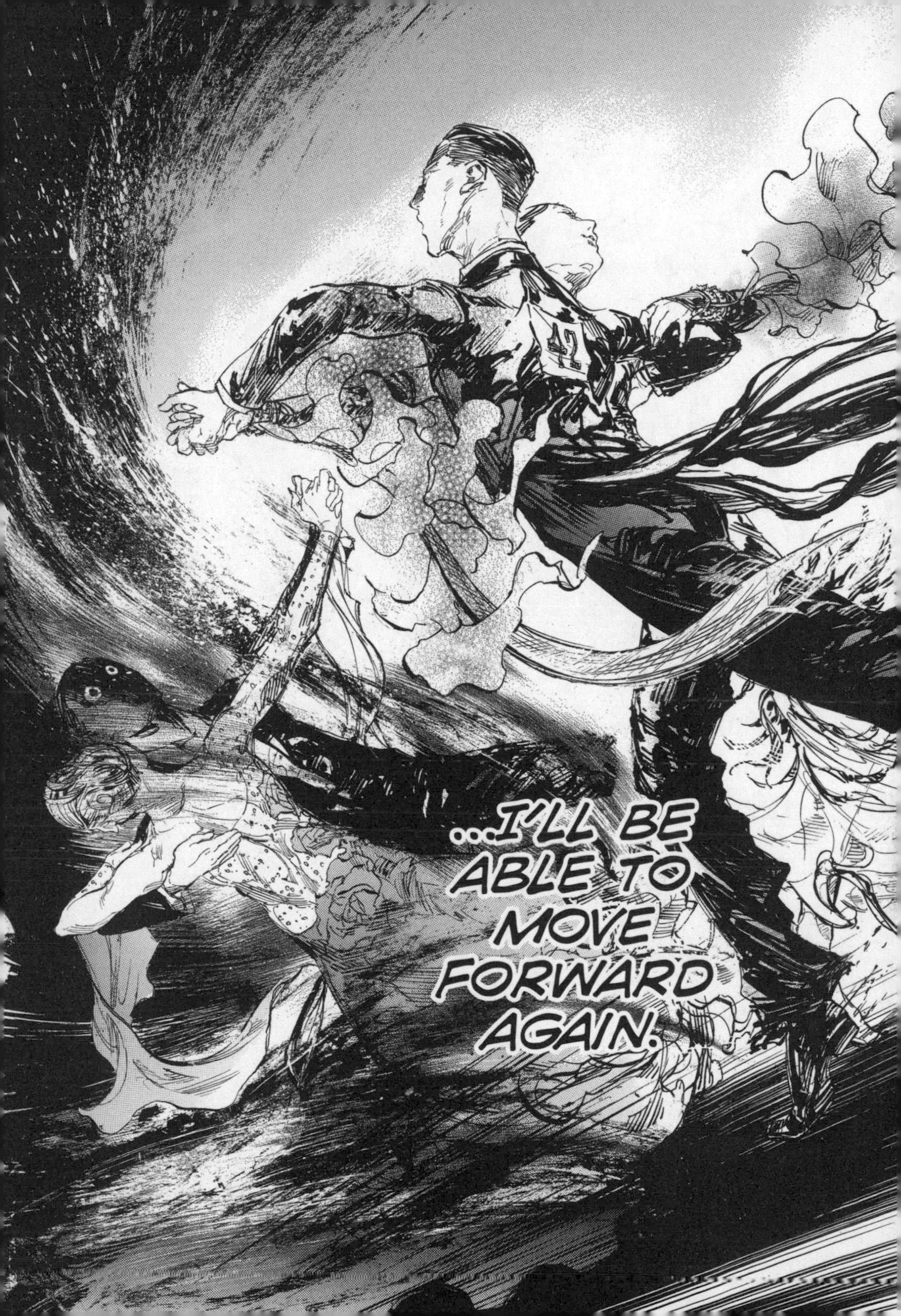
...I'LL BE ABLE TO MOVE FORWARD AGAIN.

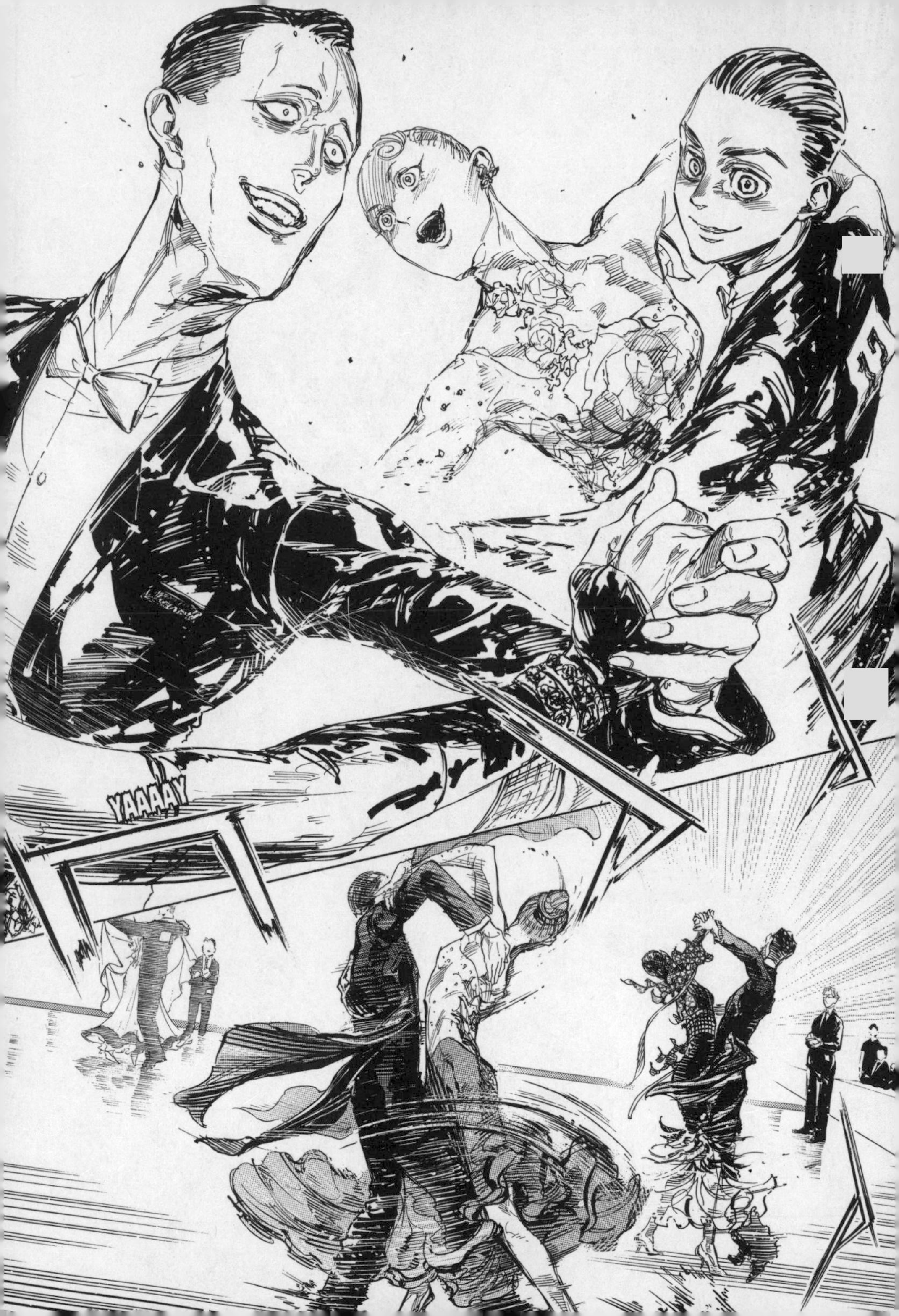
YAAAAY

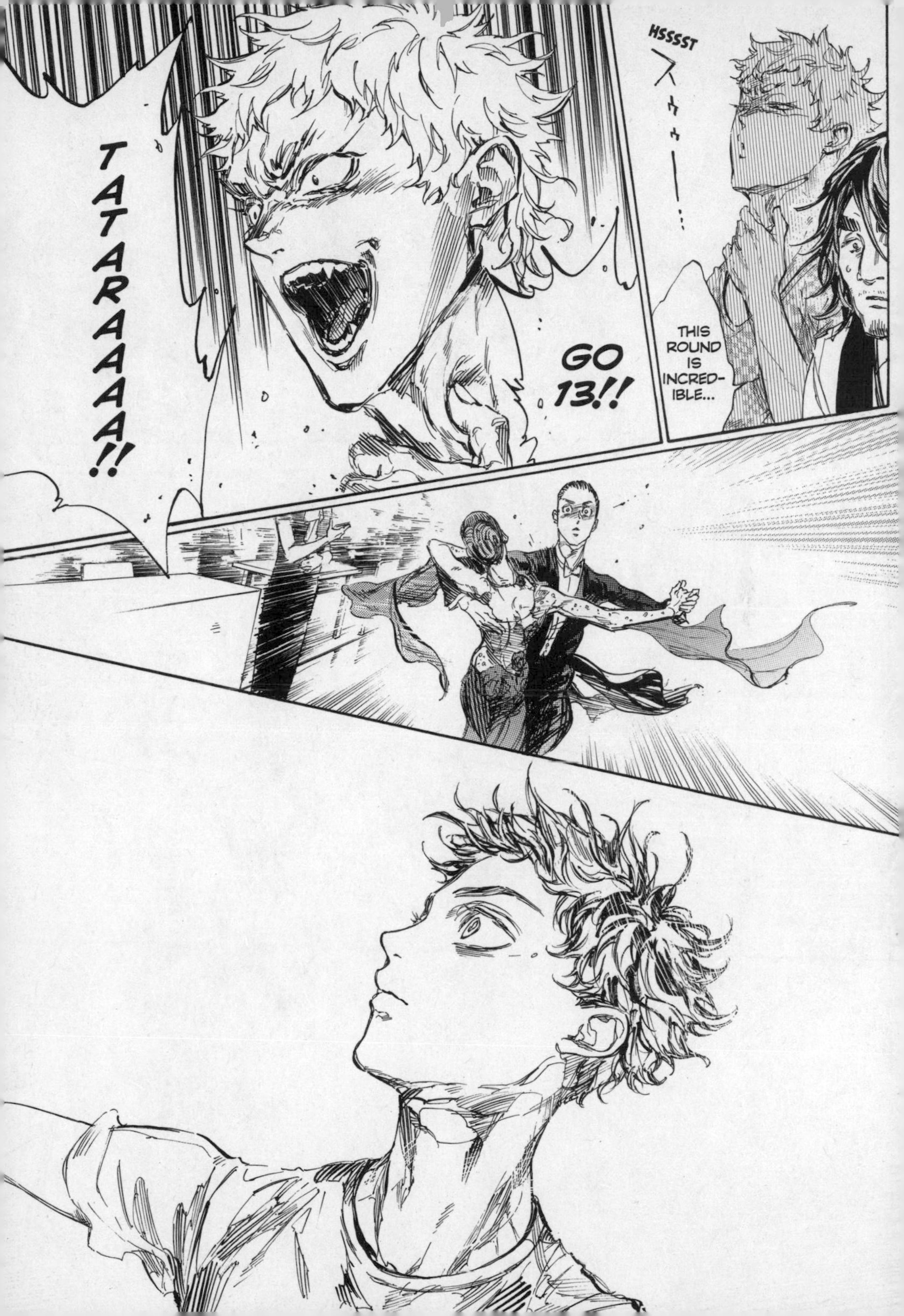
HSSSST
THIS ROUND IS INCREDIBLE...
GO 13!!
TATARAAAAA!!

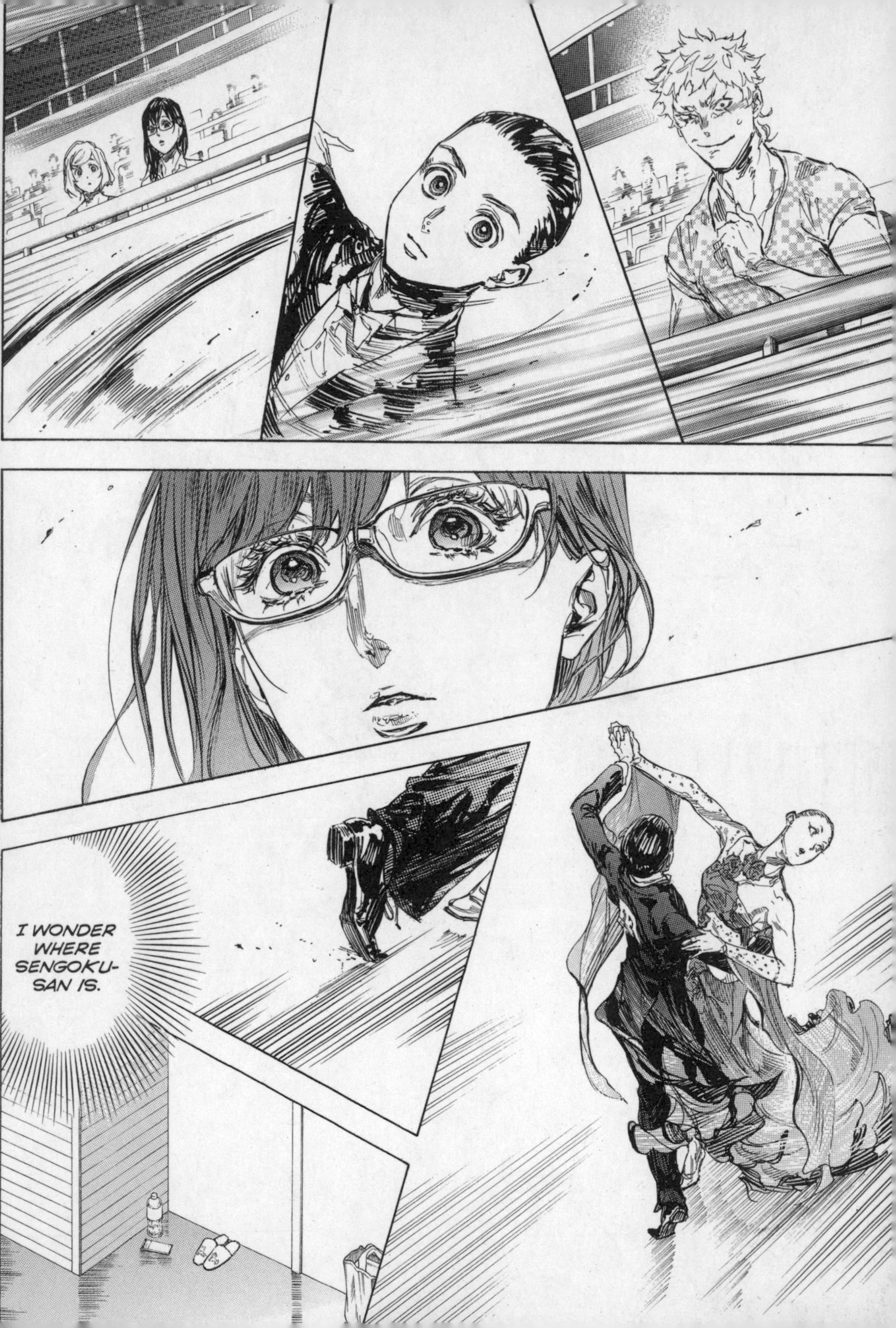
I WONDER WHERE SENGOKU-SAN IS.

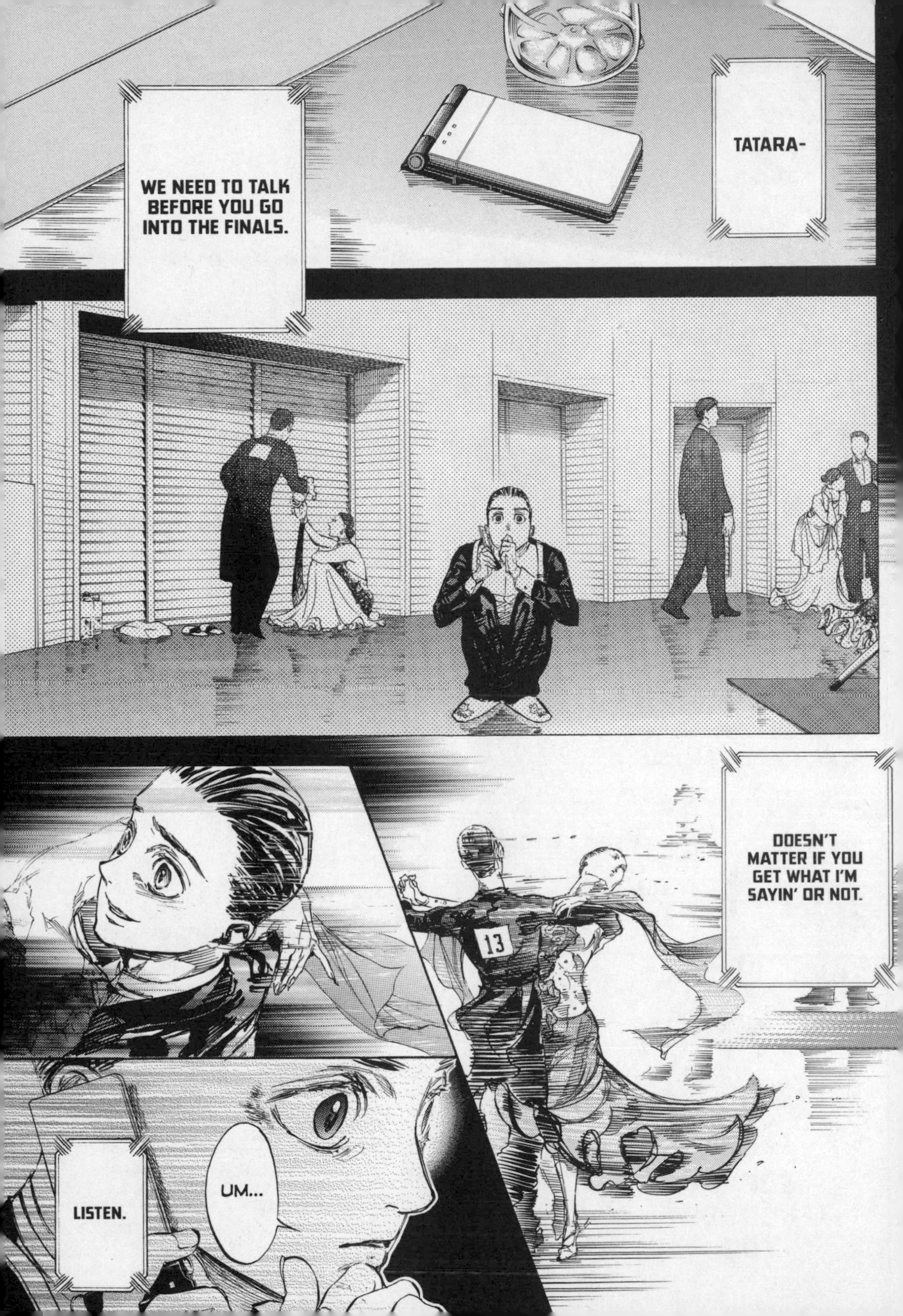
TATARA-
WE NEED TO TALK BEFORE YOU GO INTO THE FINALS.
DOESN'T MATTER IF YOU GET WHAT I'M SAYIN' OR NOT.
UM...
LISTEN.

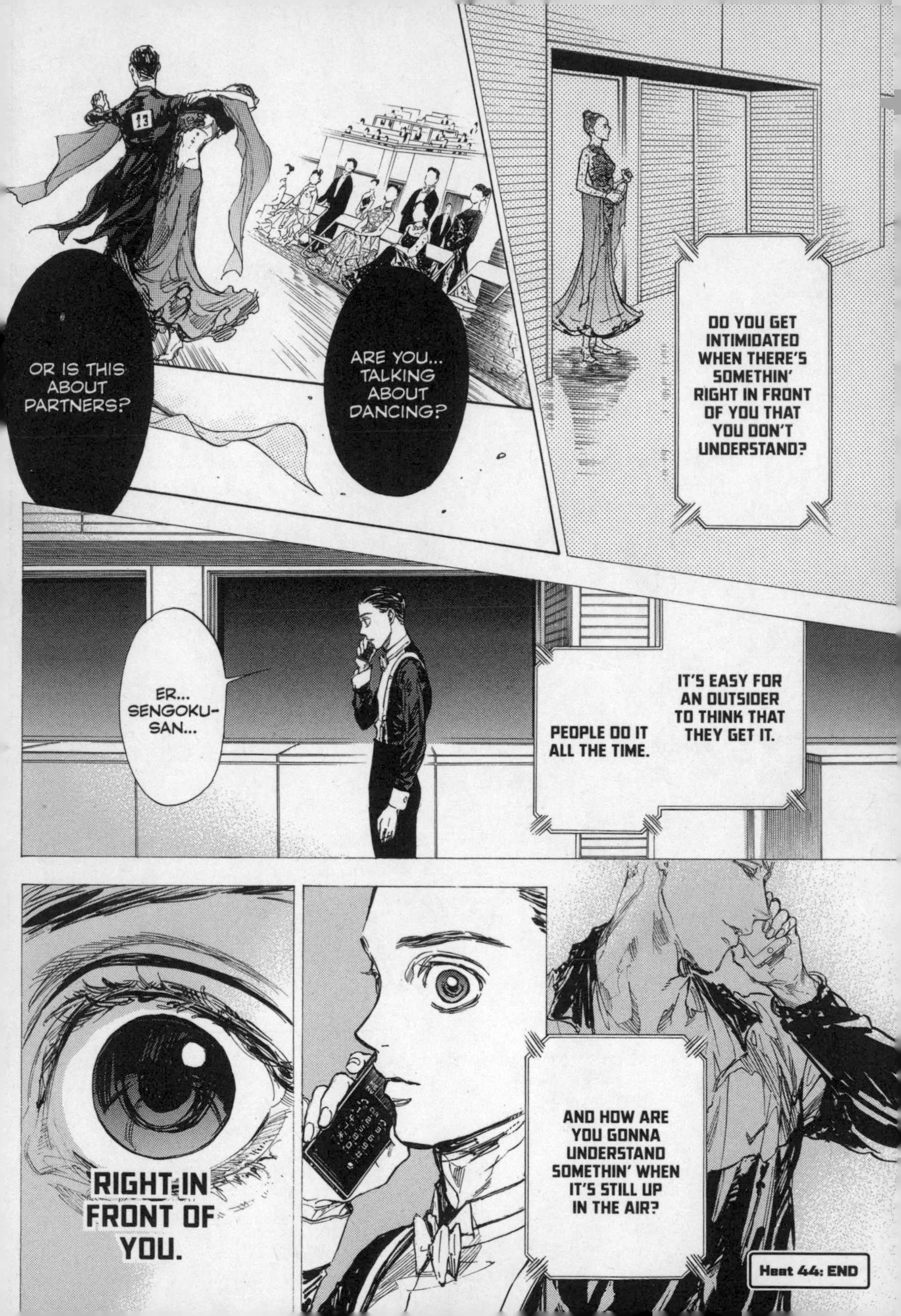
DO YOU GET INTIMIDATED WHEN THERE'S SOMETHIN' RIGHT IN FRONT OF YOU THAT YOU DON'T UNDERSTAND?
ARE YOU... TALKING ABOUT DANCING?
OR IS THIS ABOUT PARTNERS?
IT'S EASY FOR AN OUTSIDER TO THINK THAT THEY GET IT.
PEOPLE DO IT ALL THE TIME.
ER... SENGOKU-SAN...
AND HOW ARE YOU GONNA UNDERSTAND SOMETHIN' WHEN IT'S STILL UP IN THE AIR?
RIGHT IN FRONT OF YOU.
Heat 44: END

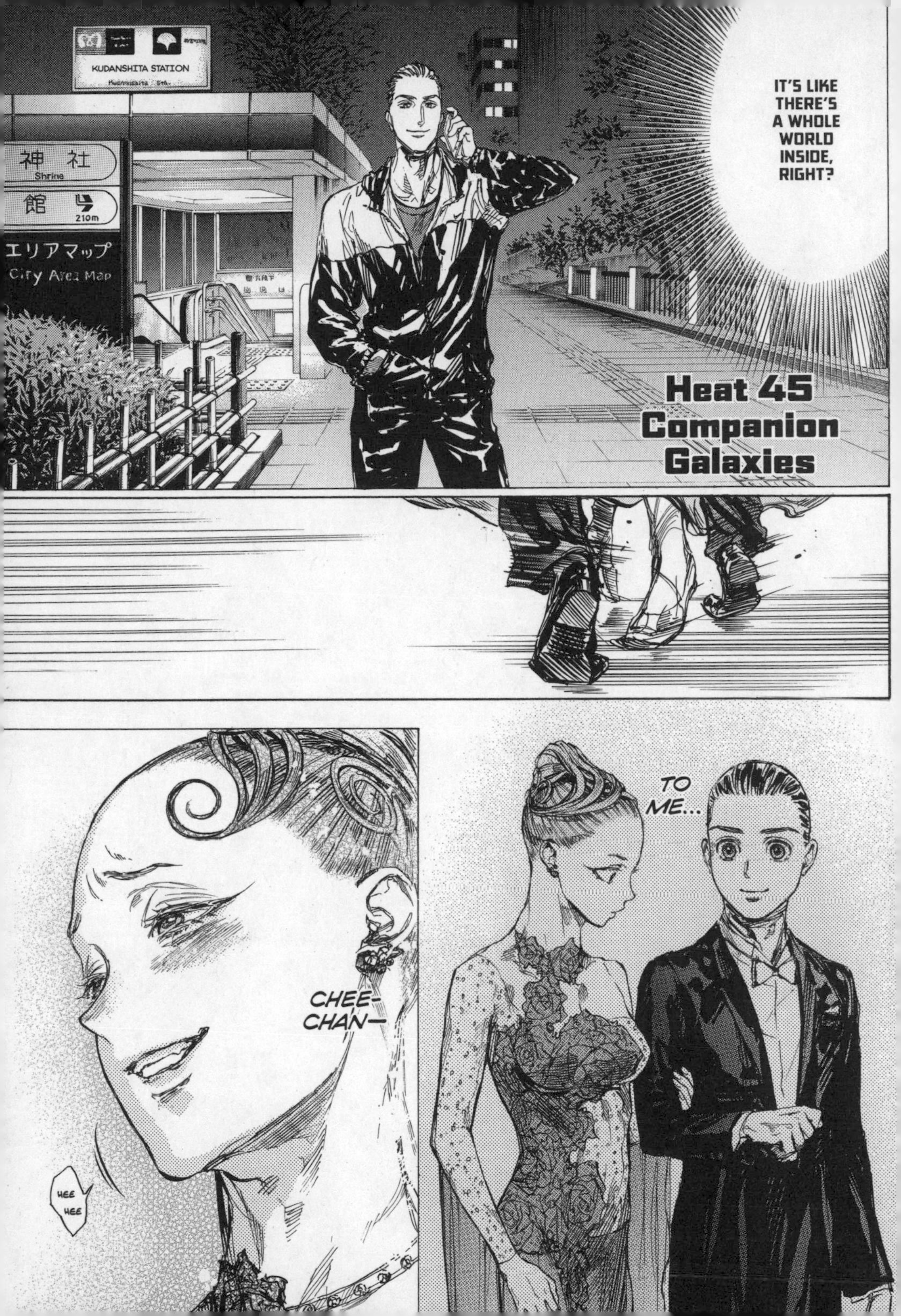
KUDANSHITA STATION
神社
Shrine
館
210m
エリアマップ
City Area Map
IT'S LIKE THERE'S A WHOLE WORLD INSIDE, RIGHT?
Heat 45
Companion Galaxies
TO ME...
CHEE-CHAN—
HEE HEE

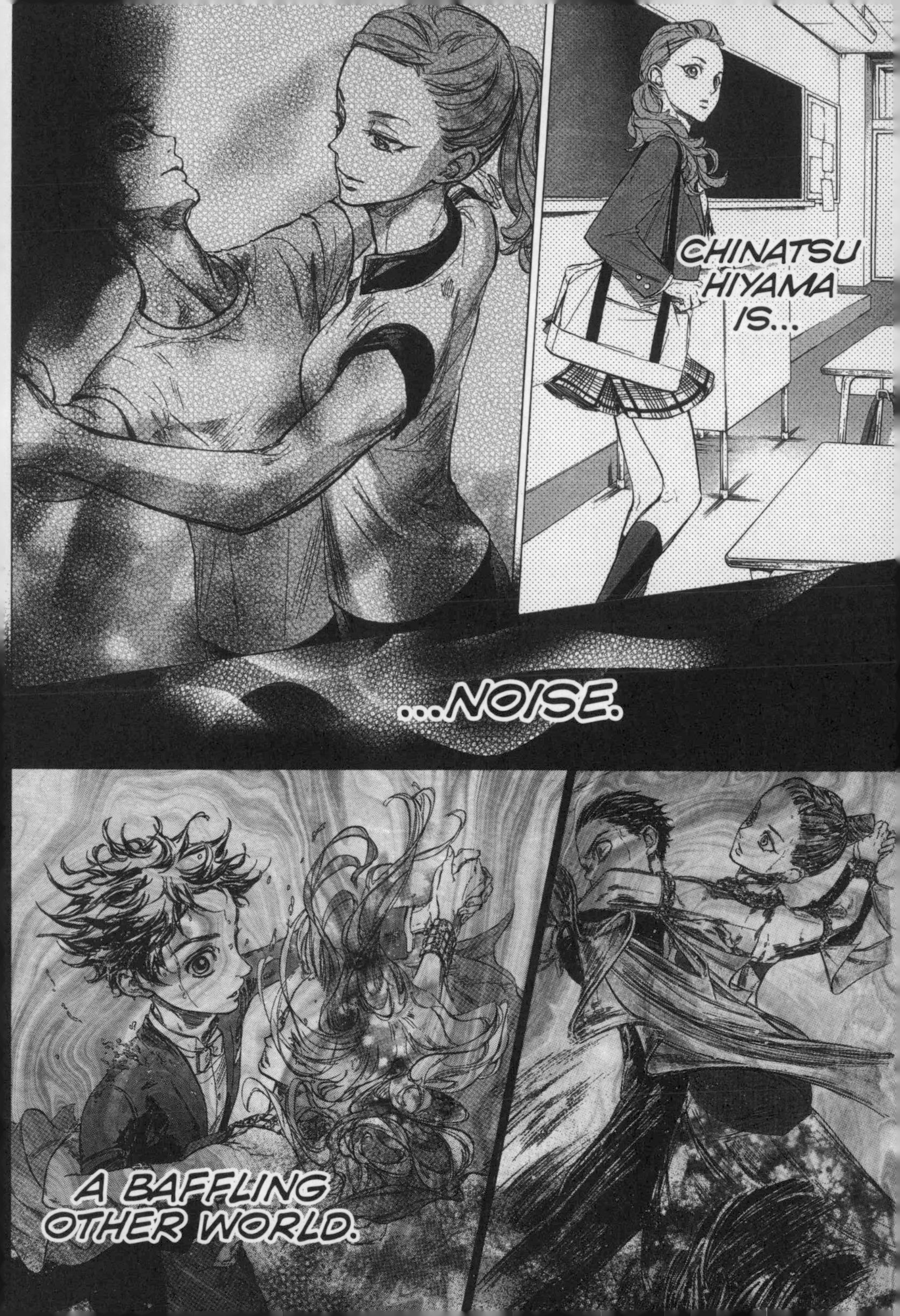
CHINATSU HIYAMA IS...
...NOISE.
A BAFFLING OTHER WORLD.

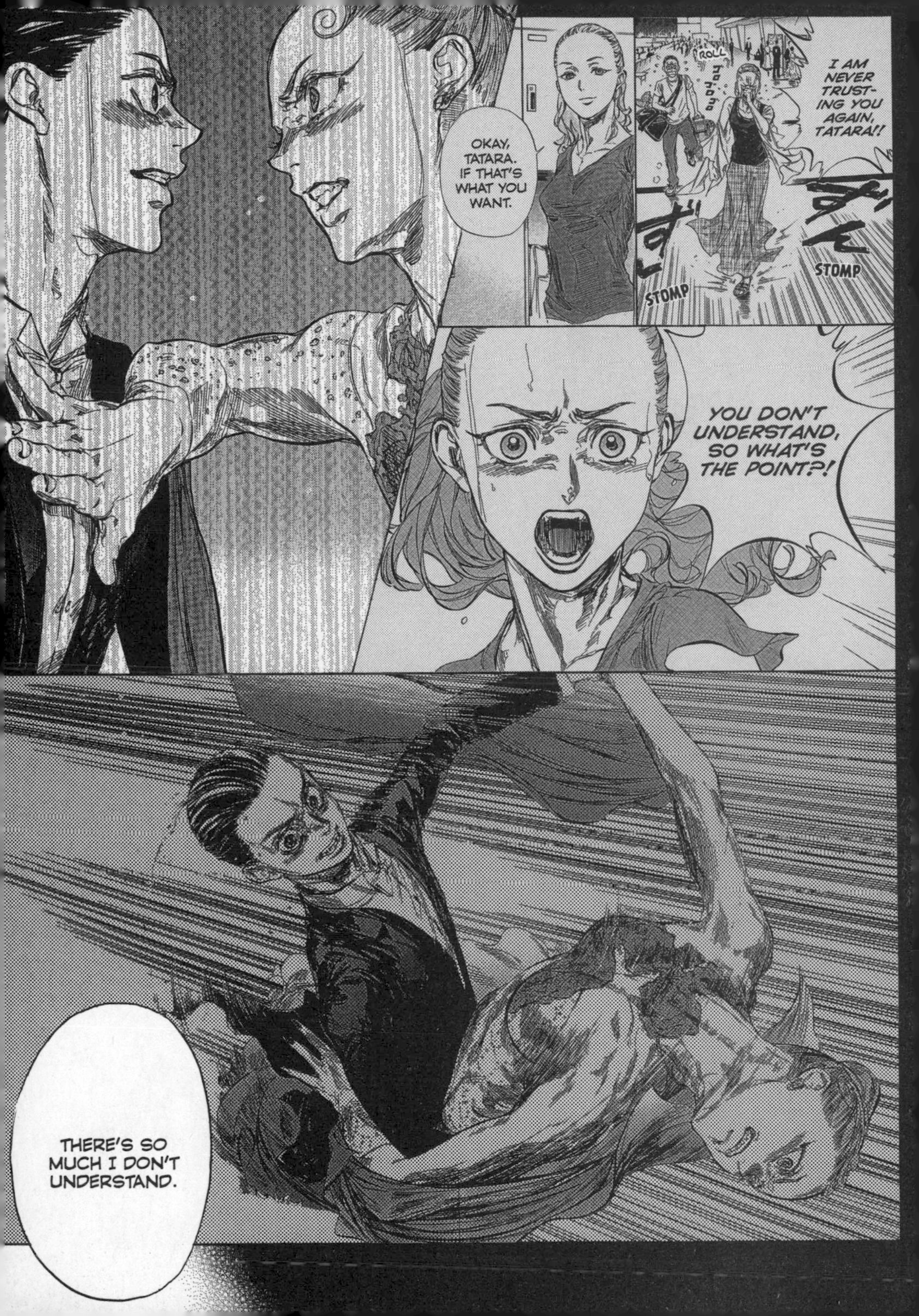
I AM NEVER TRUSTING YOU AGAIN, TATARA!!
ROLL
STOMP
STOMP
OKAY, TATARA. IF THAT'S WHAT YOU WANT.
YOU DON'T UNDERSTAND, SO WHAT'S THE POINT?!
THERE'S SO MUCH I DON'T UNDERSTAND.

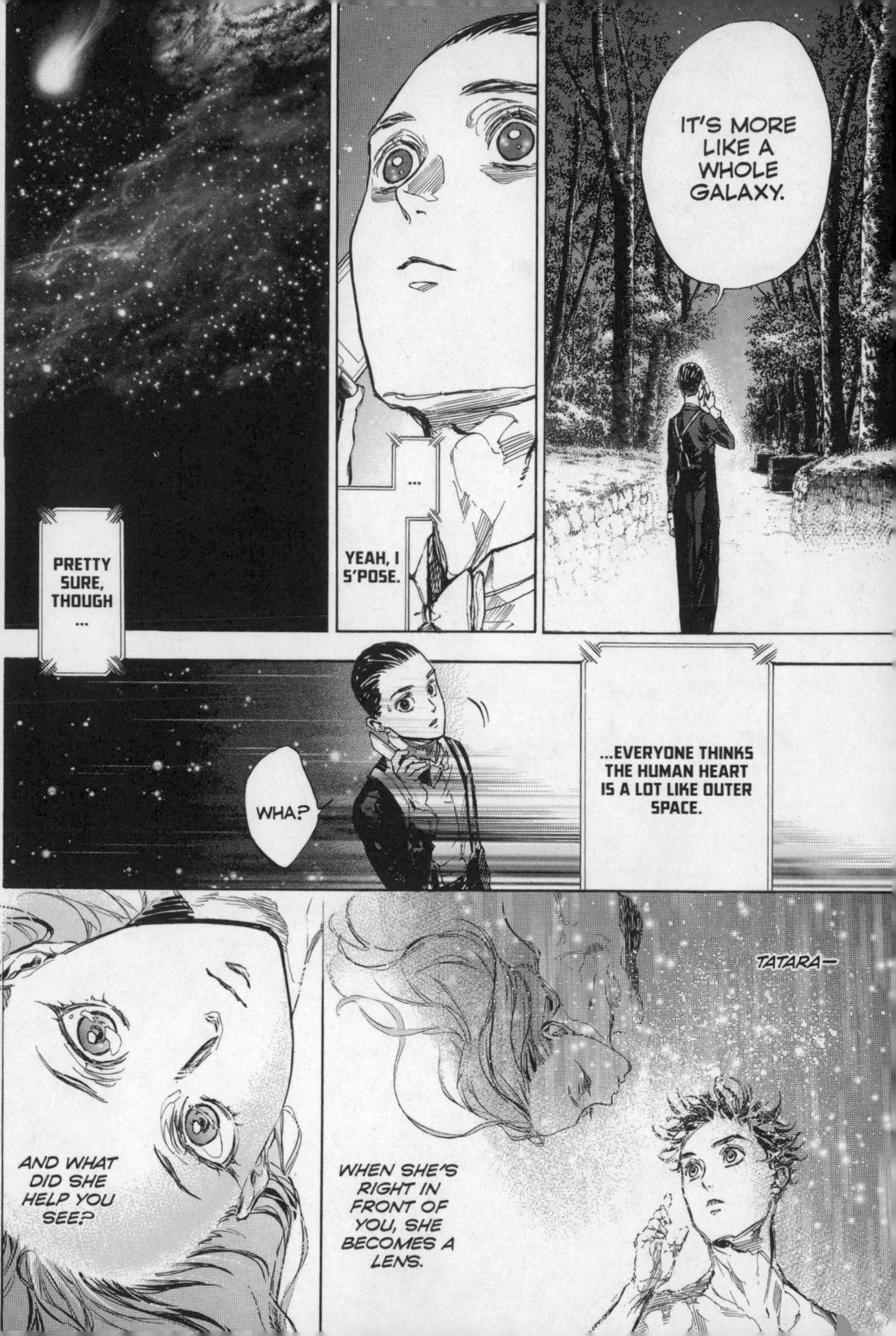
IT'S MORE LIKE A WHOLE GALAXY.
...
YEAH, I S'POSE.
PRETTY SURE, THOUGH ...
...EVERYONE THINKS THE HUMAN HEART IS A LOT LIKE OUTER SPACE.
WHA?
TATARA—
WHEN SHE'S RIGHT IN FRONT OF YOU, SHE BECOMES A LENS.
AND WHAT DID SHE HELP YOU SEE?

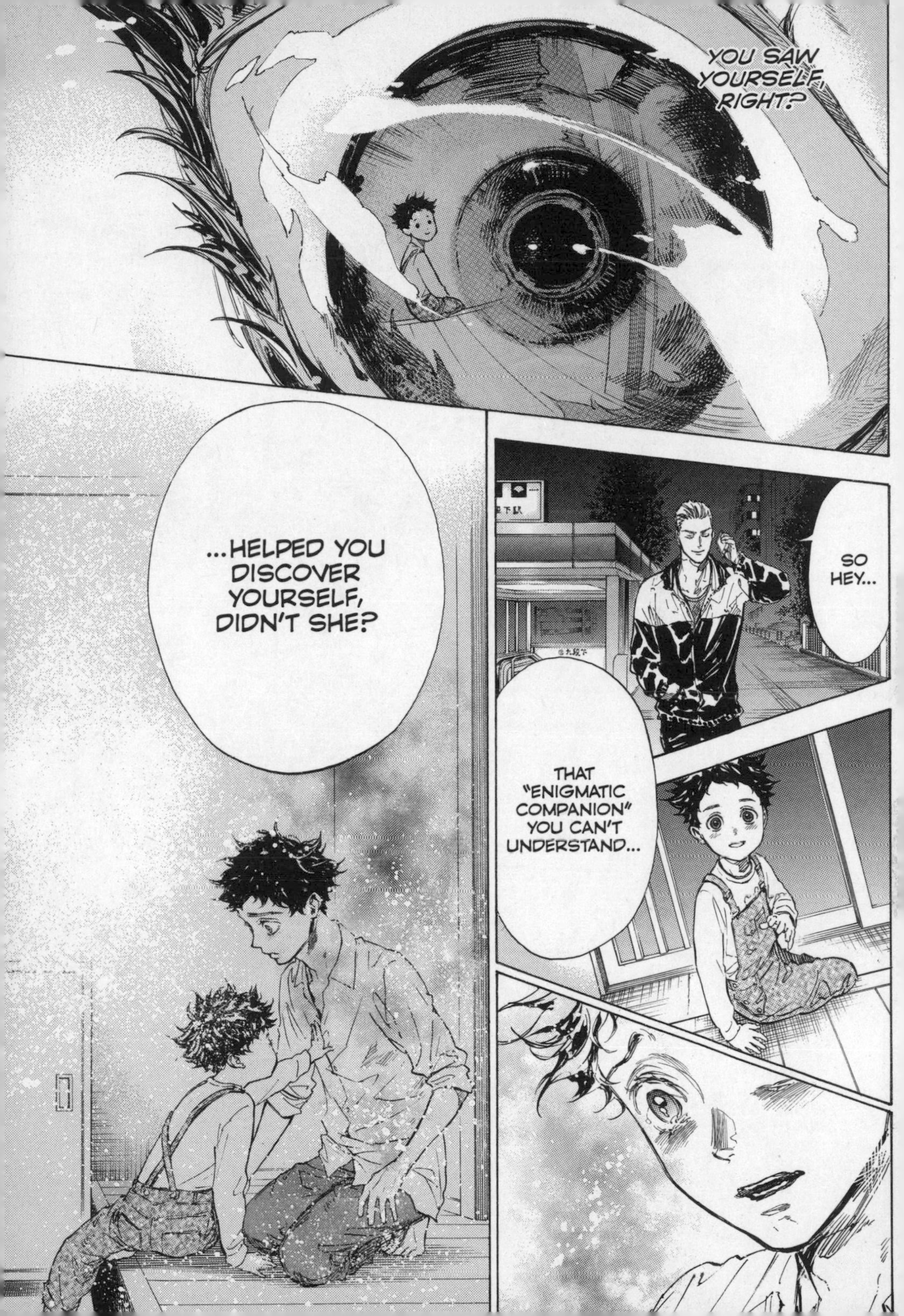
YOU SAW YOURSELF, RIGHT?
SO HEY...
THAT "ENIGMATIC COMPANION" YOU CAN'T UNDERSTAND...
...HELPED YOU DISCOVER YOURSELF, DIDN'T SHE?

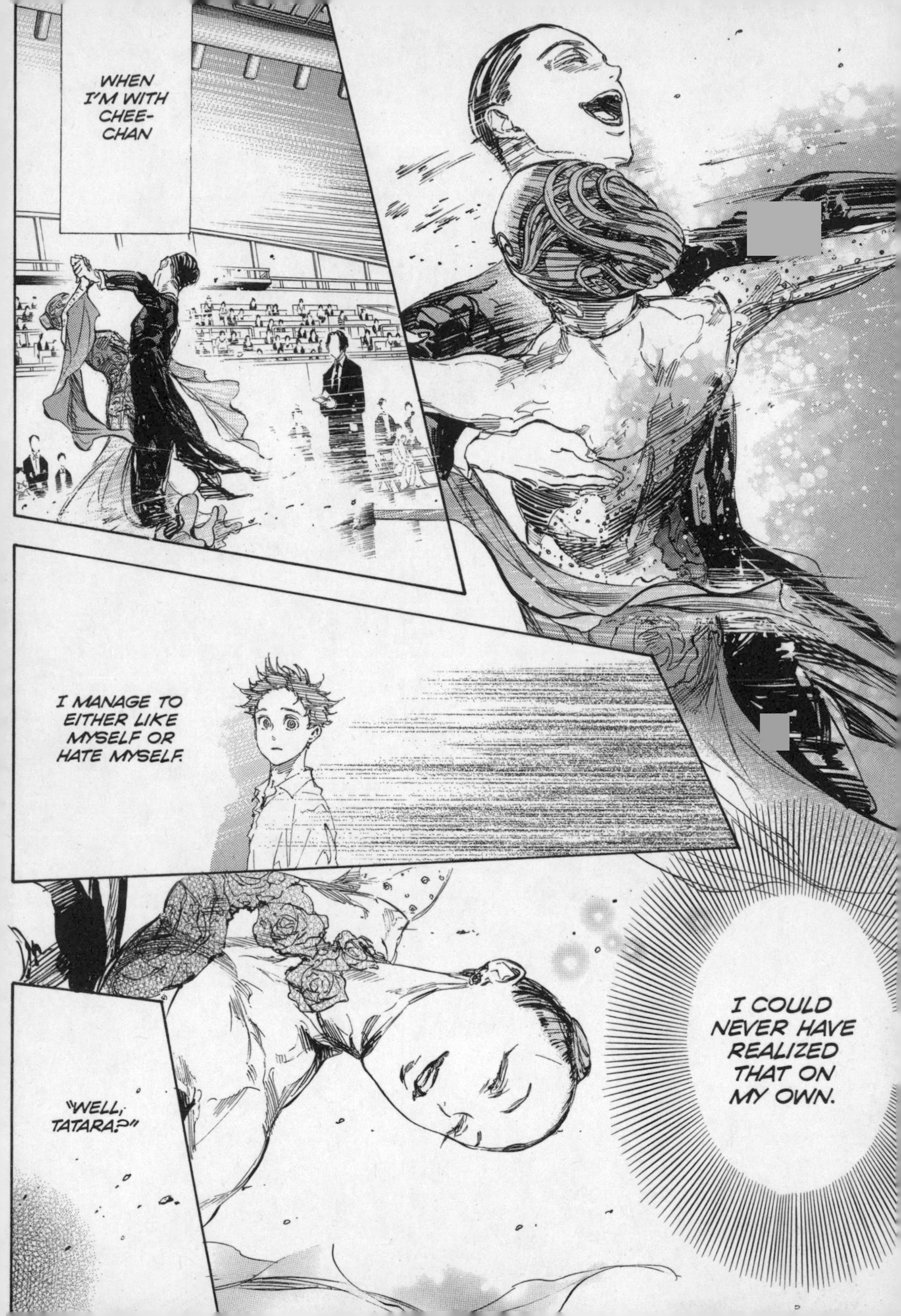
WHEN I'M WITH CHEE-CHAN
I MANAGE TO EITHER LIKE MYSELF OR HATE MYSELF.
I COULD NEVER HAVE REALIZED THAT ON MY OWN.
"WELL, TATARA?"

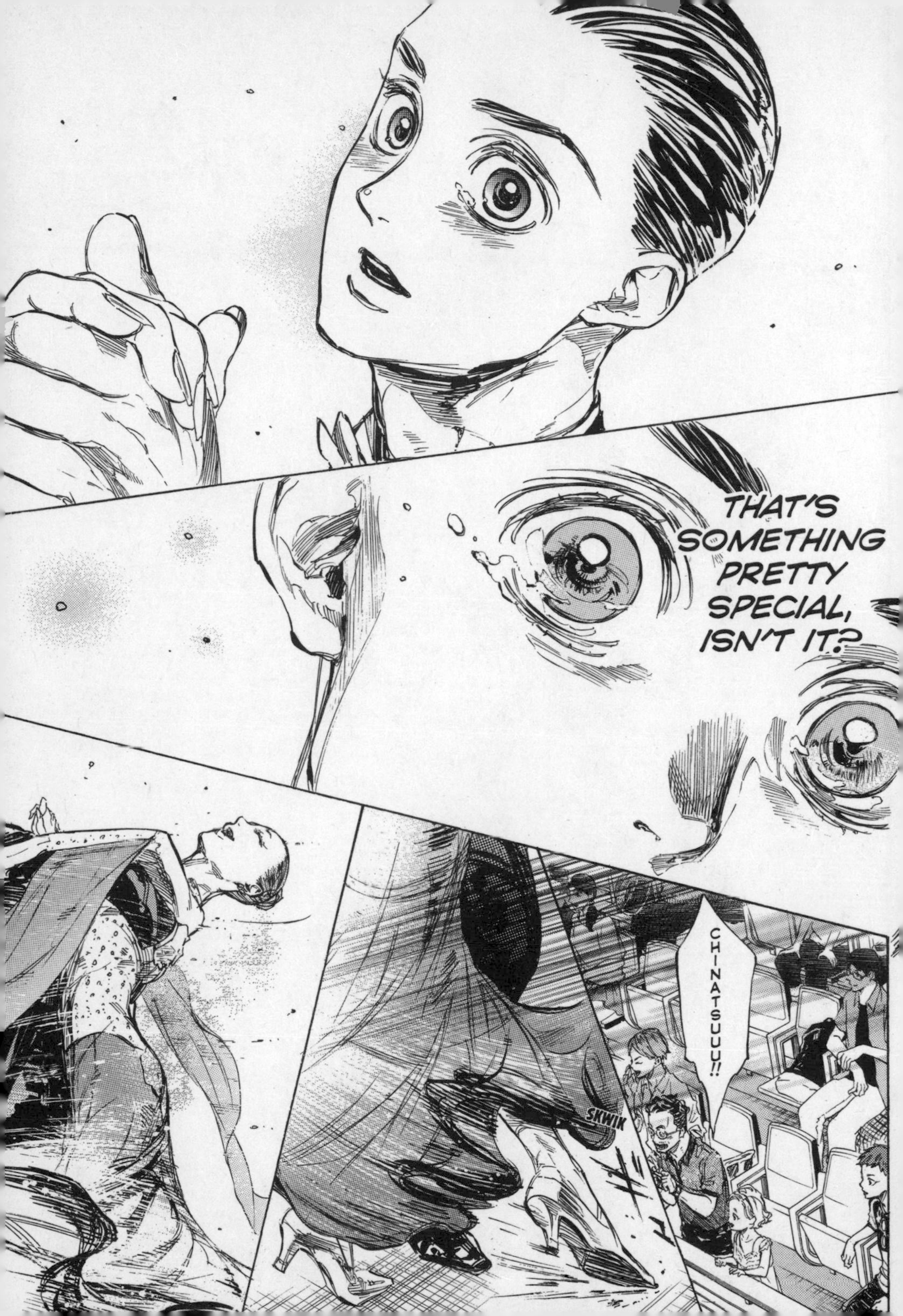
THAT'S SOMETHING PRETTY SPECIAL, ISN'T IT?
CHINATSUUU!!
SKWIK

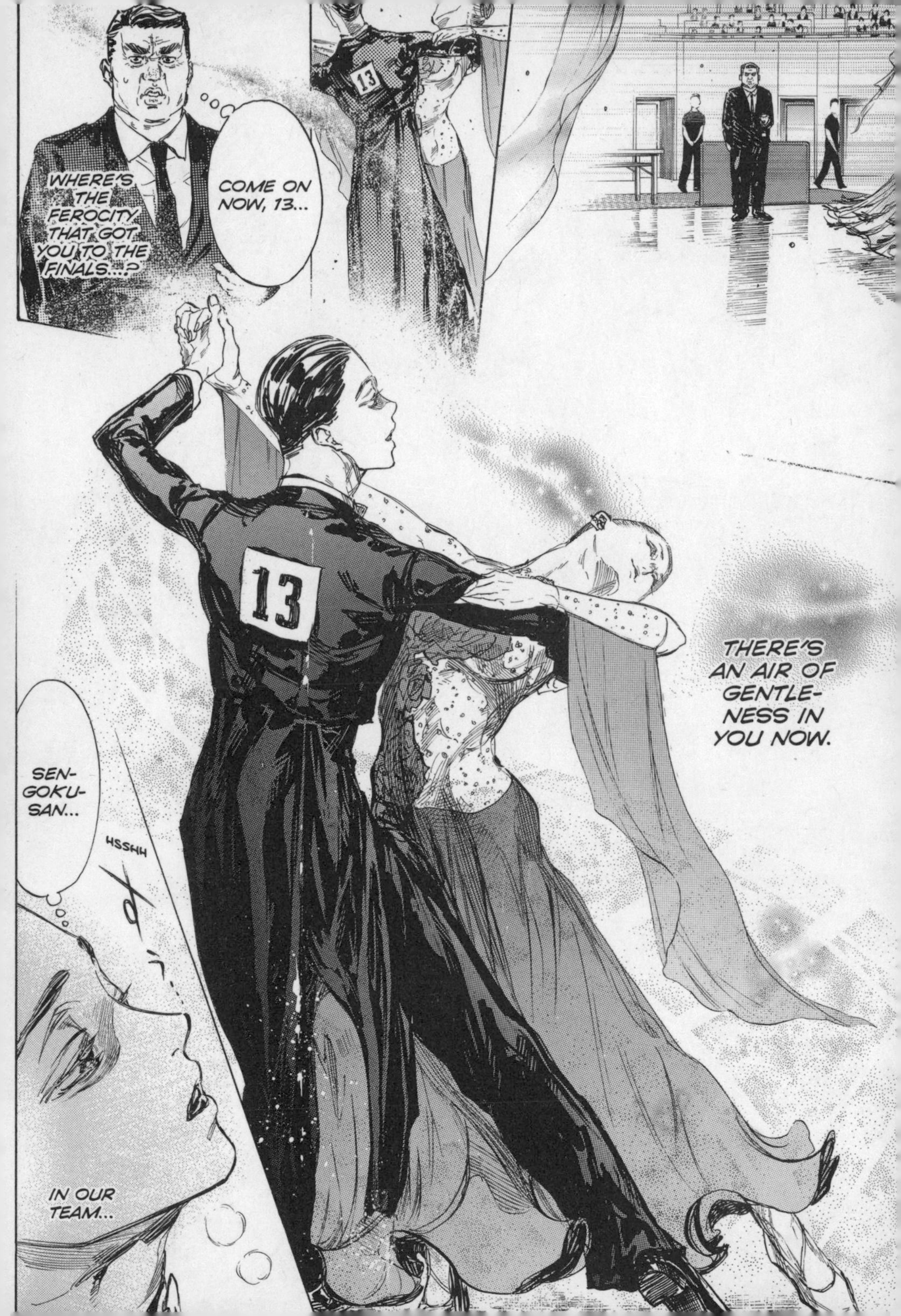
COME ON NOW, 13...
WHERE'S THE FEROCITY THAT GOT YOU TO THE FINALS...?
THERE'S AN AIR OF GENTLE-NESS IN YOU NOW.
SEN-GOKU-SAN...
HSSHH
IN OUR TEAM...

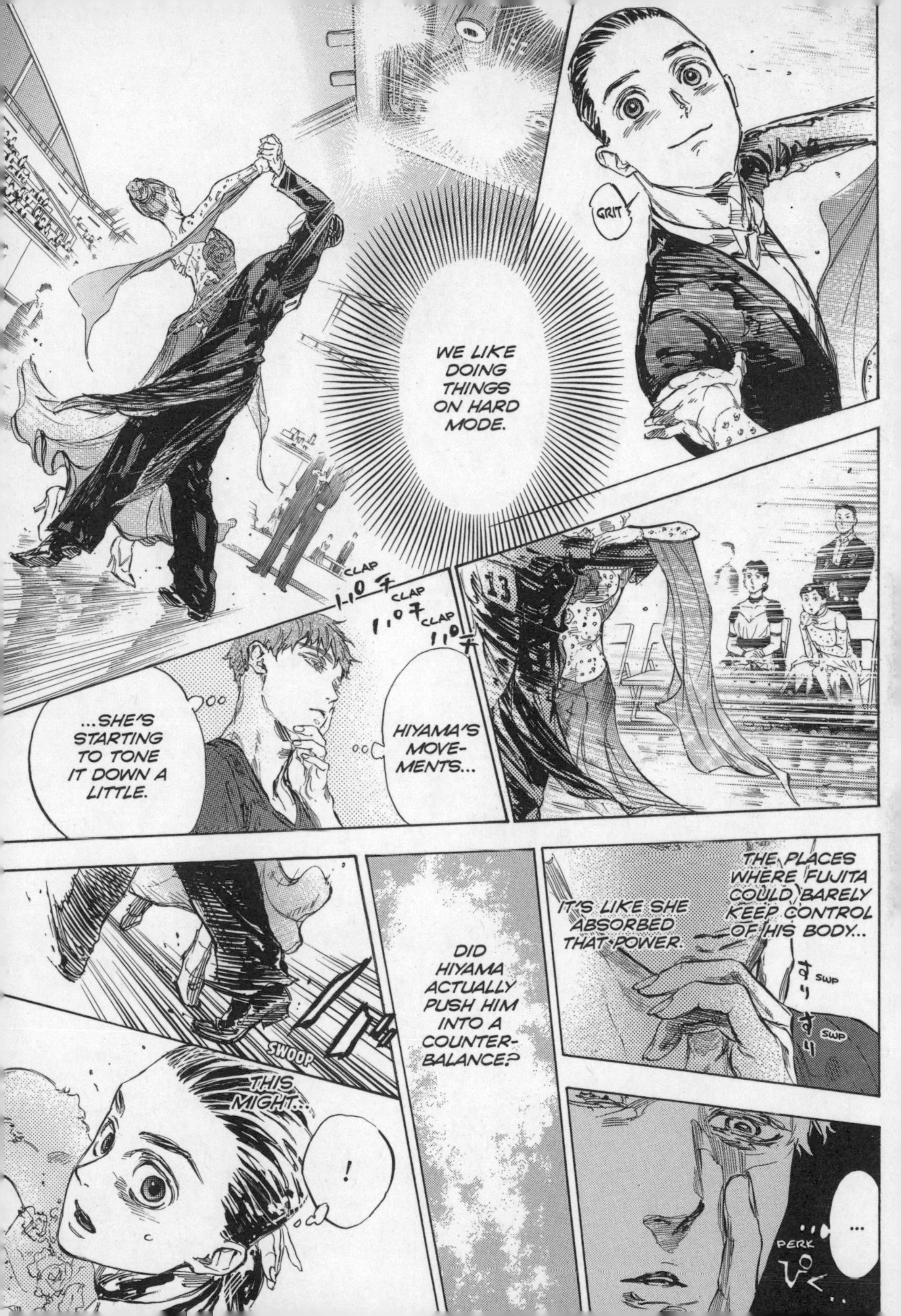
GRIT
WE LIKE DOING THINGS ON HARD MODE.
CLAP
CLAP
CLAP
HIYAMA'S MOVEMENTS...
...SHE'S STARTING TO TONE IT DOWN A LITTLE.
THE PLACES WHERE FUJITA COULD BARELY KEEP CONTROL OF HIS BODY...
IT'S LIKE SHE ABSORBED THAT POWER.
SWP
SWP
DID HIYAMA ACTUALLY PUSH HIM INTO A COUNTER-BALANCE?
SWOOP
...
PERK
THIS MIGHT...
!

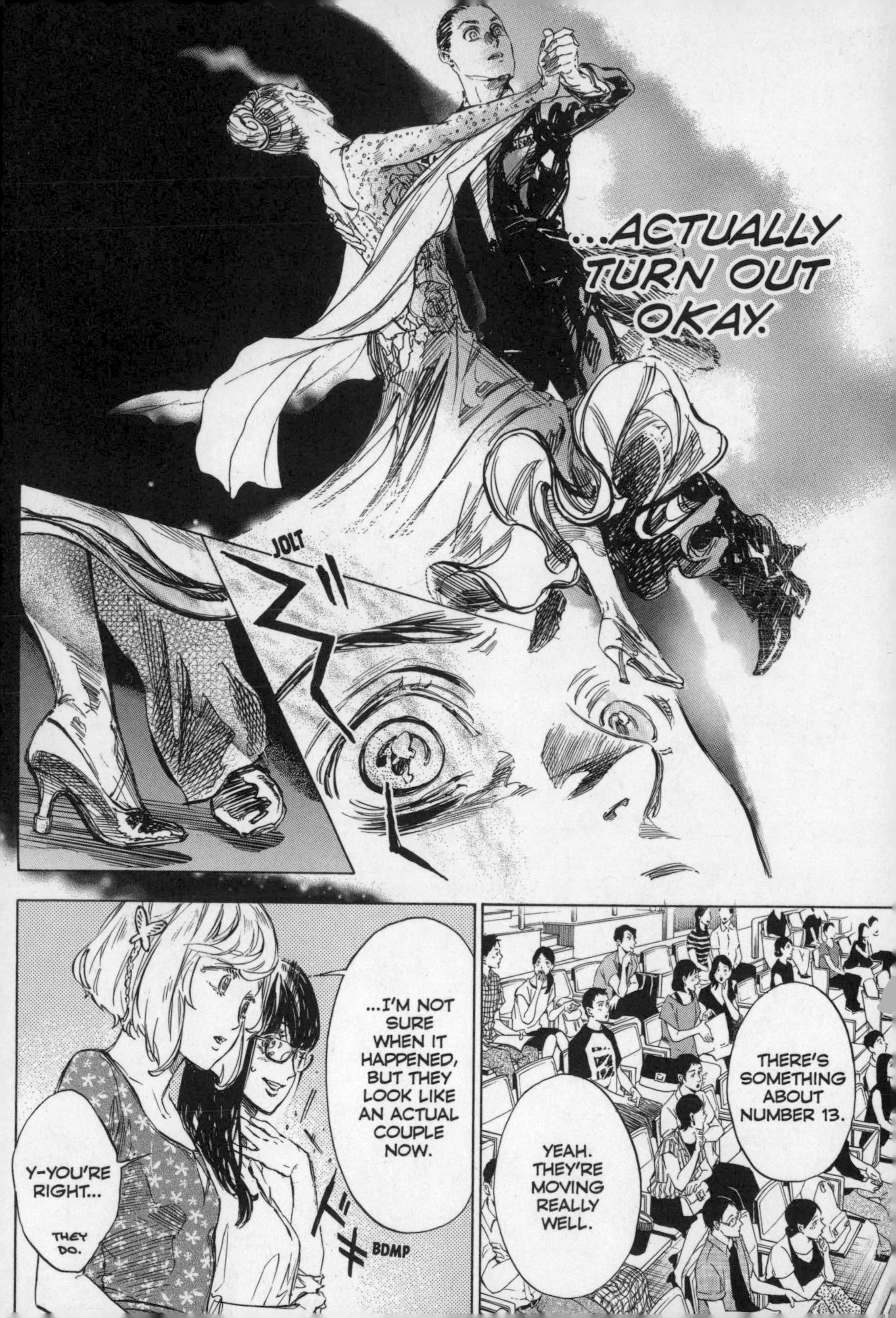
...ACTUALLY TURN OUT OKAY.
JOLT
THERE'S SOMETHING ABOUT NUMBER 13.
YEAH. THEY'RE MOVING REALLY WELL.
...I'M NOT SURE WHEN IT HAPPENED, BUT THEY LOOK LIKE AN ACTUAL COUPLE NOW.
BDMP
Y-YOU'RE RIGHT...
THEY DO.

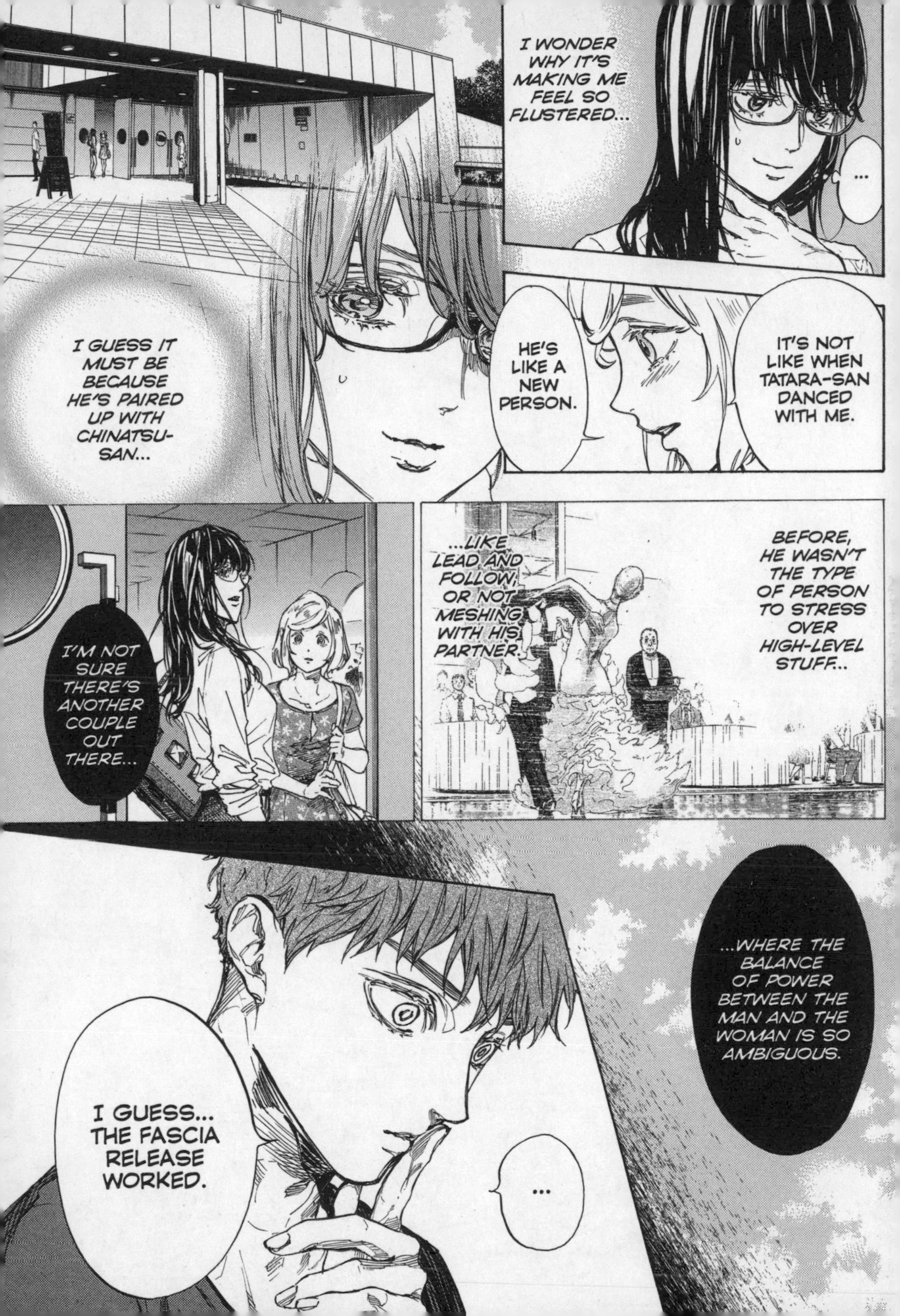
I WONDER WHY IT'S MAKING ME FEEL SO FLUSTERED...
...
IT'S NOT LIKE WHEN TATARA-SAN DANCED WITH ME.
HE'S LIKE A NEW PERSON.
I GUESS IT MUST BE BECAUSE HE'S PAIRED UP WITH CHINATSU-SAN...
BEFORE, HE WASN'T THE TYPE OF PERSON TO STRESS OVER HIGH-LEVEL STUFF...
...LIKE LEAD AND FOLLOW, OR NOT MESHING WITH HIS PARTNER.
I'M NOT SURE THERE'S ANOTHER COUPLE OUT THERE...
...WHERE THE BALANCE OF POWER BETWEEN THE MAN AND THE WOMAN IS SO AMBIGUOUS.
...
I GUESS... THE FASCIA RELEASE WORKED.

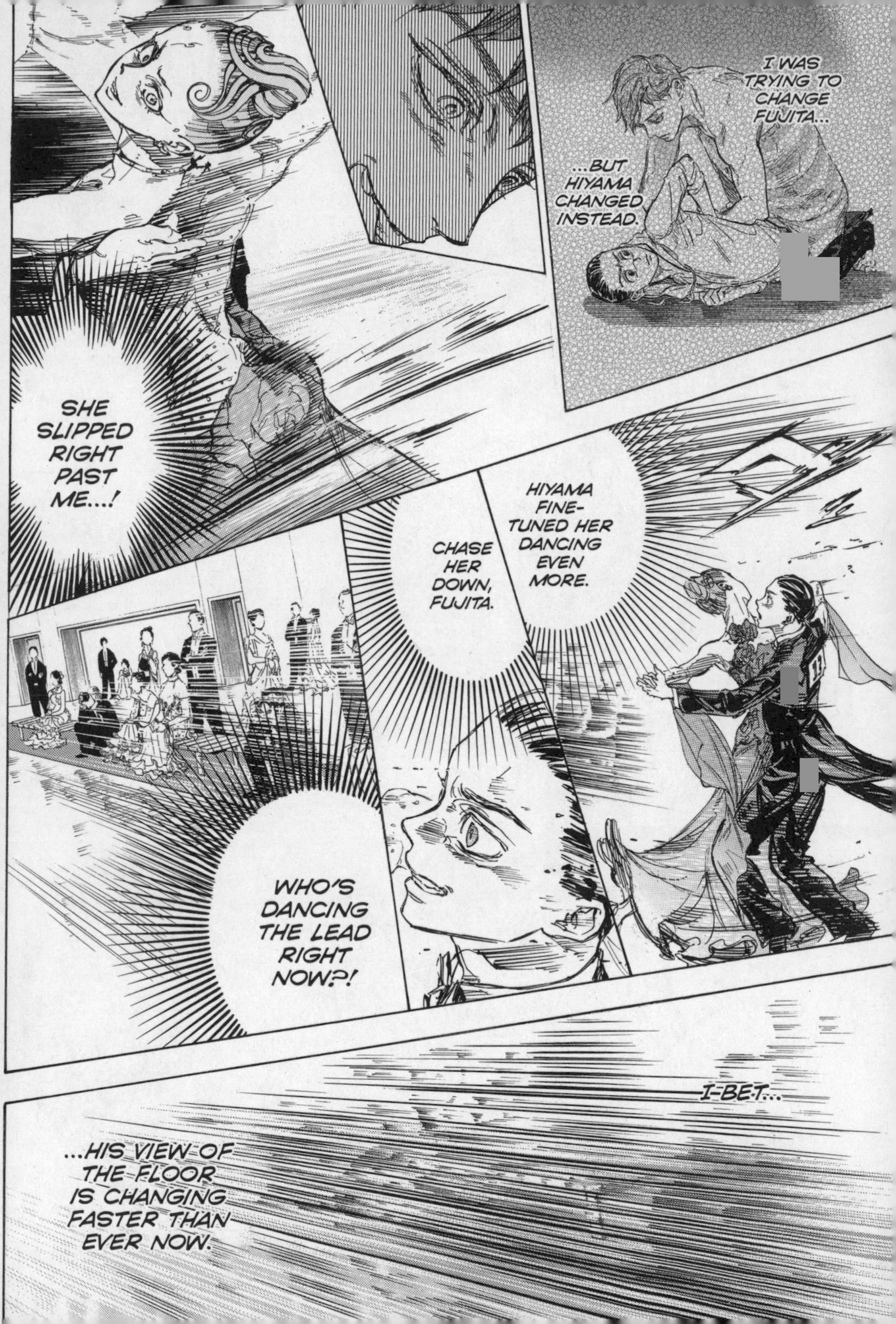
I WAS TRYING TO CHANGE FUJITA...
...BUT HIYAMA CHANGED INSTEAD.
SHE SLIPPED RIGHT PAST ME...!
HIYAMA FINE-TUNED HER DANCING EVEN MORE.
CHASE HER DOWN, FUJITA.
WHO'S DANCING THE LEAD RIGHT NOW?!
I BET...
...HIS VIEW OF THE FLOOR IS CHANGING FASTER THAN EVER NOW.

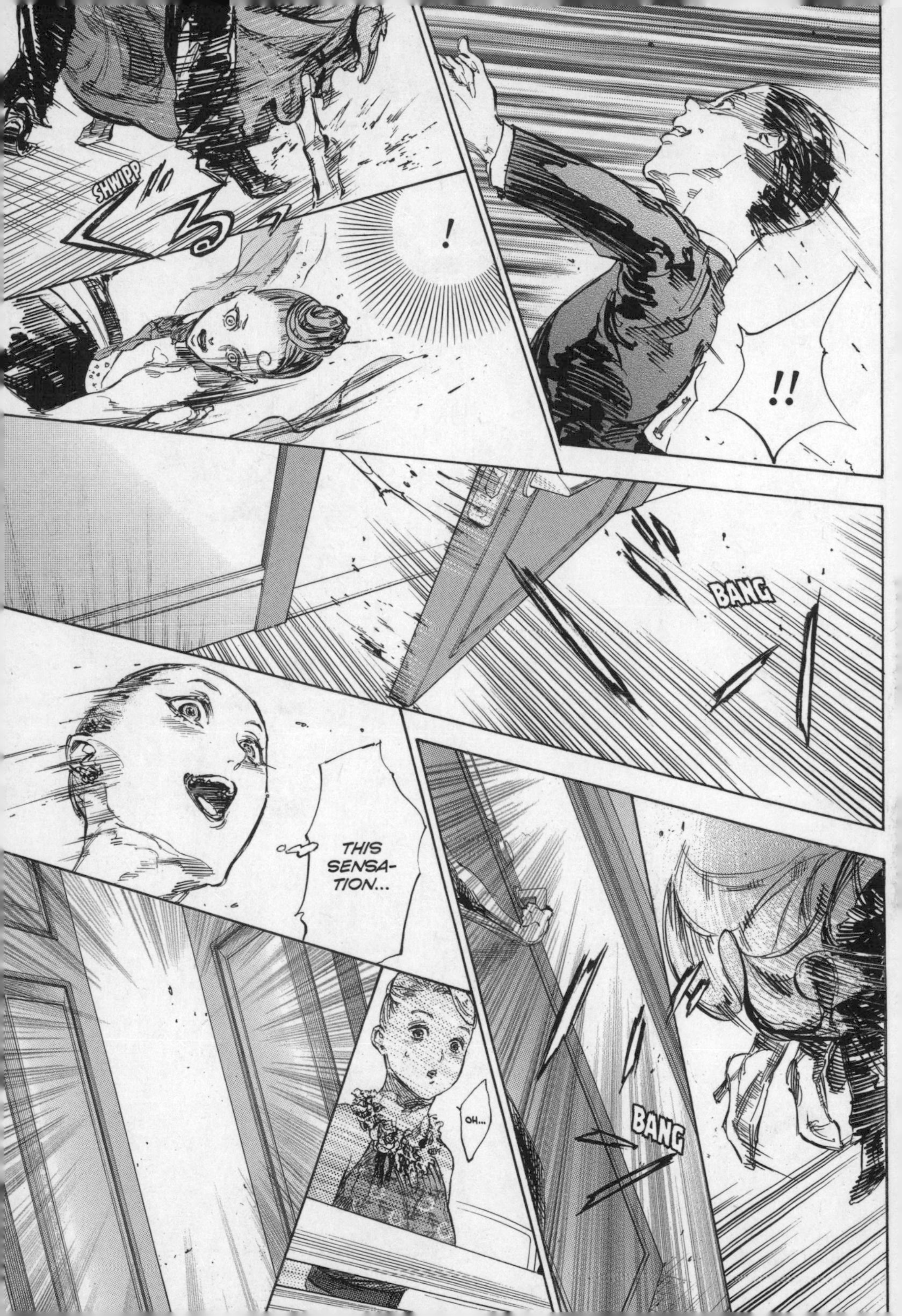
!!
SHWIPP
!
BANG
THIS SENSA-TION...
BANG
OH...

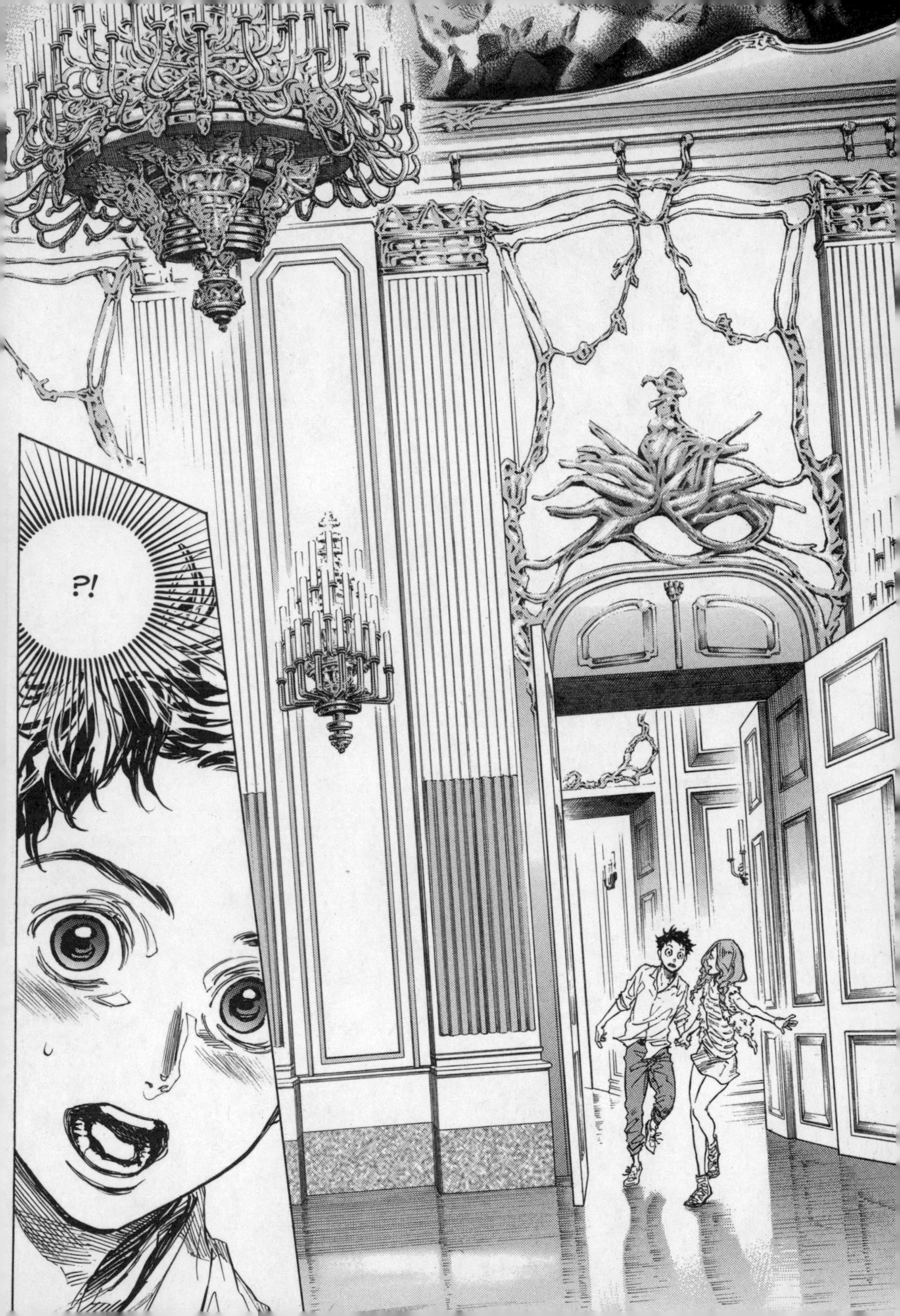
?!

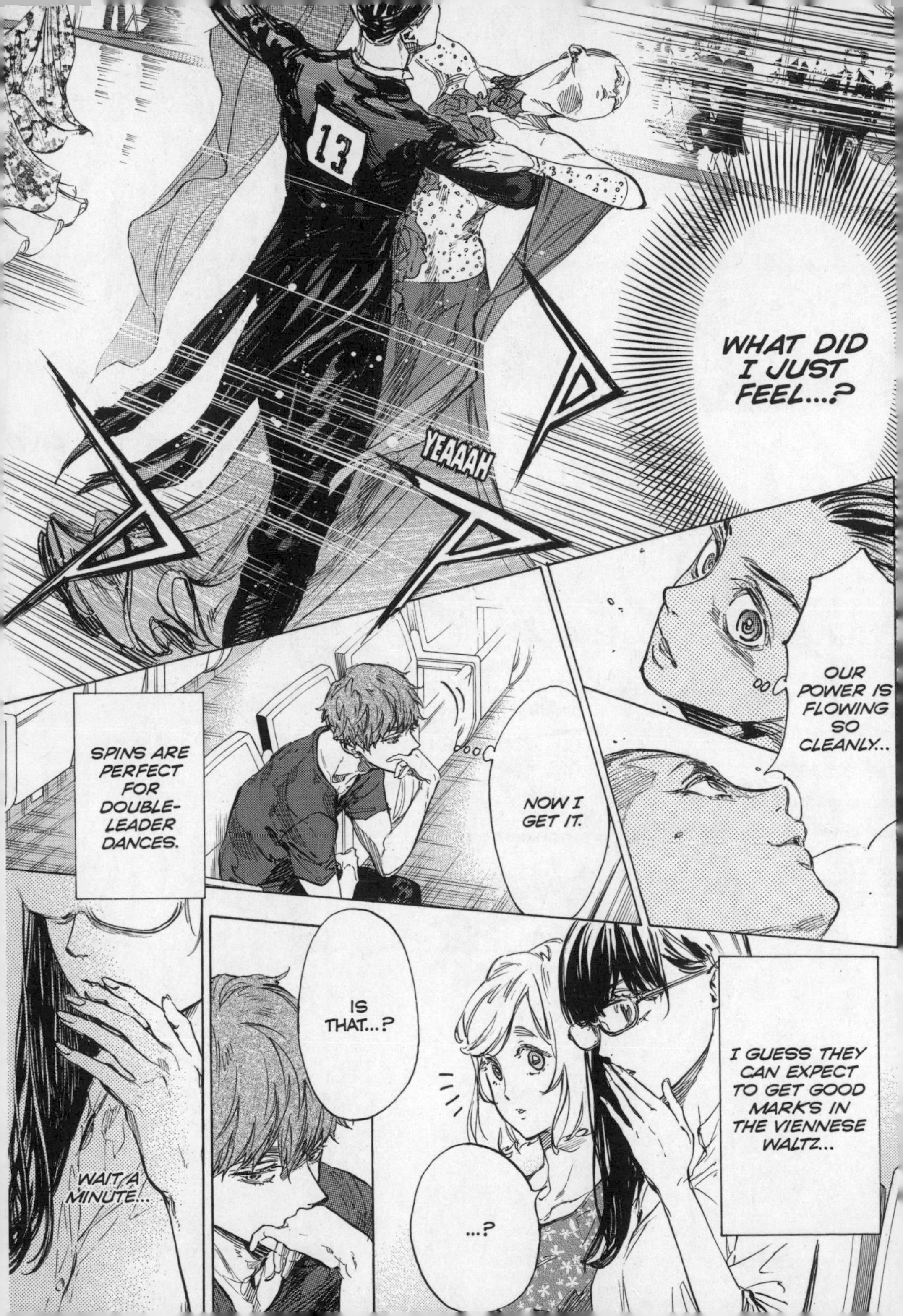

WHAT DID I JUST FEEL...?
YEAAAH
OUR POWER IS FLOWING SO CLEANLY...
NOW I GET IT.
SPINS ARE PERFECT FOR DOUBLE-LEADER DANCES.
I GUESS THEY CAN EXPECT TO GET GOOD MARKS IN THE VIENNESE WALTZ...
IS THAT...?
...?
WAIT A MINUTE...

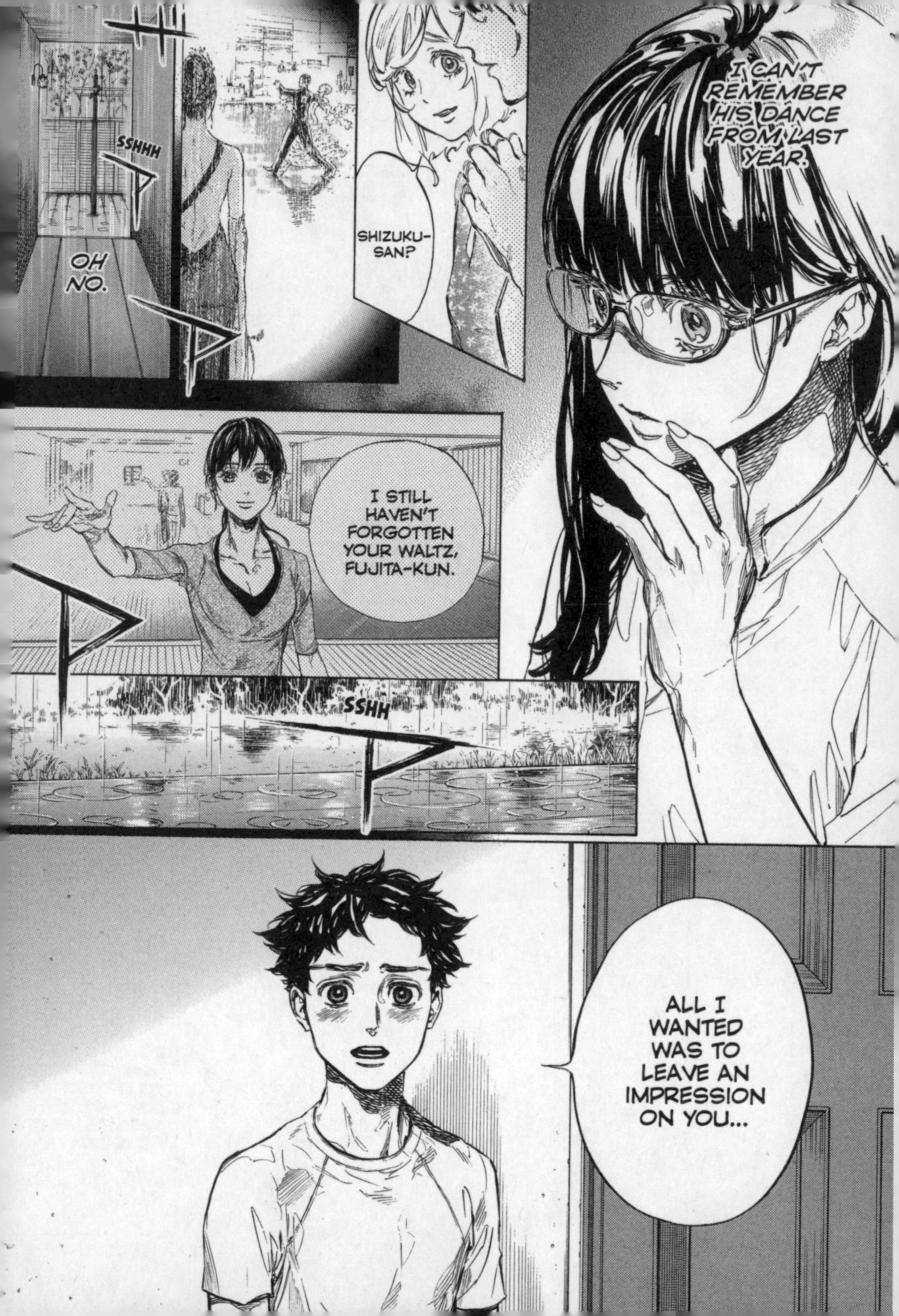
I CAN'T REMEMBER HIS DANCE FROM LAST YEAR.
SHIZUKU-SAN?
SSHHH
OH NO.
I STILL HAVEN'T FORGOTTEN YOUR WALTZ, FUJITA-KUN.
SSHH
ALL I WANTED WAS TO LEAVE AN IMPRESSION ON YOU...

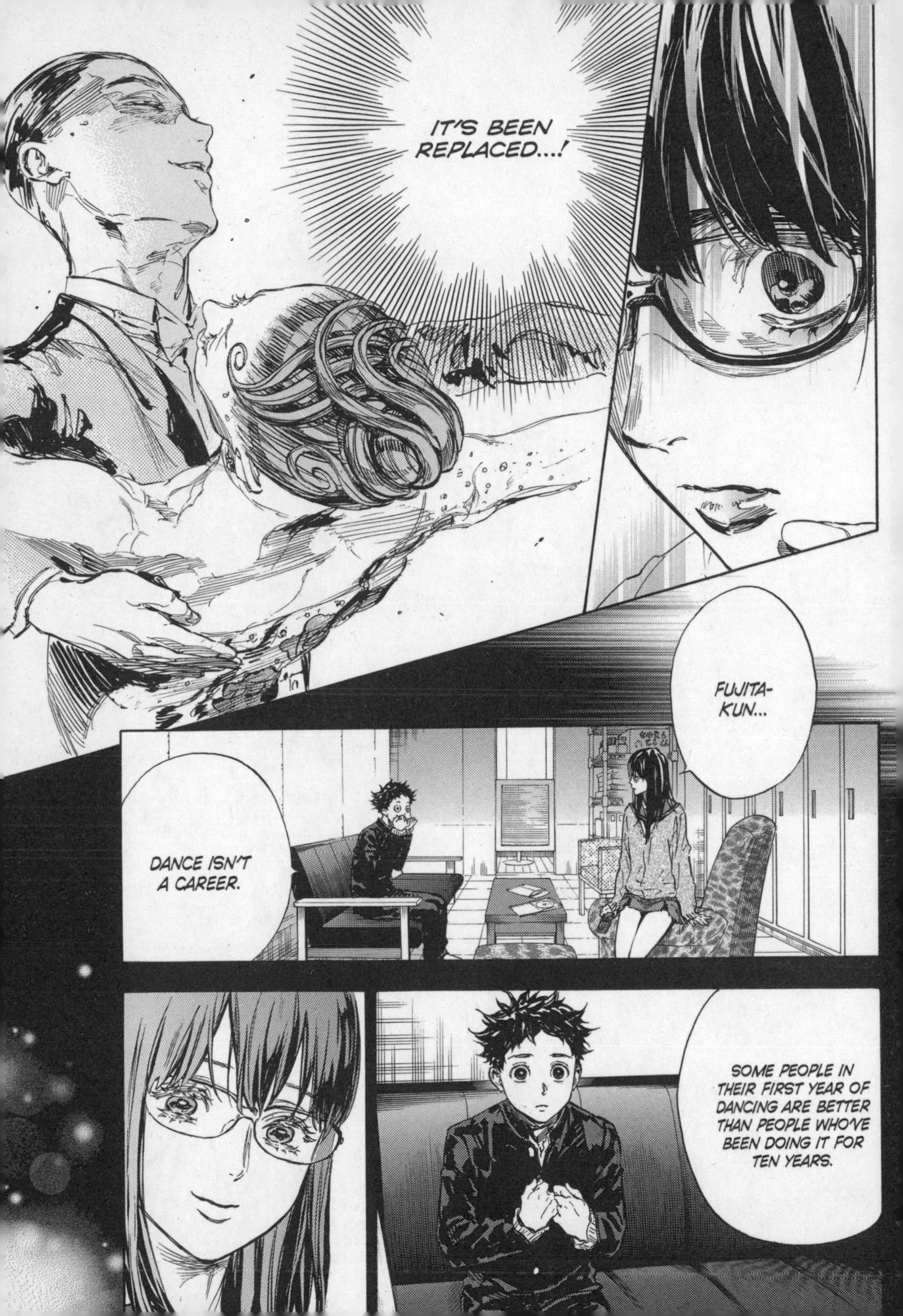
IT'S BEEN REPLACED...!
FUJITA-KUN...
DANCE ISN'T A CAREER.
SOME PEOPLE IN THEIR FIRST YEAR OF DANCING ARE BETTER THAN PEOPLE WHO'VE BEEN DOING IT FOR TEN YEARS.

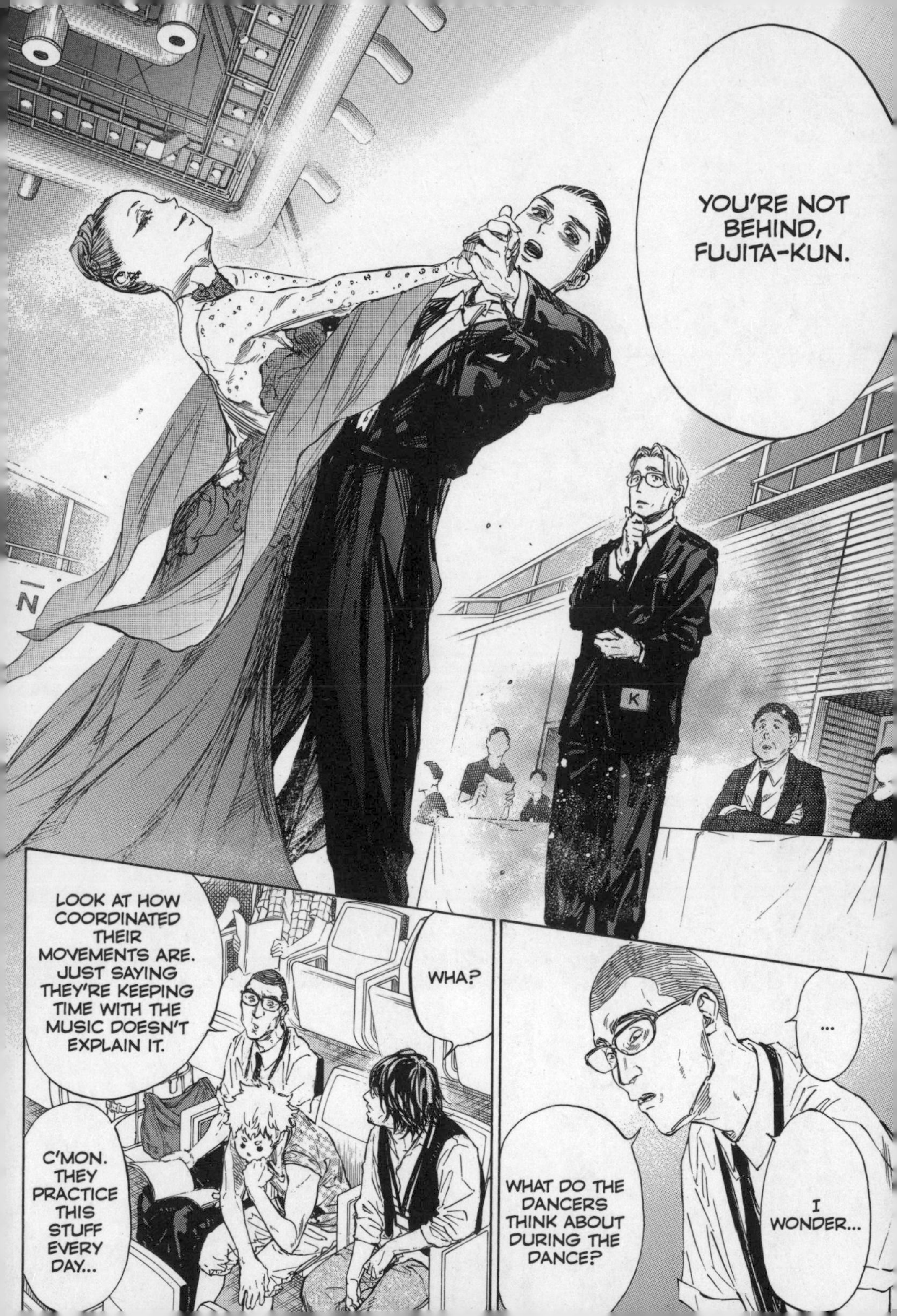
YOU'RE NOT BEHIND, FUJITA-KUN.
...
I WONDER...
WHAT DO THE DANCERS THINK ABOUT DURING THE DANCE?
LOOK AT HOW COORDINATED THEIR MOVEMENTS ARE. JUST SAYING THEY'RE KEEPING TIME WITH THE MUSIC DOESN'T EXPLAIN IT.
WHA?
C'MON. THEY PRACTICE THIS STUFF EVERY DAY...

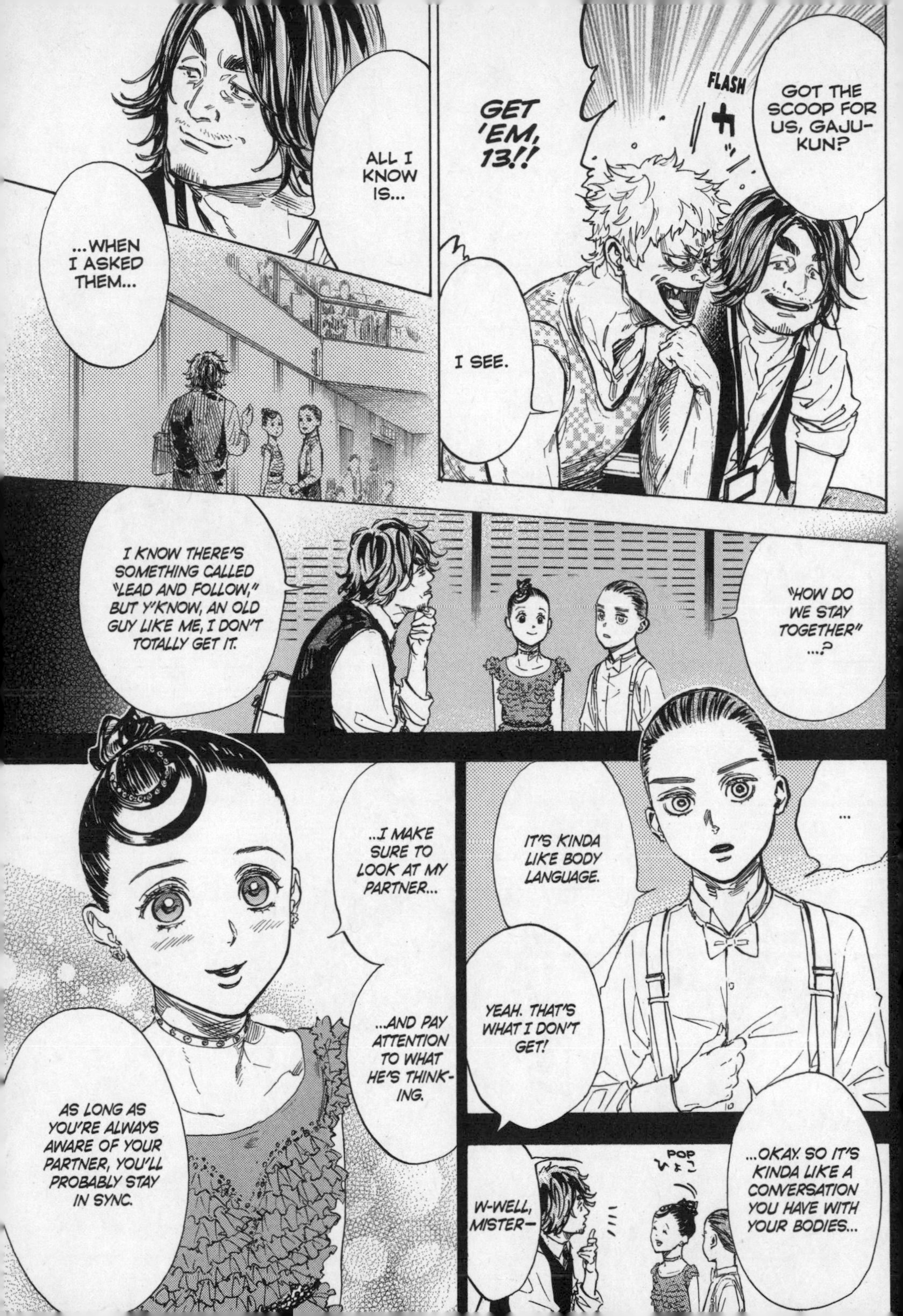

GOT THE SCOOP FOR US, GAJU-KUN?
FLASH
カ
GET 'EM, 13!!
I SEE.
ALL I KNOW IS...
...WHEN I ASKED THEM...
"HOW DO WE STAY TOGETHER" ...?
I KNOW THERE'S SOMETHING CALLED "LEAD AND FOLLOW," BUT Y'KNOW, AN OLD GUY LIKE ME, I DON'T TOTALLY GET IT.
...
IT'S KINDA LIKE BODY LANGUAGE.
YEAH. THAT'S WHAT I DON'T GET!
...OKAY. SO IT'S KINDA LIKE A CONVERSATION YOU HAVE WITH YOUR BODIES...
POP
ひょこ
W-WELL, MISTER—
...I MAKE SURE TO LOOK AT MY PARTNER...
...AND PAY ATTENTION TO WHAT HE'S THINKING.
AS LONG AS YOU'RE ALWAYS AWARE OF YOUR PARTNER, YOU'LL PROBABLY STAY IN SYNC.

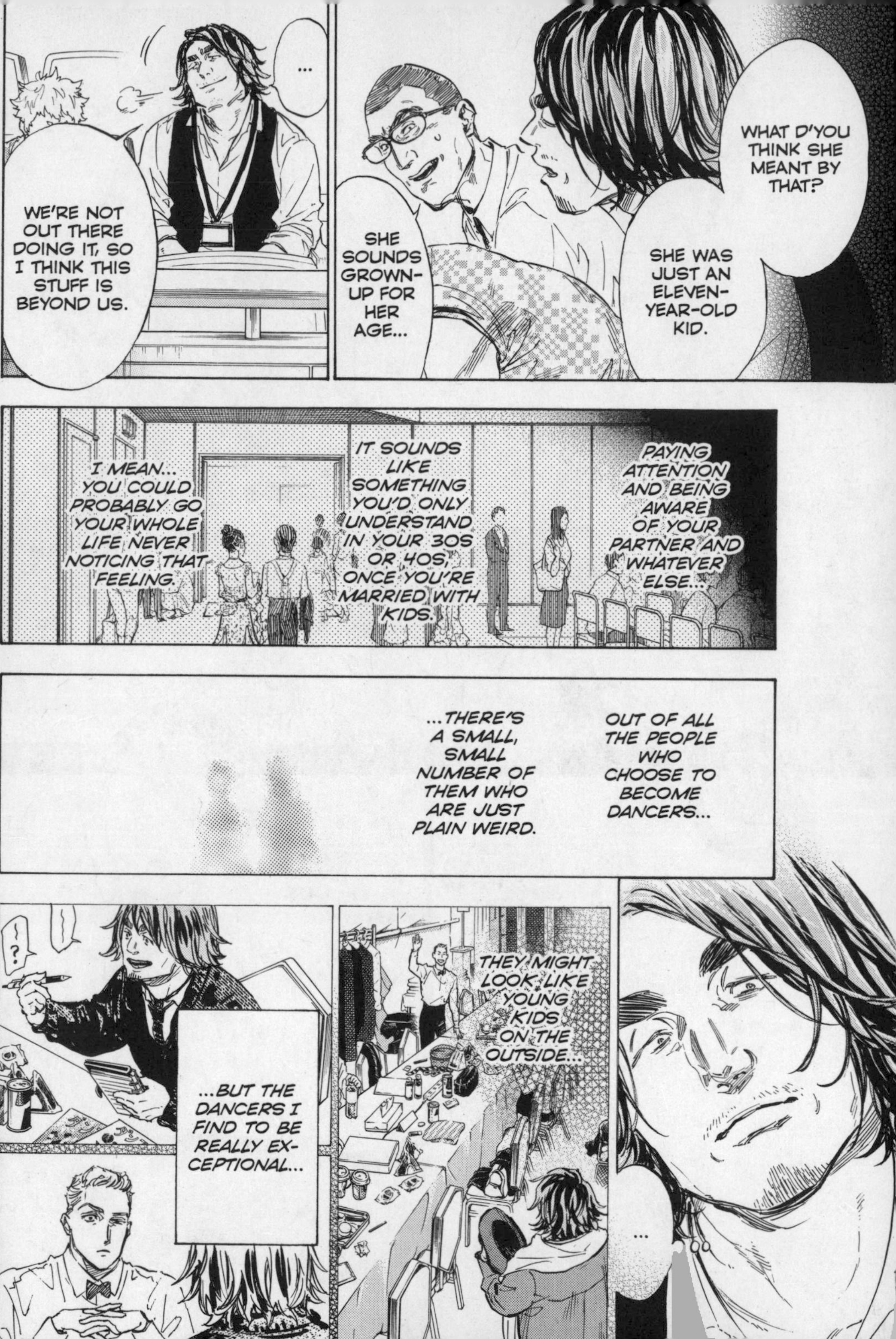
WHAT D'YOU THINK SHE MEANT BY THAT?
SHE WAS JUST AN ELEVEN-YEAR-OLD KID.
SHE SOUNDS GROWN-UP FOR HER AGE...
...
WE'RE NOT OUT THERE DOING IT, SO I THINK THIS STUFF IS BEYOND US.
PAYING ATTENTION AND BEING AWARE OF YOUR PARTNER AND WHATEVER ELSE...
IT SOUNDS LIKE SOMETHING YOU'D ONLY UNDERSTAND IN YOUR 30S OR 40S, ONCE YOU'RE MARRIED WITH KIDS.
I MEAN... YOU COULD PROBABLY GO YOUR WHOLE LIFE NEVER NOTICING THAT FEELING.
OUT OF ALL THE PEOPLE WHO CHOOSE TO BECOME DANCERS...
...THERE'S A SMALL, SMALL NUMBER OF THEM WHO ARE JUST PLAIN WEIRD.
...
THEY MIGHT LOOK LIKE YOUNG KIDS ON THE OUTSIDE...
...BUT THE DANCERS I FIND TO BE REALLY EXCEPTIONAL...
?

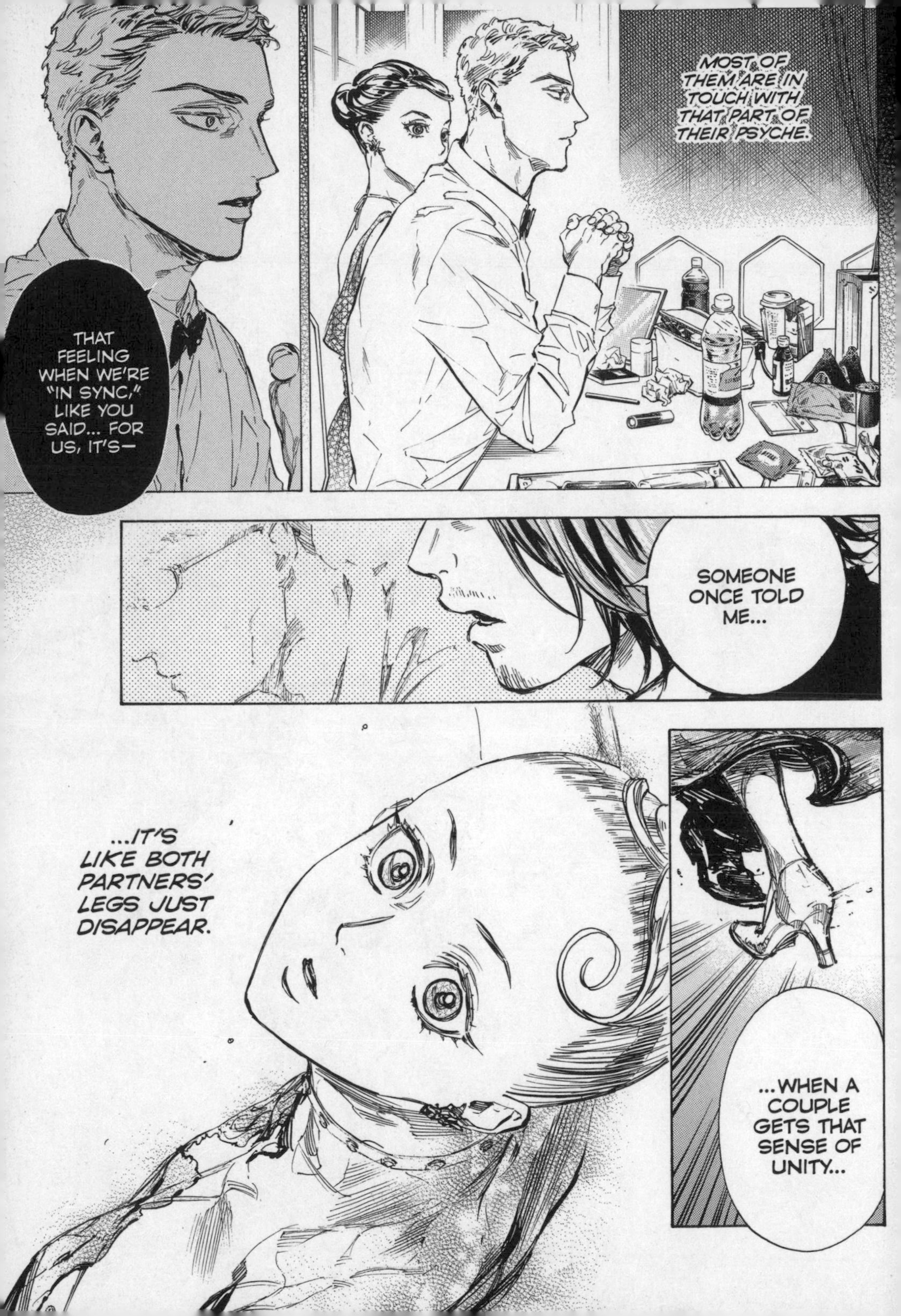
MOST OF THEM ARE IN TOUCH WITH THAT PART OF THEIR PSYCHE.
THAT FEELING WHEN WE'RE "IN SYNC," LIKE YOU SAID... FOR US, IT'S—
SOMEONE ONCE TOLD ME...
...WHEN A COUPLE GETS THAT SENSE OF UNITY...
...IT'S LIKE BOTH PARTNERS' LEGS JUST DISAPPEAR.

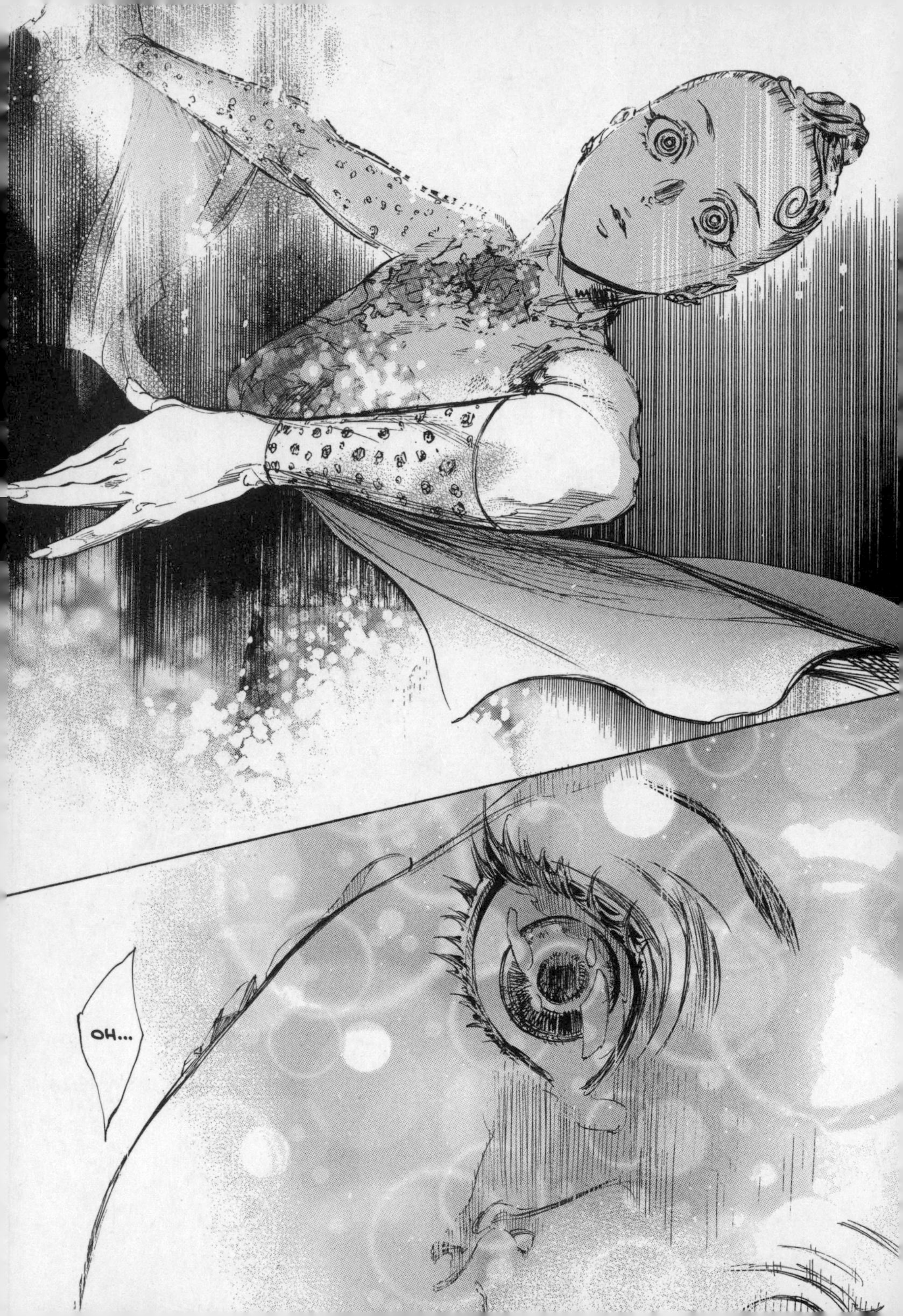
OH...

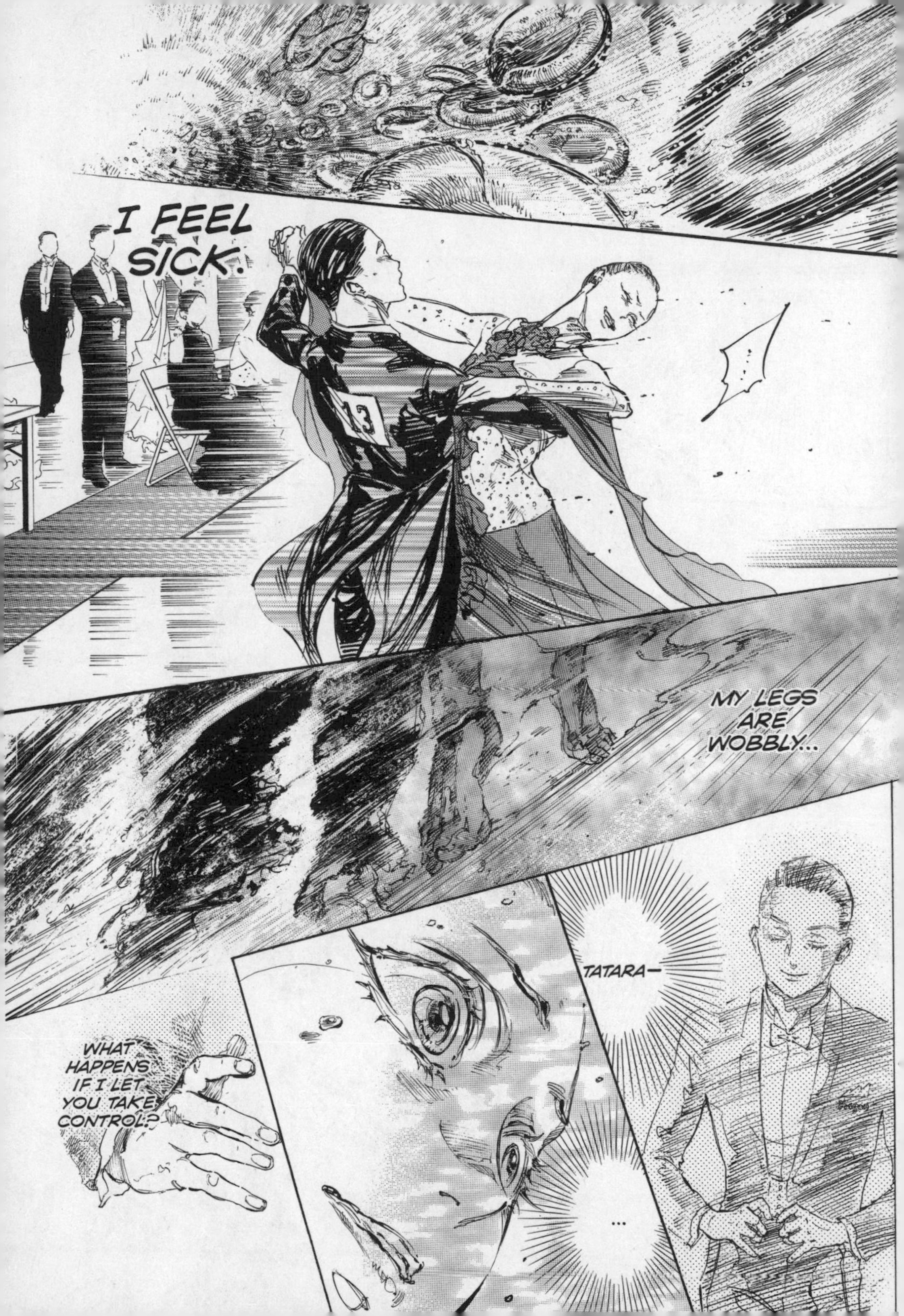
I FEEL SICK.
MY LEGS ARE WOBBLY...
TATARA—
...
WHAT HAPPENS IF I LET YOU TAKE CONTROL?

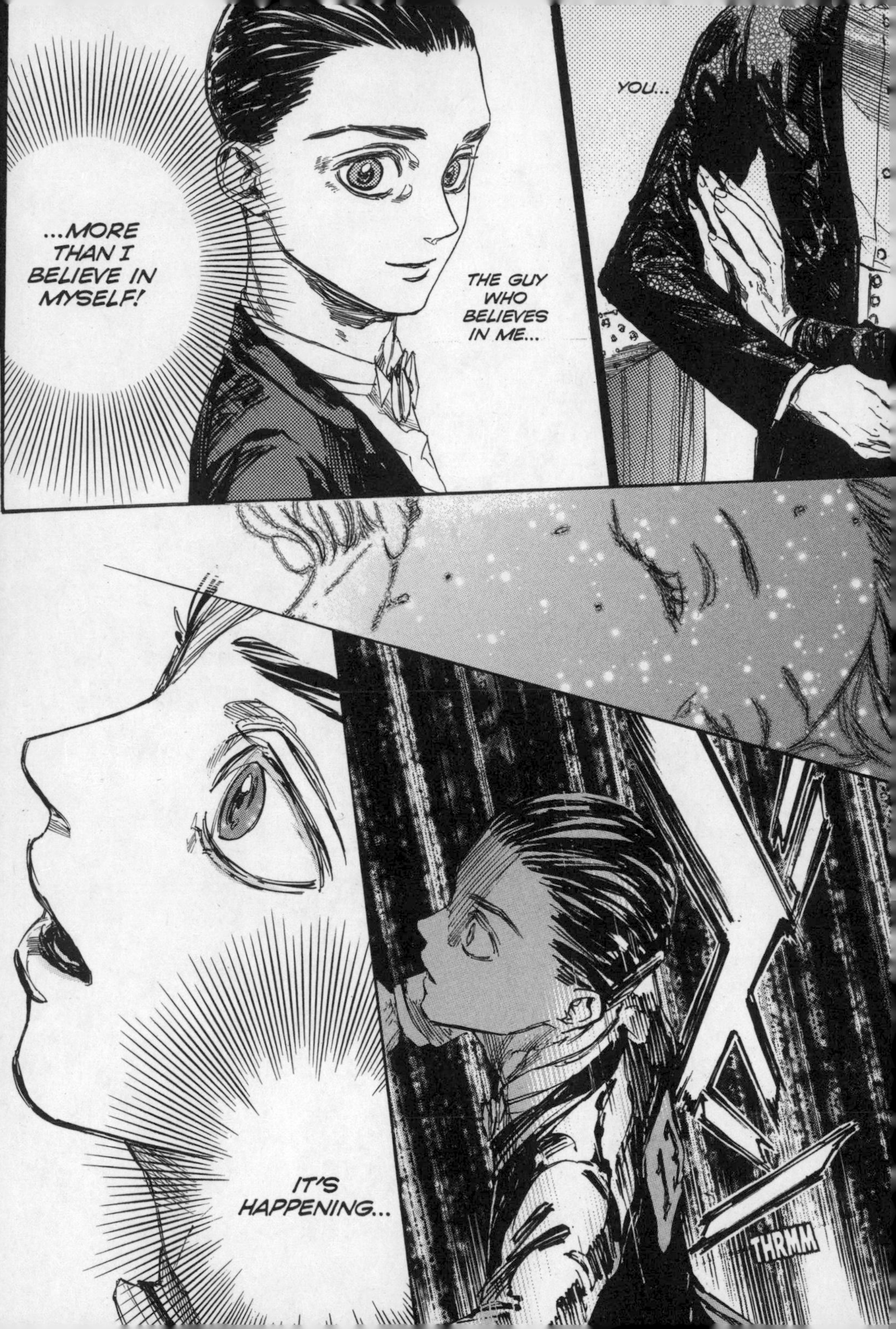
YOU...
THE GUY WHO BELIEVES IN ME...
...MORE THAN I BELIEVE IN MYSELF!
THRMM
IT'S HAPPENING...

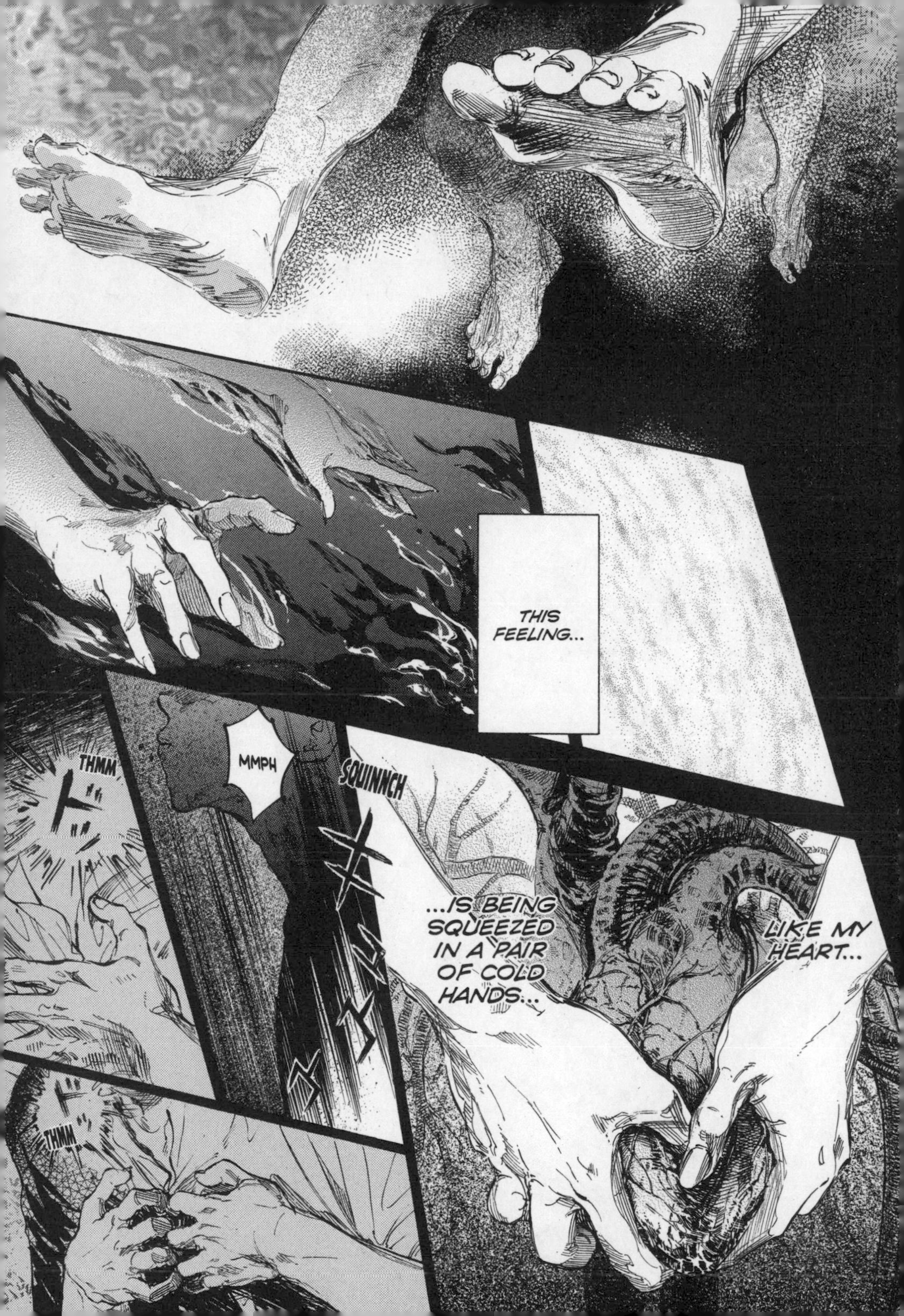
THIS FEELING...
LIKE MY HEART...
...IS BEING SQUEEZED IN A PAIR OF COLD HANDS...
SQUINNCH
MMPH
THMM
THMM

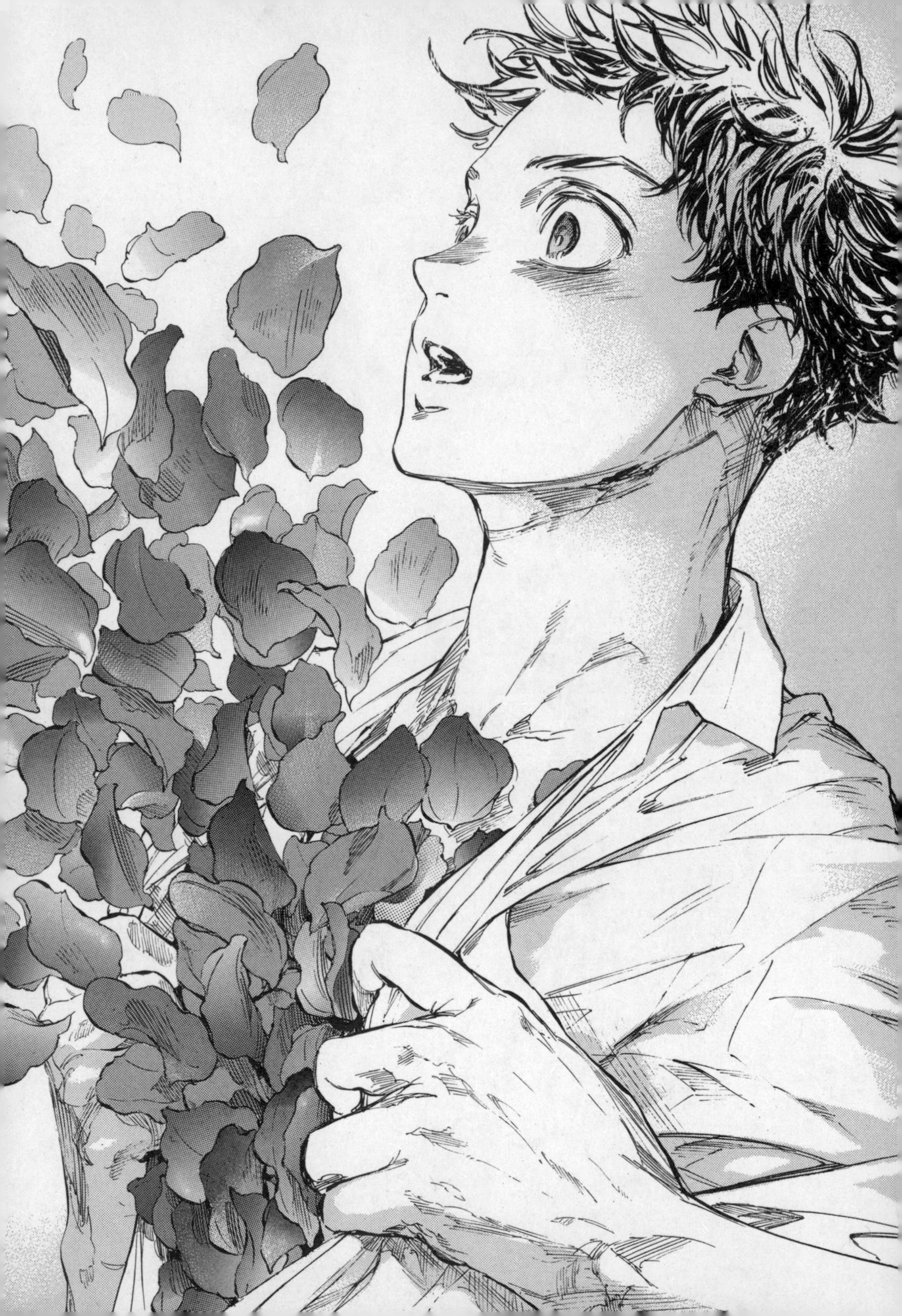

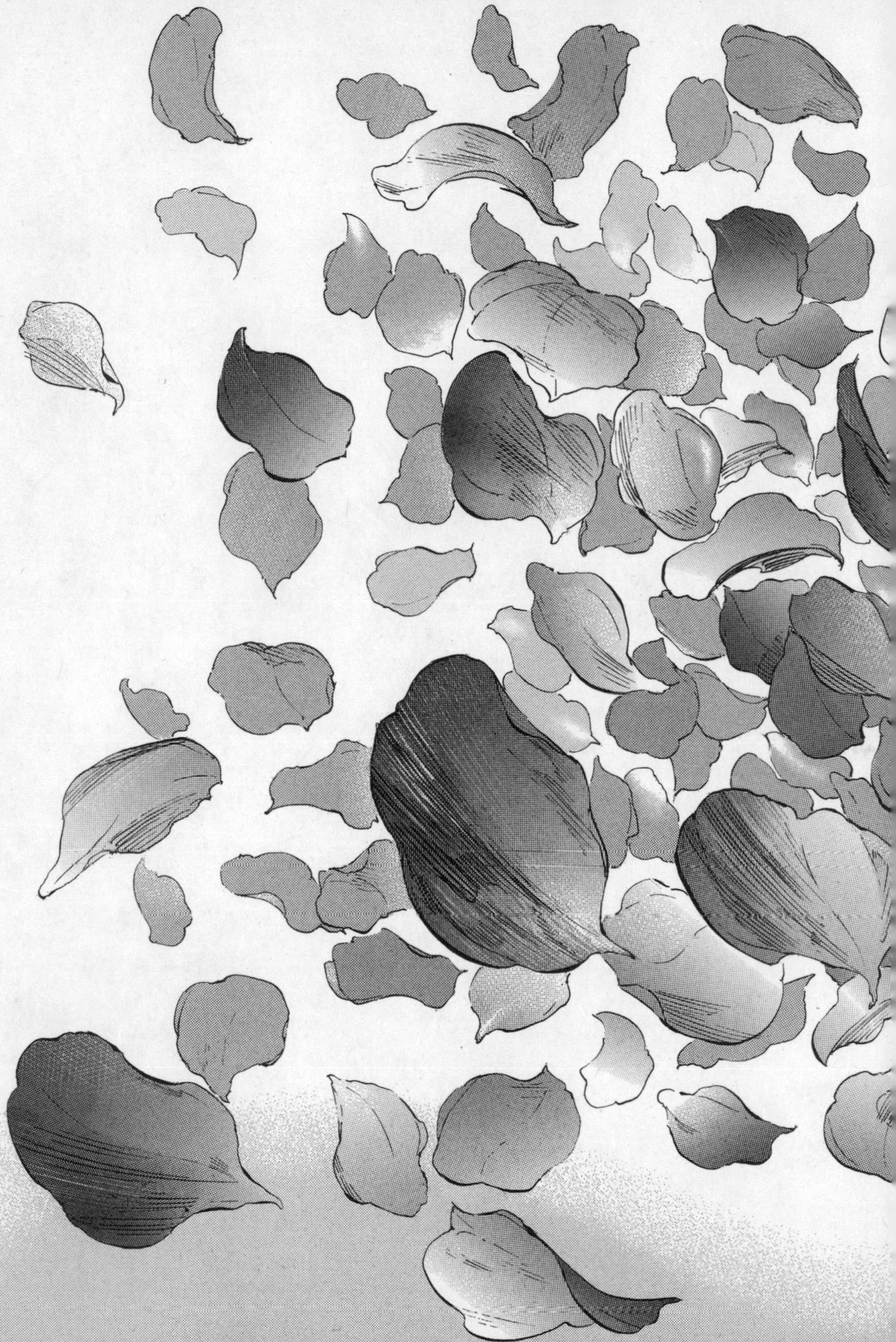

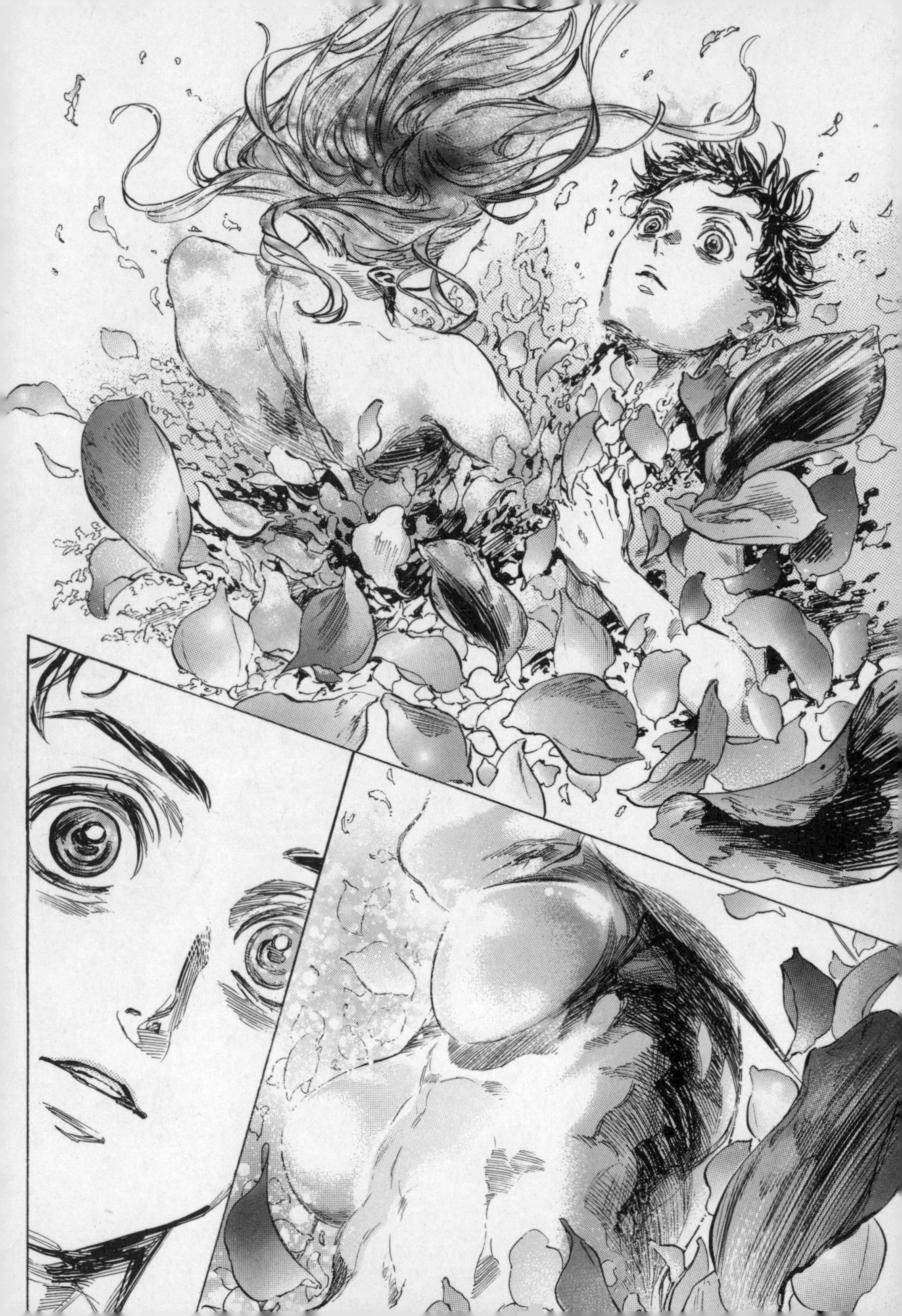

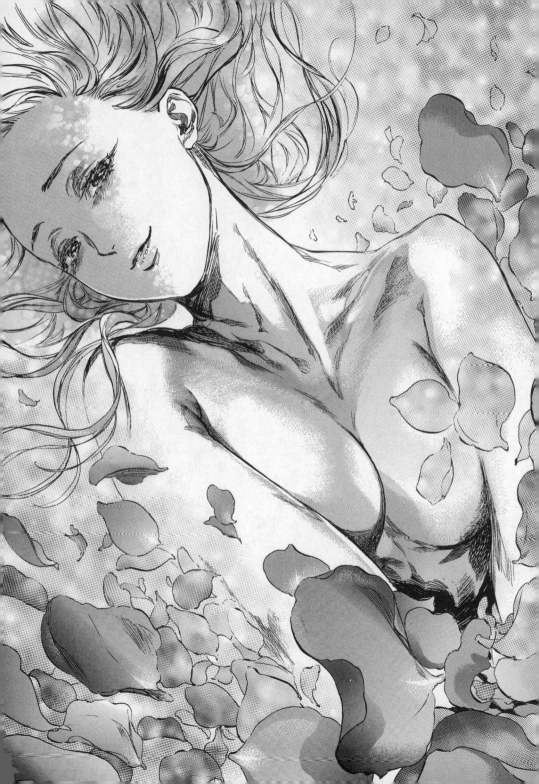

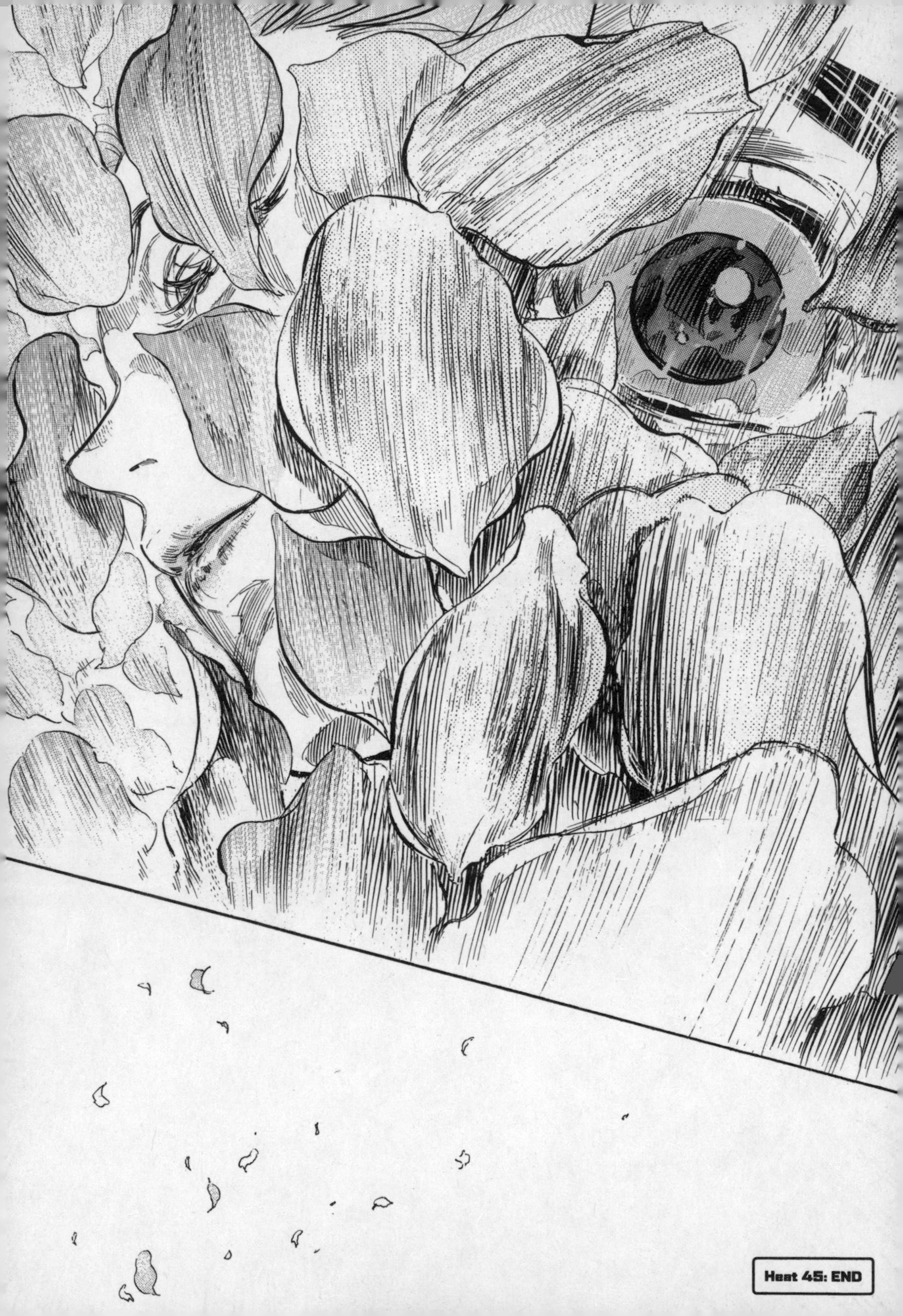
Heat 45: END

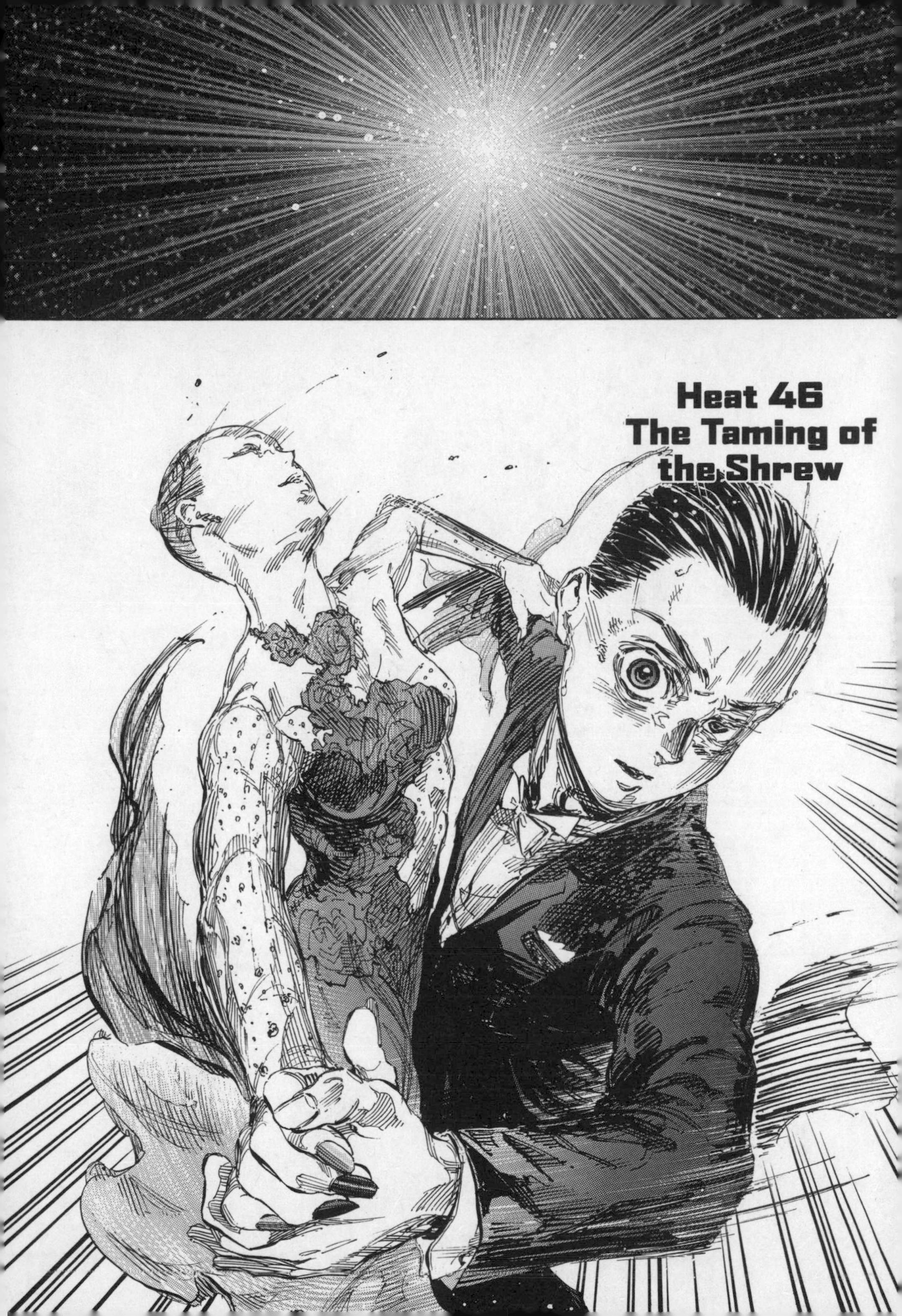
Heat 46
The Taming of the Shrew

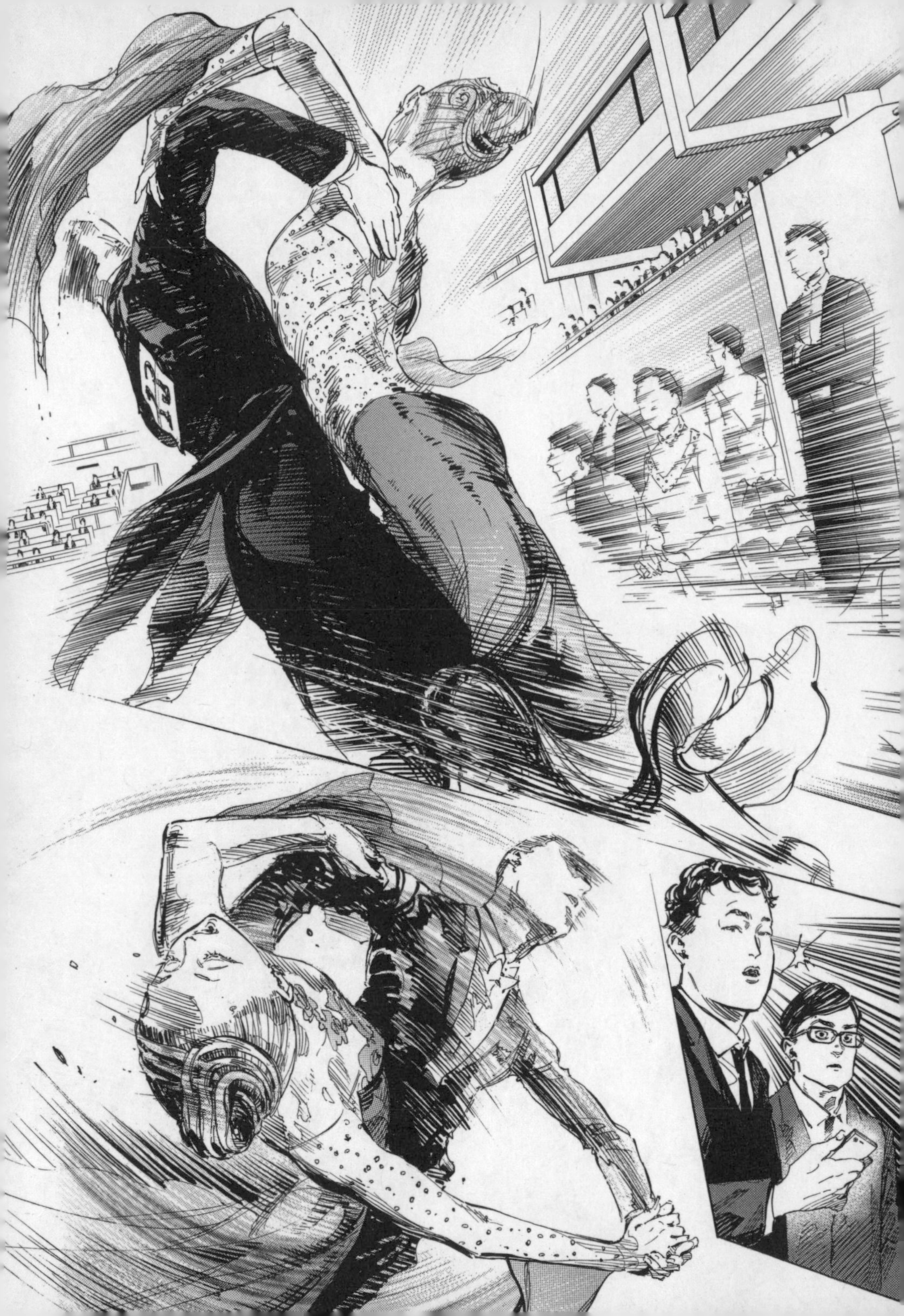

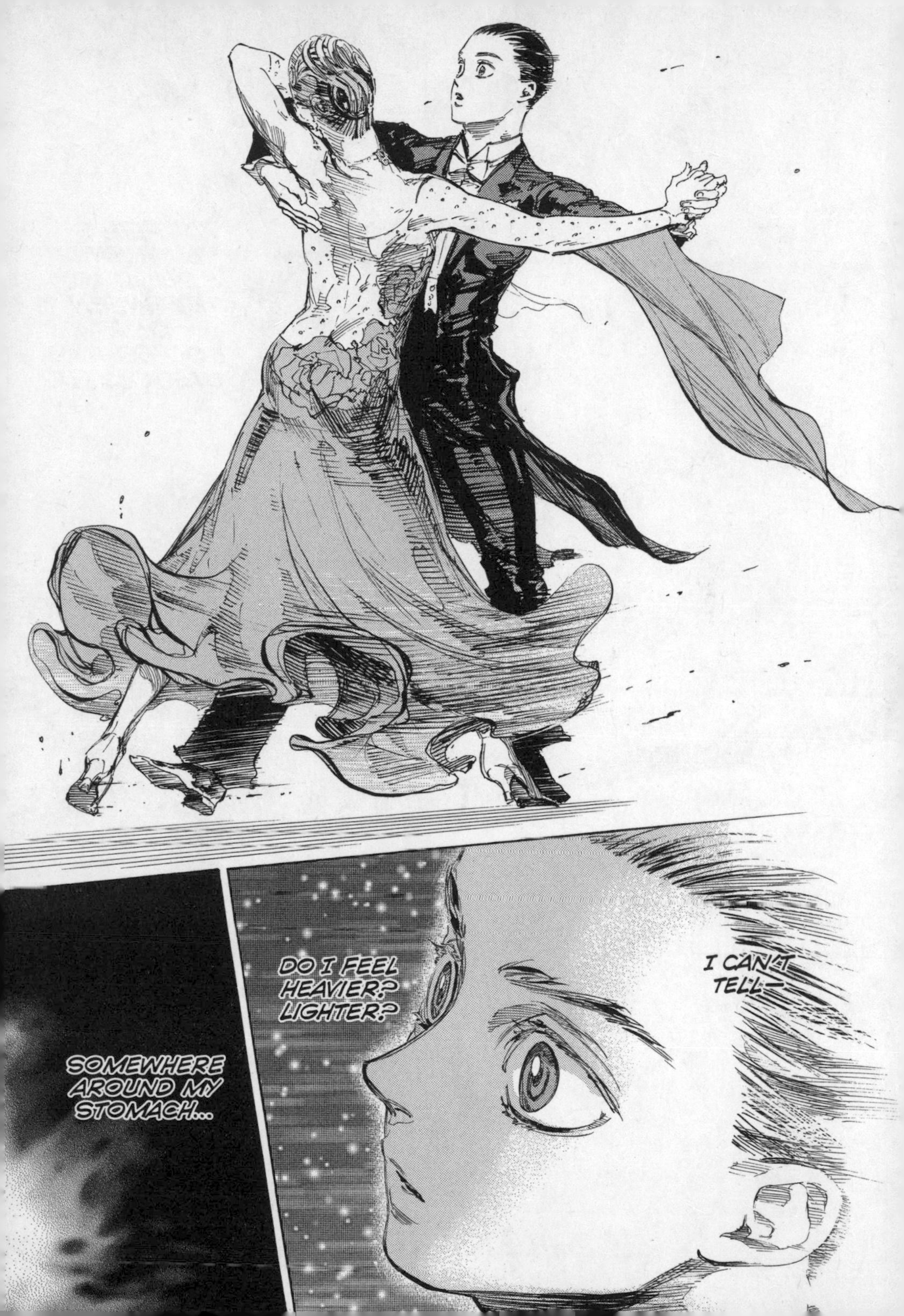
I CAN'T TELL—
DO I FEEL HEAVIER? LIGHTER?
SOMEWHERE AROUND MY STOMACH...

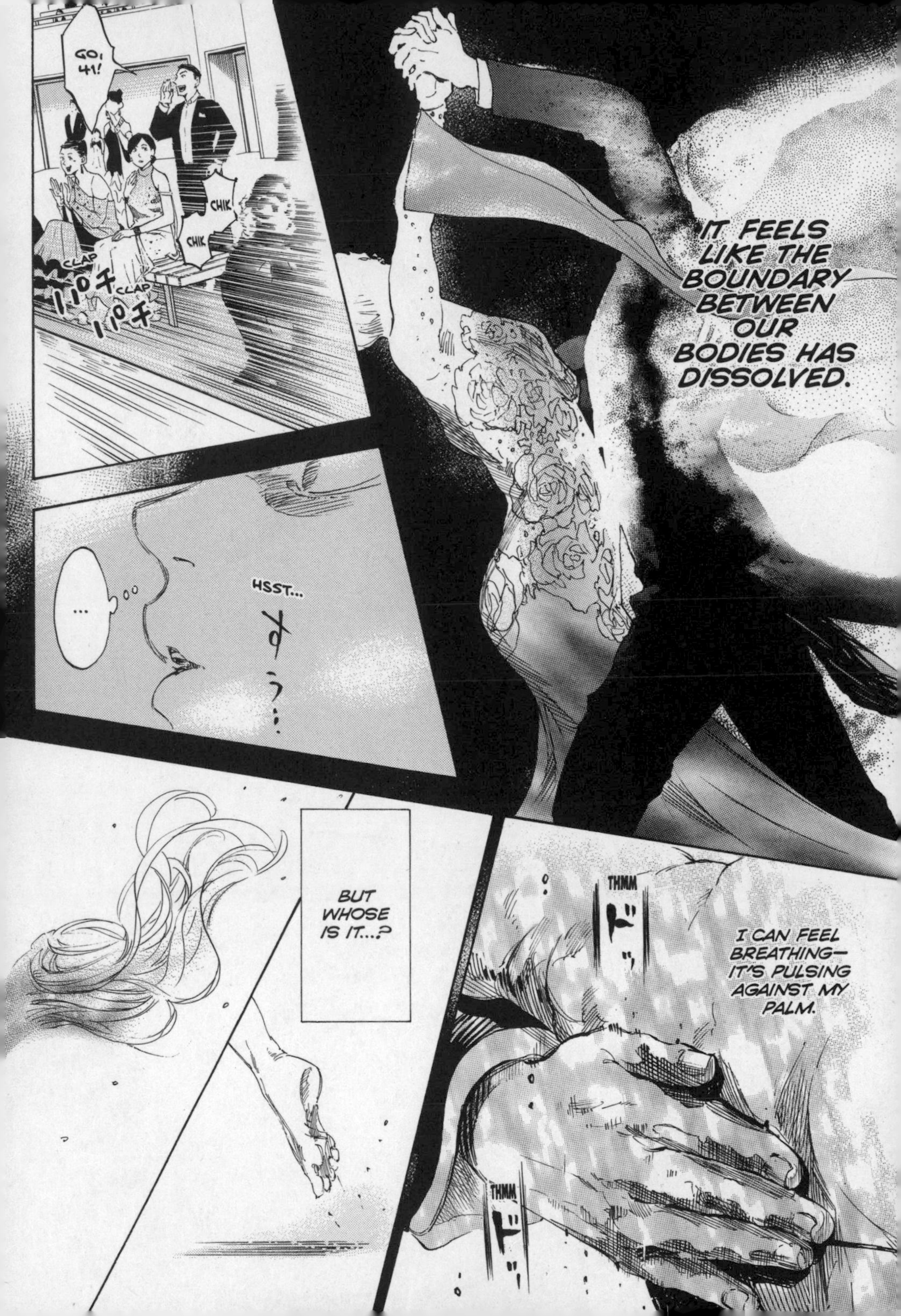
IT FEELS LIKE THE BOUNDARY BETWEEN OUR BODIES HAS DISSOLVED.
GO, 41!
CHIK
CHIK
CLAP パチ
CLAP パチ
...
HSST... すぅ...
THMM ド
I CAN FEEL BREATHING— IT'S PULSING AGAINST MY PALM.
THMM ド
BUT WHOSE IS IT...?

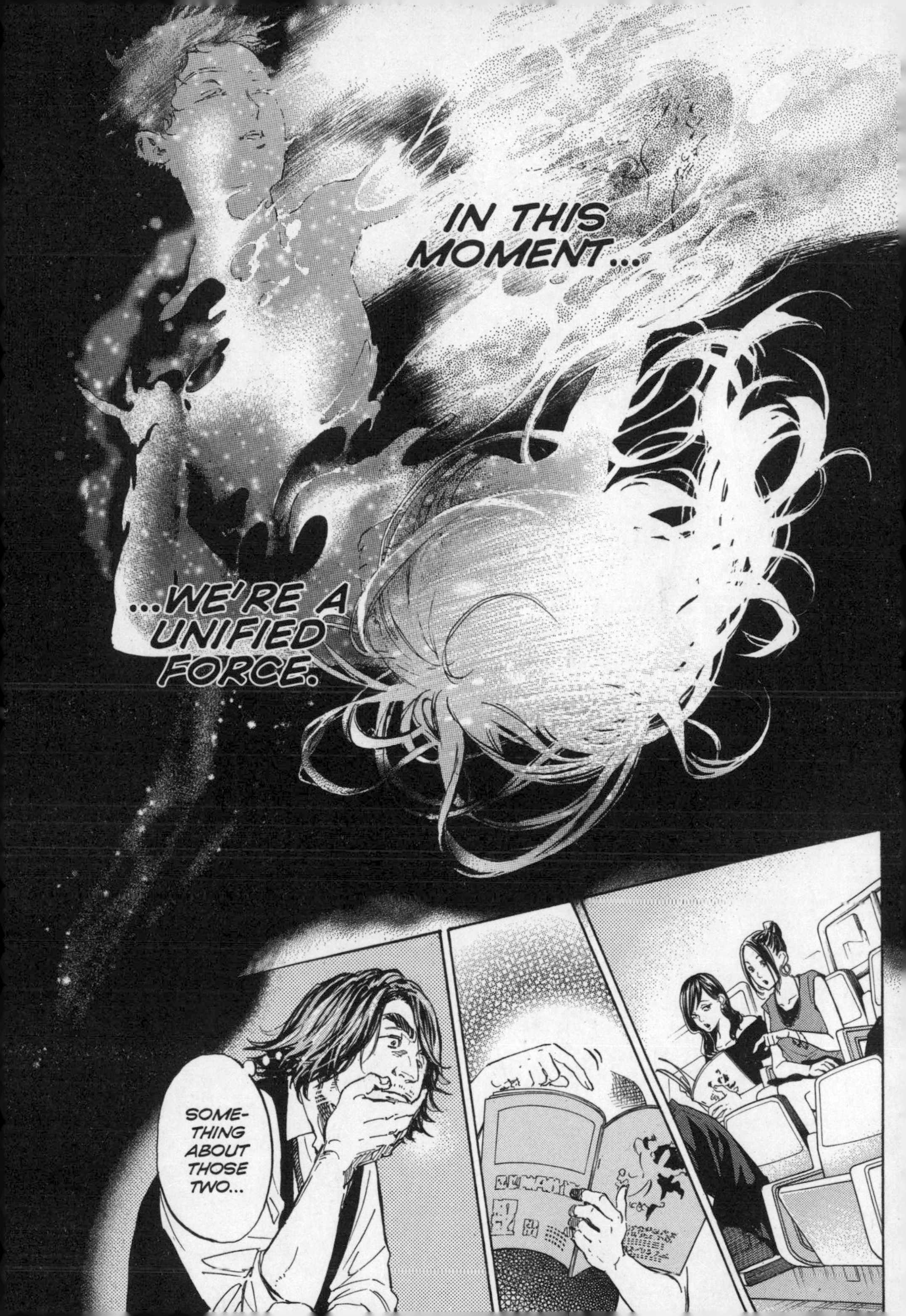
IN THIS MOMENT...
...WE'RE A UNIFIED FORCE.
SOME-THING ABOUT THOSE TWO...

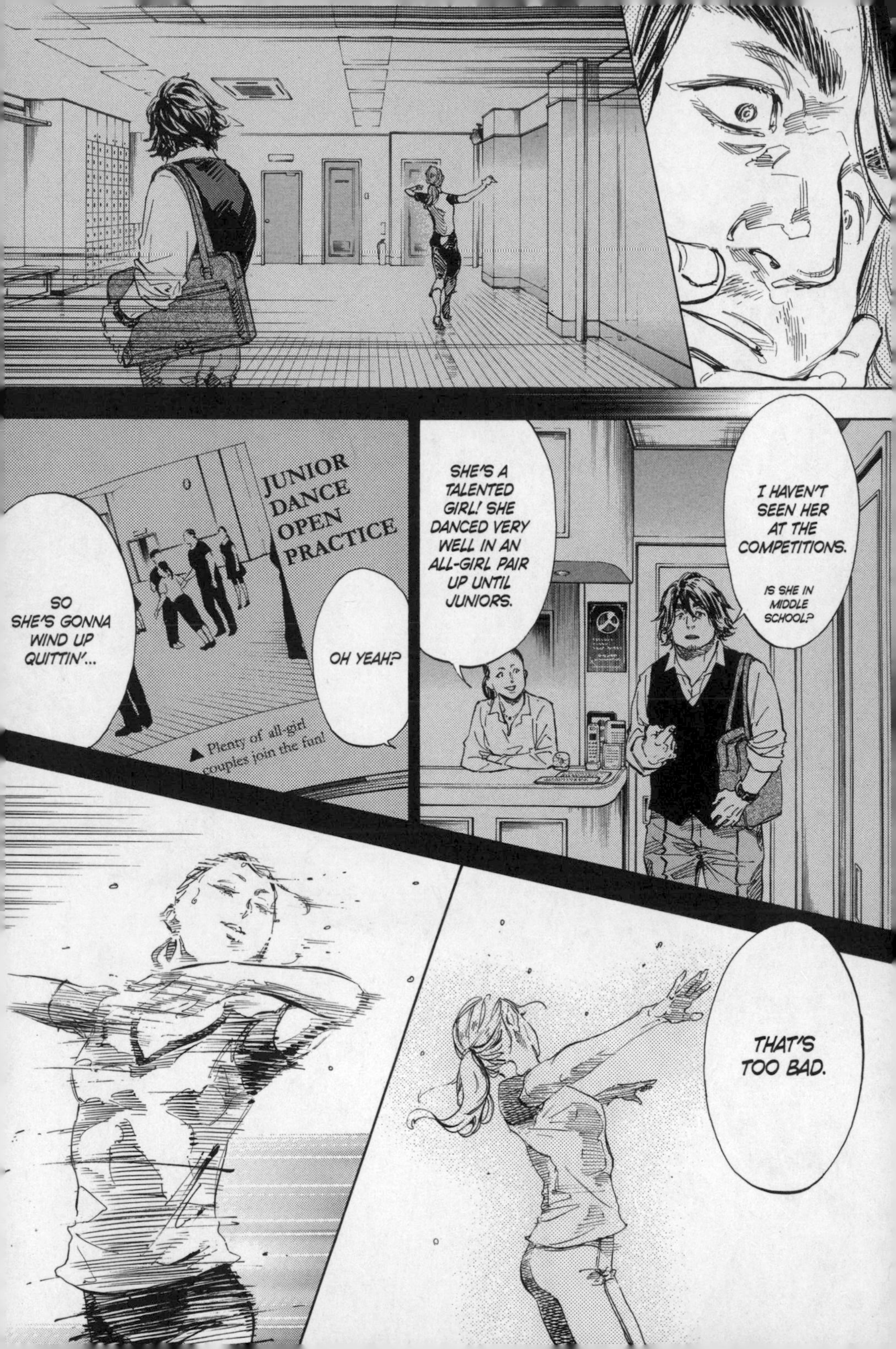
I HAVEN'T SEEN HER AT THE COMPETITIONS.
IS SHE IN MIDDLE SCHOOL?
SHE'S A TALENTED GIRL! SHE DANCED VERY WELL IN AN ALL-GIRL PAIR UP UNTIL JUNIORS.
OH YEAH?
JUNIOR DANCE OPEN PRACTICE
▲ Plenty of all-girl couples join the fun!
SO SHE'S GONNA WIND UP QUITTIN'...
THAT'S TOO BAD.

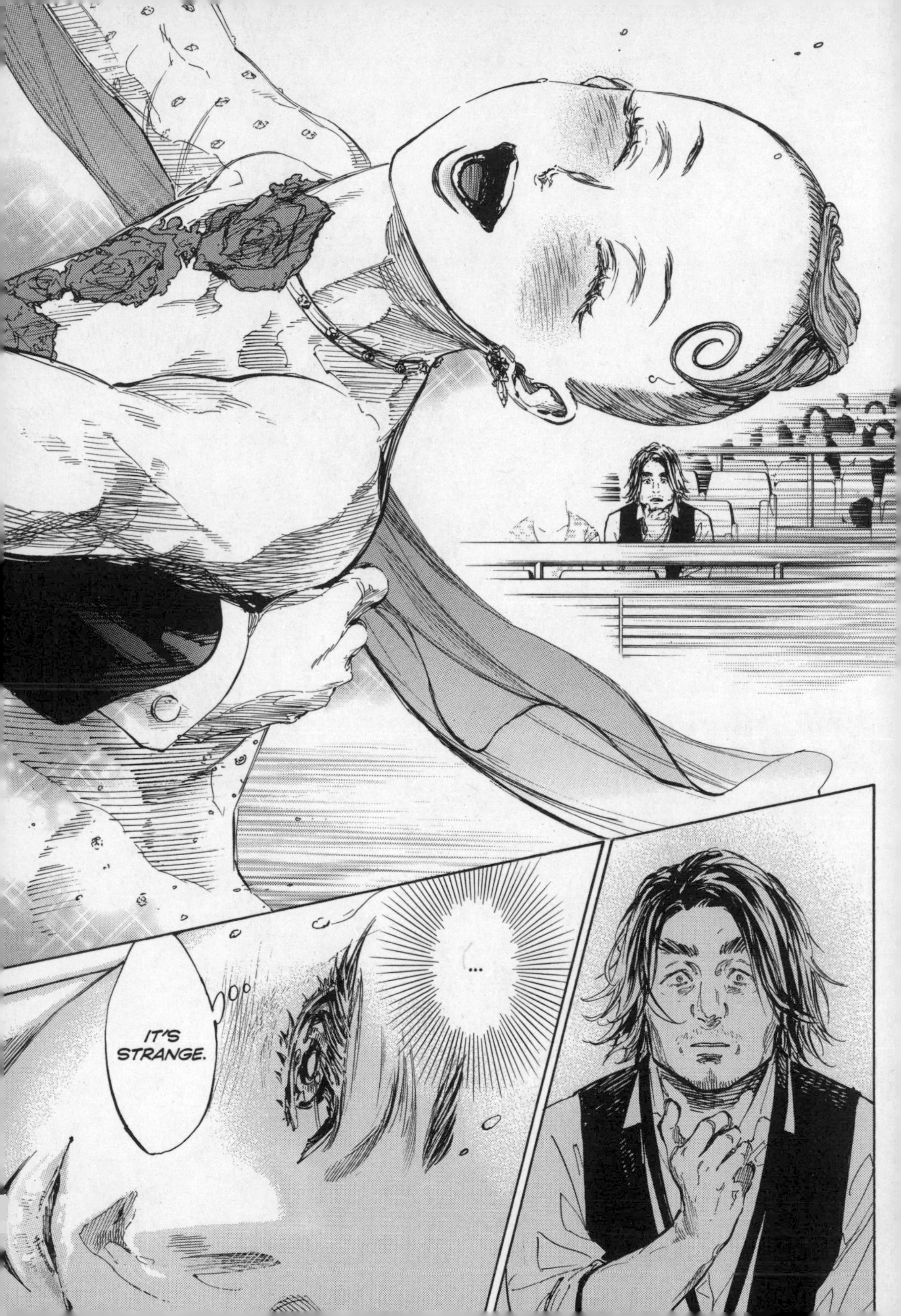
...
IT'S STRANGE.

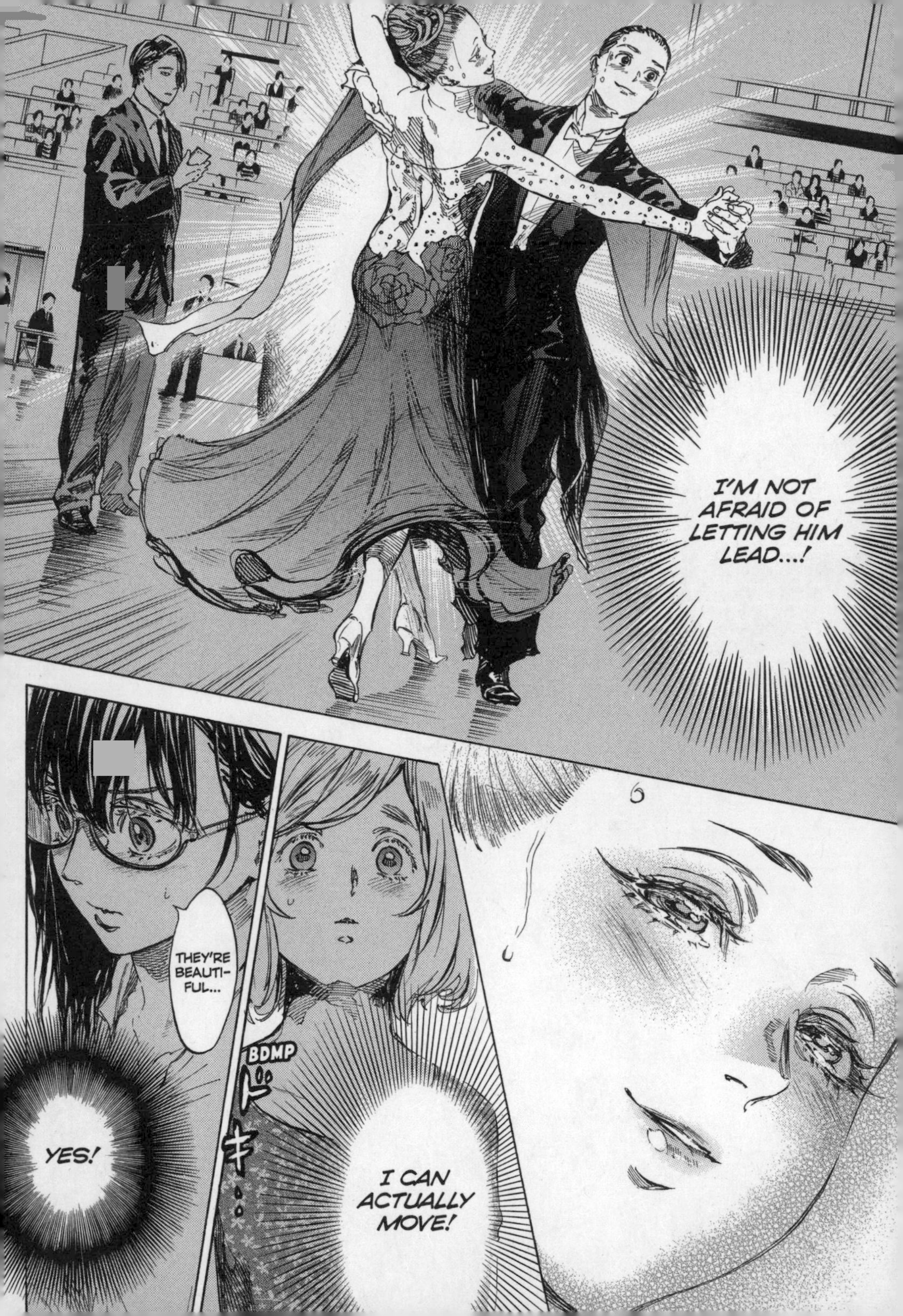
I'M NOT AFRAID OF LETTING HIM LEAD...!
BDMP
ドキ...
I CAN ACTUALLY MOVE!
THEY'RE BEAUTI-FUL...
YES!

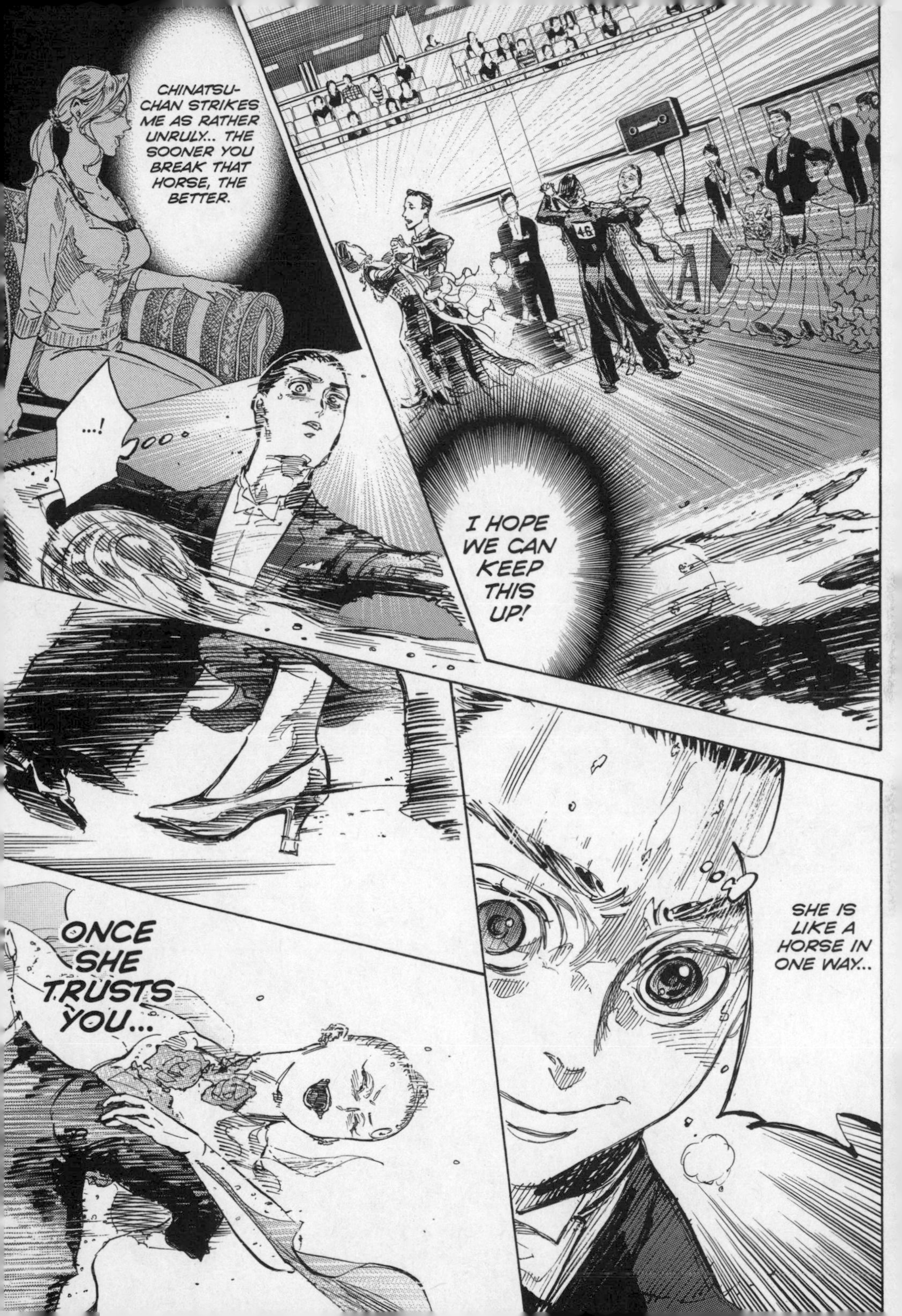
I HOPE WE CAN KEEP THIS UP!
CHINATSU-CHAN STRIKES ME AS RATHER UNRULY... THE SOONER YOU BREAK THAT HORSE, THE BETTER.
...!
SHE IS LIKE A HORSE IN ONE WAY...
ONCE SHE TRUSTS YOU...

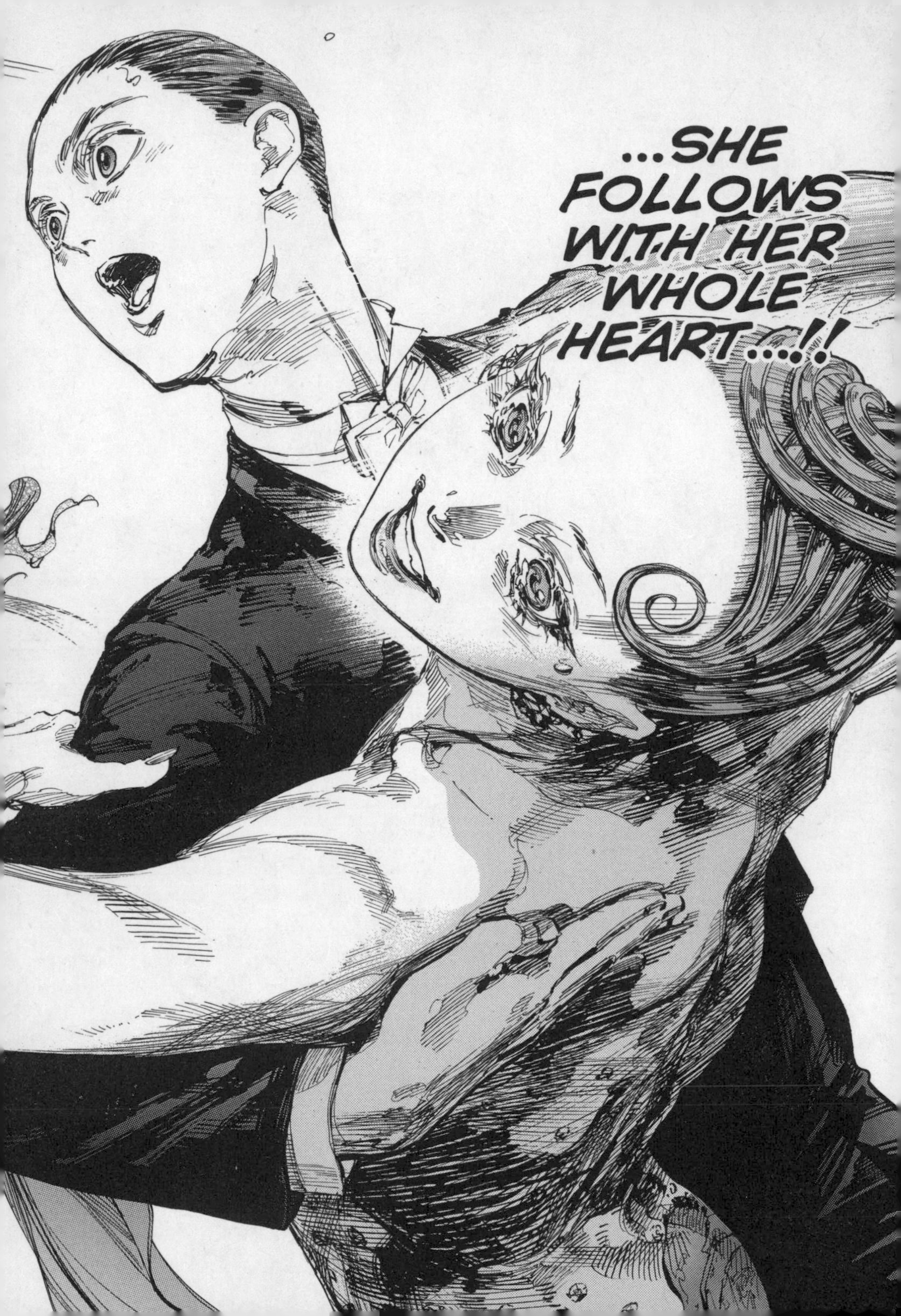
...SHE FOLLOWS WITH HER WHOLE HEART...!!

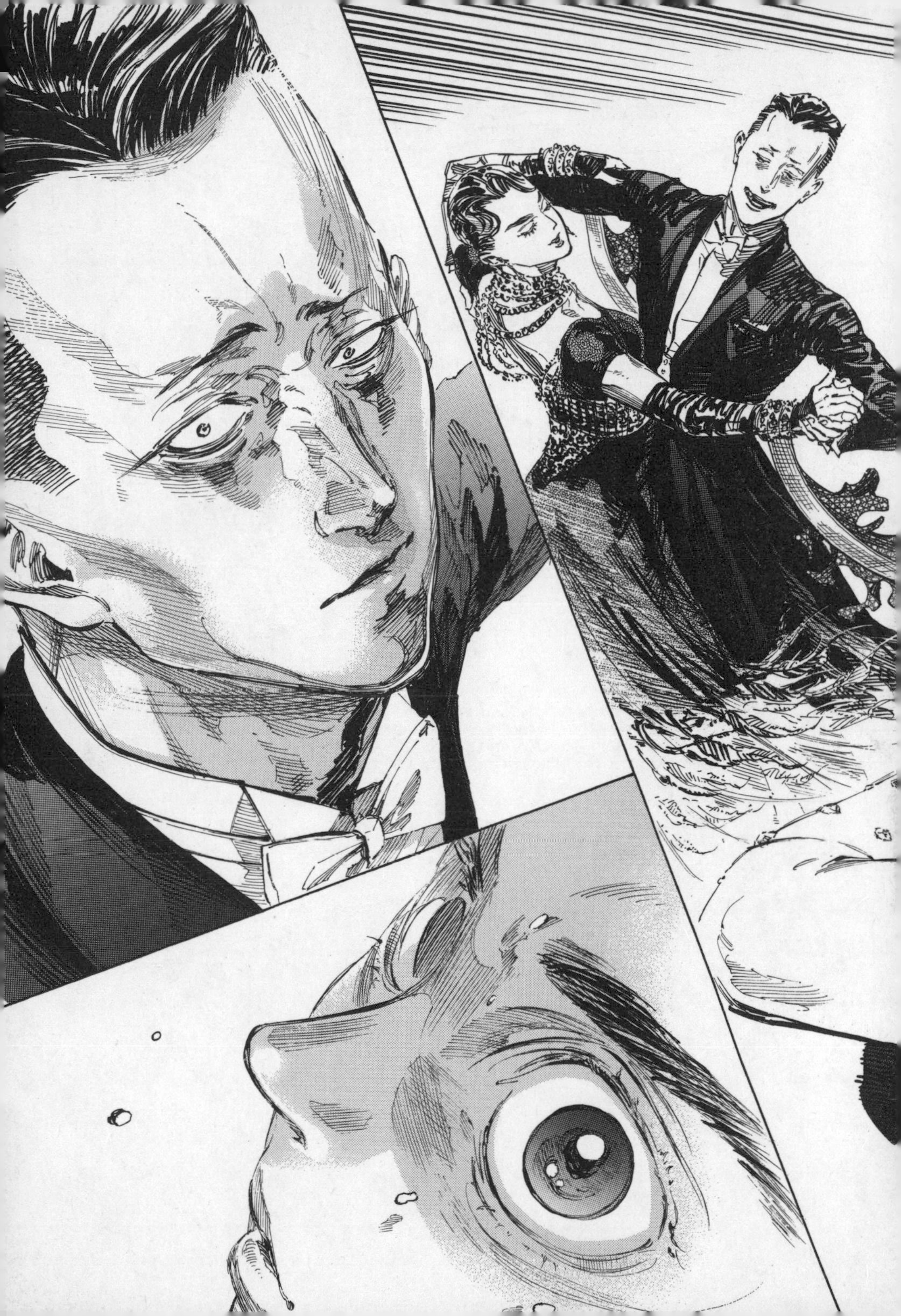

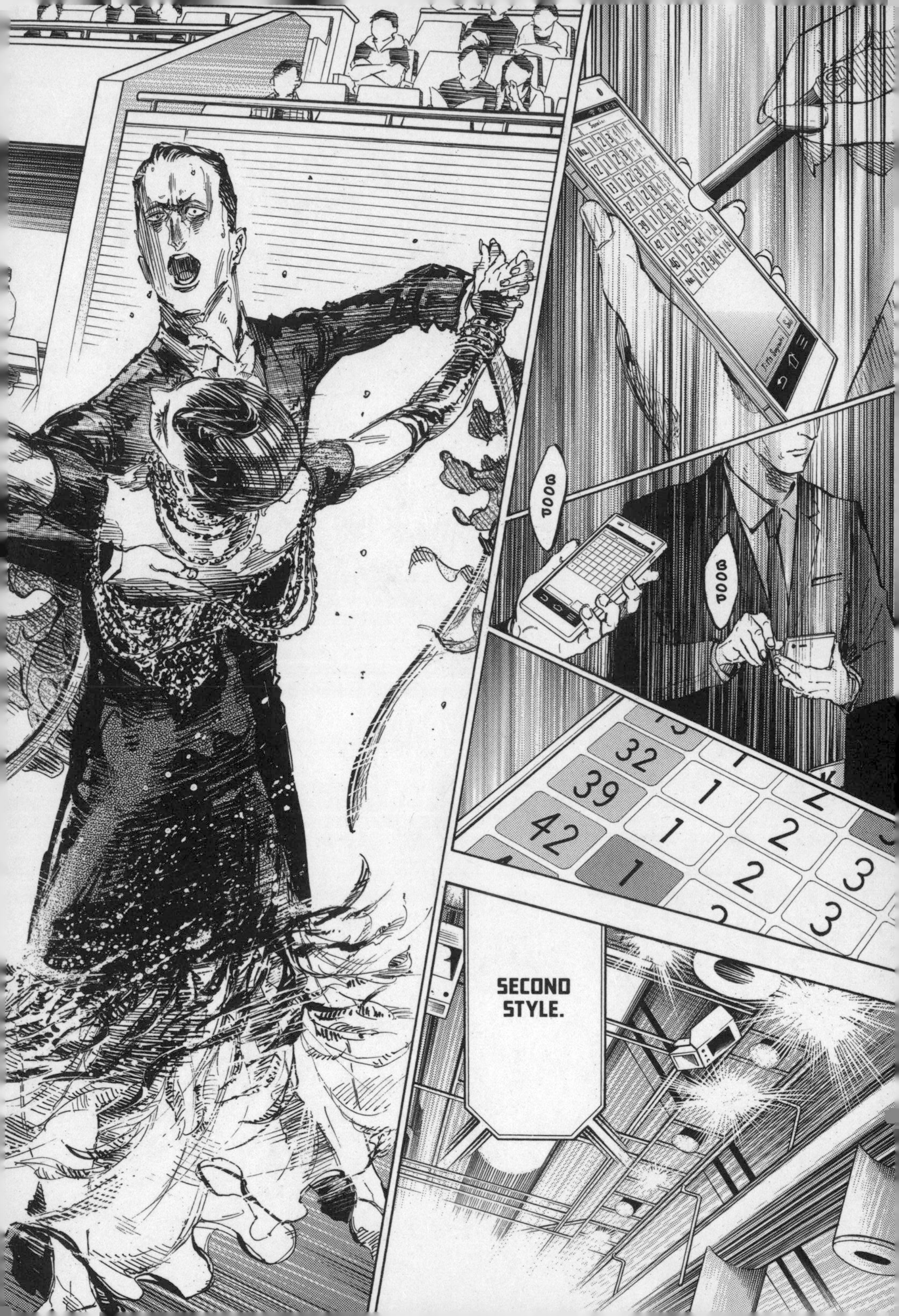
BOOP
BOOP
SECOND STYLE.

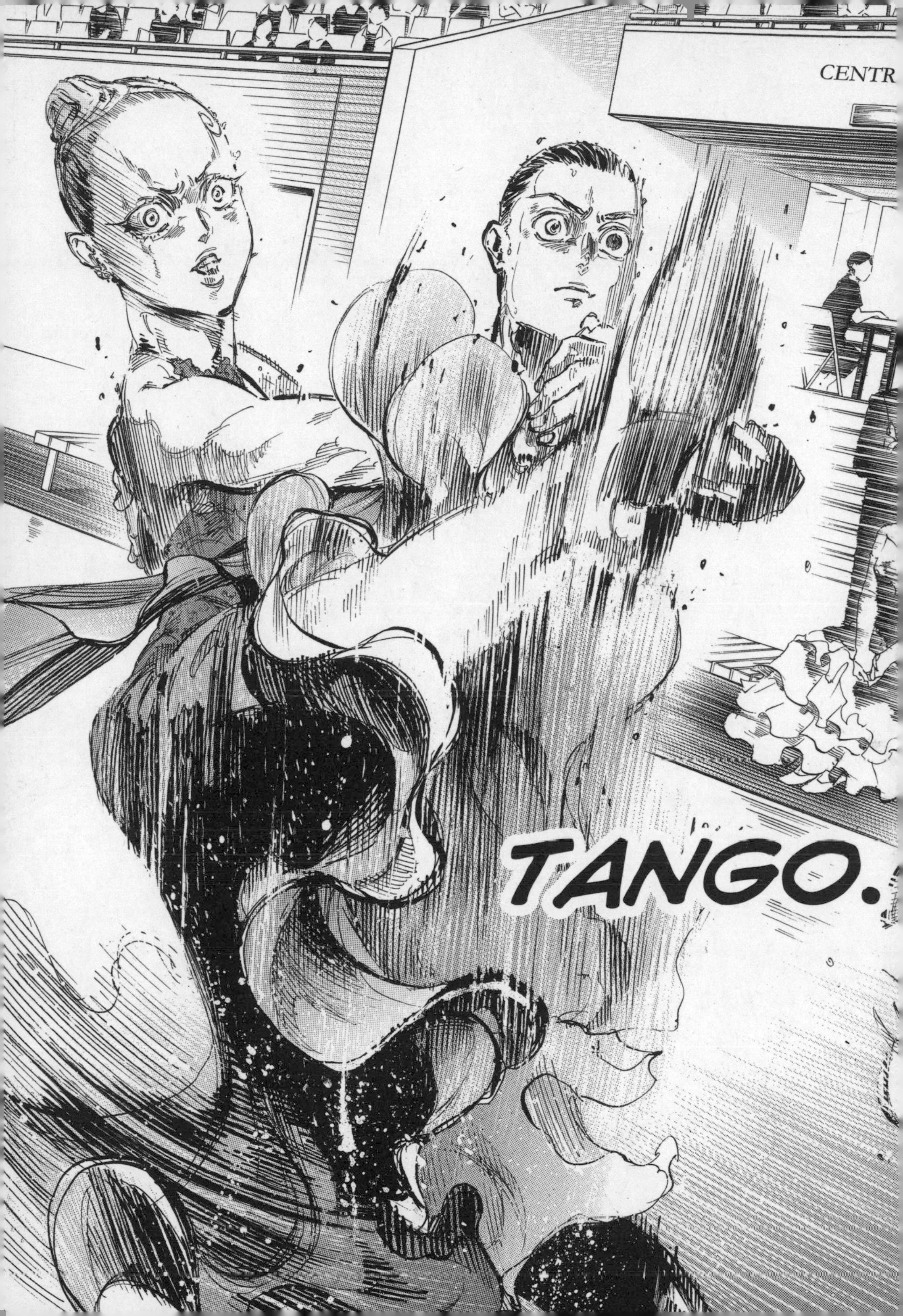
CENTR
TANGO.

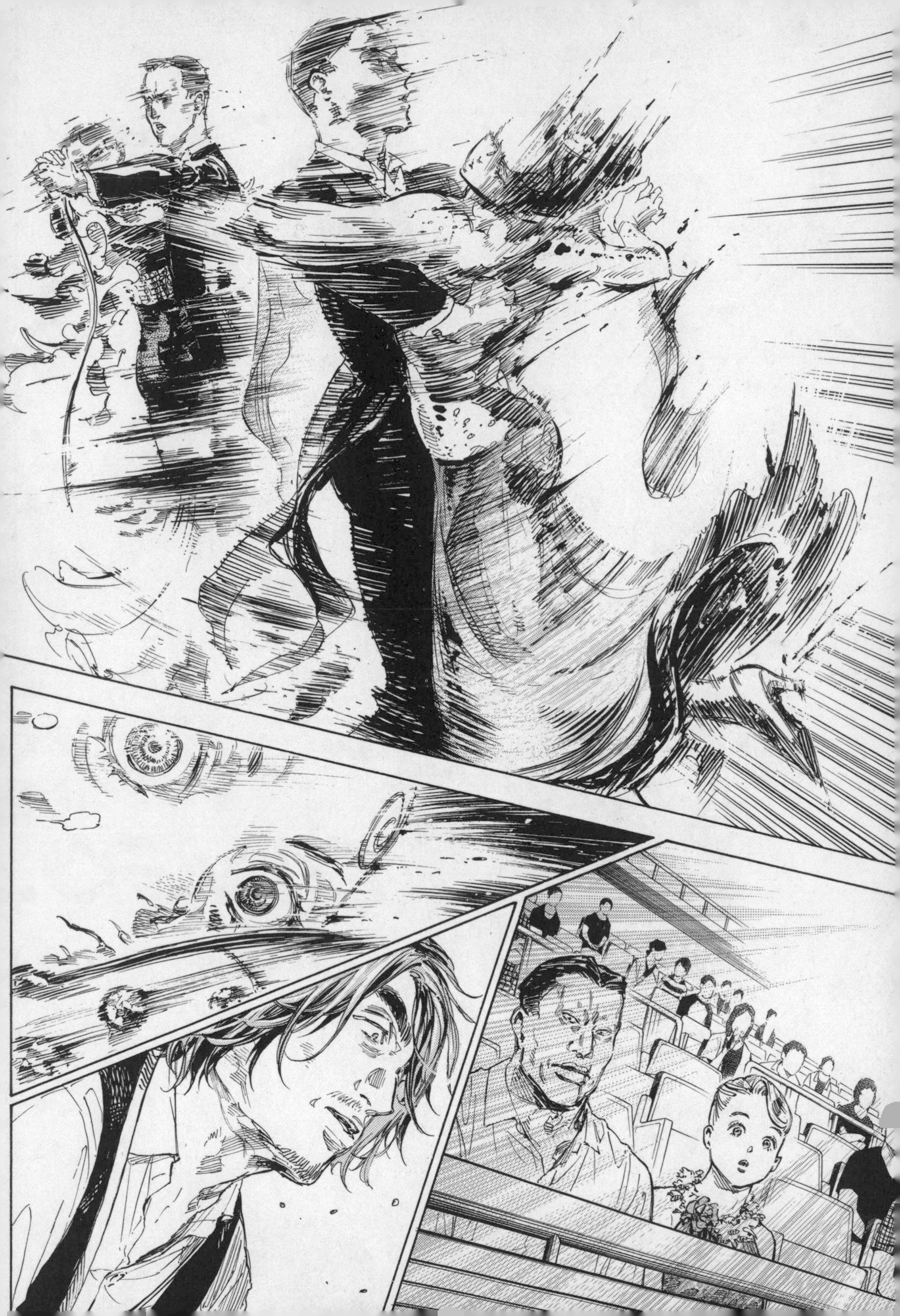

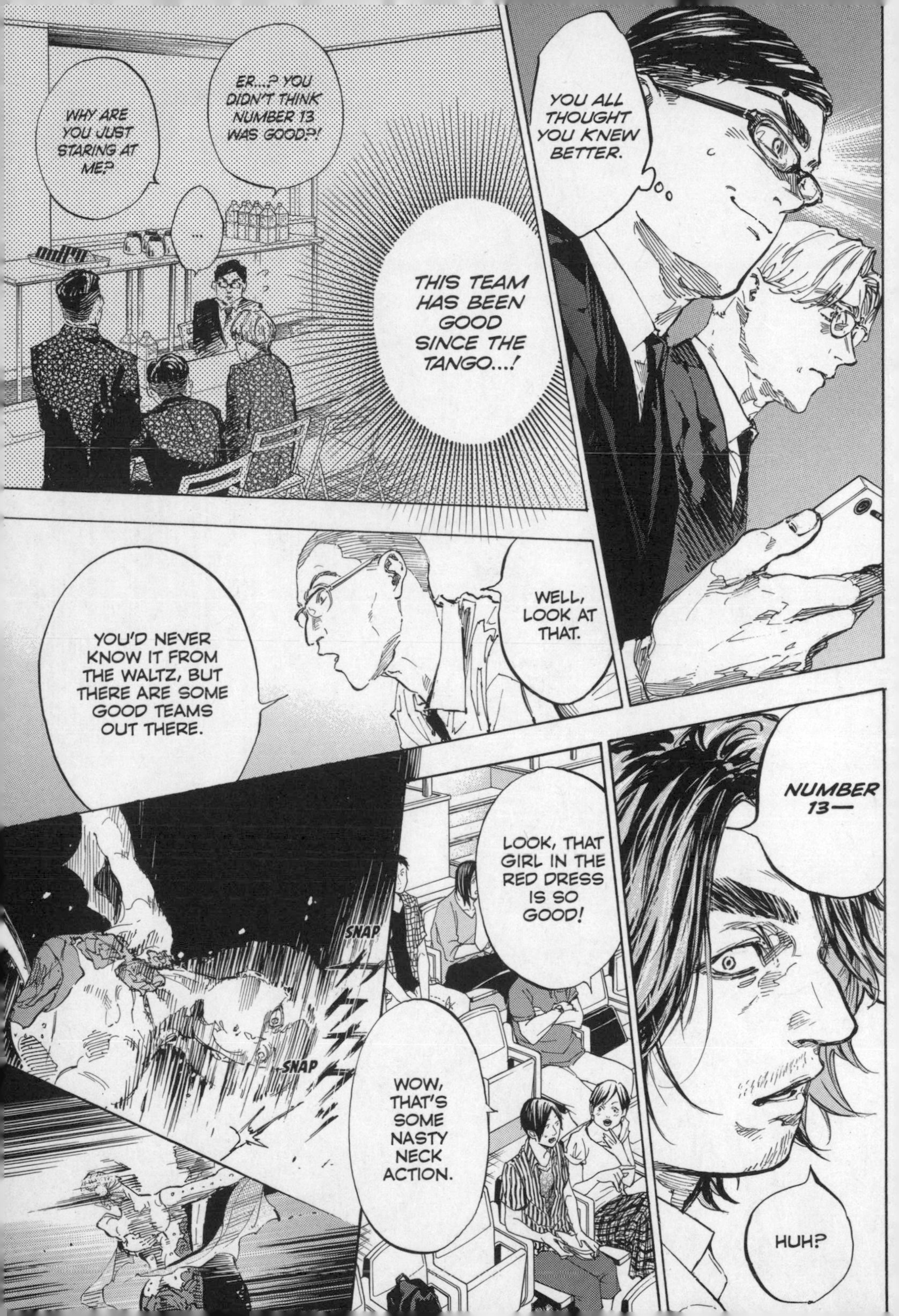
YOU ALL THOUGHT YOU KNEW BETTER.
THIS TEAM HAS BEEN GOOD SINCE THE TANGO...!
ER...? YOU DIDN'T THINK NUMBER 13 WAS GOOD?!
...
WHY ARE YOU JUST STARING AT ME?
WELL, LOOK AT THAT.
YOU'D NEVER KNOW IT FROM THE WALTZ, BUT THERE ARE SOME GOOD TEAMS OUT THERE.
NUMBER 13—
HUH?
LOOK, THAT GIRL IN THE RED DRESS IS SO GOOD!
WOW, THAT'S SOME NASTY NECK ACTION.
SNAP
SNAP

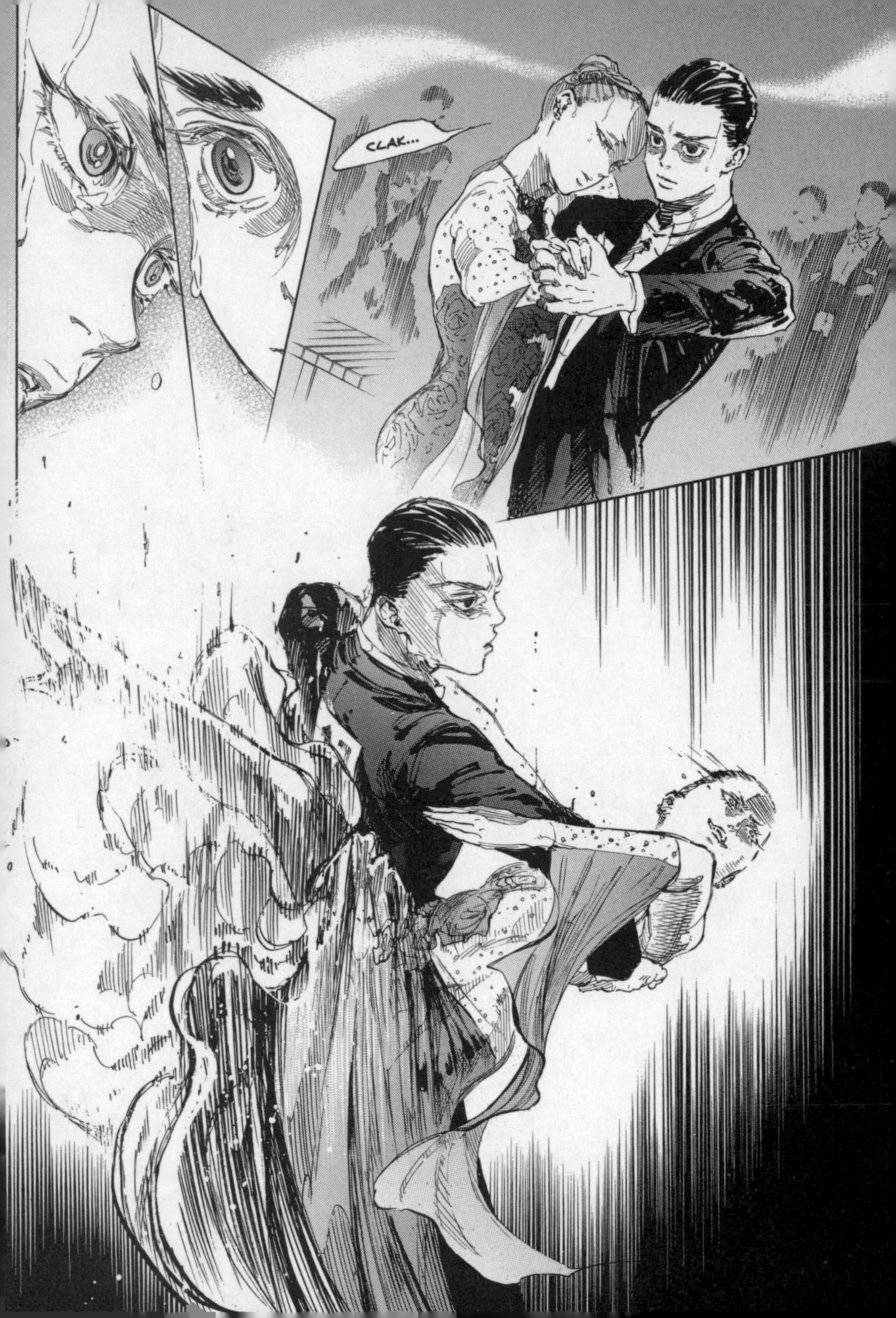
CLAK...

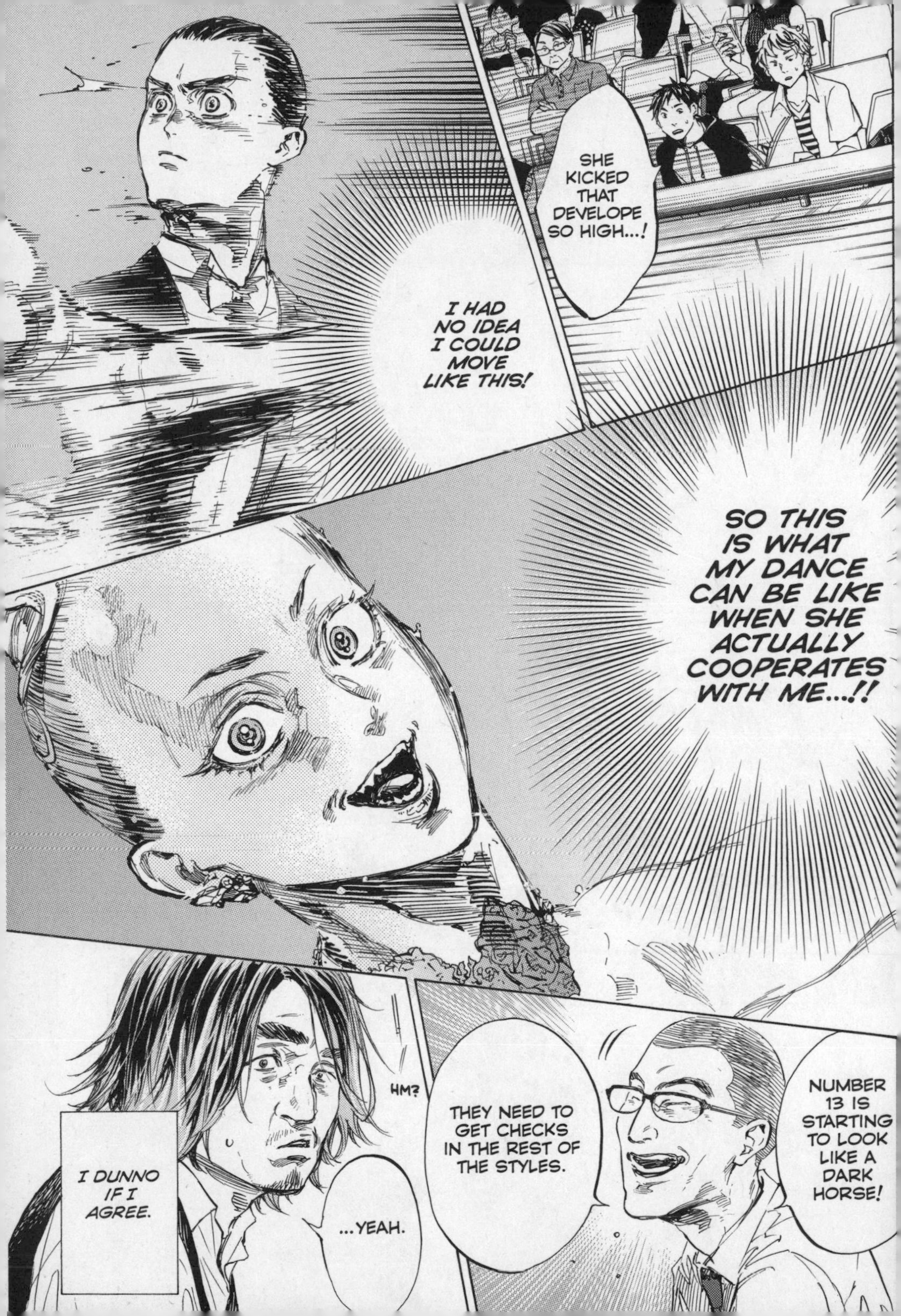
SHE KICKED THAT DEVELOPE SO HIGH...!
I HAD NO IDEA I COULD MOVE LIKE THIS!
SO THIS IS WHAT MY DANCE CAN BE LIKE WHEN SHE ACTUALLY COOPERATES WITH ME...!!
NUMBER 13 IS STARTING TO LOOK LIKE A DARK HORSE!
THEY NEED TO GET CHECKS IN THE REST OF THE STYLES.
HM?
...YEAH.
I DUNNO IF I AGREE.

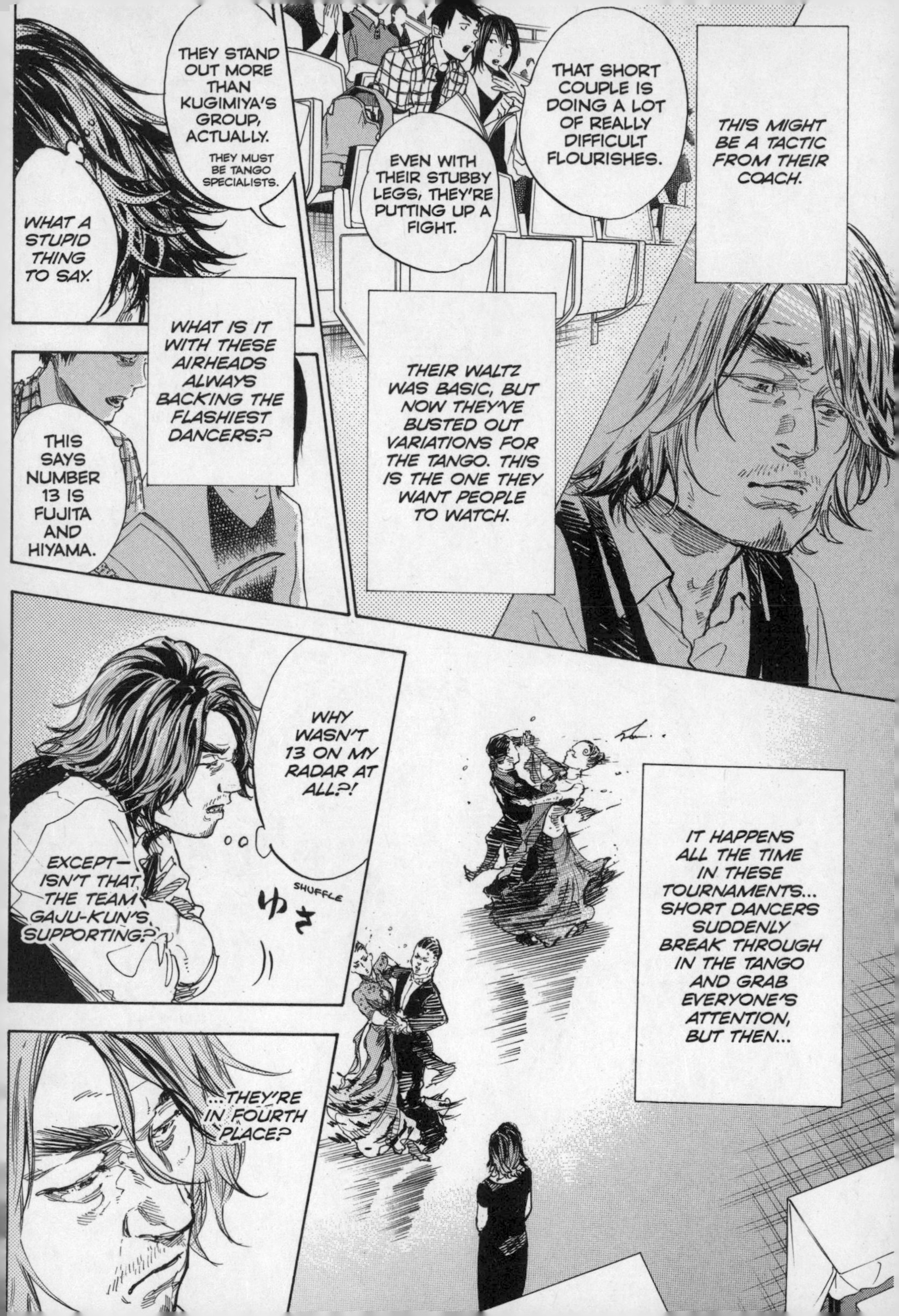
THIS MIGHT BE A TACTIC FROM THEIR COACH.
THEIR WALTZ WAS BASIC, BUT NOW THEY'VE BUSTED OUT VARIATIONS FOR THE TANGO. THIS IS THE ONE THEY WANT PEOPLE TO WATCH.
THAT SHORT COUPLE IS DOING A LOT OF REALLY DIFFICULT FLOURISHES.
EVEN WITH THEIR STUBBY LEGS, THEY'RE PUTTING UP A FIGHT.
THEY STAND OUT MORE THAN KUGIMIYA'S GROUP, ACTUALLY.
THEY MUST BE TANGO SPECIALISTS.
WHAT A STUPID THING TO SAY.
WHAT IS IT WITH THESE AIRHEADS ALWAYS BACKING THE FLASHIEST DANCERS?
THIS SAYS NUMBER 13 IS FUJITA AND HIYAMA.
IT HAPPENS ALL THE TIME IN THESE TOURNAMENTS... SHORT DANCERS SUDDENLY BREAK THROUGH IN THE TANGO AND GRAB EVERYONE'S ATTENTION, BUT THEN...
WHY WASN'T 13 ON MY RADAR AT ALL?!
SHUFFLE
ゆさ
EXCEPT— ISN'T THAT THE TEAM GAJU-KUN'S SUPPORTING?
...THEY'RE IN FOURTH PLACE?

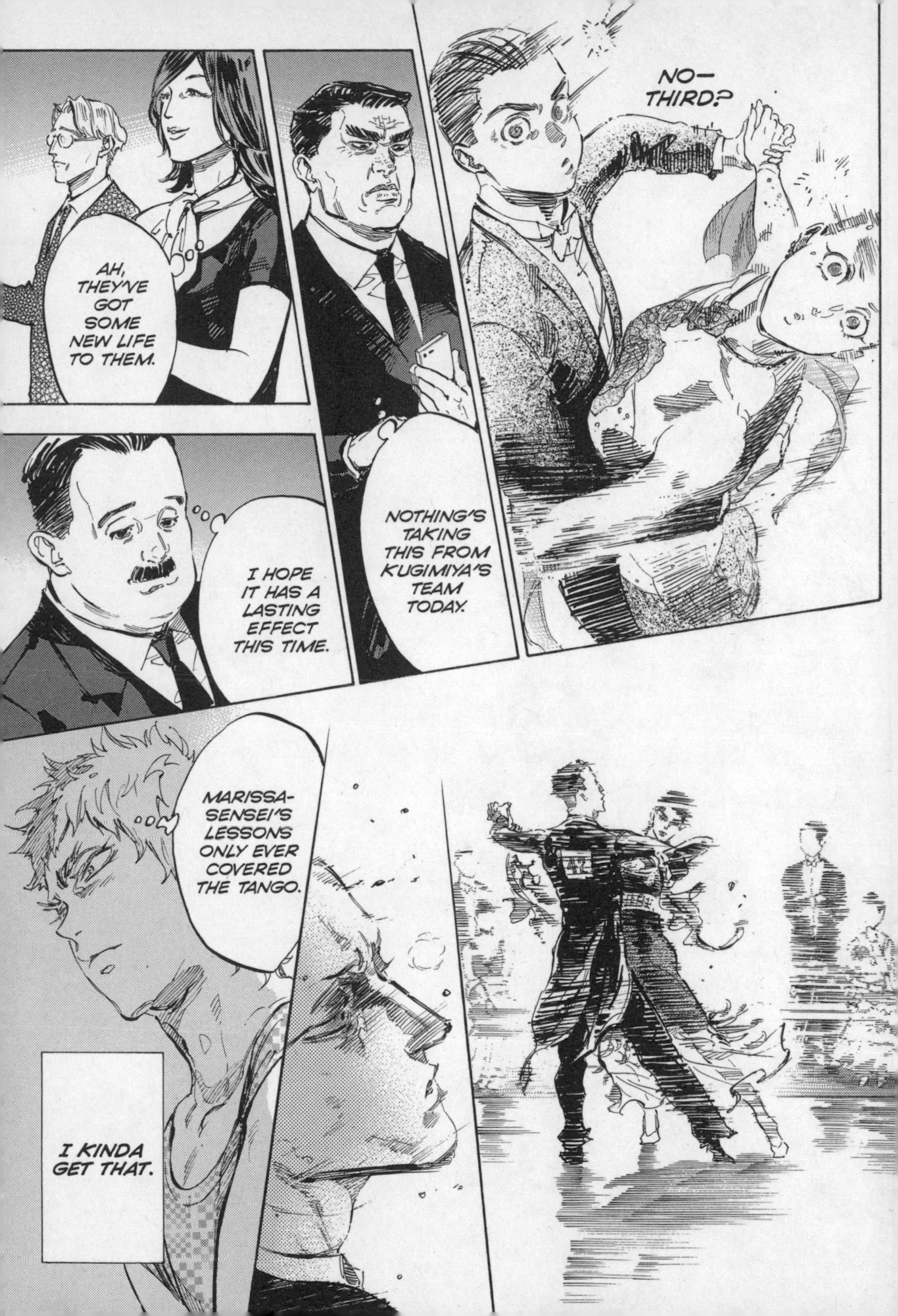
NO— THIRD?
NOTHING'S TAKING THIS FROM KUGIMIYA'S TEAM TODAY.
AH, THEY'VE GOT SOME NEW LIFE TO THEM.
I HOPE IT HAS A LASTING EFFECT THIS TIME.
MARISSA-SENSEI'S LESSONS ONLY EVER COVERED THE TANGO.
I KINDA GET THAT.

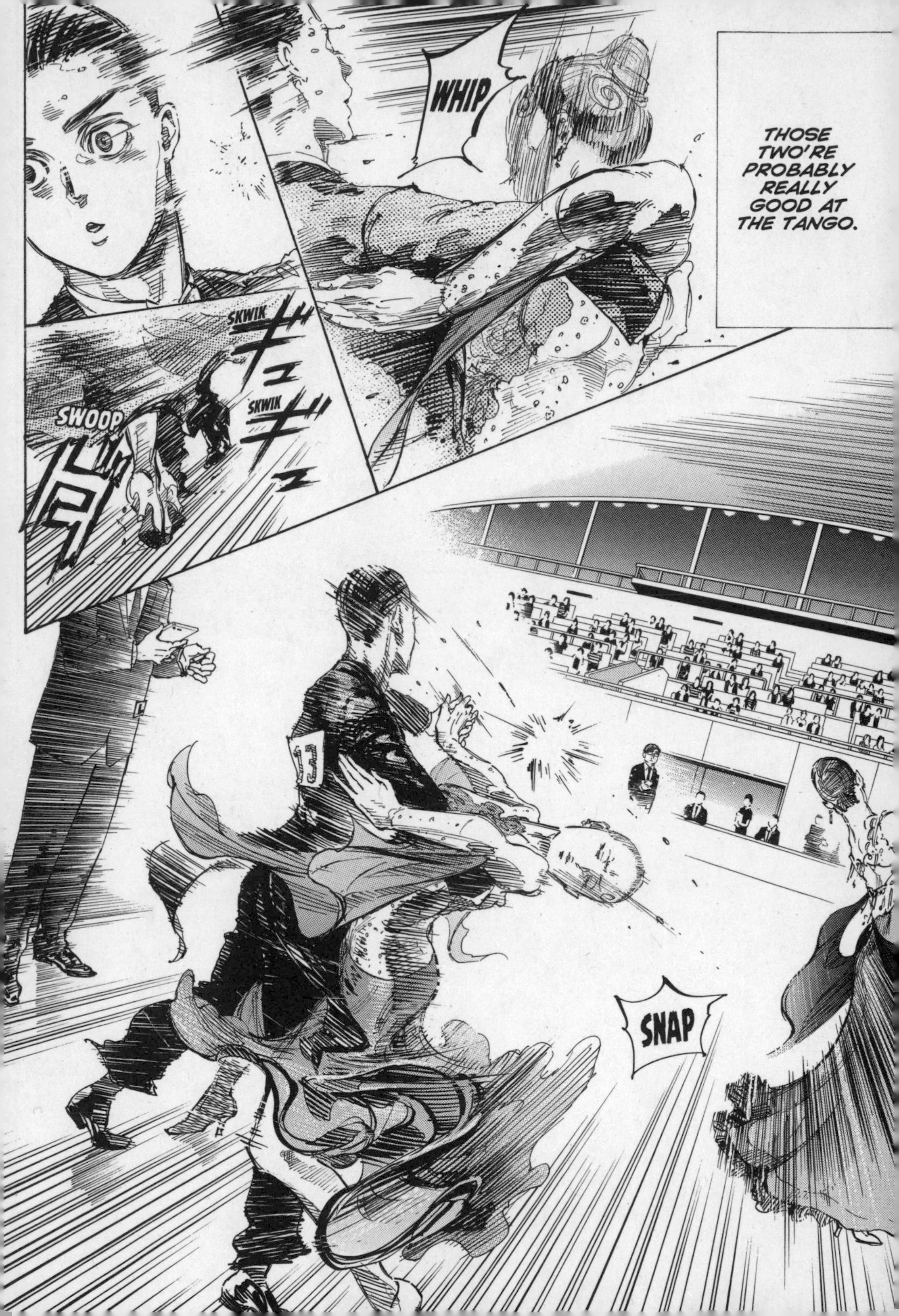
THOSE TWO'RE PROBABLY REALLY GOOD AT THE TANGO.
WHIP
SKWIK
SKWIK
SWOOP
SNAP

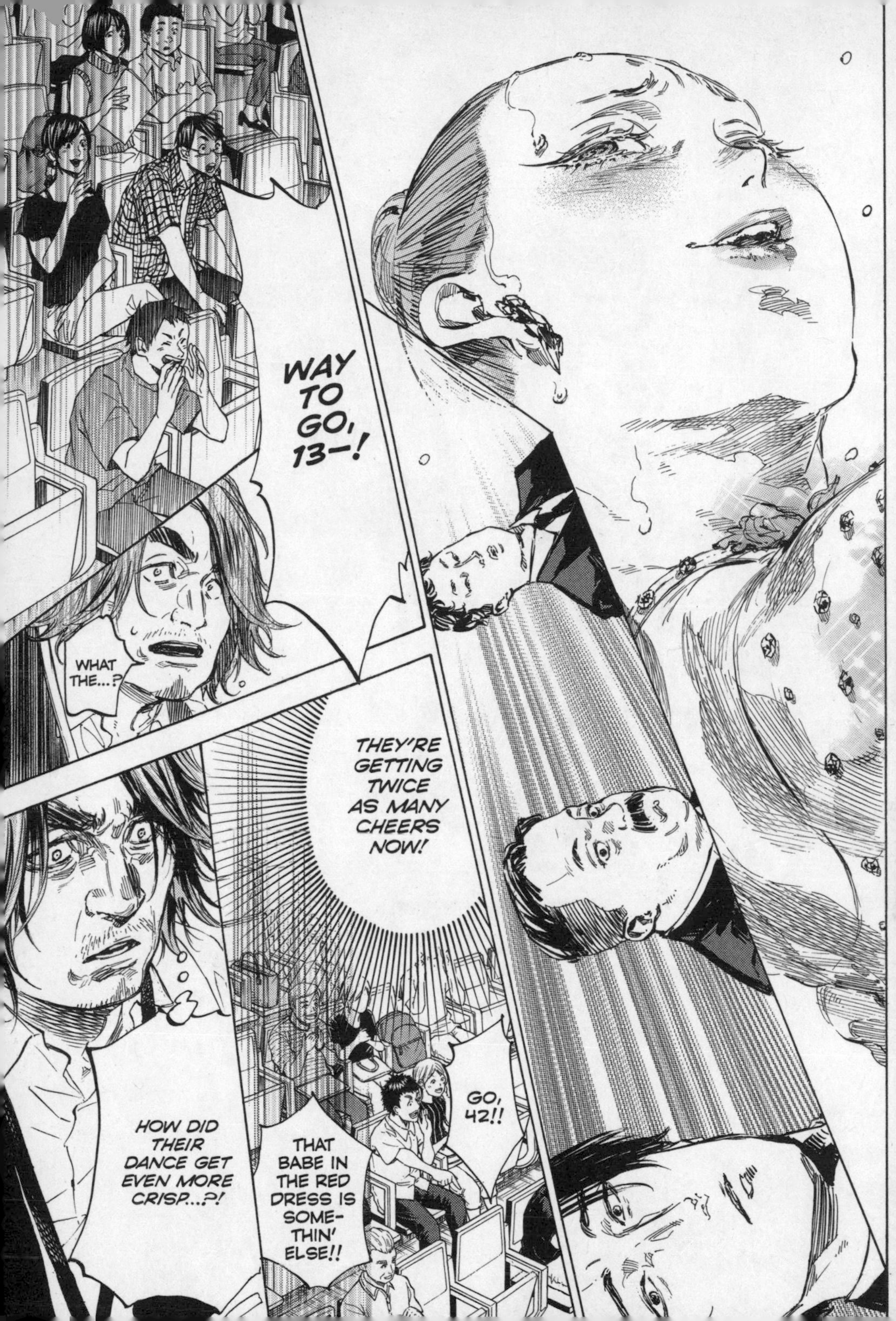
WAY TO GO, 13—!
WHAT THE...?
THEY'RE GETTING TWICE AS MANY CHEERS NOW!
GO, 42!!
THAT BABE IN THE RED DRESS IS SOME-THIN' ELSE!!
HOW DID THEIR DANCE GET EVEN MORE CRISP...?!

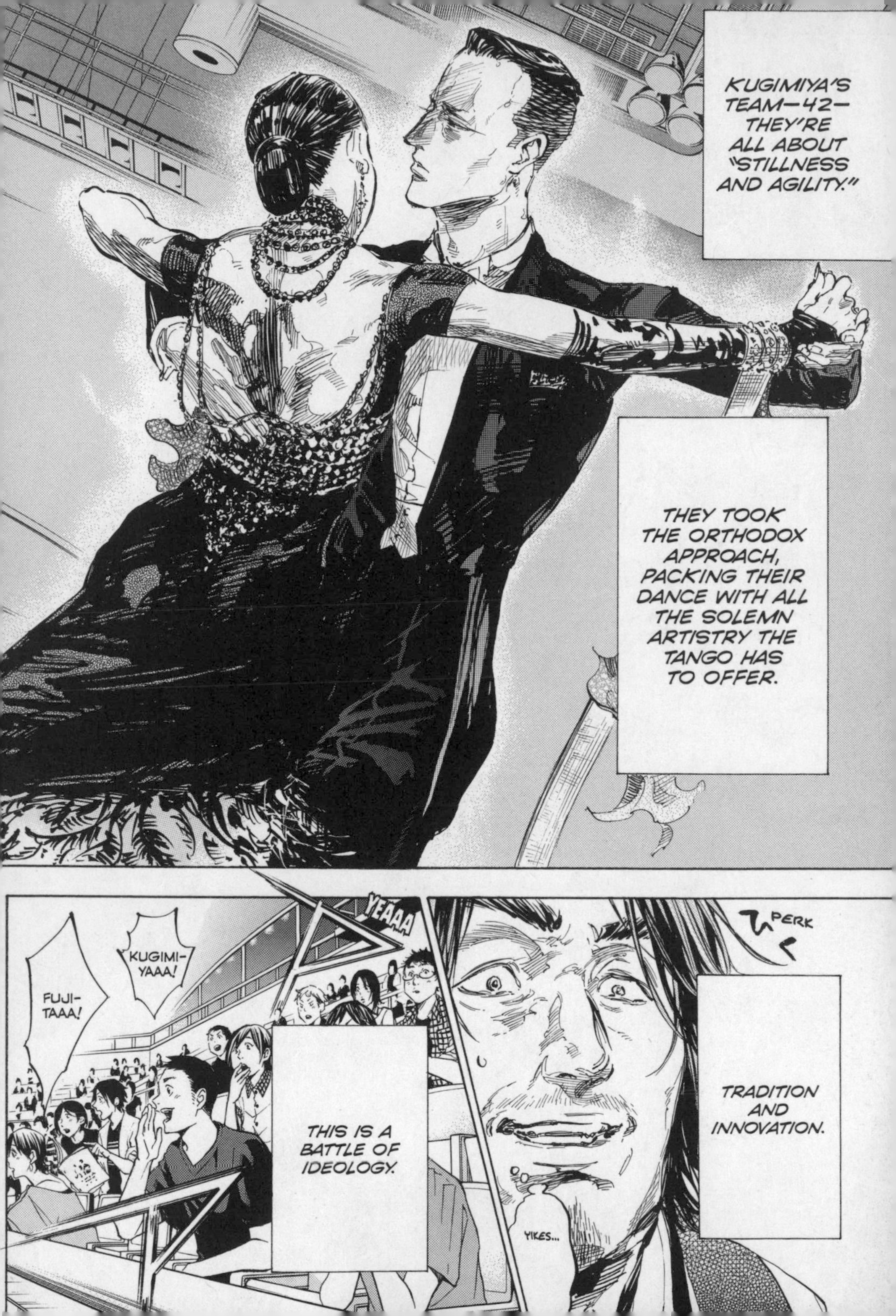
KUGIMIYA'S TEAM—42—THEY'RE ALL ABOUT "STILLNESS AND AGILITY."
THEY TOOK THE ORTHODOX APPROACH, PACKING THEIR DANCE WITH ALL THE SOLEMN ARTISTRY THE TANGO HAS TO OFFER.
PERK
TRADITION AND INNOVATION.
YIKES...
YEAAA
KUGIMI-YAAA!
FUJI-TAAA!
THIS IS A BATTLE OF IDEOLOGY.

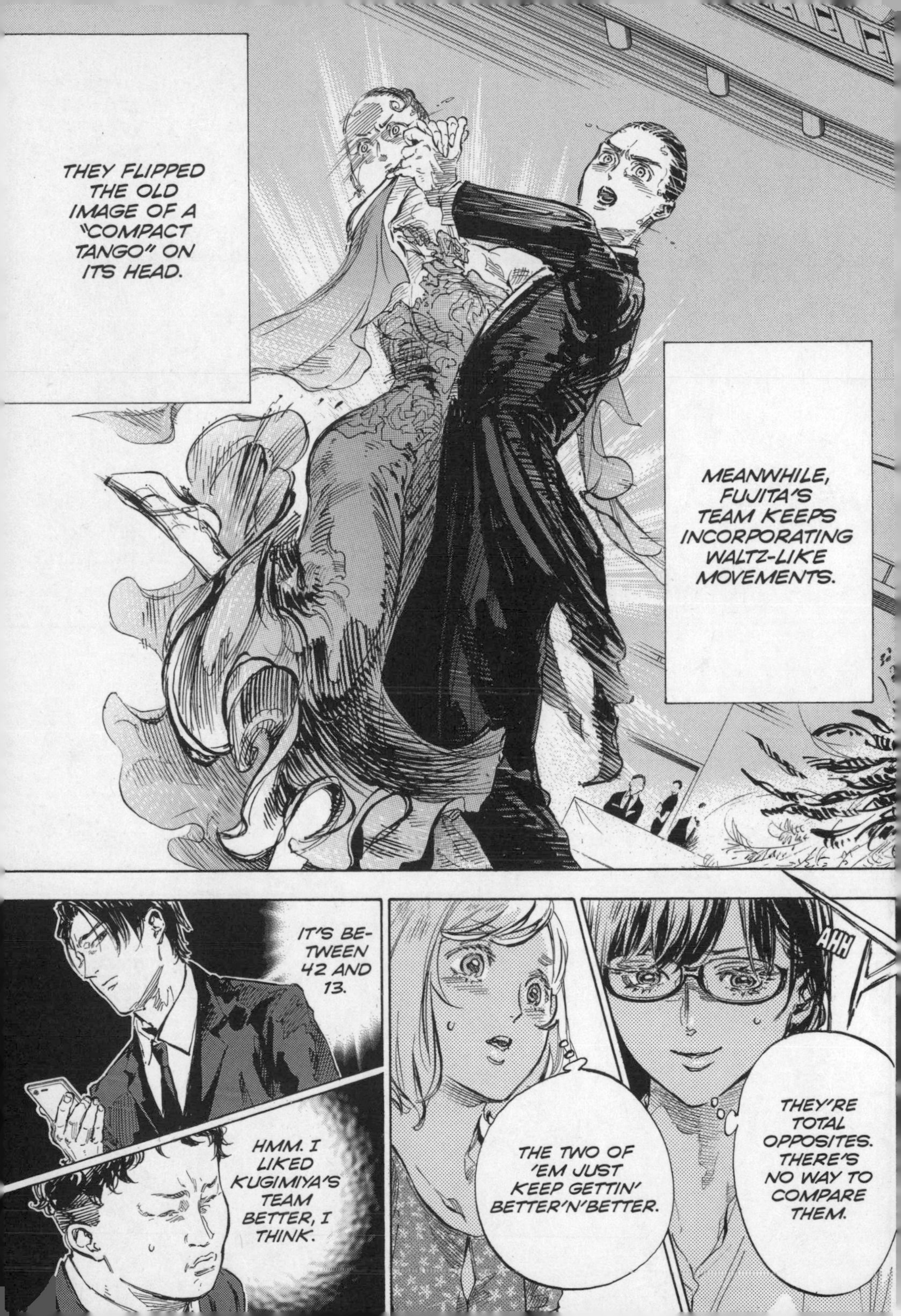
THEY FLIPPED THE OLD IMAGE OF A "COMPACT TANGO" ON ITS HEAD.
MEANWHILE, FUJITA'S TEAM KEEPS INCORPORATING WALTZ-LIKE MOVEMENTS.
AHH
THEY'RE TOTAL OPPOSITES. THERE'S NO WAY TO COMPARE THEM.
THE TWO OF 'EM JUST KEEP GETTIN' BETTER'N'BETTER.
IT'S BE-TWEEN 42 AND 13.
HMM. I LIKED KUGIMIYA'S TEAM BETTER, I THINK.

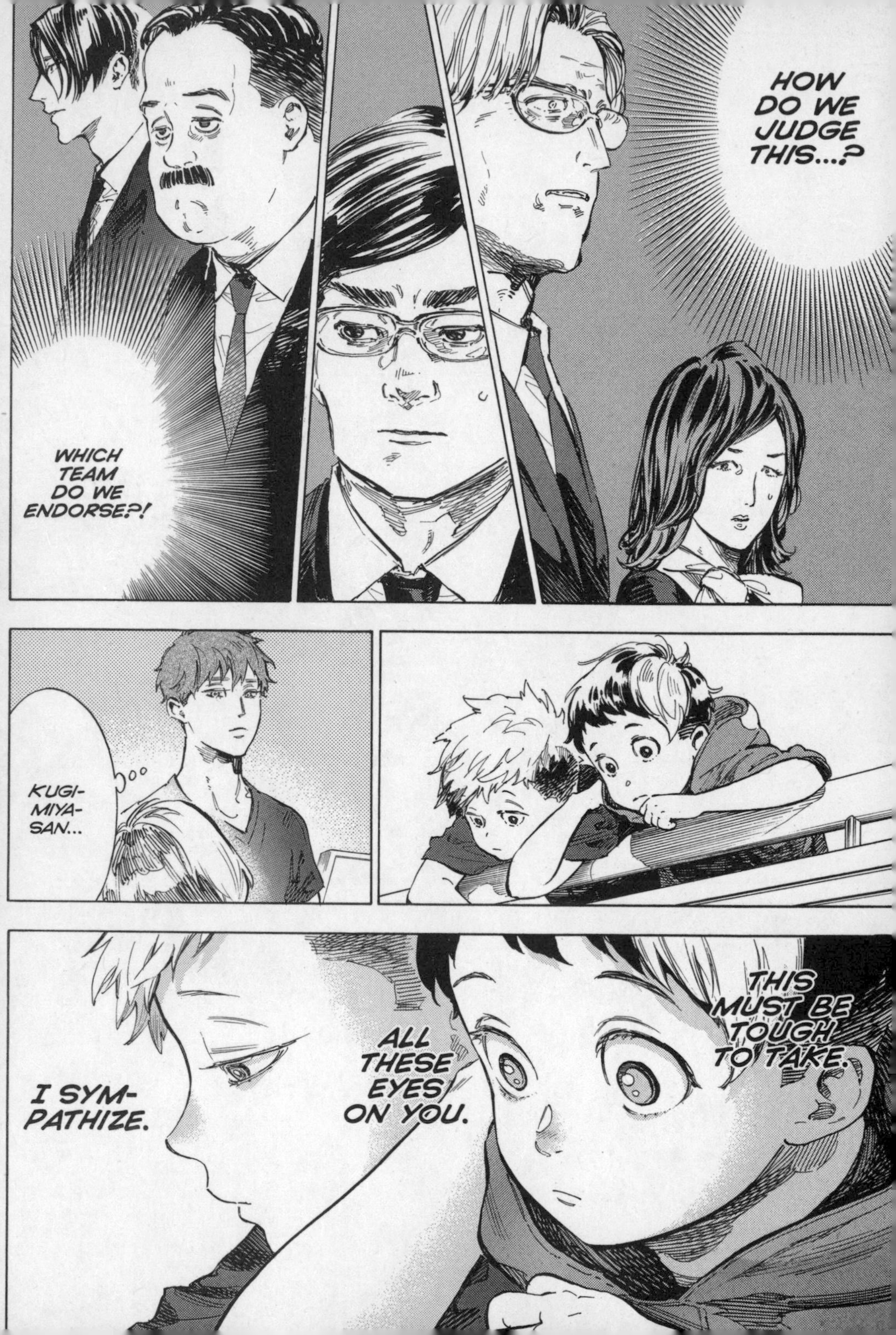
HOW DO WE JUDGE THIS...?
WHICH TEAM DO WE ENDORSE?!
KUGI-MIYA-SAN...
THIS MUST BE TOUGH TO TAKE.
ALL THESE EYES ON YOU.
I SYM-PATHIZE.

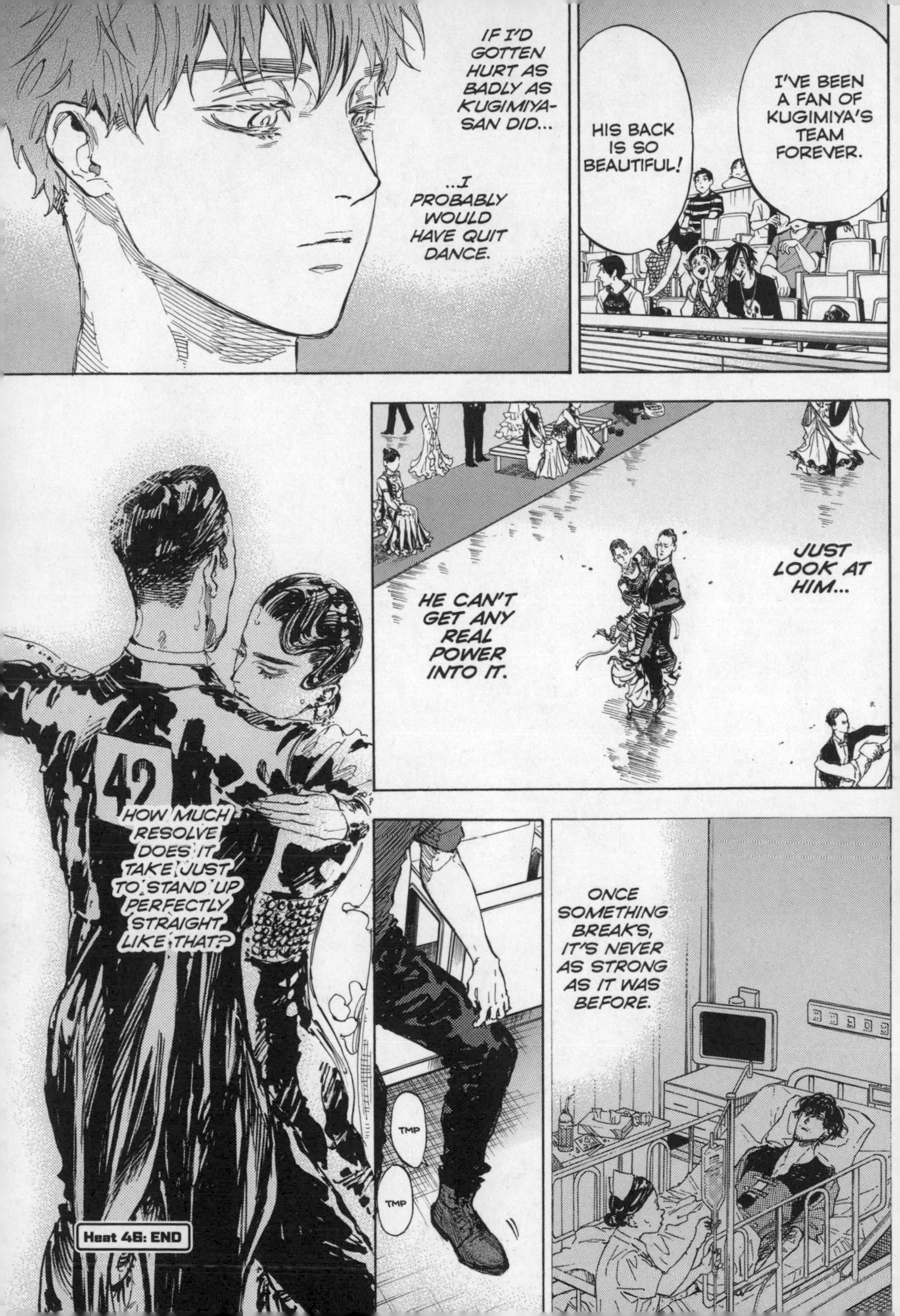
I'VE BEEN A FAN OF KUGIMIYA'S TEAM FOREVER.
HIS BACK IS SO BEAUTIFUL!
IF I'D GOTTEN HURT AS BADLY AS KUGIMIYA-SAN DID...
...I PROBABLY WOULD HAVE QUIT DANCE.
JUST LOOK AT HIM...
HE CAN'T GET ANY REAL POWER INTO IT.
ONCE SOMETHING BREAKS, IT'S NEVER AS STRONG AS IT WAS BEFORE.
TMP
TMP
HOW MUCH RESOLVE DOES IT TAKE JUST TO STAND UP PERFECTLY STRAIGHT LIKE THAT?
Heat 46: END

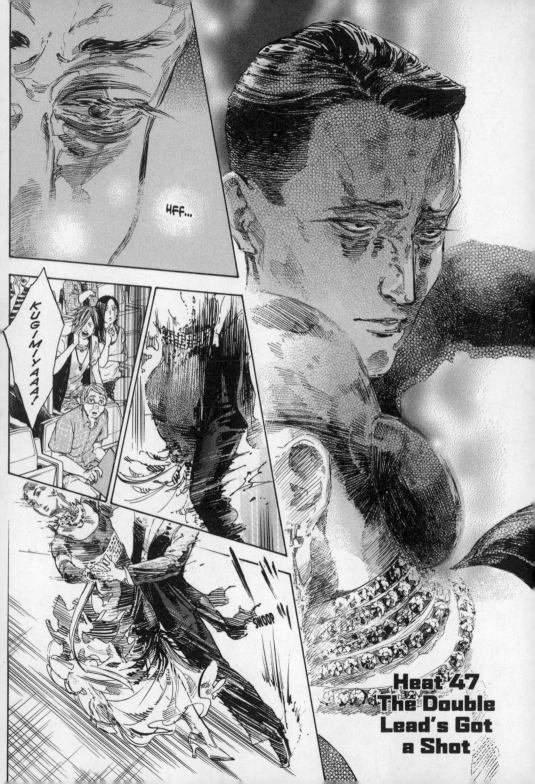

Heat 47
The Double
Lead's Got
a Shot

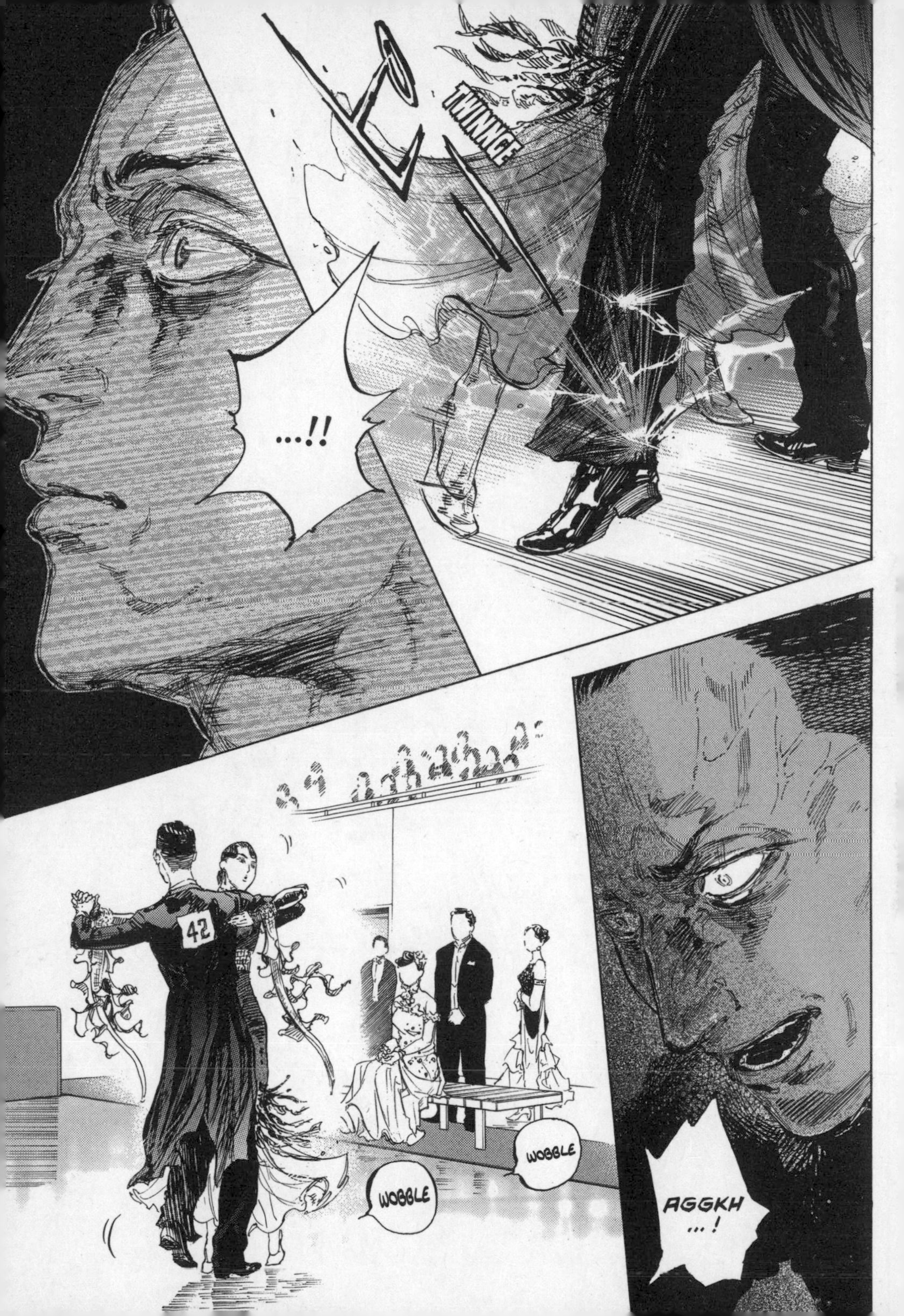
TWINNGE
...!!
AGGKH ...!
WOBBLE
WOBBLE

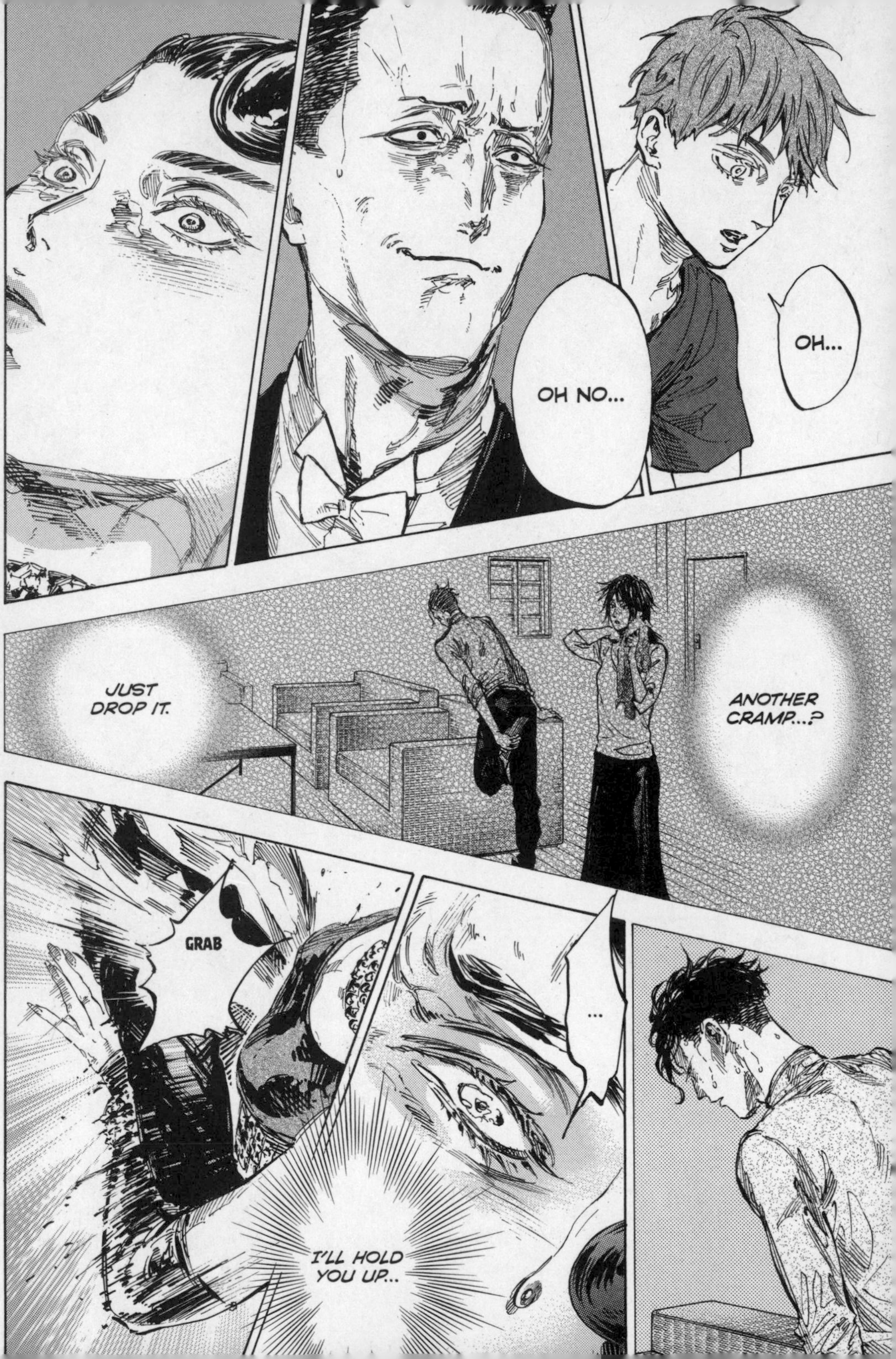
OH...
OH NO...
ANOTHER CRAMP...?
JUST DROP IT.
...
GRAB
I'LL HOLD YOU UP...

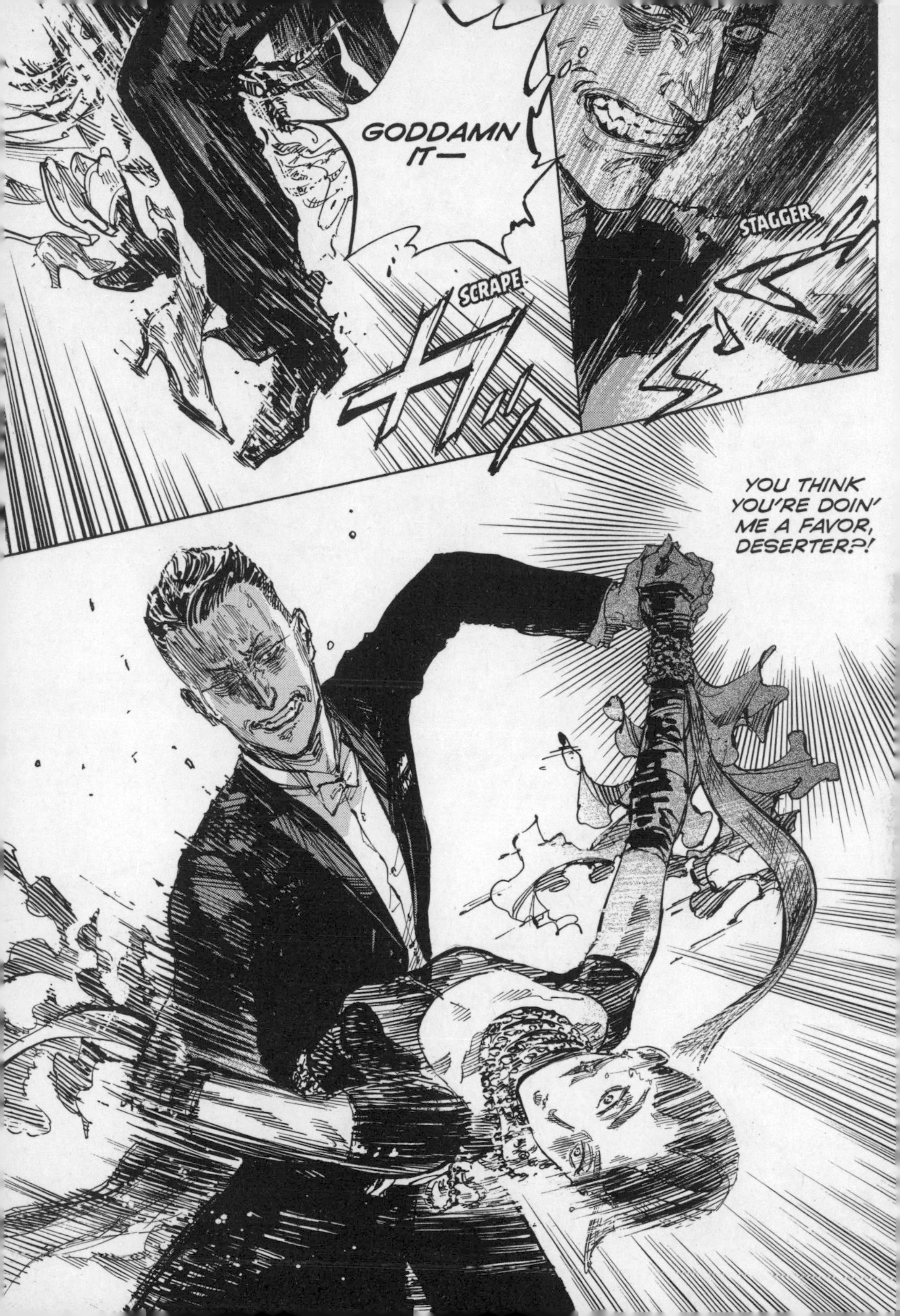
STAGGER
GODDAMN IT—
SCRAPE
YOU THINK YOU'RE DOIN' ME A FAVOR, DESERTER?!

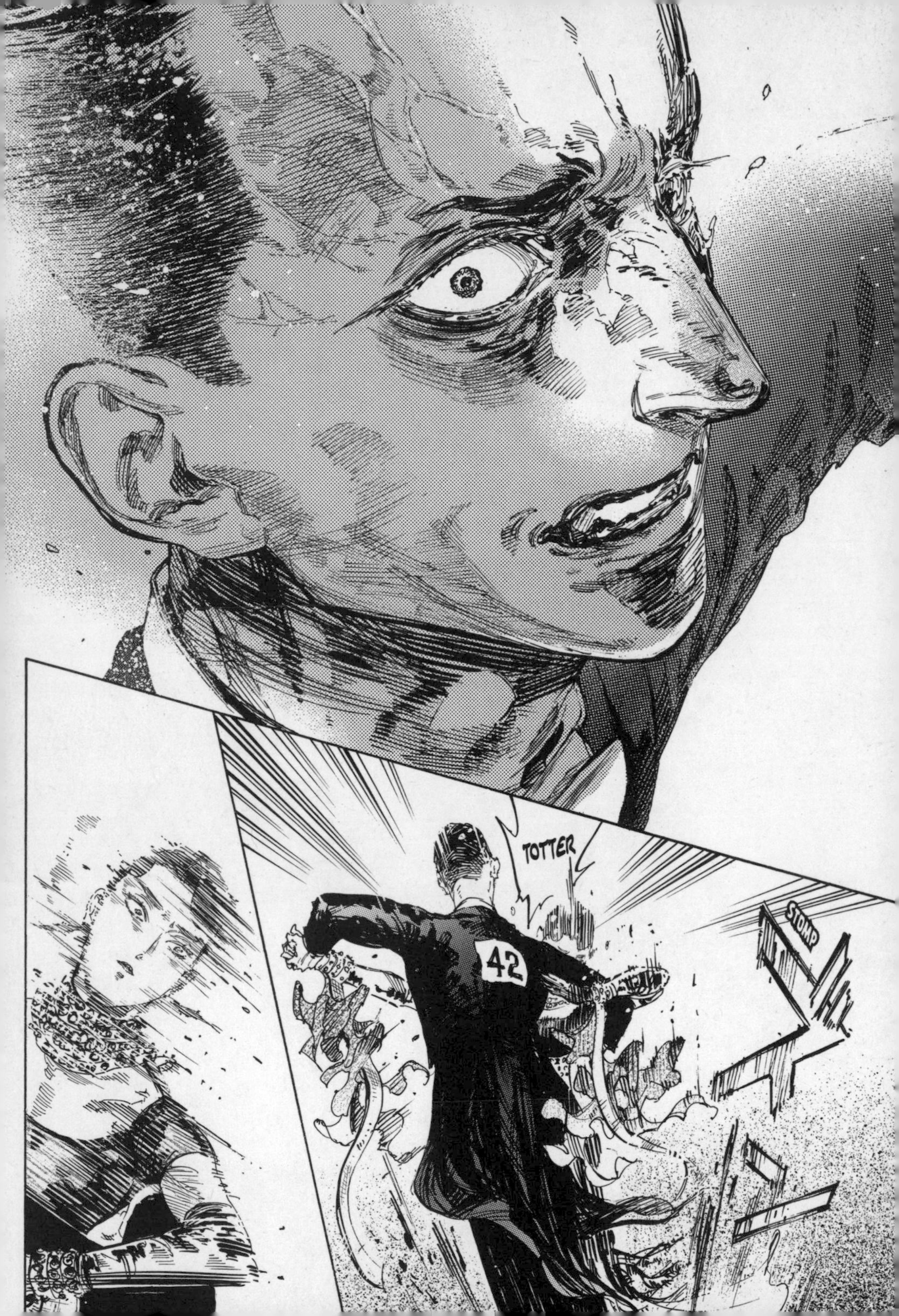
TOTTER
STOMP

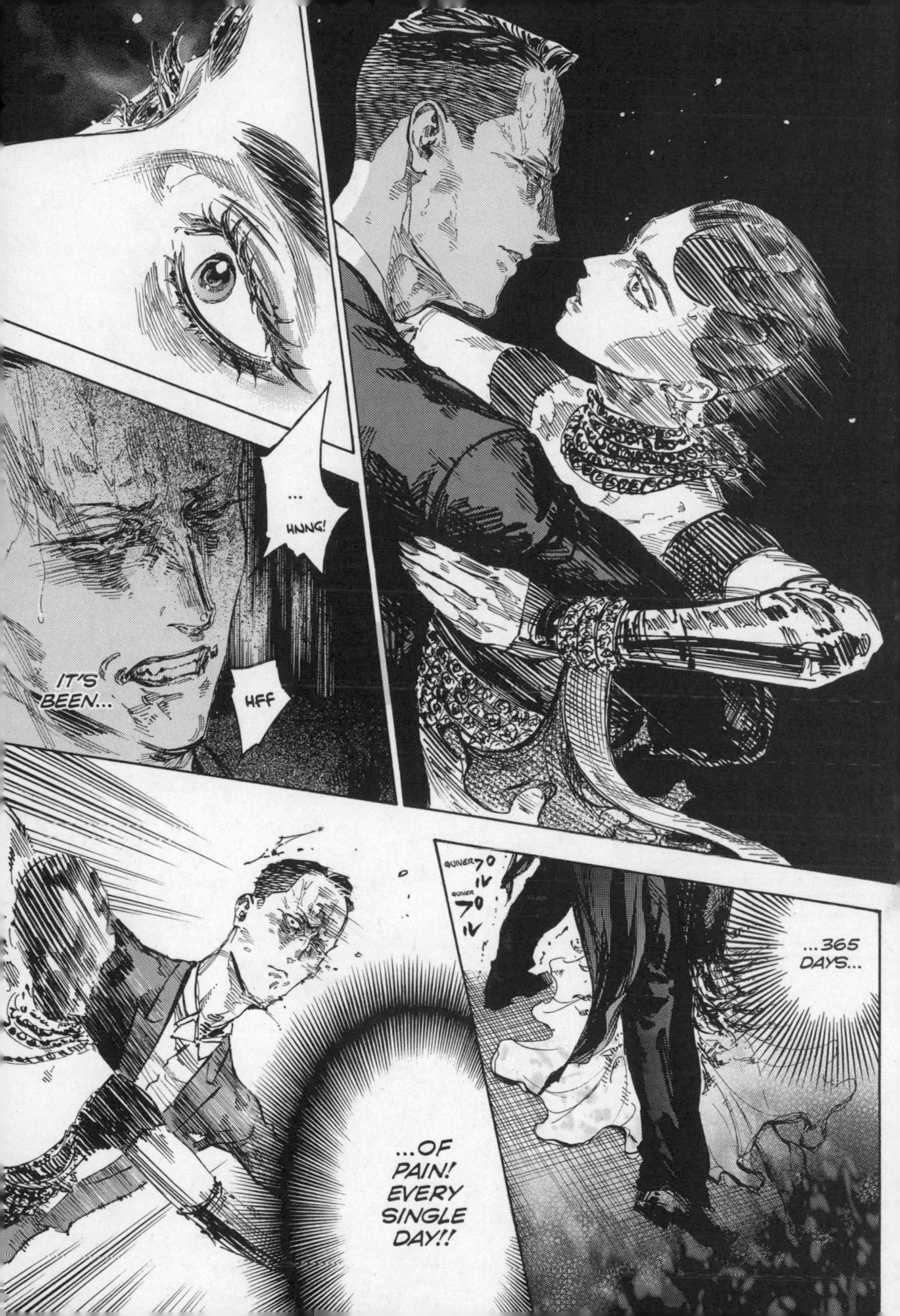

... HNNG!
HFF
IT'S BEEN...
QUIVER
QUIVER
...365 DAYS...
...OF PAIN! EVERY SINGLE DAY!!

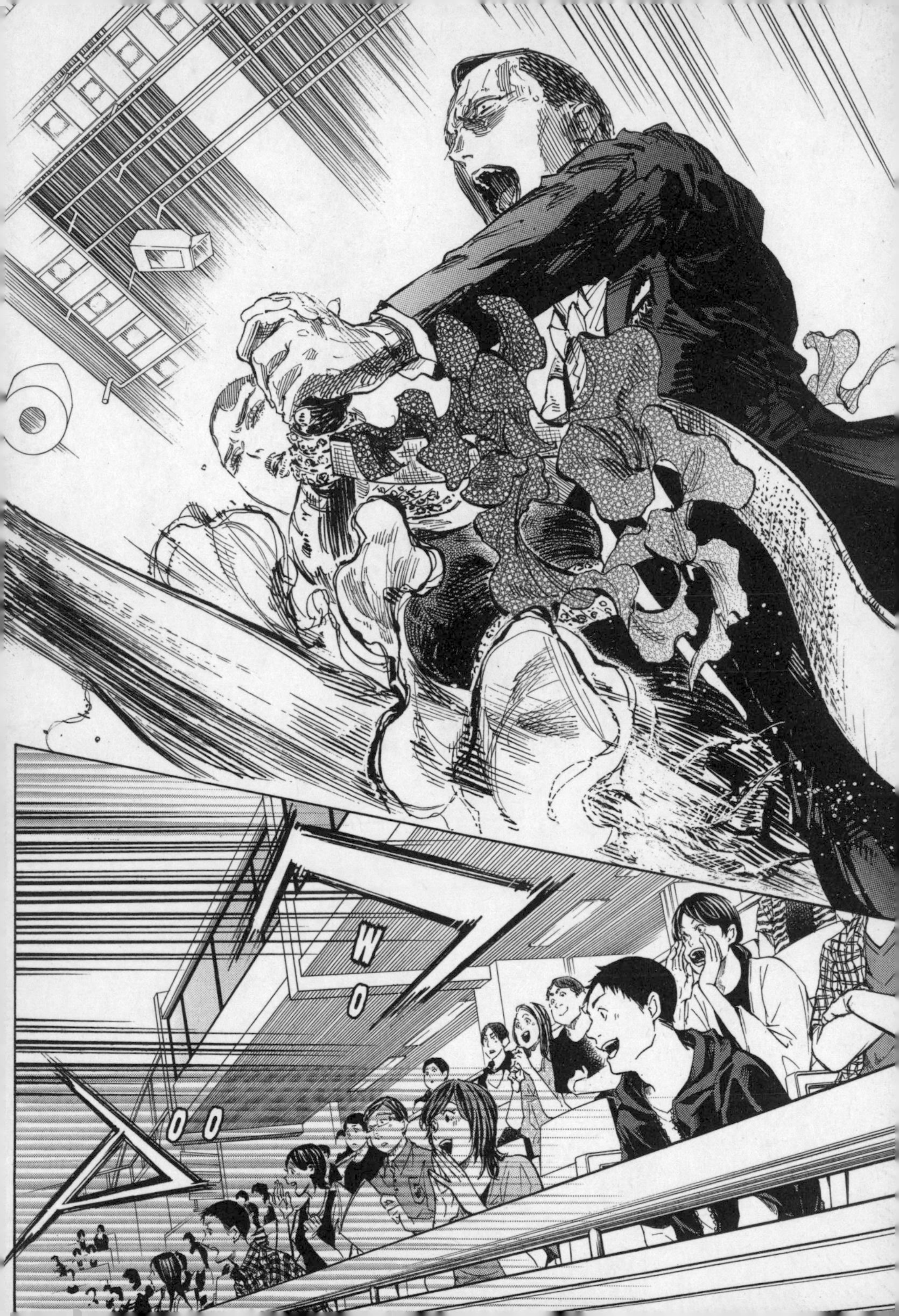
WOOO

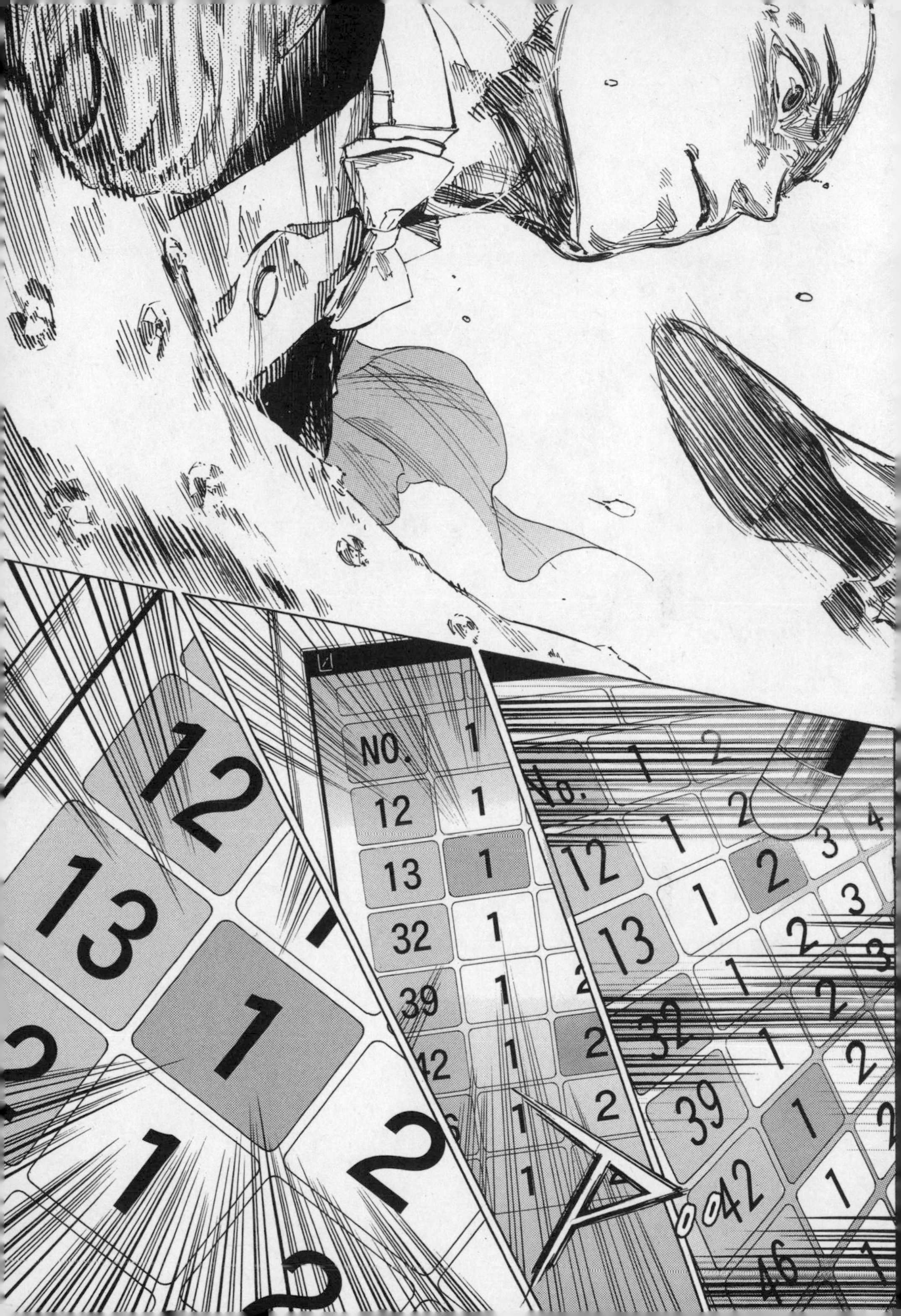
NO. 1
12 1
13 1
32 1
39 1
42 1 2

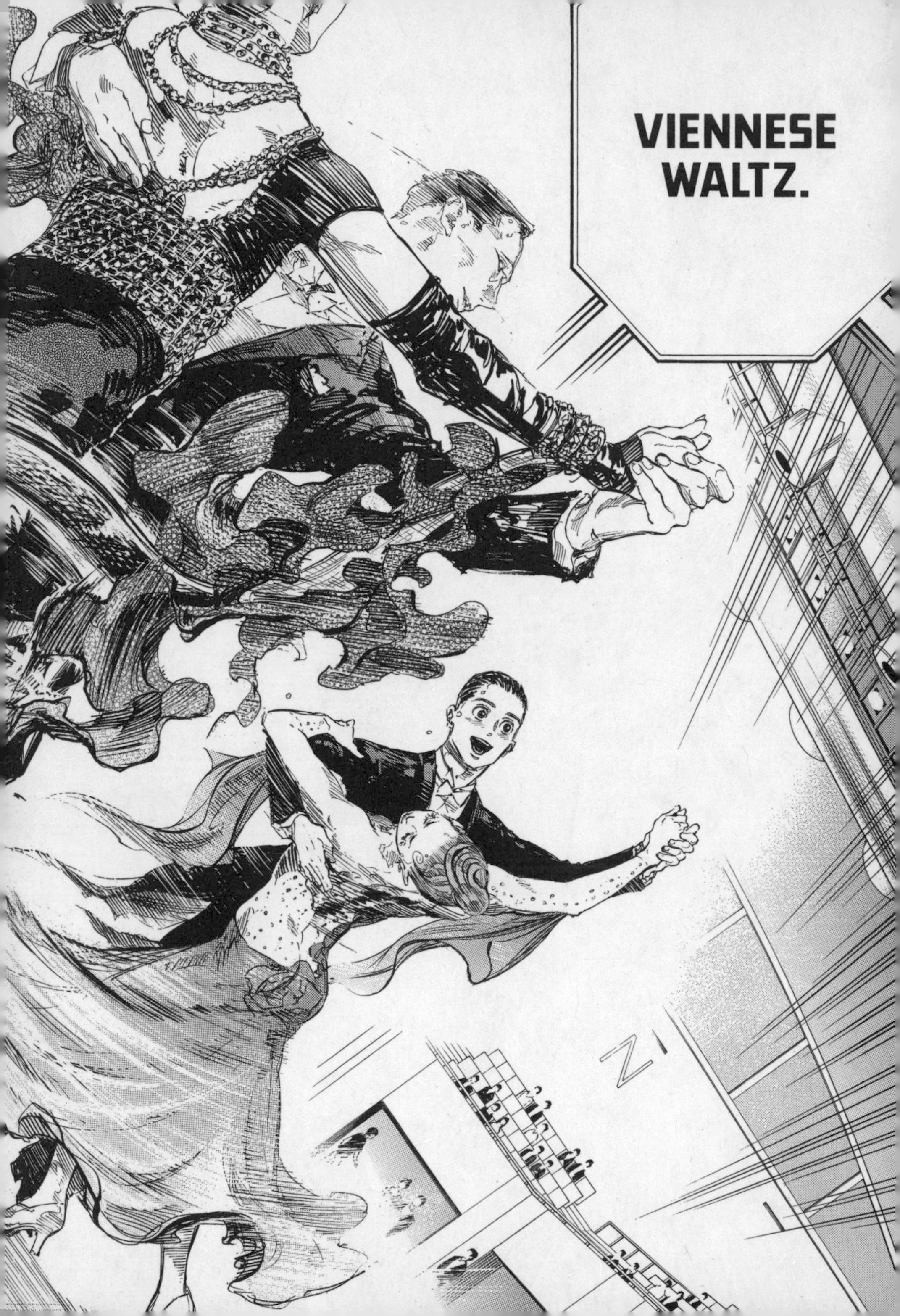
VIENNESE WALTZ.

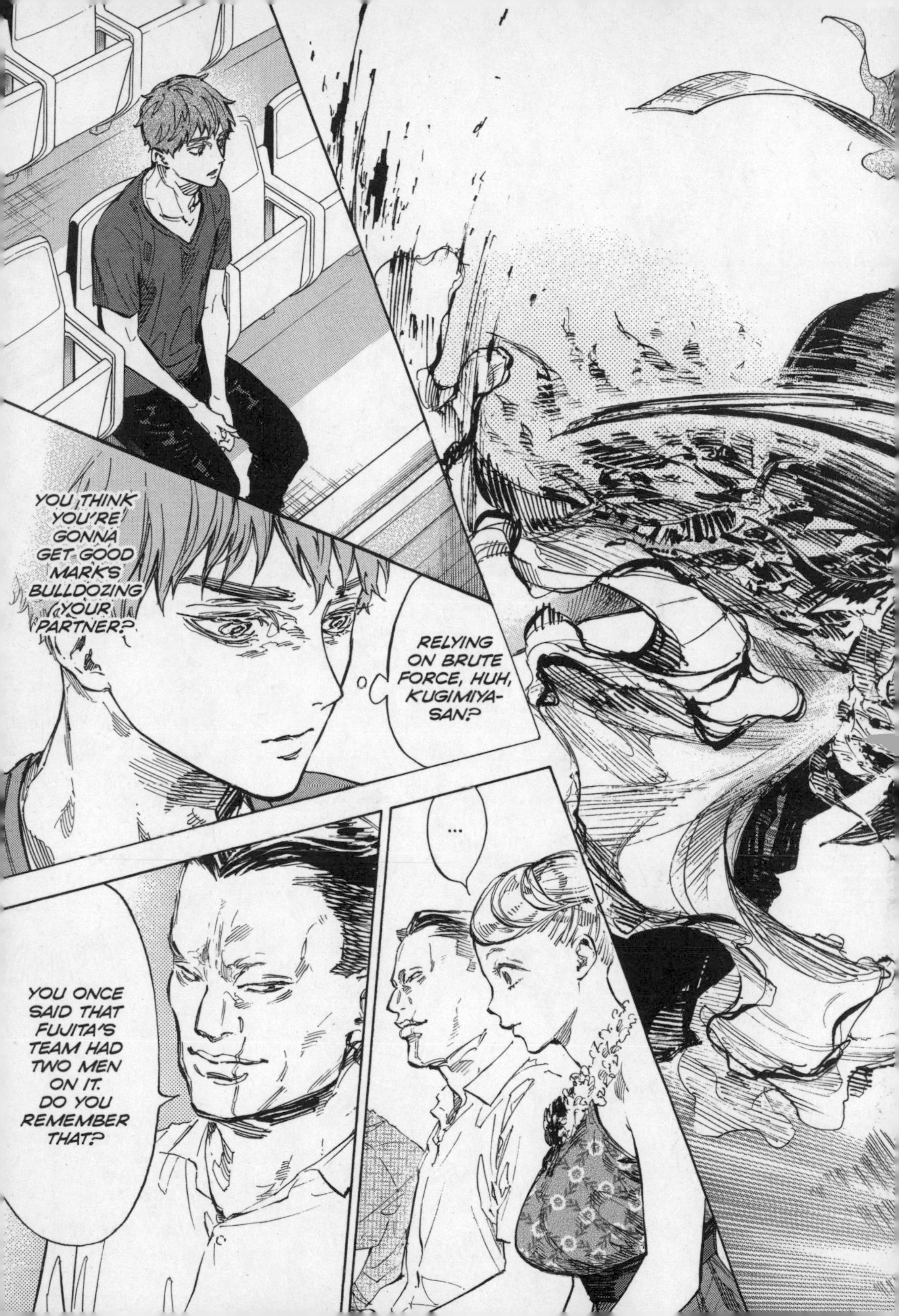
RELYING ON BRUTE FORCE, HUH, KUGIMIYA-SAN?
YOU THINK YOU'RE GONNA GET GOOD MARKS BULLDOZING YOUR PARTNER?
...
YOU ONCE SAID THAT FUJITA'S TEAM HAD TWO MEN ON IT. DO YOU REMEMBER THAT?

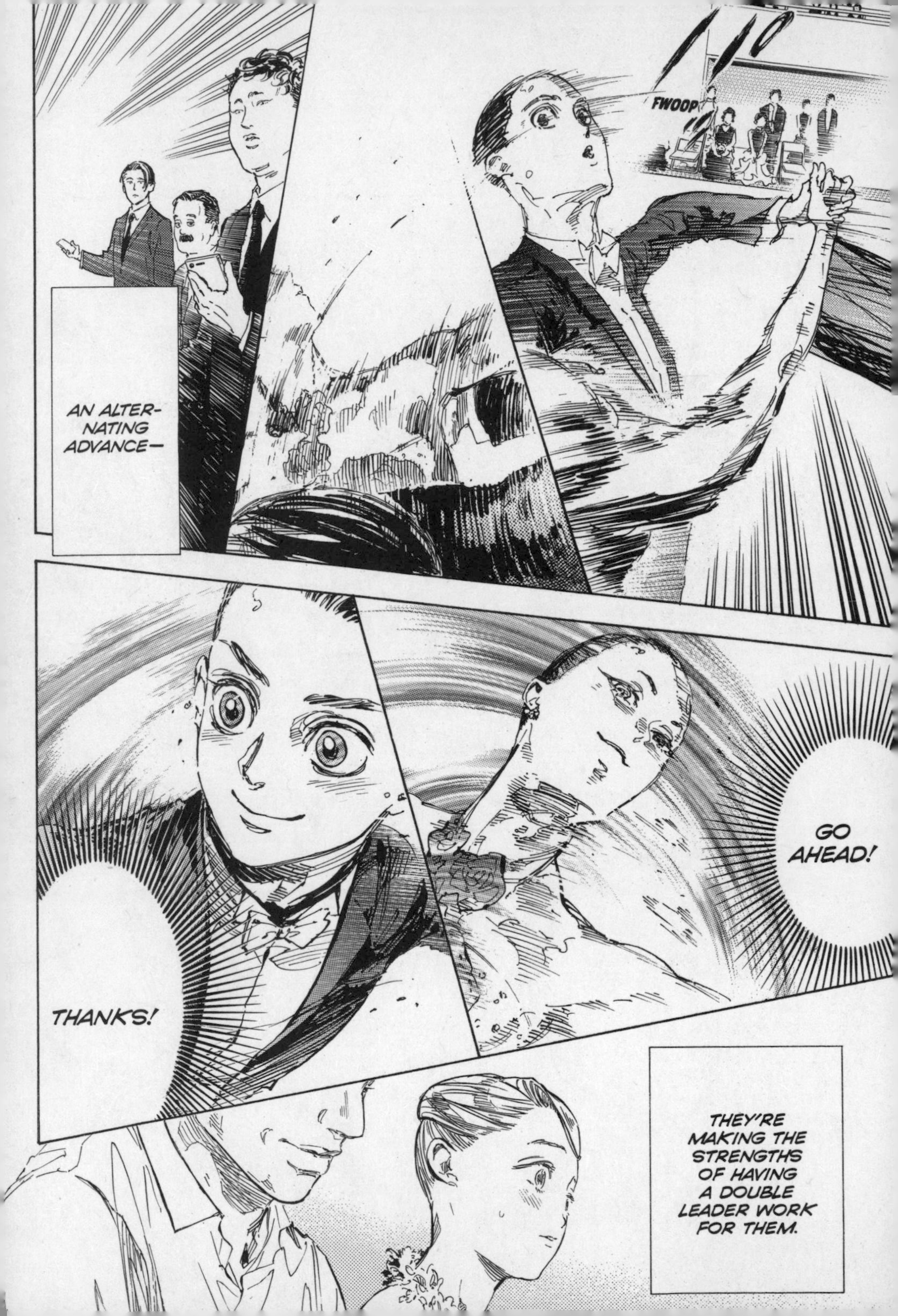
FWOOP
AN ALTER-NATING ADVANCE—
GO AHEAD!
THANKS!
THEY'RE MAKING THE STRENGTHS OF HAVING A DOUBLE LEADER WORK FOR THEM.

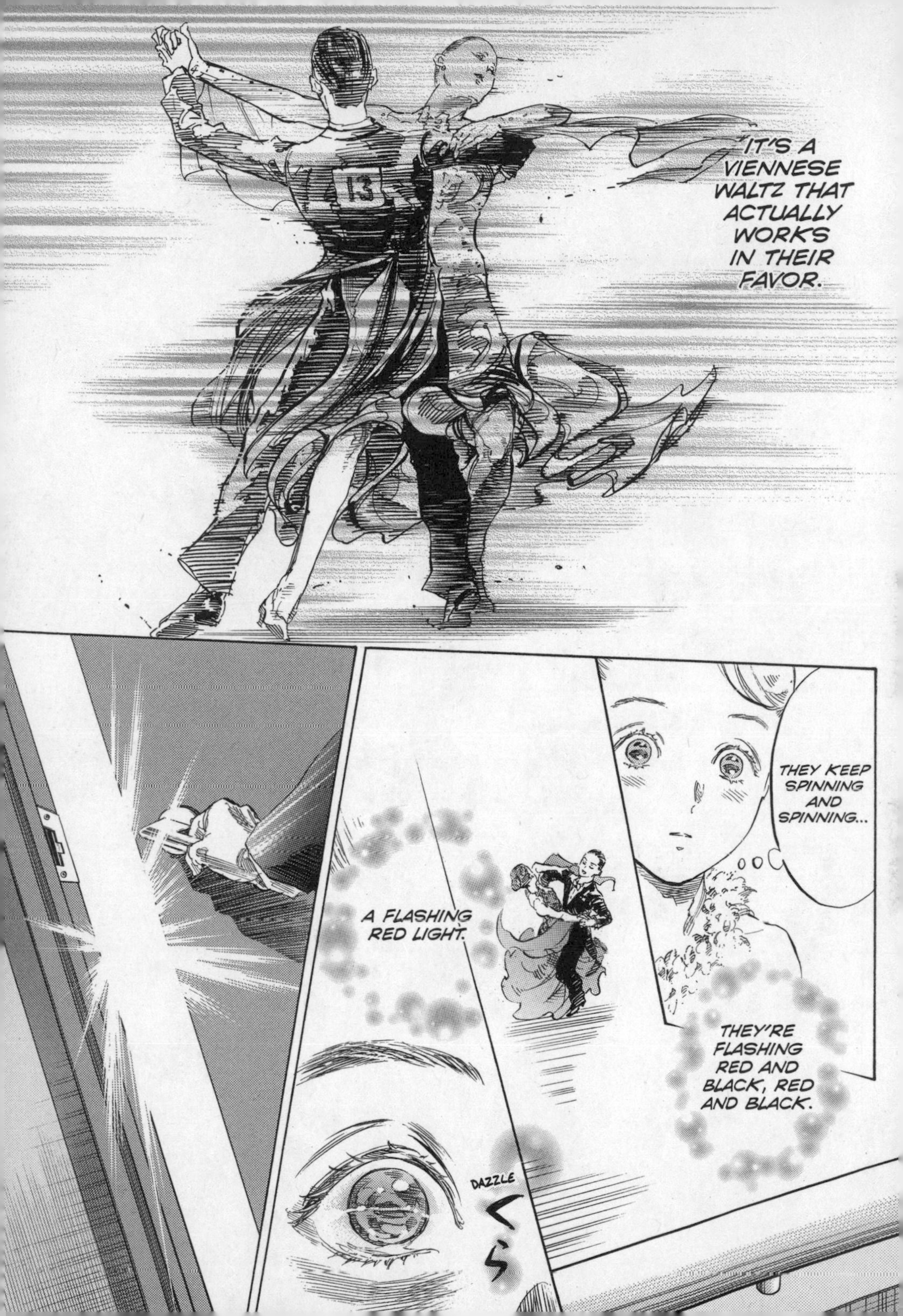
IT'S A VIENNESE WALTZ THAT ACTUALLY WORKS IN THEIR FAVOR.
THEY KEEP SPINNING AND SPINNING...
A FLASHING RED LIGHT.
THEY'RE FLASHING RED AND BLACK, RED AND BLACK.
DAZZLE

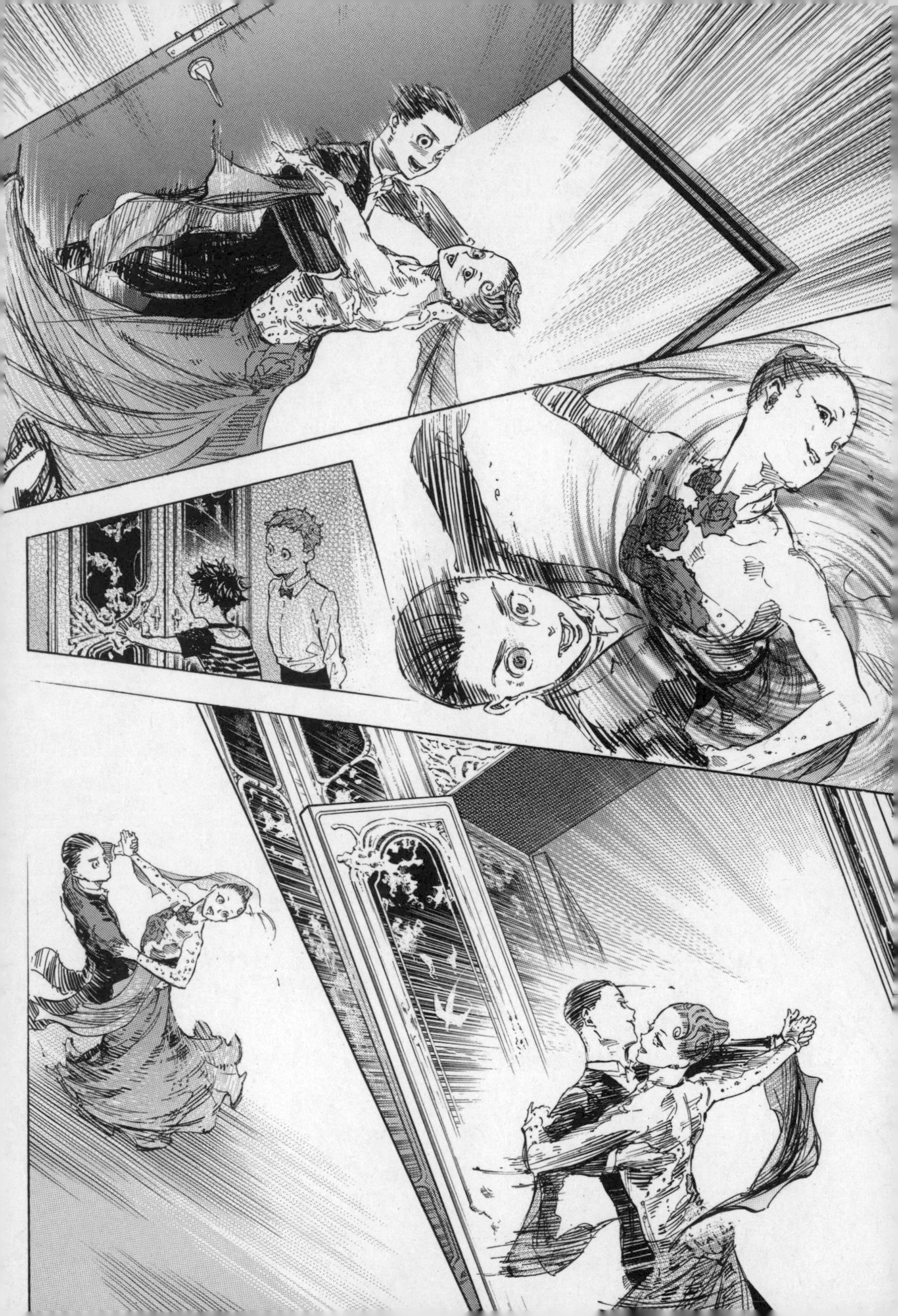

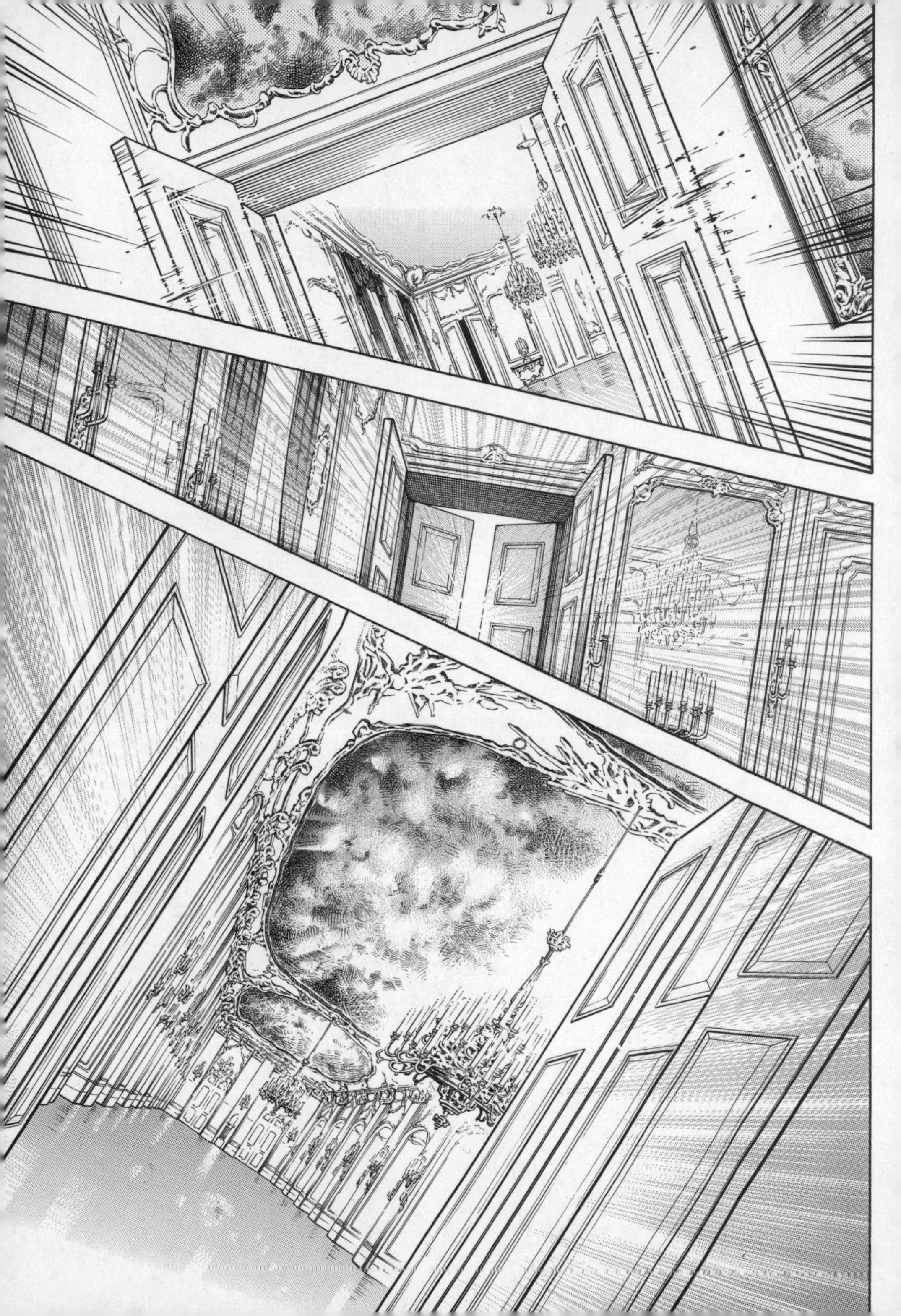

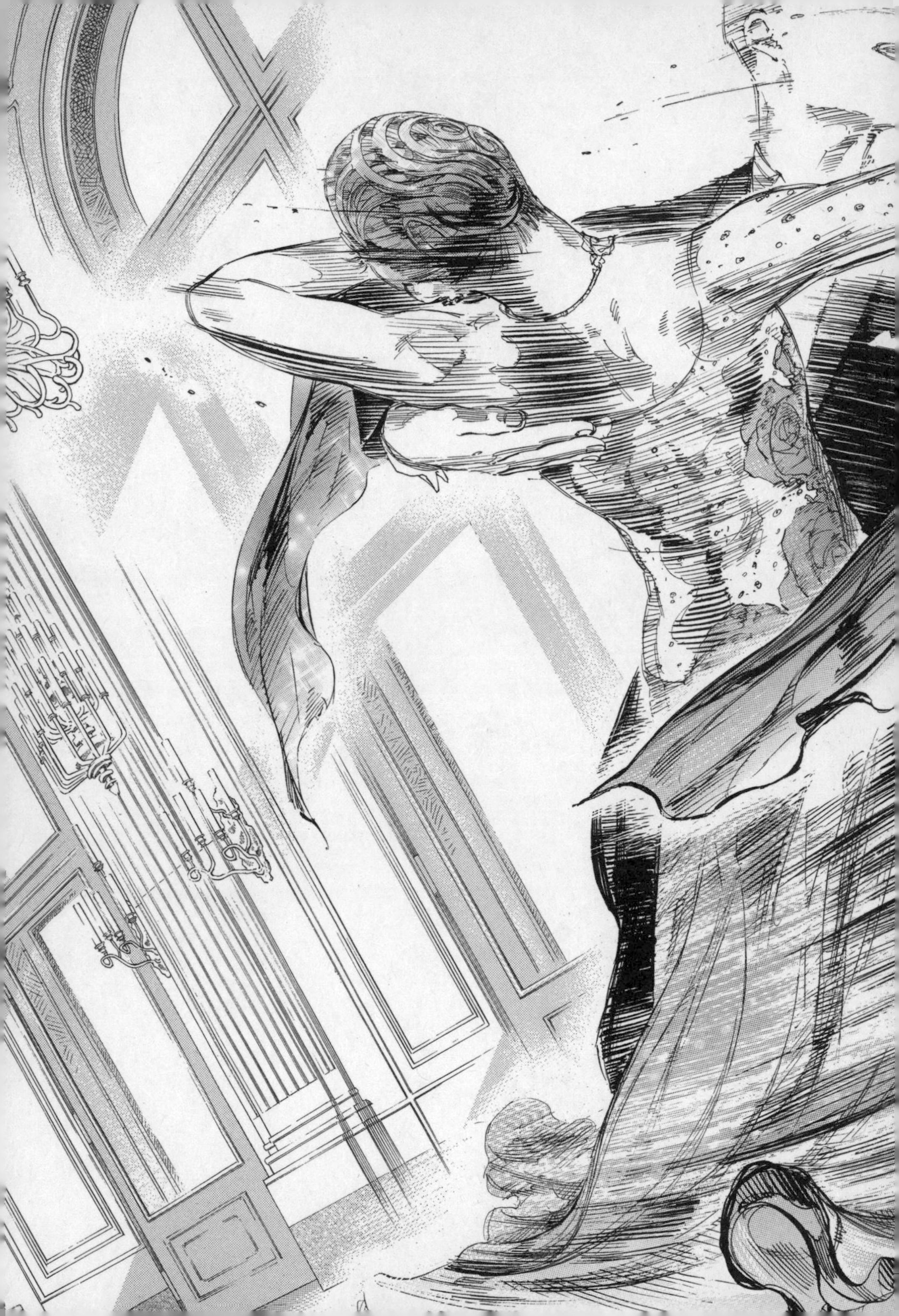

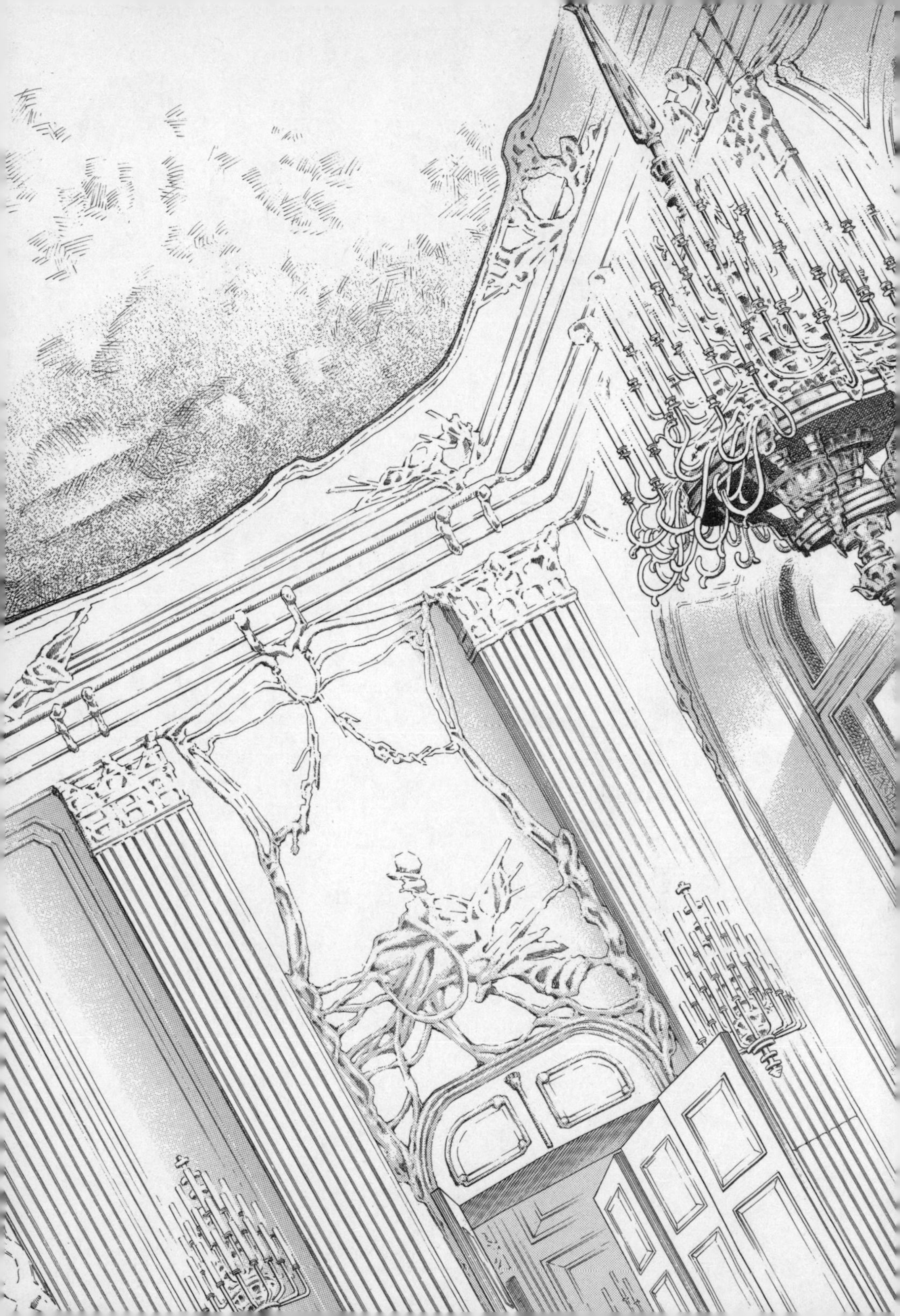

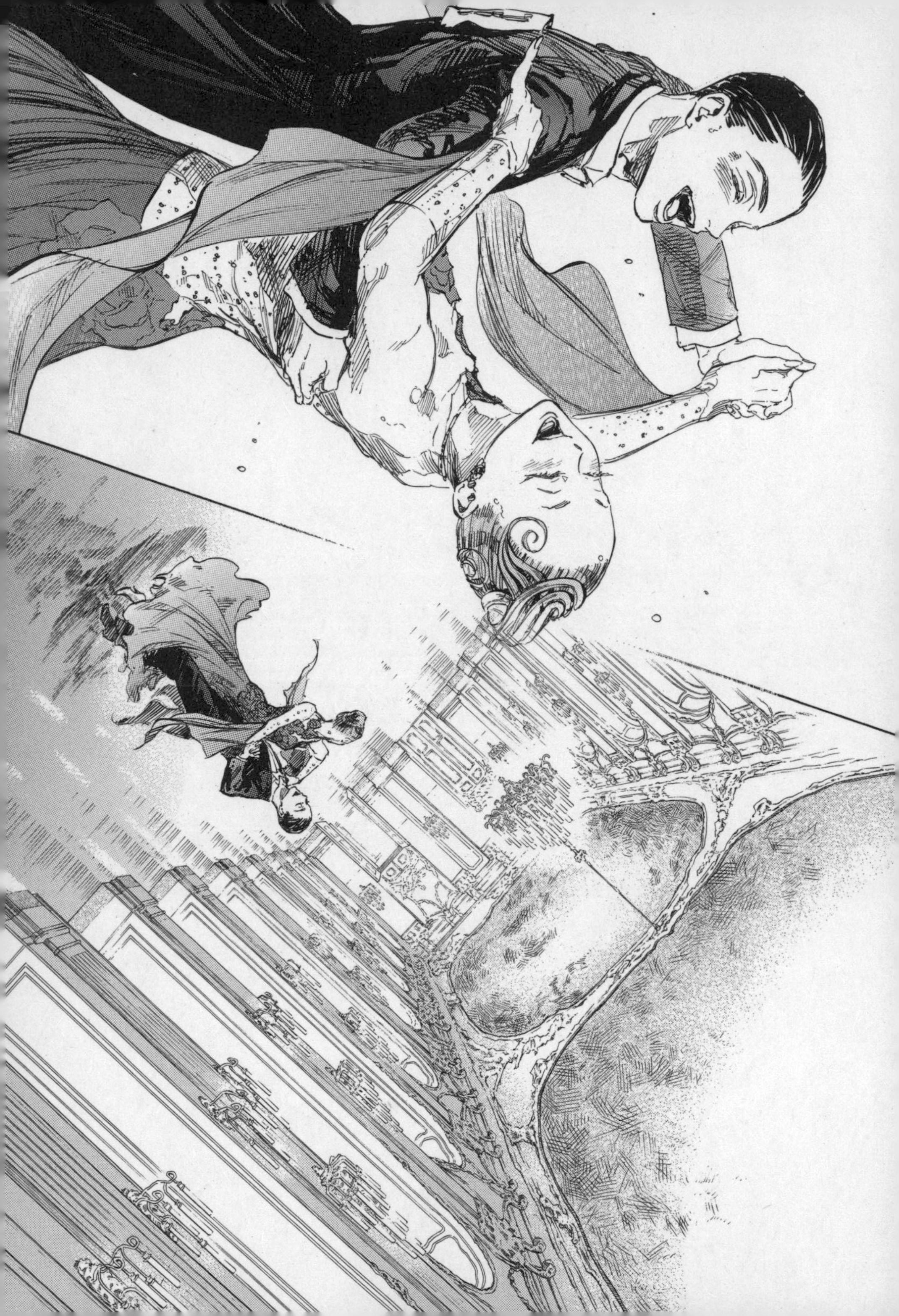

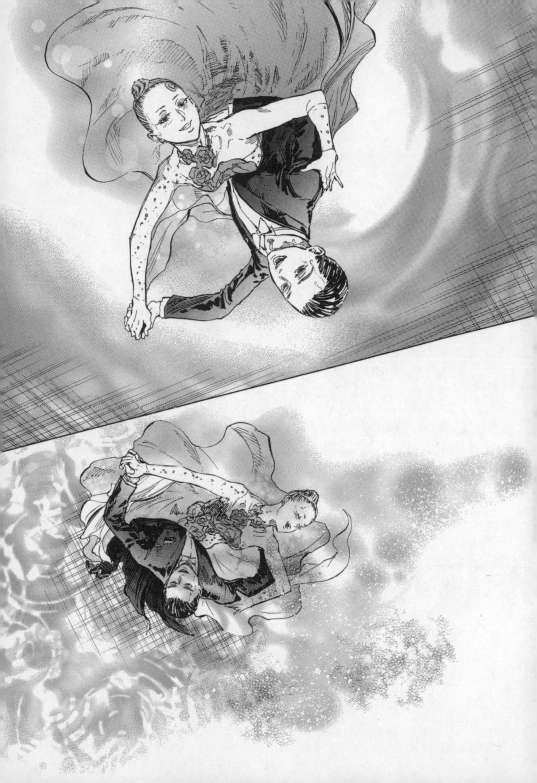

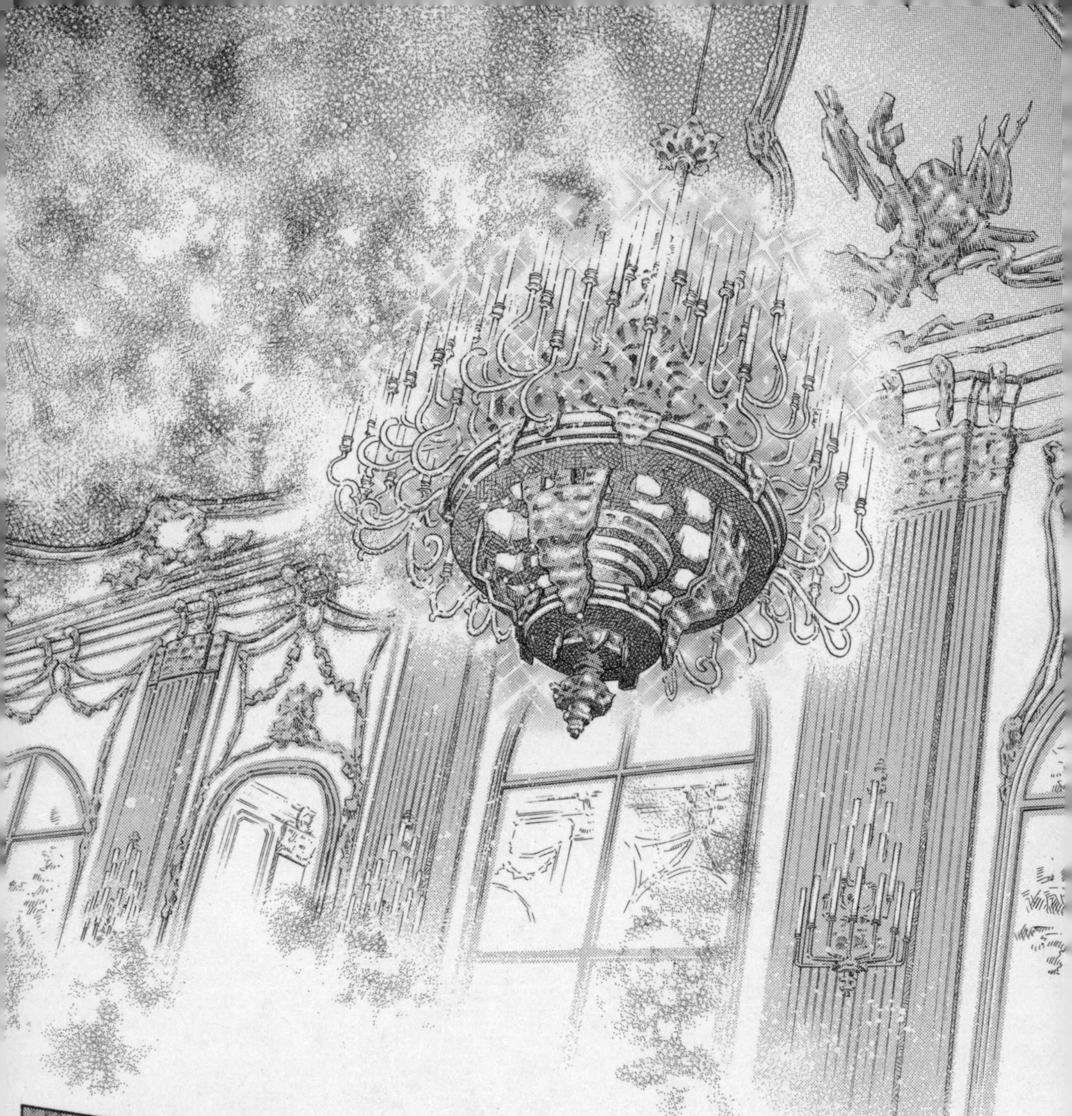
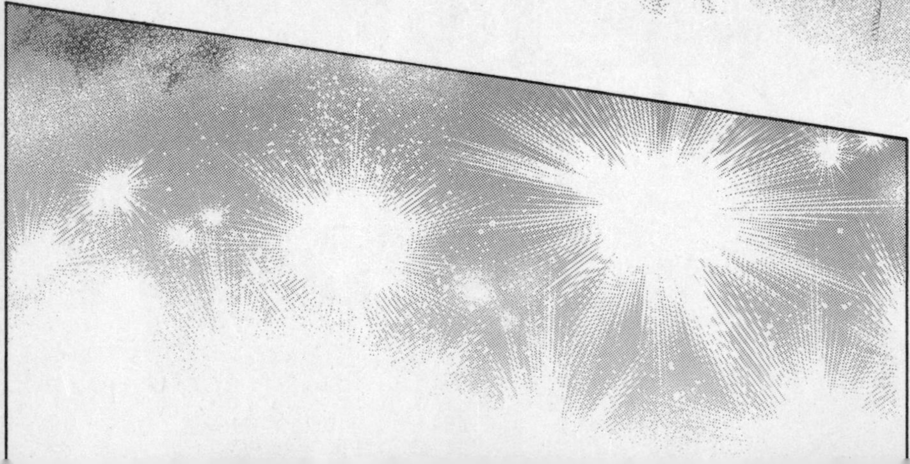

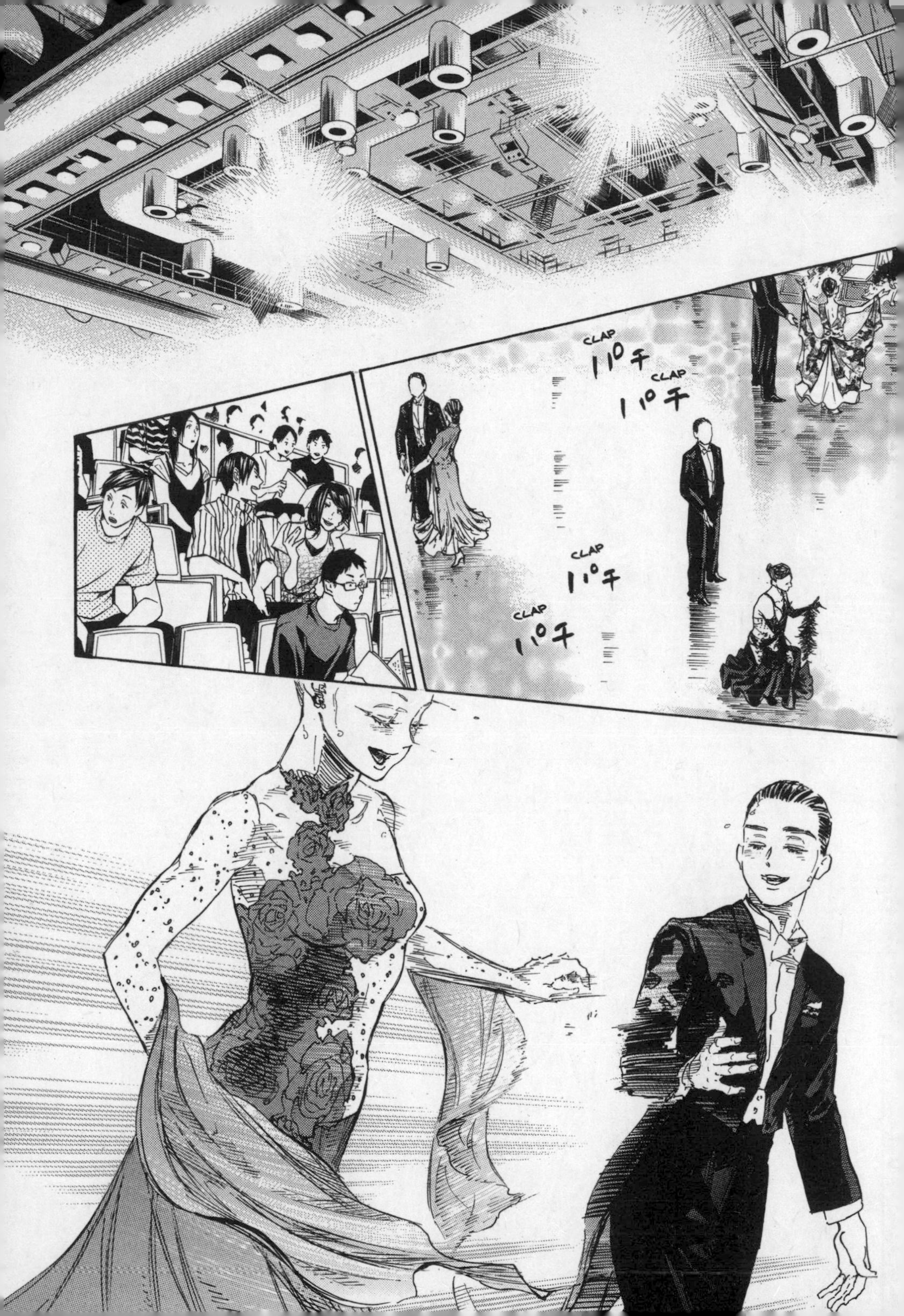
CLAP
パチ
CLAP
パチ
CLAP
パチ
CLAP
パチ

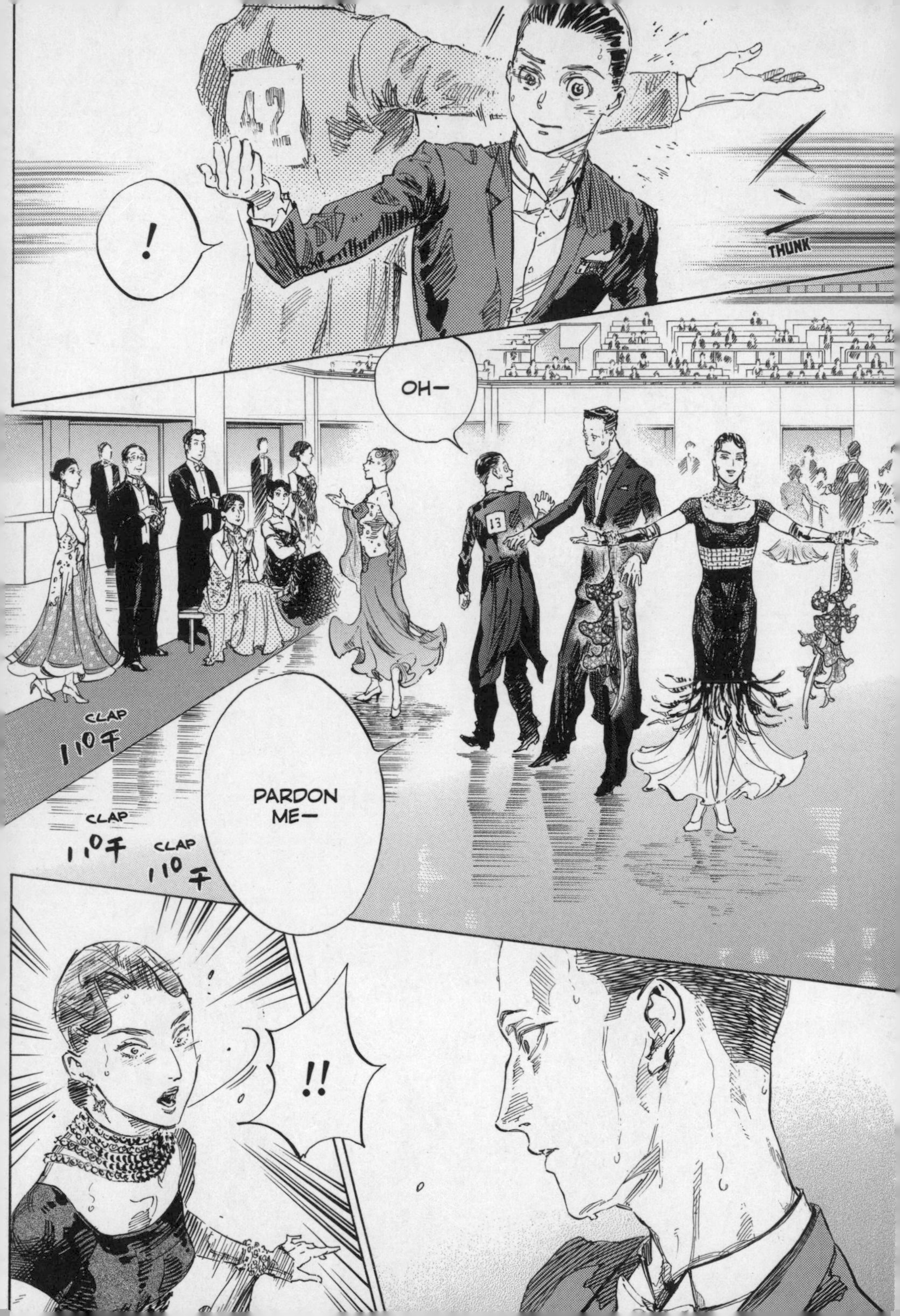
THUNK
!
OH—
CLAP
PARDON ME—
CLAP
CLAP
!!

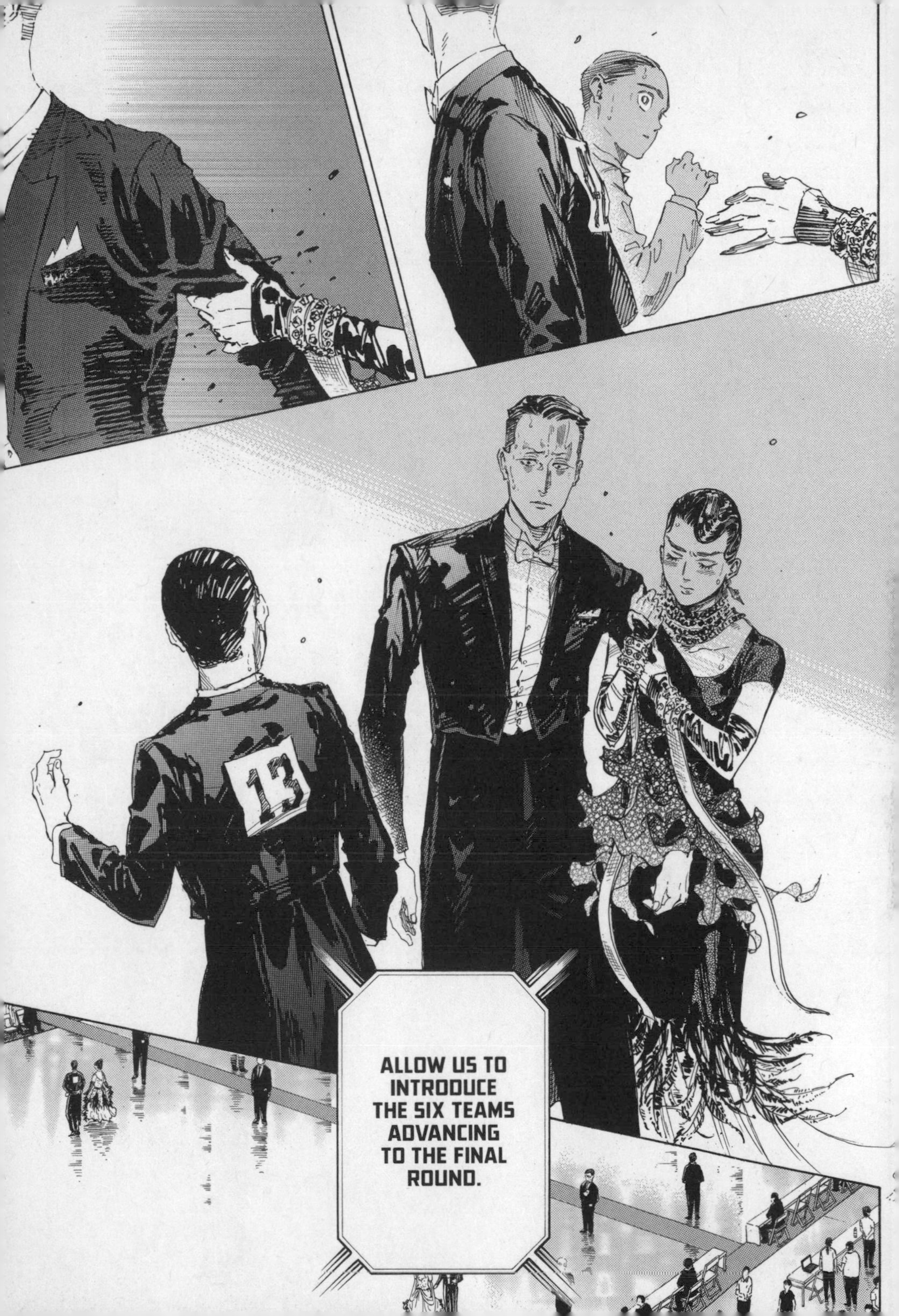
13
ALLOW US TO INTRODUCE THE SIX TEAMS ADVANCING TO THE FINAL ROUND.

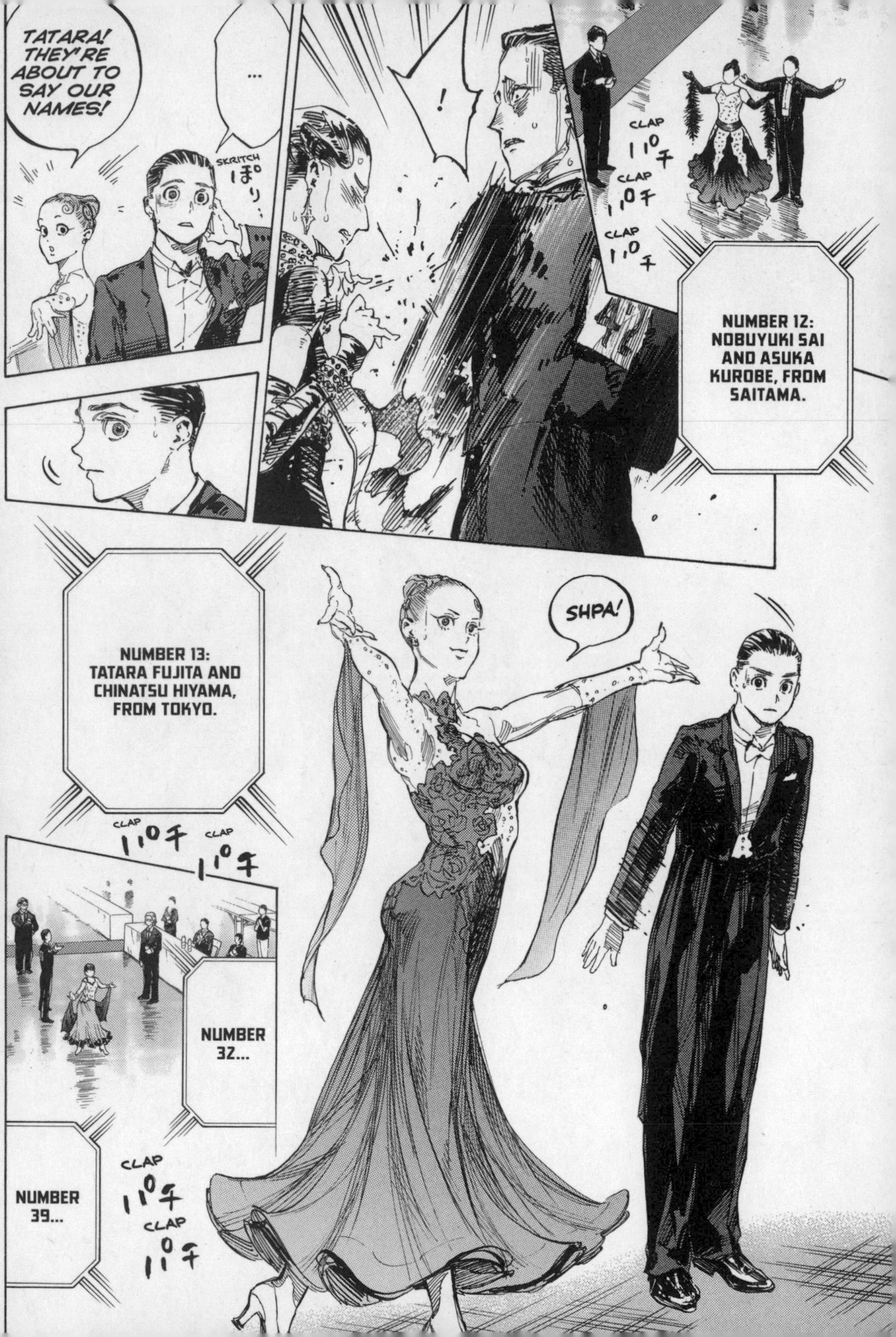

CLAP
パチ
CLAP
パチ
CLAP
パチ
NUMBER 12: NOBUYUKI SAI AND ASUKA KUROBE, FROM SAITAMA.
!
TATARA! THEY'RE ABOUT TO SAY OUR NAMES!
...
SKRITCH
ぽり
SHPA!
NUMBER 13: TATARA FUJITA AND CHINATSU HIYAMA, FROM TOKYO.
CLAP
パチ
CLAP
パチ
NUMBER 32...
CLAP
パチ
CLAP
パチ
NUMBER 39...

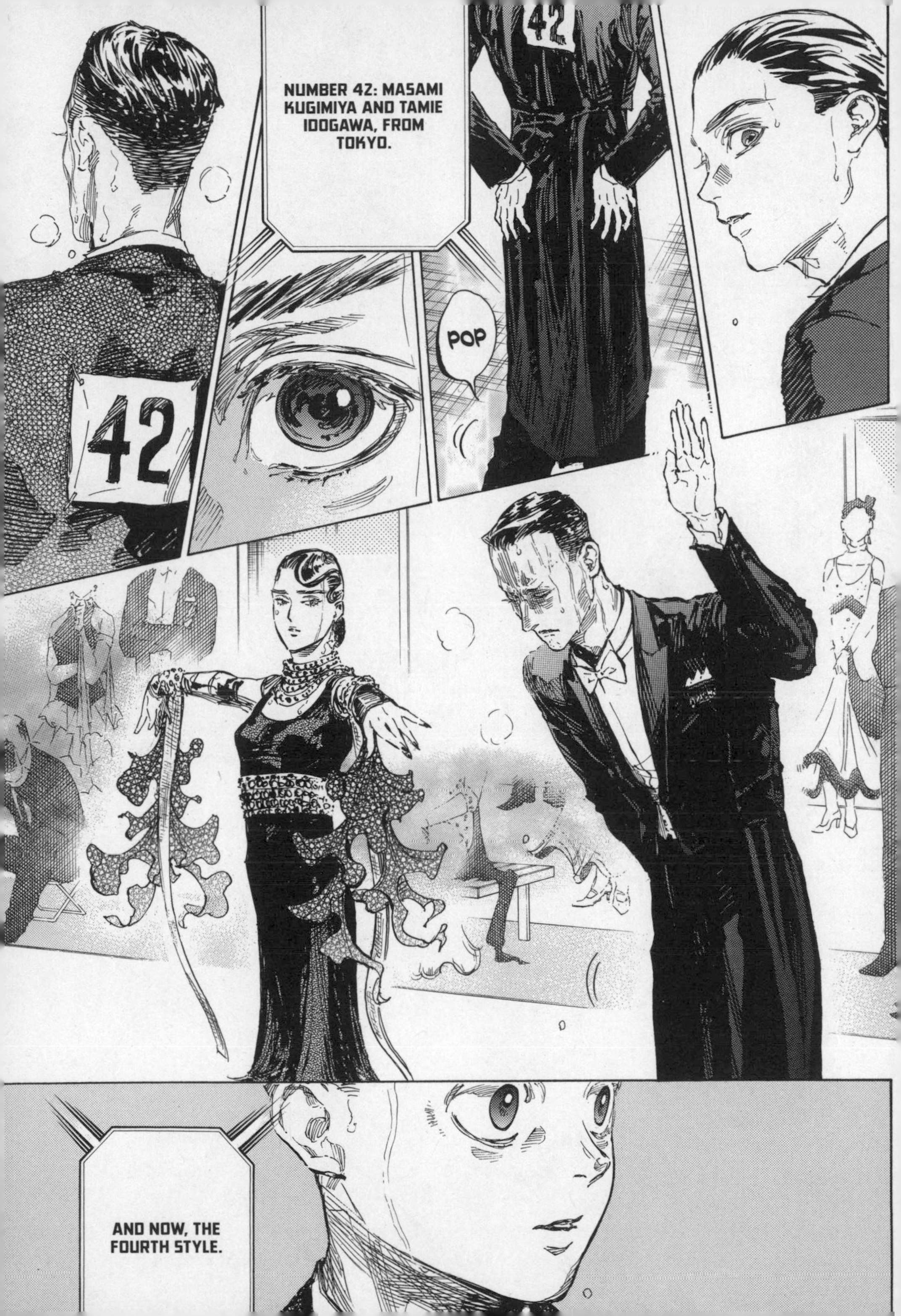
NUMBER 42: MASAMI KUGIMIYA AND TAMIE IDOGAWA, FROM TOKYO.
POP
AND NOW, THE FOURTH STYLE.

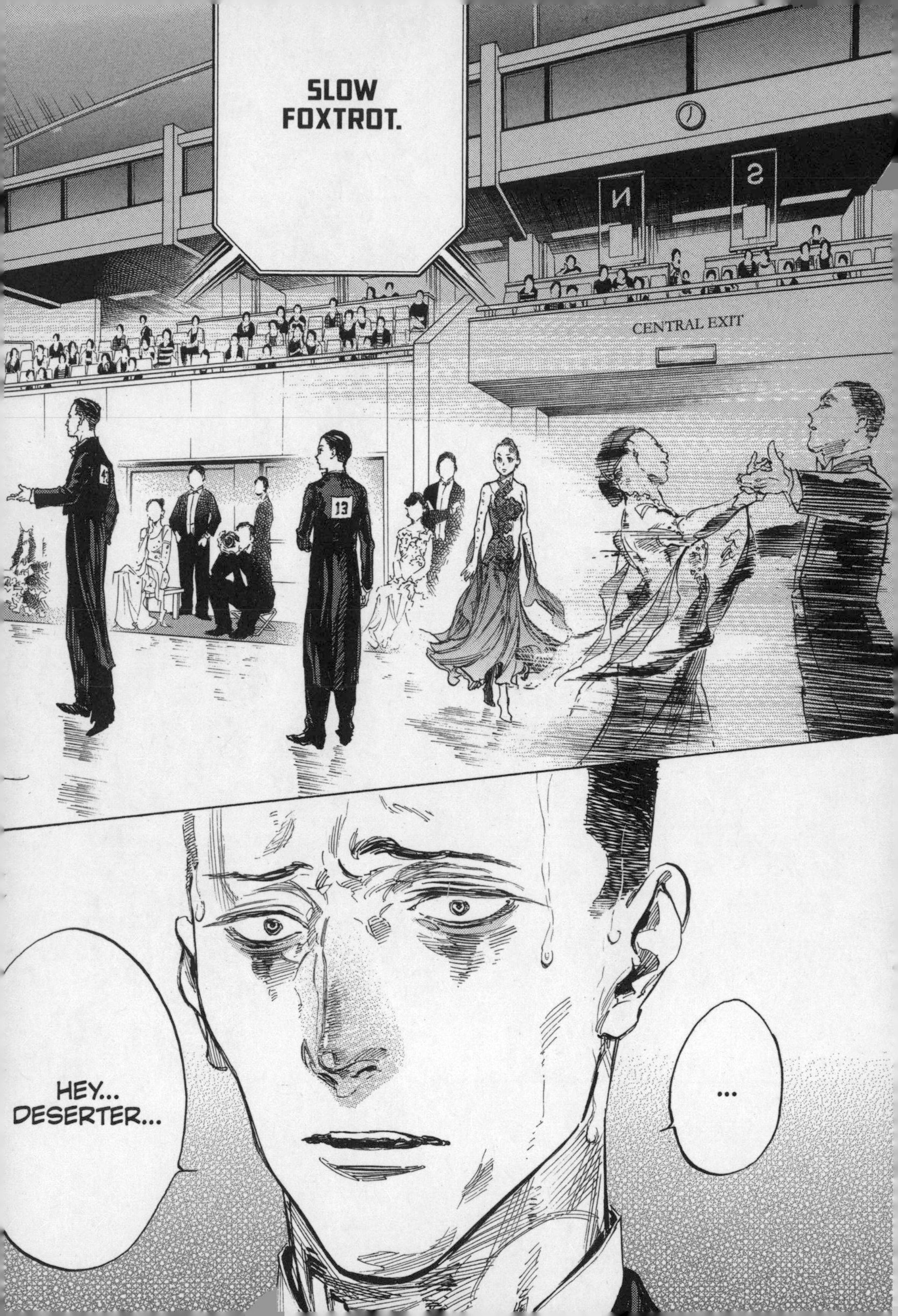
SLOW FOXTROT.
CENTRAL EXIT
...
HEY... DESERTER...

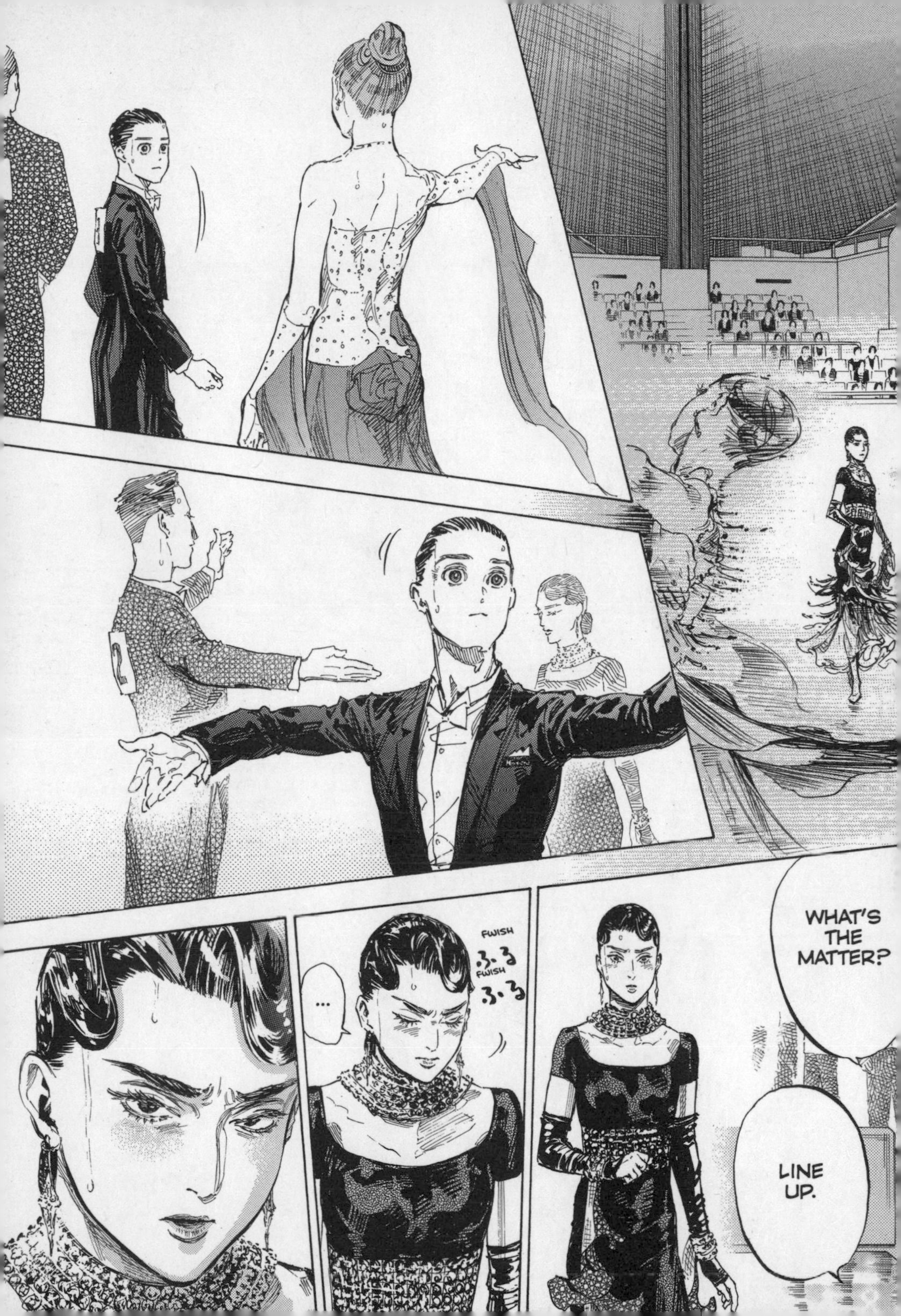
WHAT'S THE MATTER?
LINE UP.
...
FWISH
ふる
FWISH
ふる

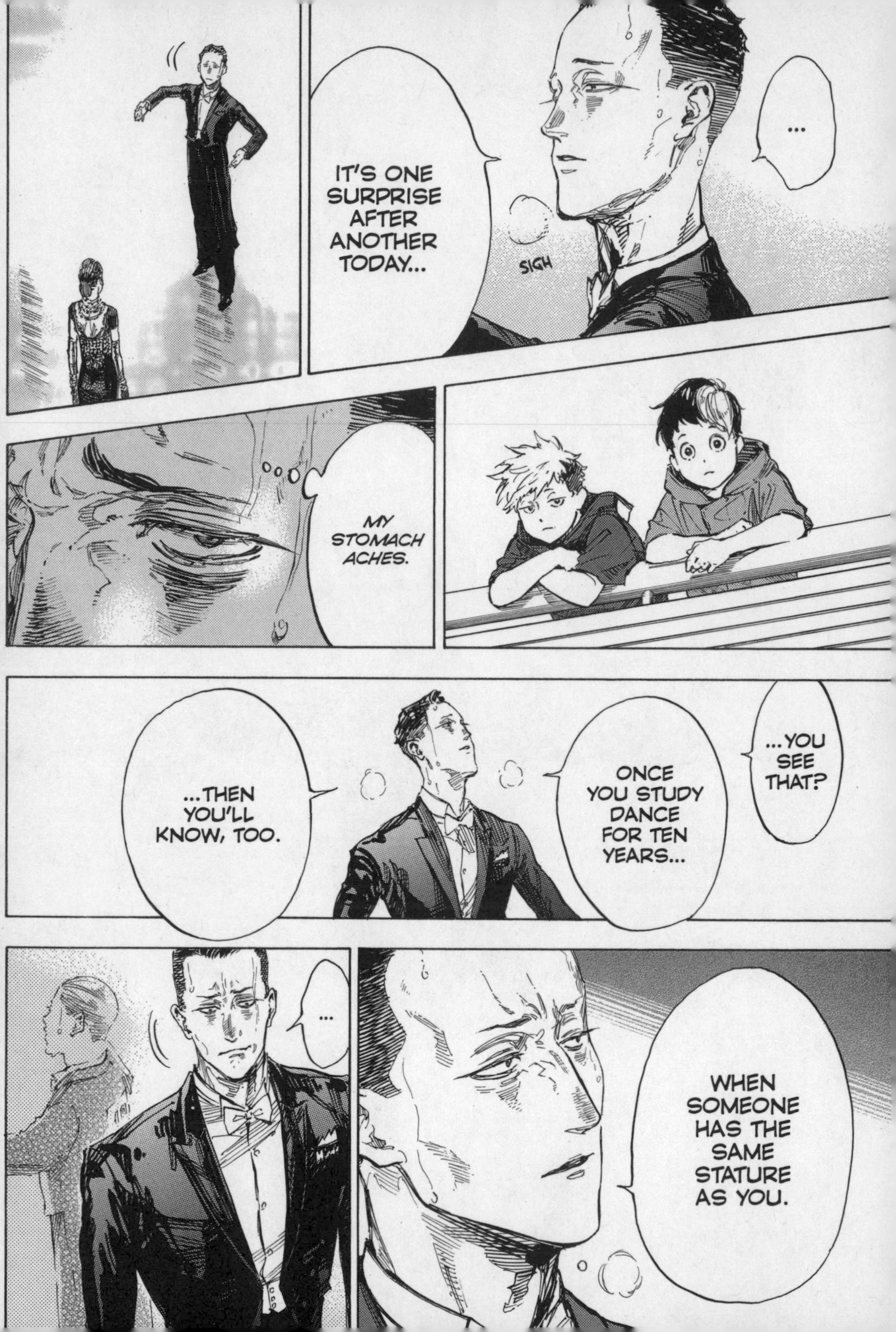
...
IT'S ONE SURPRISE AFTER ANOTHER TODAY...
SIGH
MY STOMACH ACHES.
...YOU SEE THAT?
ONCE YOU STUDY DANCE FOR TEN YEARS...
...THEN YOU'LL KNOW, TOO.
WHEN SOMEONE HAS THE SAME STATURE AS YOU.
...

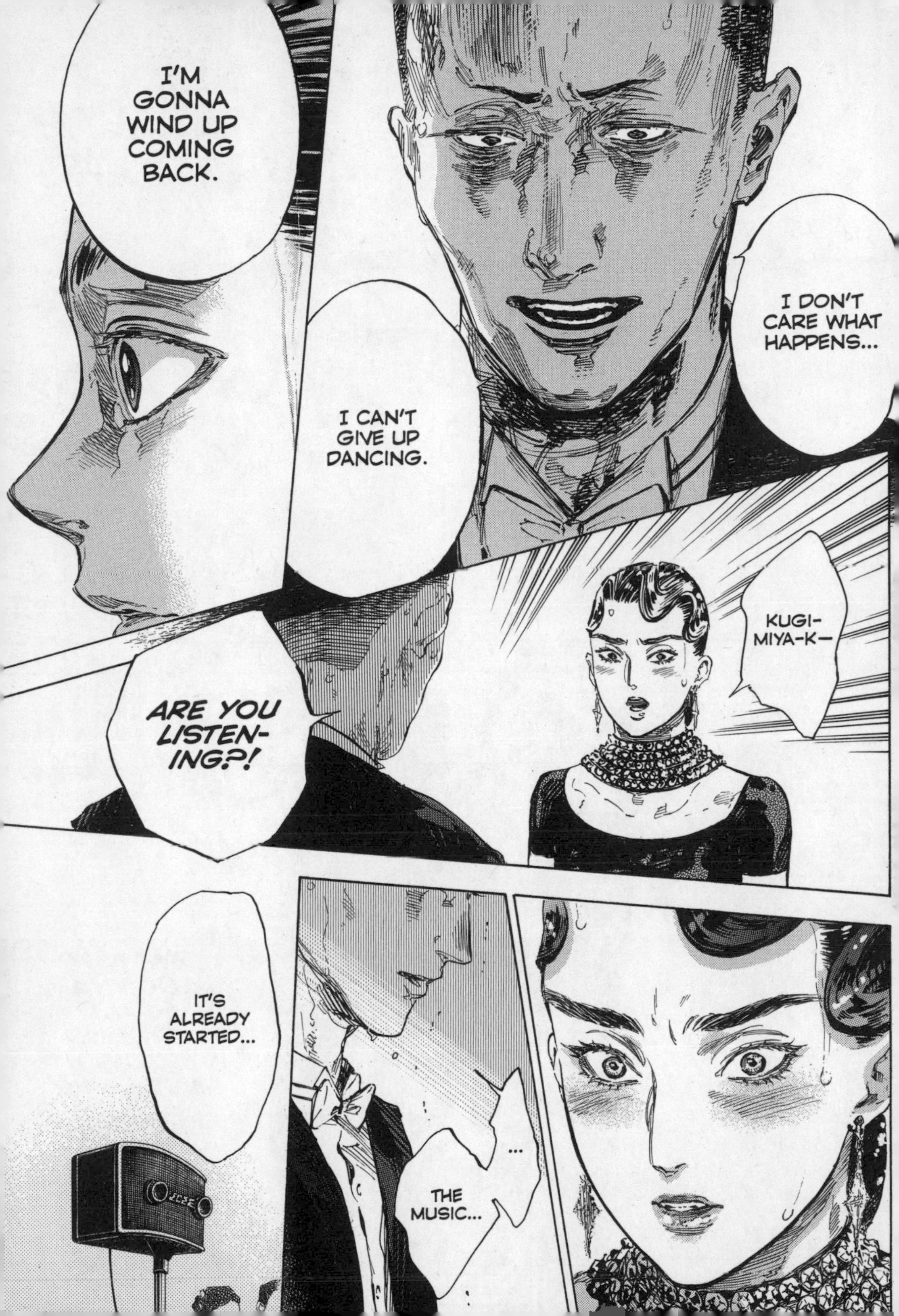
I DON'T CARE WHAT HAPPENS...
I CAN'T GIVE UP DANCING.
I'M GONNA WIND UP COMING BACK.
KUGI-MIYA-K—
ARE YOU LISTEN-ING?!
...
THE MUSIC...
IT'S ALREADY STARTED...

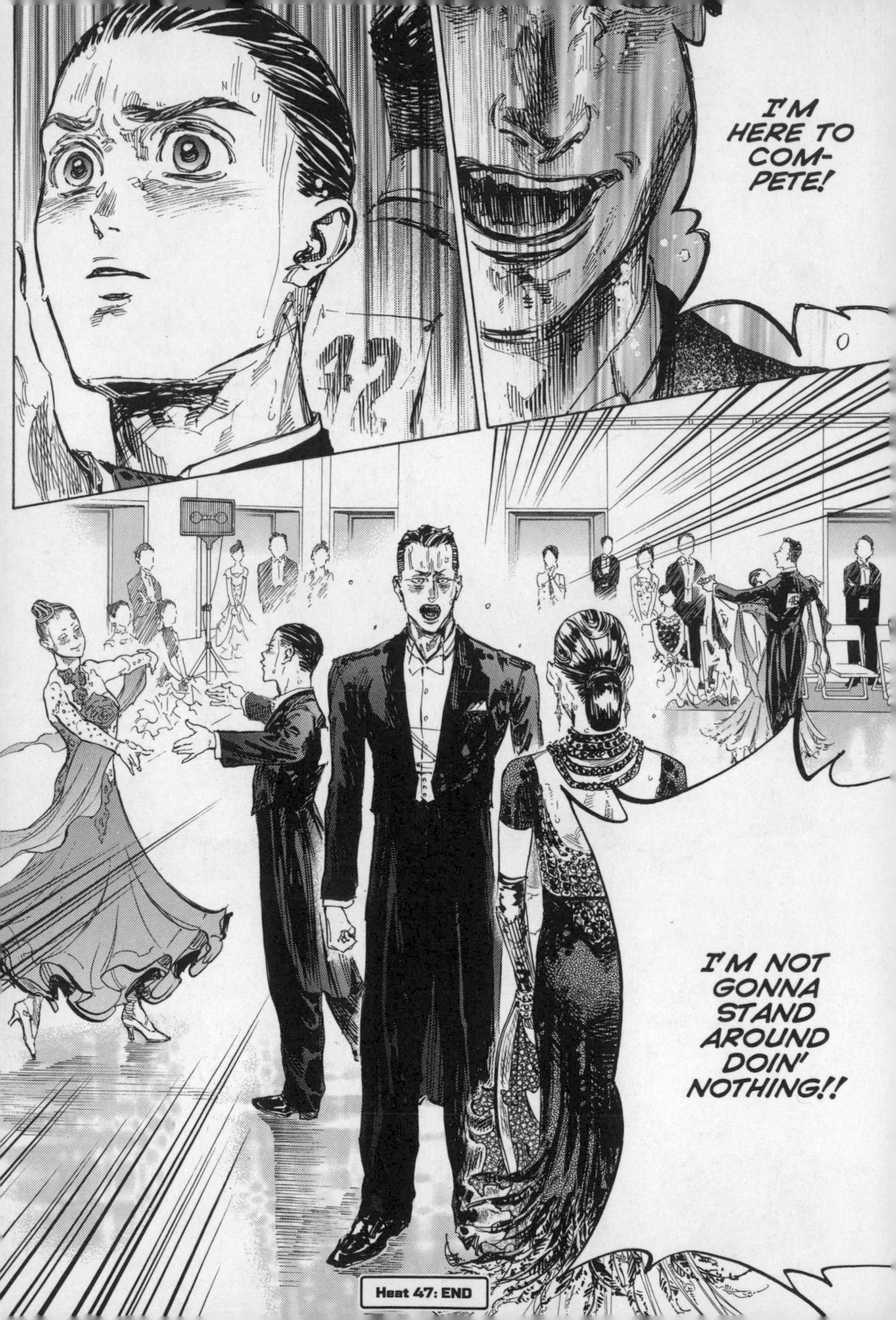
I'M HERE TO COM-PETE!
I'M NOT GONNA STAND AROUND DOIN' NOTHING!!
Heat 47: END

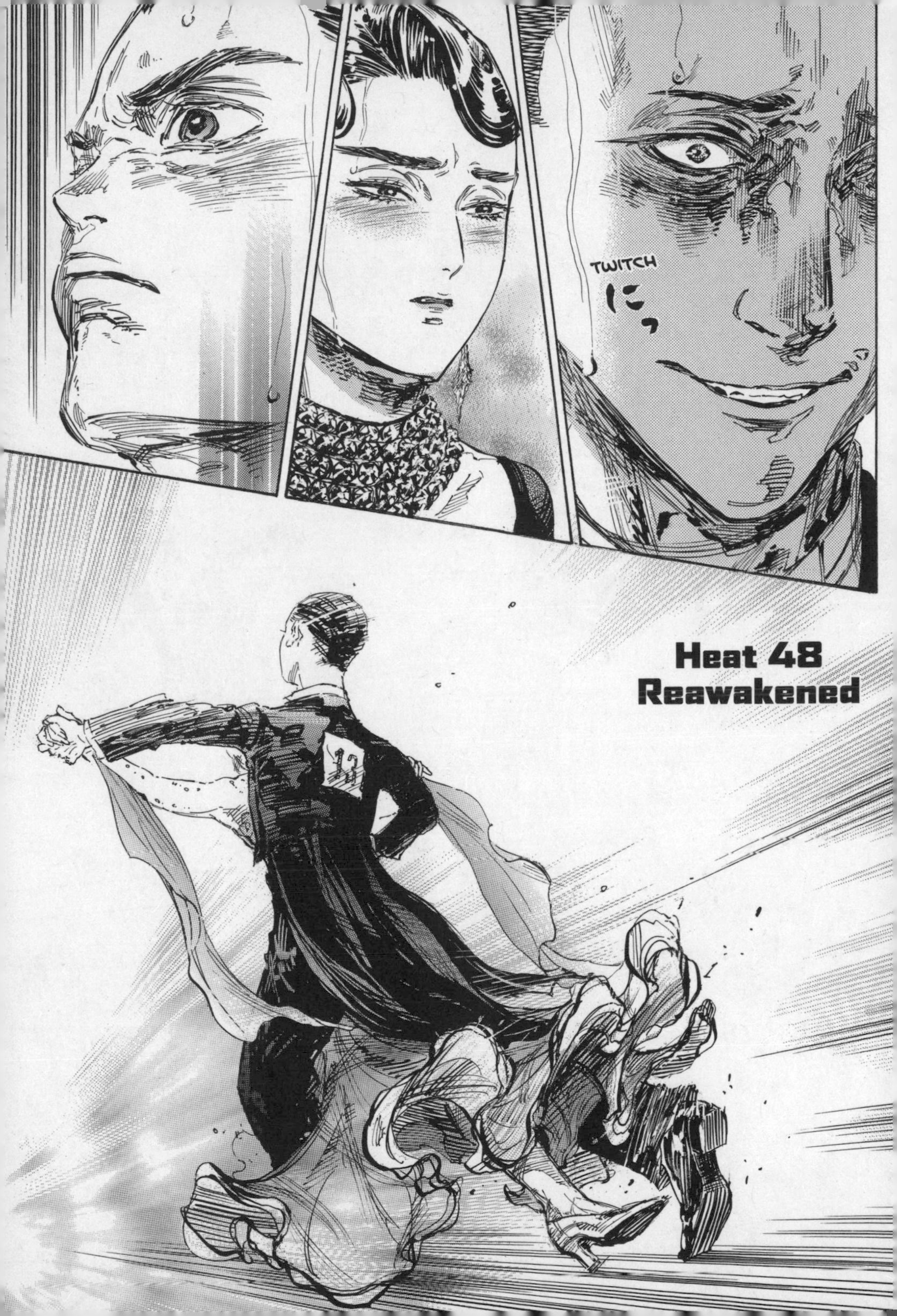
TWITCH
にっ
Heat 48
Reawakened

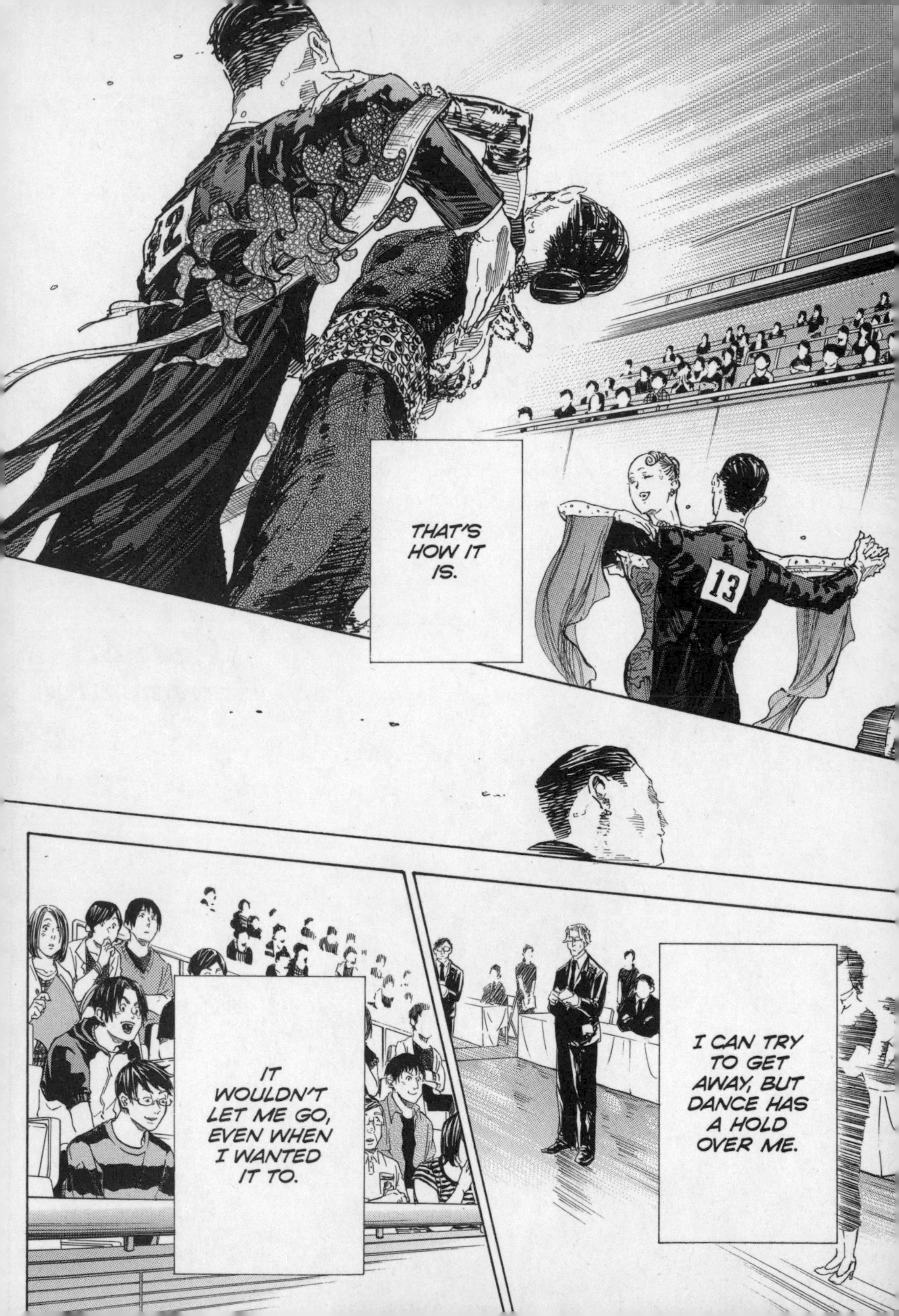
THAT'S HOW IT IS.
I CAN TRY TO GET AWAY, BUT DANCE HAS A HOLD OVER ME.
IT WOULDN'T LET ME GO, EVEN WHEN I WANTED IT TO.

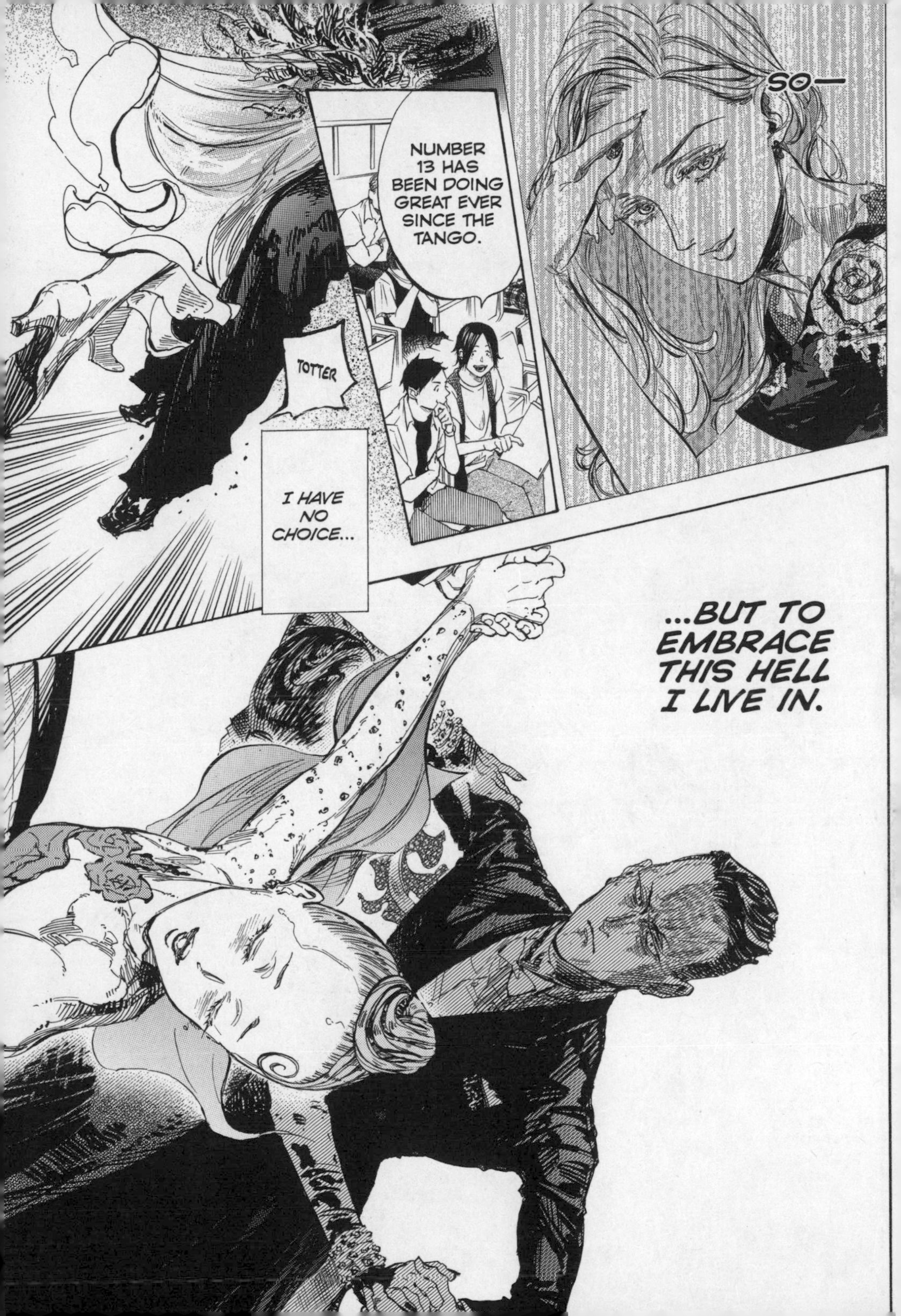
SO—
NUMBER 13 HAS BEEN DOING GREAT EVER SINCE THE TANGO.
TOTTER
I HAVE NO CHOICE...
...BUT TO EMBRACE THIS HELL I LIVE IN.

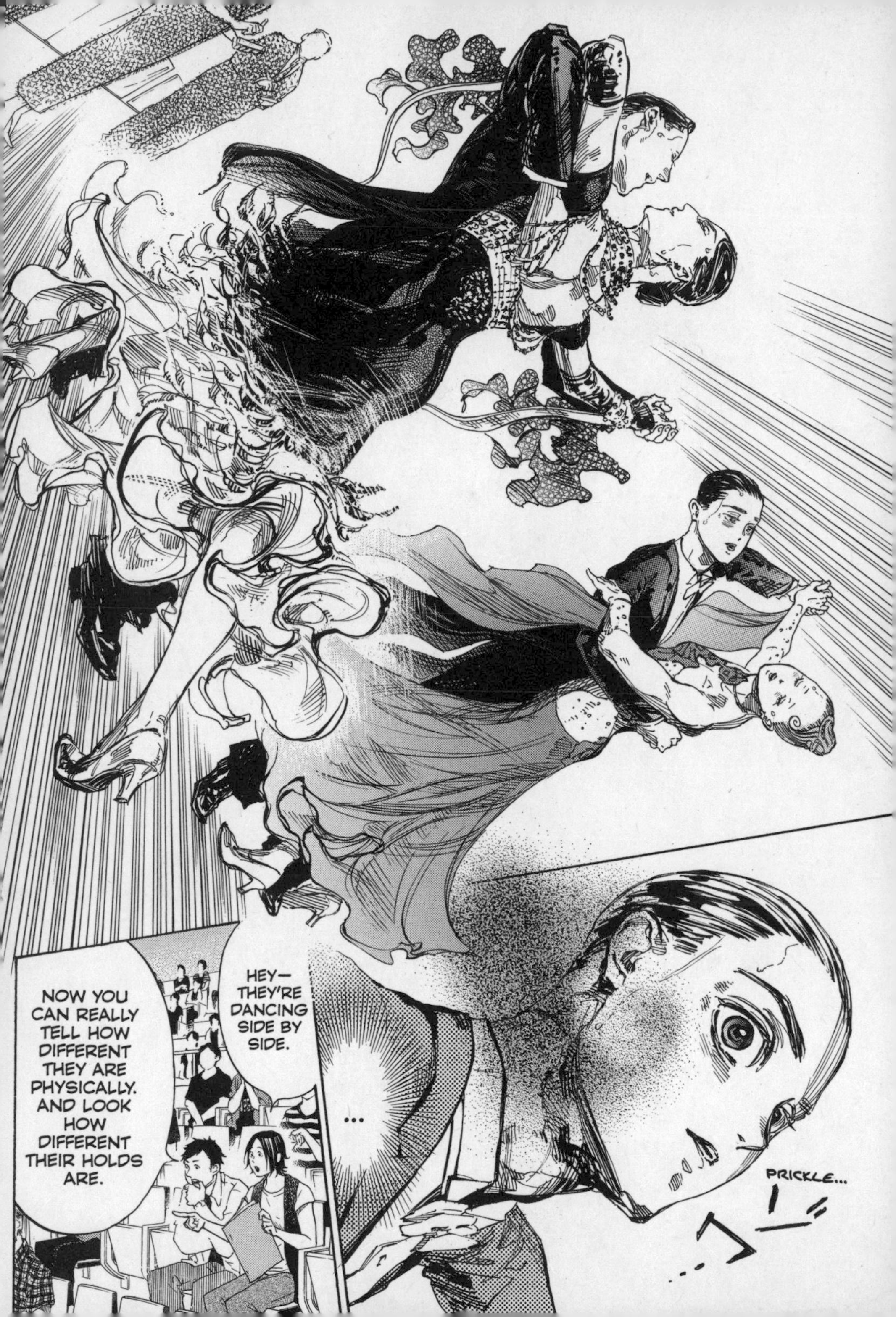
PRICKLE...
...
HEY— THEY'RE DANCING SIDE BY SIDE.
NOW YOU CAN REALLY TELL HOW DIFFERENT THEY ARE PHYSICALLY. AND LOOK HOW DIFFERENT THEIR HOLDS ARE.

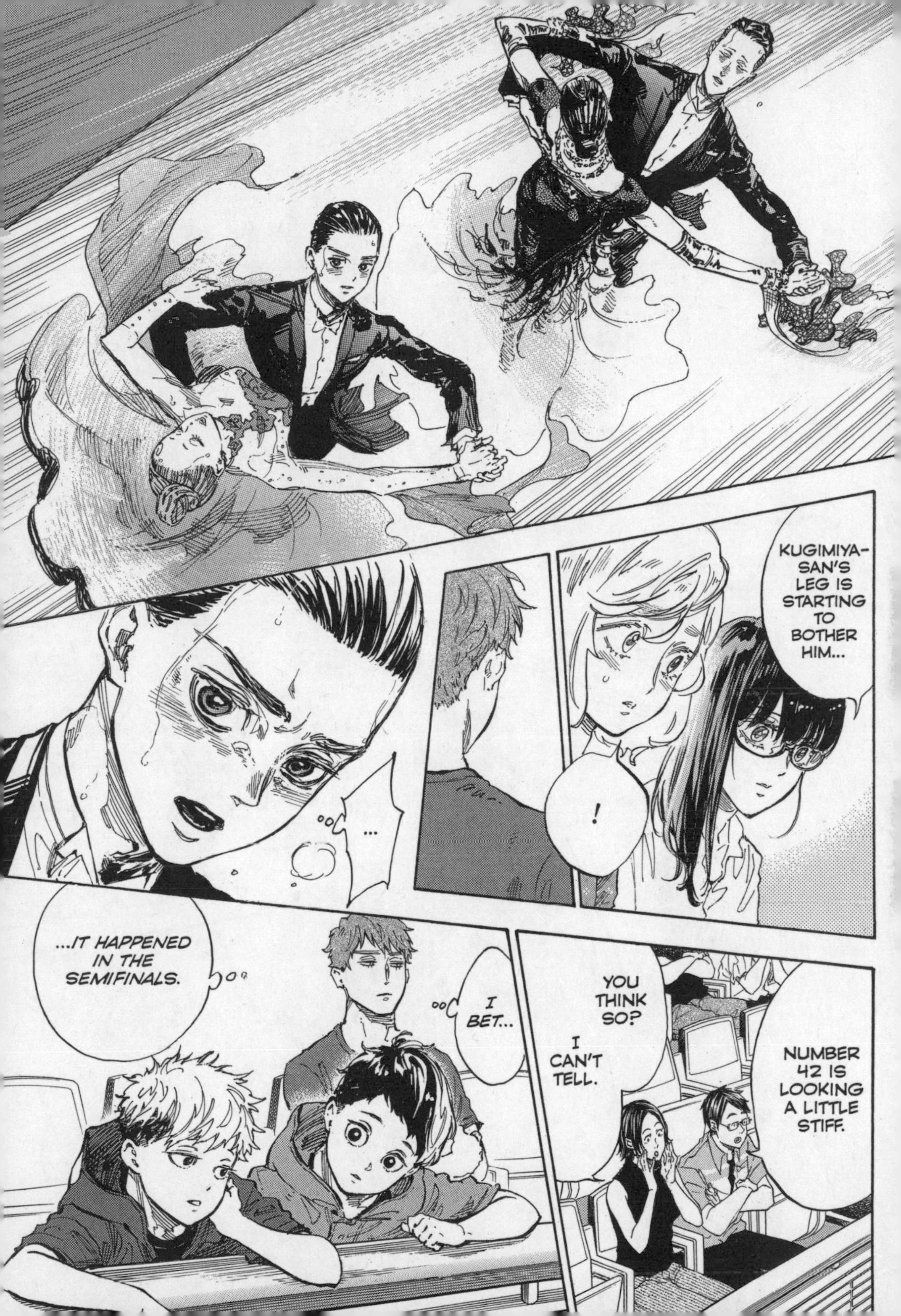
KUGIMIYA-SAN'S LEG IS STARTING TO BOTHER HIM...
!
...
NUMBER 42 IS LOOKING A LITTLE STIFF.
YOU THINK SO?
I CAN'T TELL.
I BET...
...IT HAPPENED IN THE SEMIFINALS.

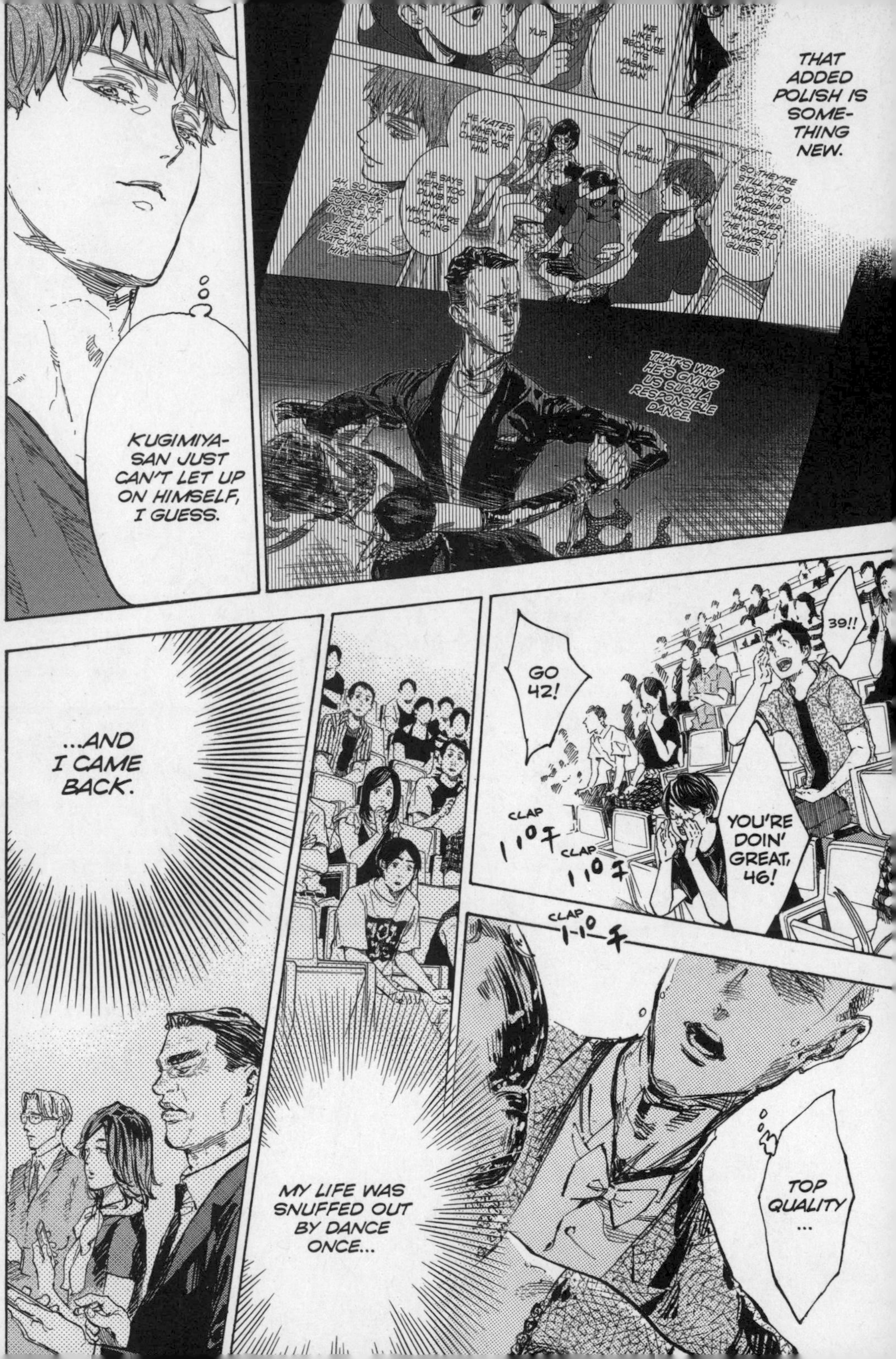
THAT ADDED POLISH IS SOMETHING NEW.
WE LIKE IT BECAUSE IT'S MASAMI-CHAN.
YUP.
BUT ACTUALLY...
HE HATES IT WHEN WE CHEER FOR HIM.
HE SAYS WE'RE TOO DUMB TO KNOW WHAT WE'RE LOOKING AT.
SO THEY'RE STILL KIDS ENOUGH TO WORSHIP "MASAMI-CHAN" OVER THE WORLD CHAMPS, I GUESS.
AH, SO IT'S BECAUSE A COUPLE OF INNOCENT LITTLE KIDS ARE WATCHING HIM.
THAT'S WHY HE'S GIVING US SUCH A RESPONSIBLE DANCE.
KUGIMIYA-SAN JUST CAN'T LET UP ON HIMSELF, I GUESS.
39!!
GO 42!
CLAP
CLAP
YOU'RE DOIN' GREAT, 46!
CLAP
TOP QUALITY...
MY LIFE WAS SNUFFED OUT BY DANCE ONCE...
...AND I CAME BACK.

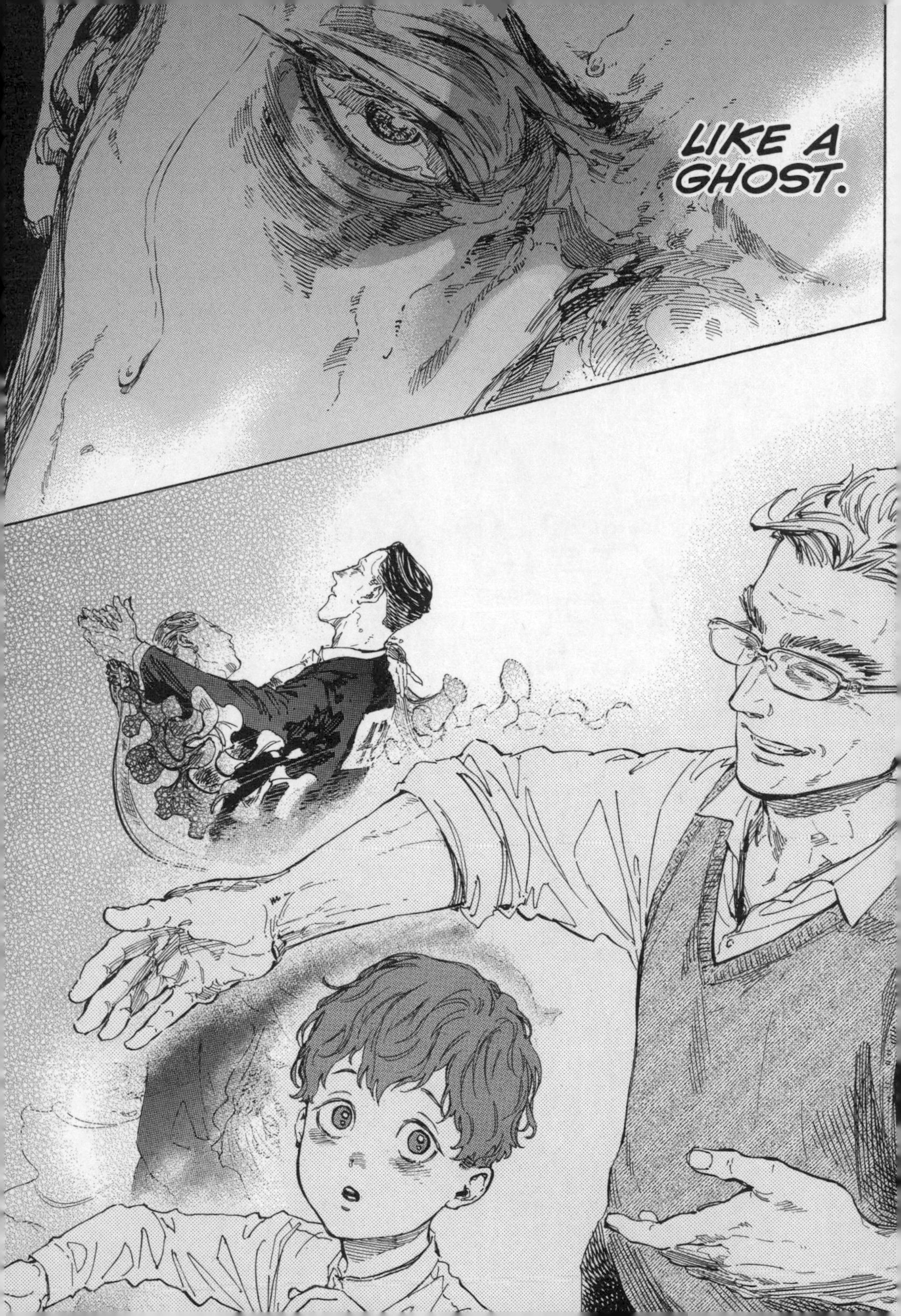
LIKE A GHOST.

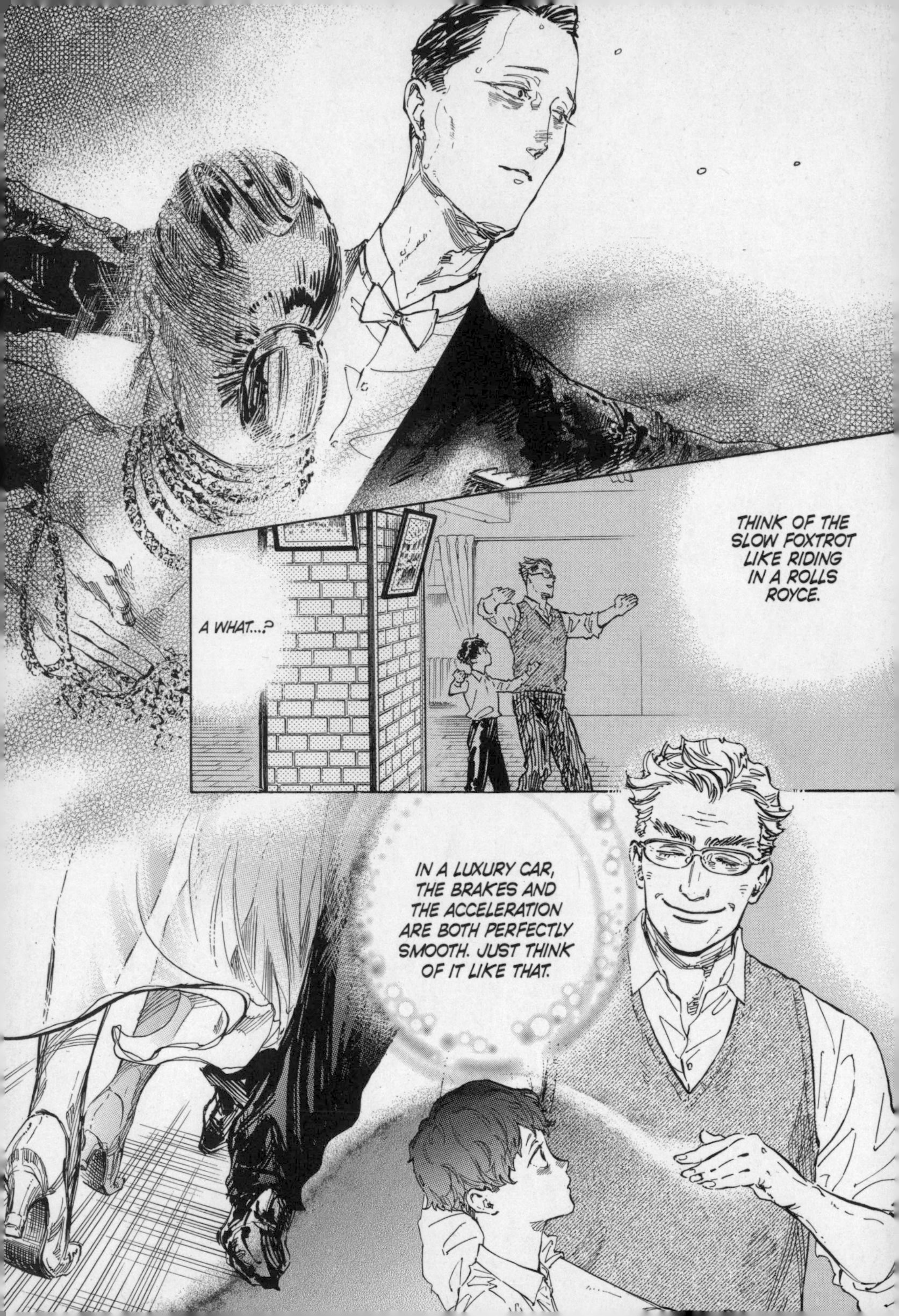
THINK OF THE SLOW FOXTROT LIKE RIDING IN A ROLLS ROYCE.
A WHAT...?
IN A LUXURY CAR, THE BRAKES AND THE ACCELERATION ARE BOTH PERFECTLY SMOOTH. JUST THINK OF IT LIKE THAT.

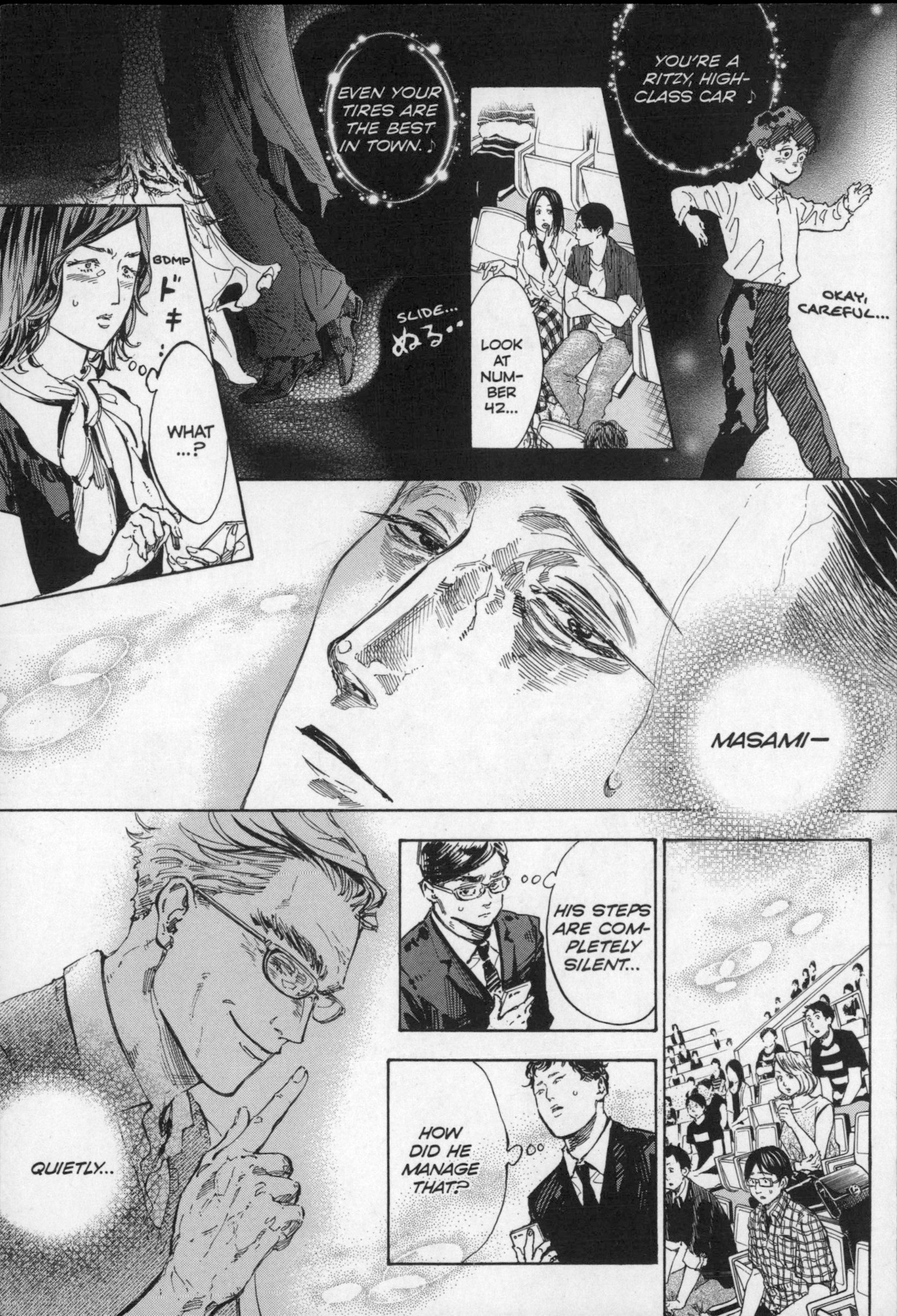
YOU'RE A RITZY, HIGH-CLASS CAR ♪
OKAY, CAREFUL...
EVEN YOUR TIRES ARE THE BEST IN TOWN. ♪
LOOK AT NUMBER 42...
SLIDE... ぬる…
BDMP ドキ
WHAT ...?
MASAMI—
HIS STEPS ARE COMPLETELY SILENT...
HOW DID HE MANAGE THAT?
QUIETLY...

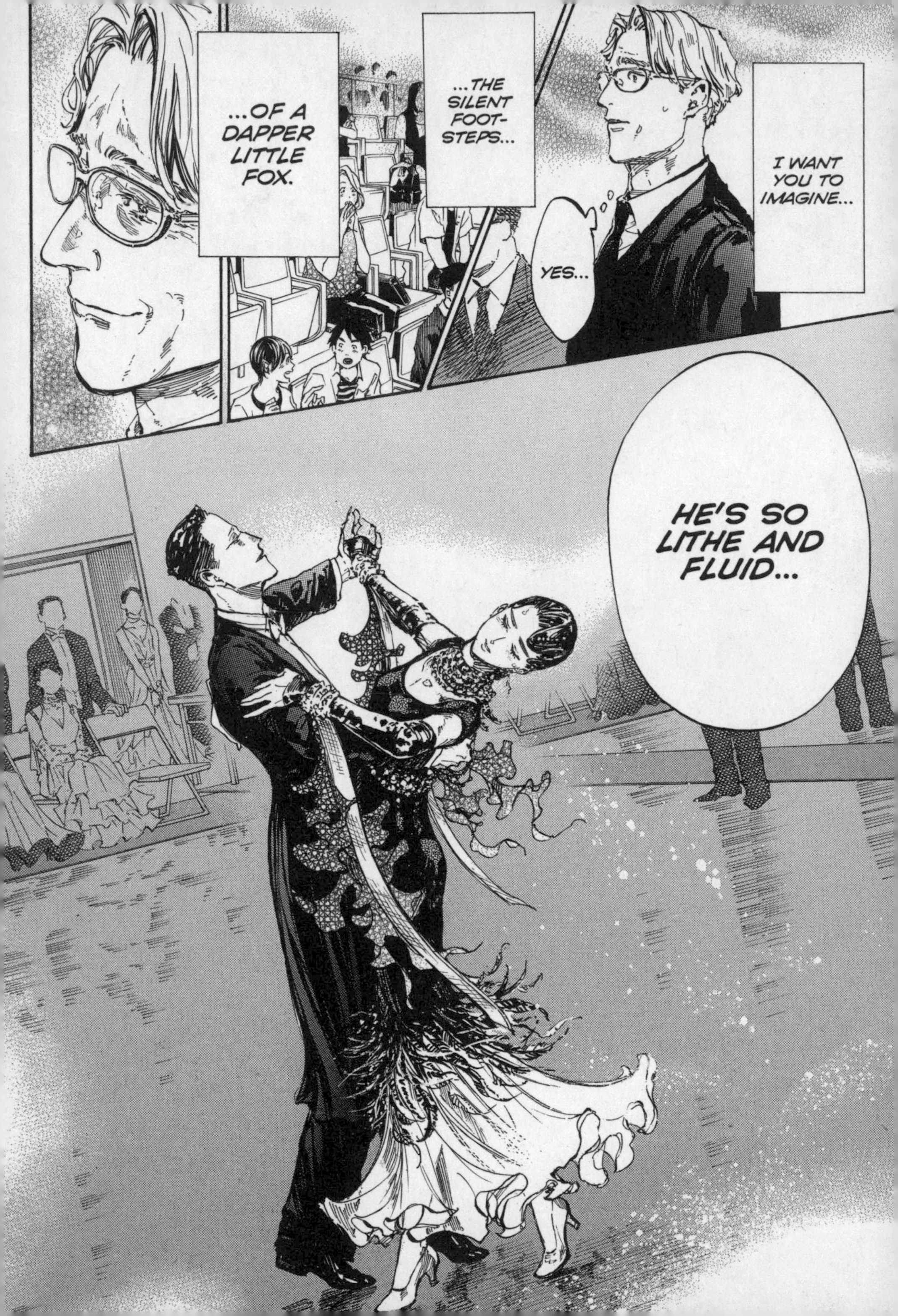
I WANT YOU TO IMAGINE...
YES...
...THE SILENT FOOT-STEPS...
...OF A DAPPER LITTLE FOX.
HE'S SO LITHE AND FLUID...

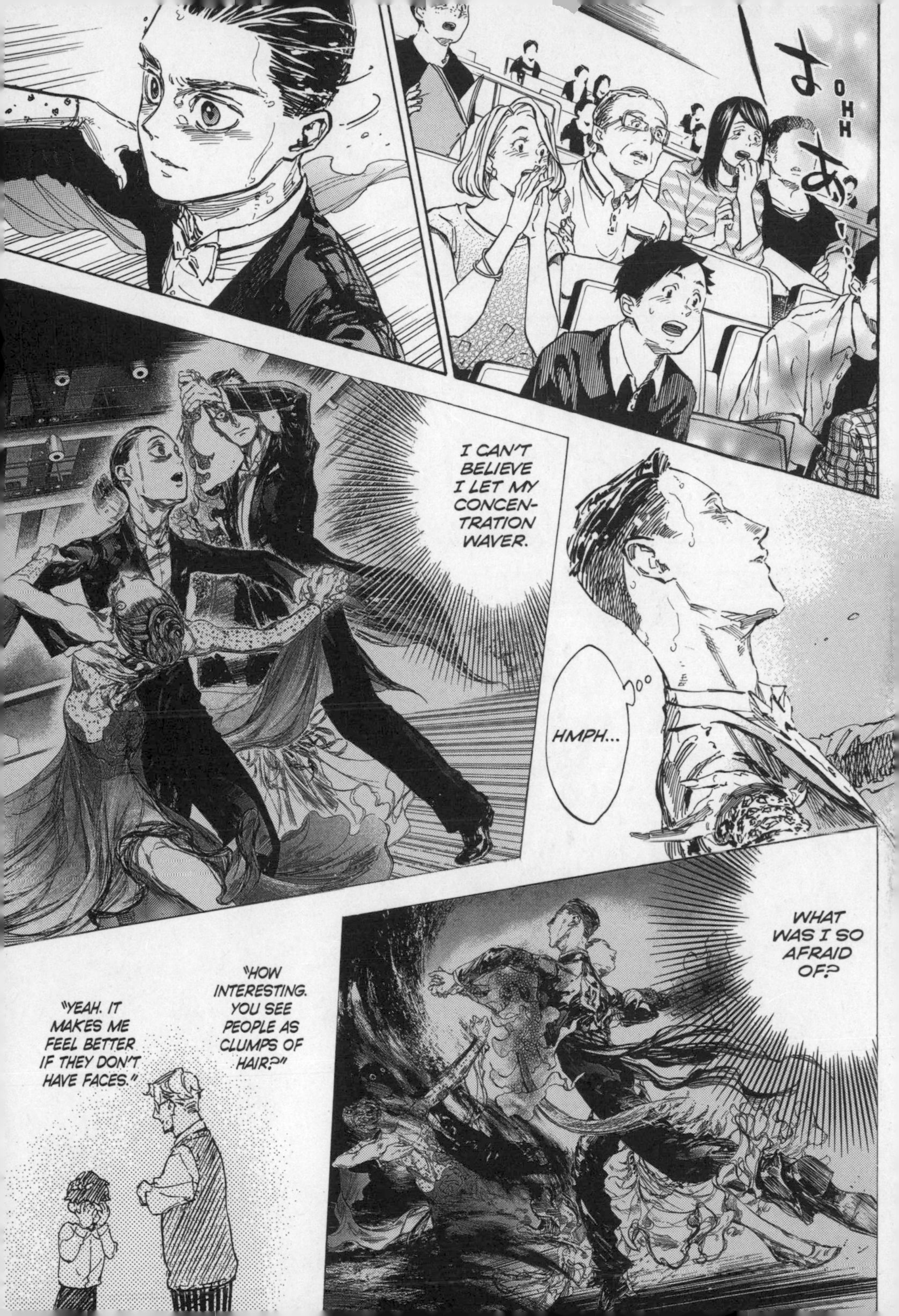
OHH
HMPH...
I CAN'T BELIEVE I LET MY CONCENTRATION WAVER.
WHAT WAS I SO AFRAID OF?
"HOW INTERESTING. YOU SEE PEOPLE AS CLUMPS OF HAIR?"
"YEAH. IT MAKES ME FEEL BETTER IF THEY DON'T HAVE FACES."

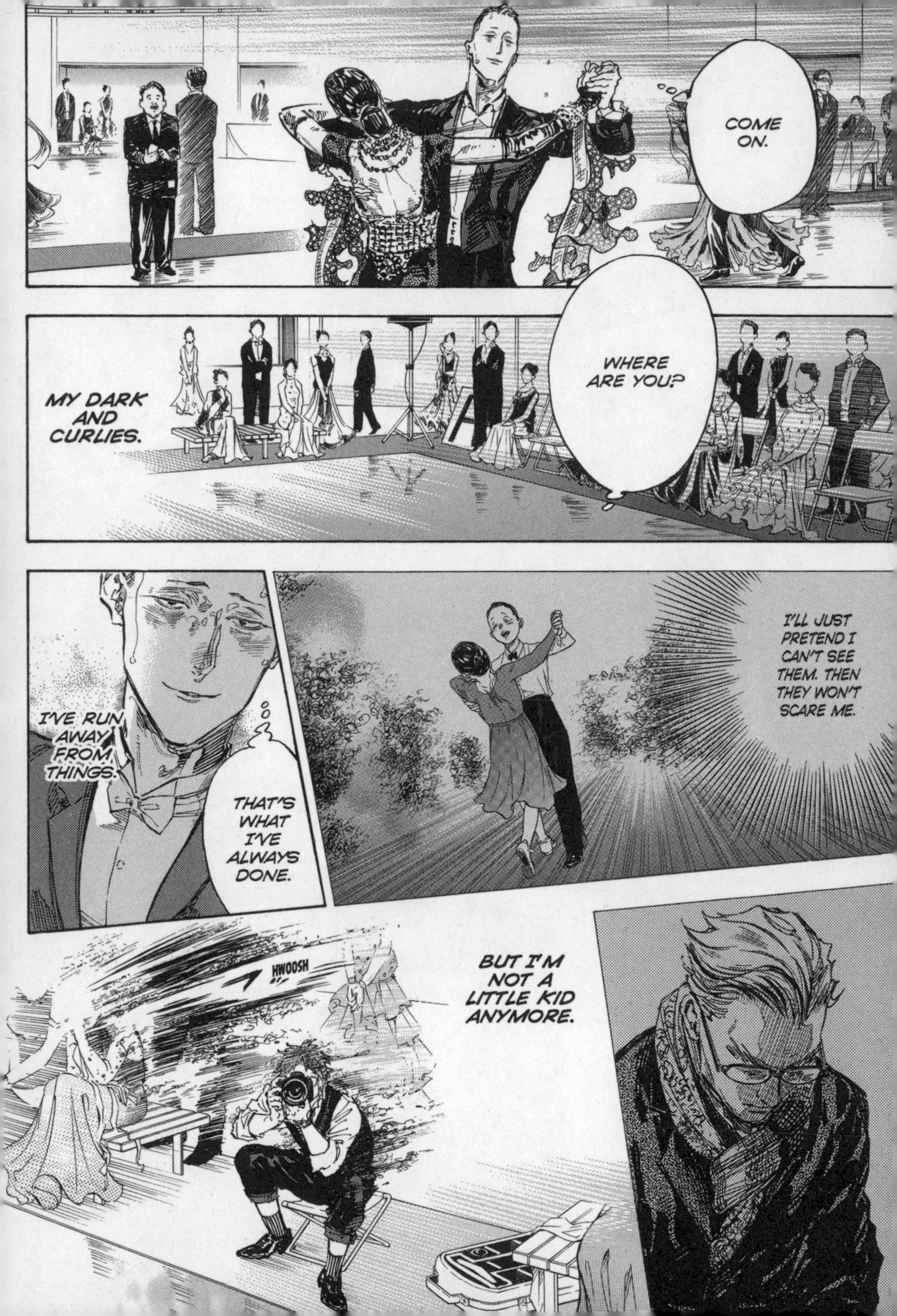
COME ON.
WHERE ARE YOU?
MY DARK AND CURLIES.
I'LL JUST PRETEND I CAN'T SEE THEM. THEN THEY WON'T SCARE ME.
I'VE RUN AWAY FROM THINGS.
THAT'S WHAT I'VE ALWAYS DONE.
BUT I'M NOT A LITTLE KID ANYMORE.
HWOOSH

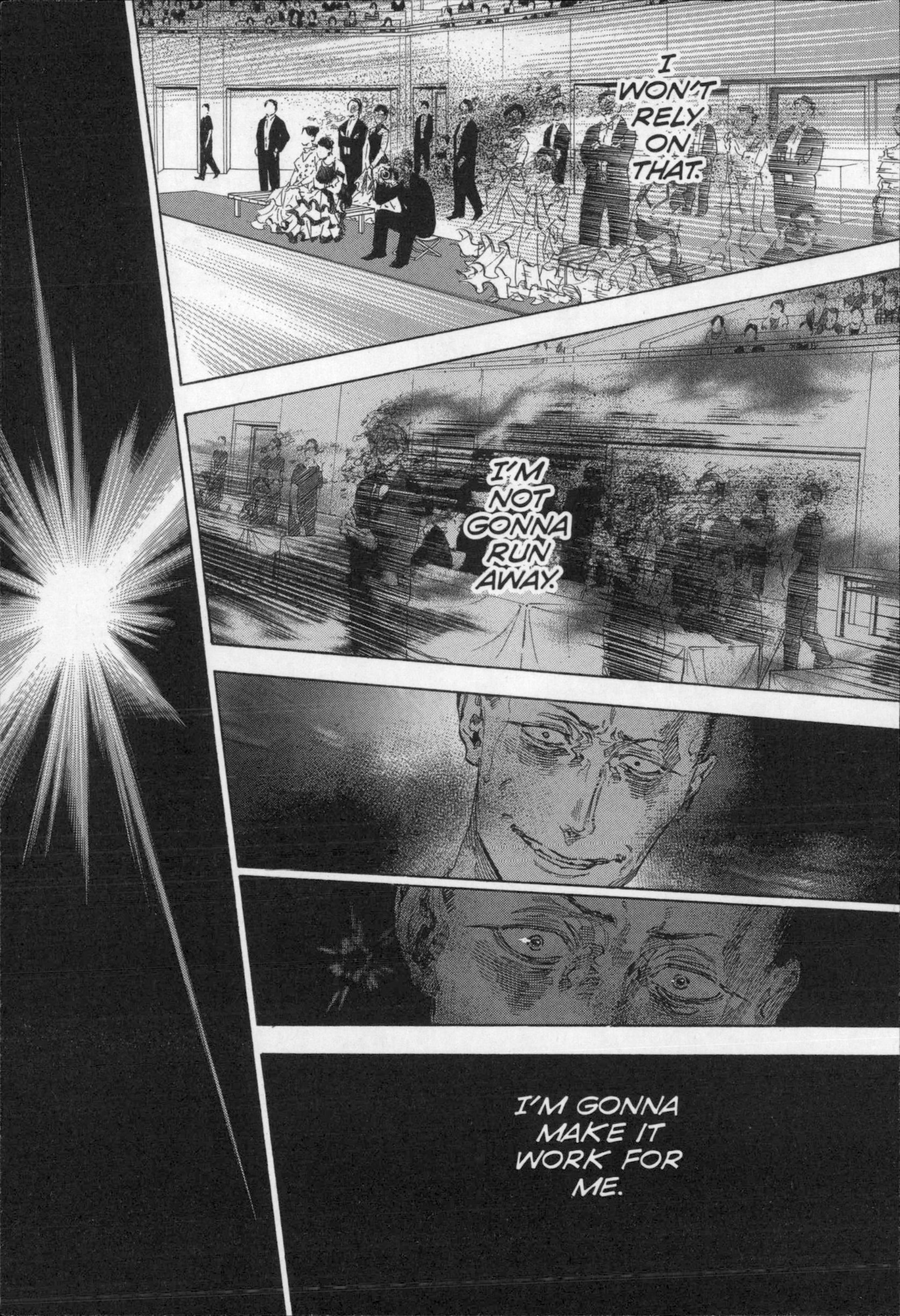
I WON'T RELY ON THAT.
I'M NOT GONNA RUN AWAY.
I'M GONNA MAKE IT WORK FOR ME.

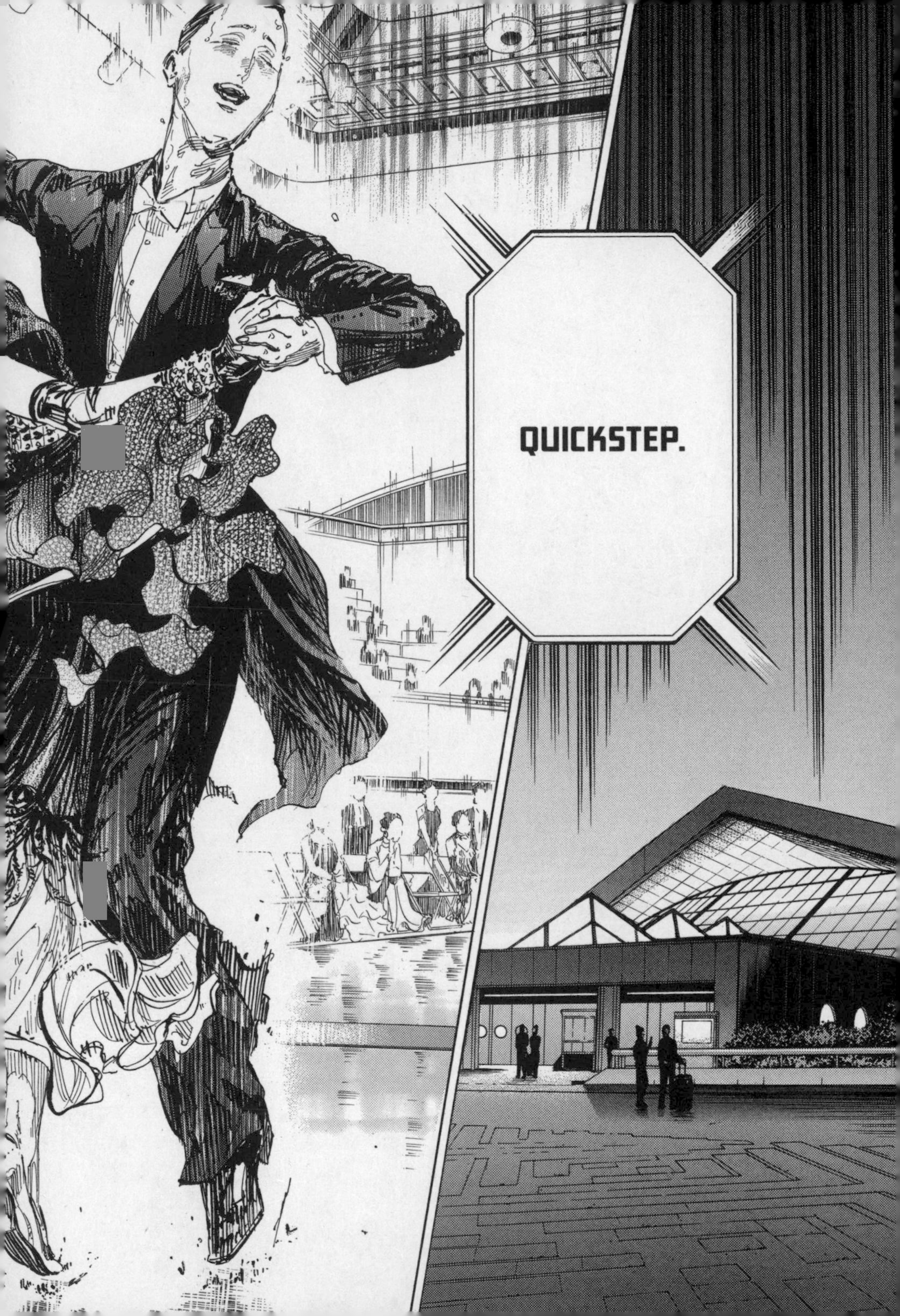
QUICKSTEP.

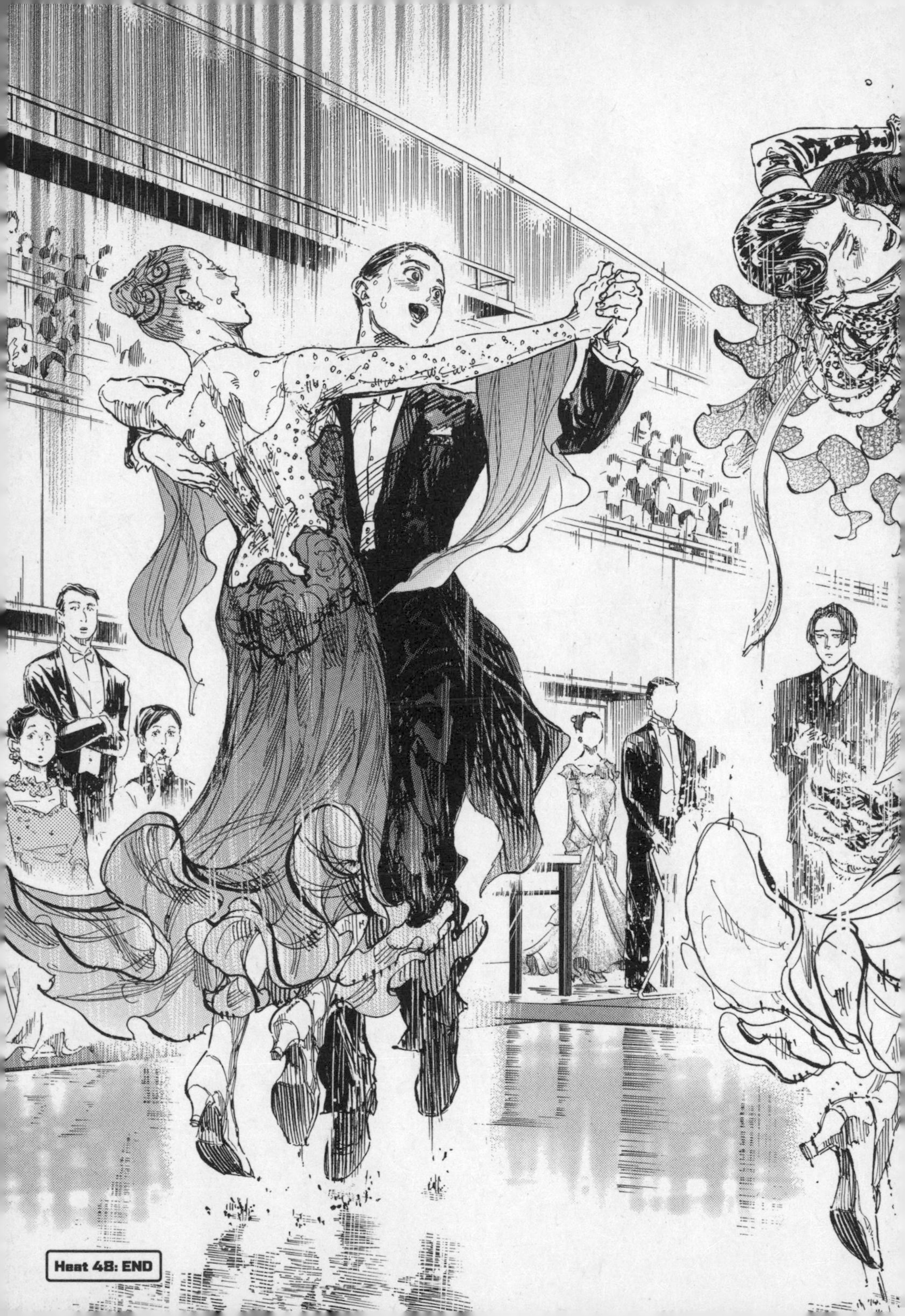
Heat 48: END

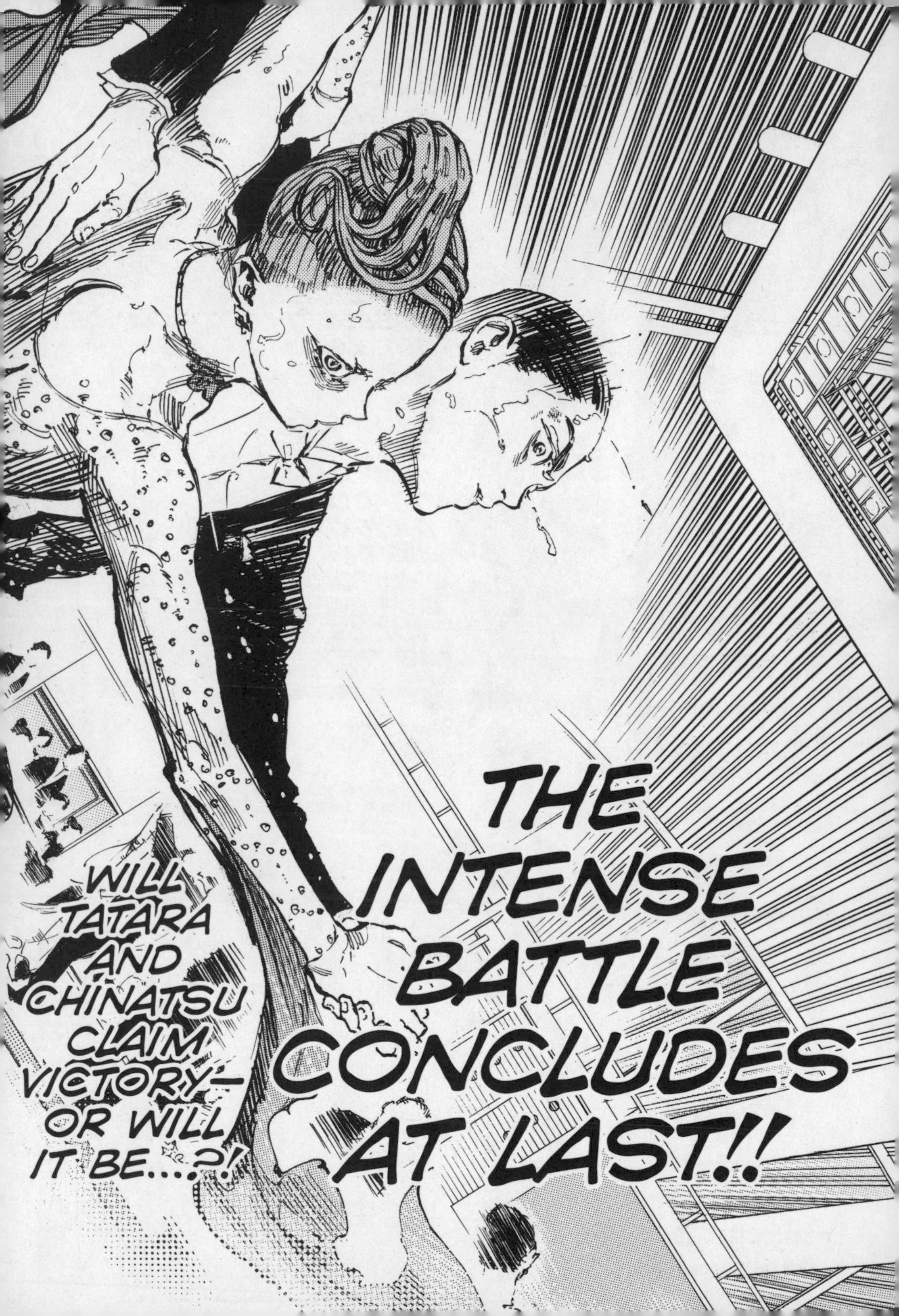
THE INTENSE BATTLE CONCLUDES AT LAST!!
WILL TATARA AND CHINATSU CLAIM VICTORY— OR WILL IT BE...?!

Welcome to the Ballroom

THE DANCERS HAVE FINISHED ALL STYLES AT THE LEVEL A MATCH AT THE METROPOLITAN TOURNAMENT!! TATARA AND CHINATSU HAVE MASTERED THEMSELVES AND DANCED AS ONE. KUGIMIYA HAS PROVEN HIS TENACIOUS OBSESSION WITH DANCE. BUT WHICH OF THEM WILL CLAIM VICTORY?!

AND FOR HYODO AND SHIZUKU, GAJU AND MAKO, WHO ALL WATCHED THE COMPETITION UNFOLD, THE EXPERIENCE SPARKS BIG EMOTIONAL CHANGES... THE TOURNAMENT IS OVER, BUT EVERYDAY LIFE MIGHT NOT BE AS STRESS-FREE AS THEY HOPED...

AND CHINATSU TRANSFORMS?!

HEH
OH, WHO CARES.

WE GET BACK TO DAILY LIFE, TOO ★

Volume 11, scheduled for winter 2020!!

Special Thanks!

For help with background
Tominaga Dance Factory

Translation Notes

Page 151

"develope"
This is a move that involves sliding one foot up
the other leg and then extending the foot forward,
almost like a kick.

A Kodansha Comics Trade Paperback Original
Welcome to the Ballroom 10 copyright © 2020 Tomo Takeuchi
English translation copyright © 2020 Tomo Takeuchi

All rights reserved.

Published in the United States by Kodansha Comics, an imprint of Kodansha USA Publishing, LLC, New York.

Publication rights for this English edition arranged through Kodansha Ltd., Tokyo.

First published in Japan in 2020 by Kodansha Ltd., Tokyo as *Booruruumu e Youkoso*, volume 10.

ISBN 978-1-63236-581-1

Printed in the United States of America.

www.kodanshacomics.com

9 8 7 6 5 4 3 2 1
Translation: Karen McGillicuddy
Lettering: Brndn Blakeslee
Editing: David Yoo
Kodansha Comics edition cover design by My Truong
Kodansha Comics edition logo deisgn by Phil Balsman

Publisher: Kiichiro Sugawara

Director of publishing services: Ben Applegate
Associate director of operations: Stephen Pakula
Publishing services managing editor: Noelle Webster
Assistant production manager: Emi Lotto, Angela Zurlo